SECRETS OF
Executive
SUCCESS

SECRETS OF Executive SUCCESS

HOW ANYONE CAN HANDLE THE HUMAN SIDE OF WORK AND GROW THEIR CAREER

By Mark Golin, Mark Bricklin, David Diamond,
and the Rodale Center for Executive Development
Edited by John Feltman

Rodale Press, Emmaus, Pennsylvania

The Rodale Center for Executive Development is a special section within Rodale Press that researches and disseminates practical information to help managers develop the best in themselves and in those who work with and for them.

Printed in the United States of America on acid-free ∞, recycled ♻ paper

Book Designer: Acey Lee
Cover Designer: Stan Green
Copy Editor: Barbara Webb
Indexer: Ed Yeager

If you have any questions or comments concerning this book, please write:

Rodale Press
Book Reader Service
33 East Minor Street
Emmaus, PA 18098

Library of Congress Cataloging-in-Publication Data

Golin, Mark.
    Secrets of executive success : how anyone can handle the human
side of work and grow their career / by Mark Golin, Mark Bricklin,
David Diamond, and the Rodale Center for Executive Development :
edited by John Feltman.
       p. cm.
  Includes index.
  ISBN 0–87857–973–7   hardcover
  1. Executive ability. 2. Management. I. Bricklin, Mark.
II. Diamond, David, 1952-   III. Feltman, John. IV. Rodale
Center for Executive Development. V. Title. HD38.2.G65 1991
658.4′09—dc20
                                                       91–19377
                                                         CIP

Distributed in the book trade by St. Martin's Press

4 6 8 10 9 7 5   hardcover

CONTENTS

v

5 Simple Rules to Add Authority to the Way You Look
How to Look Like a Million without Spending It

When Someone Challenges Your Leadership
How to Be a Leader Who's Not a Threat to Your Manager

How After-Work Pastimes Energize
Is Your Leisure Activity Right for You?
Golf and Other Ways to Network

Disclosures: Risks That Build Trust
Reflections: Acts of Empathy
Interpretations: Reshaping the Message
Questions: The Innocent and the Wicked

Finding Out What's Expected
Accepting the Challenge
Learning How to Give Orders
Accepting Responsibility for Employees' Mistakes

When a Maverick Alienates Peers
Avoiding 3 Versions of the Flash-in-the-Pan Syndrome
A Few Final Thoughts for Mavericks or Would-Be
    Mavericks

Is This Meeting Necessary?
Double Your Efficiency: Cut Meeting Time in Half
Orchestrating and Conducting a Harmonious Meeting
How to Solicit Honest Opinions
When You Want to Stand Out

The Biggest Memory Secret of All Time
Tricks of the Memory Trade

FOREWORD

It wasn't too long ago that I received a call from Rodale Press asking me to take a look at a new book they had just completed. Having admired Rodale for years, I was glad to do them a favor. . .but I was also mildly confused. Why would they want my opinion on what was surely going to be a gardening or health book? After all, I run an ice cream business. However, when I found out that the topic was management, my confusion turned to curiosity. I told them to send it on over.

When it arrived, I almost regretted ever getting involved. The advance manuscript deposited on my desk was a stack of paper nearly a foot high. It seemed to chuckle at me. It told me that I may as well forget any plans I had for the weekend.

As I lugged the monster home, I couldn't help wondering why the leading publisher of gardening and health information was venturing into the management market. It is, to put it mildly, quite a leap. But after reading a few chapters of this book, I thought I had the answer. Every time a reader picks up a health or gardening book it is for one of two primary reasons. The first possibility is that there's a problem that needs to be solved. Maybe it's high blood pressure. Perhaps aphids are laying waste to the lettuce patch. Either way, a solution needs to be found . . . and found quickly. The second reason is, pure and simple, improvement. Your health is fine, the garden looks great . . . but maybe you can learn to make them even better.

Well, people pick up management books for the same two reasons: to find a solution for a current problem or to improve their abilities in general. As I read this book, I couldn't help but feel that the same practical instincts

Rodale has for the needs of their gardening and health readers seemed to be operating equally well in the management arena.

The book is (to my immense relief) highly readable. Its light approach deals with complex topics of concern without getting bogged down in jargon. The material comes to the point as quickly as possible. And having come to the point, the book then serves up handfuls of practical tips to deal with any situation.

As I looked at the table of contents, one word came to mind: encyclopedic. There's a chapter on virtually every subject of interest to first-time managers. Naturally, everything can't be covered in great depth. This is not an advanced management book. But what Rodale has seemed to aim for (and nicely achieved) is the creation of a sensible manual for the newly made executive. A field guide that can be referred to time and time again when problems arise. A kind of hardbound mentor for success. And I might add that even the experienced exec might find a few techniques here that can help hone skills developed over the years.

But with all the success you're about to experience, I want you to keep one thing in mind. Business is the most powerful force in America. It's a force that can help transform our society into one that values environmental and human needs above short-term profits. Or it can use its enormous clout and political power as a means of preserving the status quo—a society that spends $300 billion a year on the military while steadfastly refusing to spend significant resources on education or the war against hunger, disease, and poverty.

As you work your way to the top, I encourage you to integrate personal values into your everyday office decisions. Believe it or not, it is possible to not only help yourself, but help the environment and the community at the same time. Start small. Perhaps the next time you order paper supplies you might buy recyclables. When you find out how easy it is . . . get more involved. At Ben & Jerry's we have a program called Caring Capitalism, which strives to integrate a concern for the community into every decision we make. I invite you to start the same trend in your own company. After all . . . why not make the world's future as bright as your own?

Ben Cohen, CEO
Ben & Jerry's Homemade, Inc.

INTRODUCTION

WHY DO YOU NEED

ANOTHER MANAGEMENT BOOK?

W alk into any fairly large bookstore, amble on over to the business section, and what you'll find are enough management and career how-to books to build a life-sized replica of the World Trade Center. Books that will tell you the five secrets of being a great CEO, books that will show you how to cut costs in a $5,000,000 division in 5 minutes, and sets of five books written by five corporate presidents bragging about the five smartest moves they made in their lives. So why do you need *this* book?

Because as an executive who hasn't quite made it to the absolute throne of power (yet), you have informational needs that are probably not met by many of the other books on the market. For example, it may be fun to read about how Lee Iacocca turned around Chrysler or why Michael Eisner is the patron saint of upper-level management, but how is this going to help you deal with the fact that you've got to give an unfavorable performance review to an employee who is trying his damnedest but doesn't have the necessary talent? How is knowing the right way to write an inspiring corporate mission statement going to help you finally nail down that elusive promotion when you're simply trying to encourage your team of five employees to stop bickering and start producing?

That is why we wrote this book and why you may find it useful. Specific people at specific times in their lives need specific information. What we've tried to do here is provide a wide range of information covering many of the areas in which first-time and middle managers currently face their most challenging problems. The reason you won't find technical business infor- mation presented here is because we've found that the most trying management problems (and indeed the ones that dog most of us throughout our careers) have to do with people rather than profits, with motivation rather than manufacturing, and with creativity rather than costs. In dealing with the human side of career success, we've made the additional attempt to tailor all the information to your needs as an executive on the way up. For example, rather than discuss how to carry on high-level negotiations between corporations, we explore the ways to negotiate with a co-worker on a particular project. In this book, "organization" does not refer to the operating structure of a company but rather to a way to handle the endless stream of papers that has hidden your desk from sight for the last three months.

Another criterion we had for this book was that it provide fast information in a convenient format. You won't find everything there is to know about brainstorming or intuition in this book, but you will find what we considered to be the most useful, pertinent, and easily implemented tips and techniques culled from the advice of hundreds of management experts. Rather than writing a textbook, we've chosen to create a field guide—the sort of book you might read at your leisure or turn to minutes before a meeting for a fast tip on how to streamline the proceedings.

One more thing. It seems we are living in a corporate world of almost mythic proportions. We are not executives anymore: We're ancient Japanese samurai, tigers on the prowl, Zen archers, sharks, dinosaurs, or Huns. It seems that a new management book can't be written these days without promoting a new and unique way in which to visualize yourself and your work arena. We don't know about you, but the last time we walked into a meeting, there was no raw meat lying on the conference room table, and the only guns anyone was carrying were staple guns. We are not warriors, and the office shouldn't be a battlefield. We are human beings working with other human beings. The least we should strive for is a humane approach to management. Therefore this book is not about crushing, stepping on, maiming, wasting, or obliterating the competition. This book is about working to the best of your abilities and encouraging the best in those who work with you and for you. Tricks don't ensure success, excellence does.

1

AGE

Frederic Chopin was 7 years old when he composed Polonaise in G Minor, and Winston Churchill was 84 when he came out of prime ministerial retirement to run for the House of Commons. (He won. And yes, he also exhibited 62 of his paintings that year.)

We raise these historical facts not to make you feel horribly inadequate but to illustrate that—despite what seems to be happening at work or on the basketball court—you're never too young or too old to pull off big accomplishments. Trouble is, it's the rare individual who is truly convinced that age is, in fact, mostly a state of mind.

We've been conditioned from birth to view age for its constraints, not for its possibilities. Remember waiting impatiently to be old enough to drive? Then to be old enough to drink? The age conditioning is reinforced everywhere, from the advertising industry (which glorifies youth) to typical corporate management (which rarely takes seriously the young or old among its ranks).

The first step in keeping your age from holding you back from success is to expand your limits. That doesn't mean trying out for your office rugby team if you know you're too slow and injury-prone to contribute much. But on the other hand, there's no reason why you should hang on to an unfulfilling or dead-end job just because it's the sort of position people your age are expected to have.

And if you ever feel over-the-hill in your business career, consider the sorry plight of professional athletes, who often watch their glory days fade into the past at an age when everyone else's career is just taking off. And then think about the successful ex-jocks like Jim Ridlon, a highly rated NFL defensive back whose chosen career peaked when he was 27 years old. He applied the same power and drive to a second career. Now, at 52, he is a renowned abstract painter, sculptor, and professor of art at Syracuse University's College of Visual and Performing Arts.

IF THEY SAY YOU'RE TOO YOUNG

You see it all the time. Young, confident, eager-beaver workers of about 26 who feel they have the smarts and expertise to run the show. Management, however, tells them they're brilliant and wonderful but simply too young to assume higher responsibilities.

Find out: Is it really your age? "Sometimes there are unspoken rules that say you must be 40 or so before you can be promoted into a certain position," says Beth Wilson, a career counselor at Philadelphia-based Options, Inc. "But it may be something else. Look at who is getting promoted and what they look like—not only their age, but their education, background, social standing in the community, and their sex." Sit down with your boss and ask, "What do I need to do to prove that I am ready for the responsibility?"

Gain a breadth of experience. Once you've made it known to your company that you want to advance, also make it known to them that you are open to new experiences. "If you're exposed to different areas of the corporation and if you know people in different areas, you'll be seen in a more favorable light for promotion," says Ann Howard, Ph.D., industrial psychologist and coauthor of *Managerial Lives in Transition*. "Don't be afraid to take the big challenges where you can show your stuff and learn from the experience." And volunteer for training or other educational programs your company offers. At the very least, those added experiences and training could help you land a position at a company that *doesn't* think you're too young.

Find a mentor who isn't old who will champion you. If you don't feel opportunities are limited at your company, look for a mentor who will help promote you. And then channel your youthful energies into doing promotable work.

If it looks impossible, cut your losses and leave. If your boss gives you a wishy-washy answer to the "What do I need to do . . . " question, and if your objective observations indicate age or your individual background really is keeping you back, it may be that there's nothing you can do. If it's a lost cause you have on your hands, it may be best to cut your losses and leave for a place with better opportunities.

Are your talents transferable to a more suitable employer? "If you're in a company or industry that's traditional, no amount of champing at the bit will do you any good," says Adele Scheele, Ph.D., a New York City career strategist and author of *Skills for Success*. Instead of biding your time, consider greener pastures. The newest and flashiest companies or fields are the most youth-oriented with regard to whom they promote. Advertising and high-tech companies routinely look to 30-year-olds as competent managers.

Take a job in a smaller company. "You can't expect to be a vice-president of a large company at age 28," says Dr. Howard. (Unless, of course, the company bears your parents' name.) "If you want to be a vice-president and are going nowhere in a large company, try a smaller one."

Myths of Success: The Earning-Your-Age Myth

About 20 years ago, before inflation rewrote the rules on everything from mortgage interest rates to the price of fly rods, it was pretty much an accepted standard that professionals in large companies located in major metropolitan areas should, after about five years on the job, be earning a salary figure equivalent to their age.

Now a slightly-above-average investment banker can earn his age every couple of weeks (and yes, if he's overzealous, wind up in prison shortly thereafter). So inflation, a few high-paying industries, and an atmosphere of striking one's own deal have made the are-you-earning-your-age question woefully out-of-date.

This is news that apparently hasn't reached everybody. Folks who work for such moderate-pay employers as nonprofit organizations and who rate their jobs as highly satisfying have been known to view themselves as underachievers because they don't earn their age. The irony is that since they enjoy their jobs, they're probably better off than 90 percent of the working population.

They also may be the role models of the future. "Using age as a guideline will be less important in the future because people will take more chances, shift careers more, take a cut in income in order to do something they enjoy or that gives them certain freedoms or perks," predicts career strategist Dr. Adele Scheele.

SUDDENLY, YOU'RE BOSS
OVER OLDER PEOPLE

You're hotshot enough to get a big promotion. But now the people reporting to you are old enough to be your older sister and brother—or your parents. This is a chance to prove your maturity.

Treat your subordinates with respect. It's not going to be easy if you're convinced that the folks below you are the walking dead (professionally speaking). So gain some respect for their experience and what they can do, suggests Dr. Scheele. And give them some independence. "If you stand over people and watch what they do every minute, they'll resent you twice as much," she says.

Give them different kinds of challenges, particularly if they've plateaued. They'll respond favorably, predicts Dr. Howard. If your management balks at the idea, put up a strong argument. Your subordinates will thank you, work hard for you, and give you some respect—despite your age.

In your head, make everyone even in age. Even though the cafeteria food hasn't changed, this isn't elementary school, where no third grader could ever hope to outrun a sixth grader. But age stereotypes die hard, which is why you should do something you never would have done back then: Act professionally. Don't reinforce the age gap by playing up the customs and accoutrements of youth. (Translation: Your older subordinates may resent your endless discussion of punk rock groups they've never heard of.) And acknowledge that you may harbor feelings of contempt. Then let go of those feelings, advises Dr. Scheele.

WHEN A YOUNGER PERSON
IS PROMOTED OVER YOU

The problem had really gotten out of hand when a division of Exxon Corporation called in Judith Hardwick, Ph.D., author of *In Transition, The Plateauing Trap,* and *The Psychology of Women.* A management-track young man in his early thirties was made boss over a group that included a 55-year-old "lead professional," which is that corporation's highest level of researcher.

The older professional felt demoted and was enraged at upper management and the young manager. As employees chose up sides and stood behind the opposing parties, productivity of the entire unit came screeching to a halt. The demoralizing conflict had lasted about eight months when Dr.

Hardwick came in to start the process of helping those involved set up clearly defined territories. Under her direction, she says, "they eventually crawled and lurched toward something more workable."

Shortly before Dr. Hardwick arrived on the scene, the lead professional approached his younger boss with the words: "We have to talk. Something has to change." That marked the beginning of the turnaround. But was it really his role to make that move?

Dr. Hardwick believes it's ordinarily the responsibility of the boss to initiate a dialogue with a distressed subordinate. "The person with the lesser status is behind the eight ball and could jeopardize what he or she has," she says.

When a younger person is promoted over you, the first thing to do is determine why the person was brought in. She got there for some reason, so try to determine objectively what it was— experience, credentials, truly amazing talent. See how you can learn from her. "Remember, she may be young, but it's unlikely that she's stupid," says Beth Wilson, who adds, "Be clear about the responsibility you have to help with her career—yes, even though you're older." Also, be clear about what your new boss expects of you.

Think of the new boss as being as uncomfortable as you are, and try to create a team, if that's possible. For instance, is he open to advice from you?

Still, you're bound to feel like a loser. But don't fall into the trap of letting those feelings devastate you. "You can't go smiling sweetly and pretend that everything's great if it's not," says Dr. Hardwick. "Work as well as you can and look for a situation where opportunities are better. You'd be in a better position to move if you're an able person, not a whiner. Nobody wants a whiner."

OLDER EXECUTIVES: HOW TO DISCOVER YOUR INVALUABLE ASSETS

It's official: People get smarter with age. When the School College Ability Test (SCAT) was given to 104 people who had been out of college for 20 years, they scored an average 20 percentile points higher in the areas of vocabulary and word usage than did recent college grads. In the SCAT version that evaluates critical thinking, 135 individuals who were out of college for 8 years scored an average 28 percentile points higher than did recent college grads. The bottom line: We communicate better and reason better as we age.

Career Advice by the Decade

No, we're not eager to perpetuate age stereotypes. But career experts have pinpointed distinct age-related developmental patterns that can't be ignored by anyone serious about career success. Here are the pros and cons of four decades.

The Twenties: The Grass-Must-Be-Greener Decade

Folks in their twenties are restless, says Dr. William Cron, a Southern Methodist University business professor who coauthored a study of the career evolution of 675 corporate managers. They search for the ideal position and tend to be negative about their present job because—due to their idealism and lack of experience—everybody else's job looks better. They are looking for a mentor, and are eager to move up rapidly. The great paradox facing folks in their twenties is that at the same time as they are trying to break away from parental and other early influences, their companies want them to be "maximally acquiescent," says Stanley Rosenberg, Ph.D., a Dartmouth Medical School professor of psychiatry.

On the plus side: They're willing to try different things. Young workers generally have a flexible personal life that facilitates long hours or job changes.

On the minus side: Since they're so flexible, they can easily go off in the wrong direction. They may devote too much energy to such often-negative endeavors as comparing pay.

The Thirties: The I've-Got-Something-to-Build Decade

This stage of life is generally characterized by settling down in both career and personal life (those who aren't married by now usually are thinking seriously about it). There's less emphasis on searching and comparing and more on trying to establish a professional identity and prove their worth. People work to build a solid base of support in a company and a base of transferable experience. In *Seasons of a Man's Life,* Yale professor and psychologist Daniel Levinson refers to the years 36 to 40 as the BOOM years—Becoming One's Own Man. Hobbies take a back seat.

On the plus side: People move ahead in their organization, assume more responsibilities, make more money, grow professionally. They may leave their mentor's side and assert their independence.

On the minus side: Moving ahead also means closing off one's options, says Dr. Cron. He adds that tension between home and work is strongest during this decade, as people try to juggle advancing careers and growing family responsibilities. "If their focus is only on their professional life, they may win the battle but lose the war," he cautions.

The Forties: The Is-This-Really-What-I-Want? Decade

Thinning hair and incipient paunch are daily reminders of advancing years. So as folks in their forties come face to face with their mortality, it's only natural that they start to look for the payoff. They've made trade-offs over the years and now want to know if they were worthwhile. A common result? Midlife crisis.

Then there's the issue of stalled careers. "In their forties, people need to evaluate their lives because that is when plateauing at work and plateauing at home—plateauing in life—tend to occur," wrote Dr. Judith Hardwick in *The Plateauing Trap.*

Frequently, it's workplace woes that midlifers tend to obsess about. That may be because it's easier to concentrate on unhappiness at work than to deal with "the awful issues of aging and death and the existential anchor of a long-term marriage," according to Dr. Hardwick.

On the plus side: Those who are unsatisfied in work can rely on experience, well-honed skills, and a strong network of colleagues to put a career move in action. Sometimes, those who embark on a midlife-crisis type of career evaluation eventually decide that they've already made the right career decisions—which is a satisfying thing to realize.

On the minus side: Those who find their work unrewarding may fear making a career move, crippled by a dread of the unknown and of earning less money.

The Fifties: The Most-Issues-Have-Been-Resolved Decade

In their fifties, most folks have resolved their midlife work conflicts and are either progressing in a second career or have reached a level of satisfaction with their original career. "The fifties are a pretty comfortable decade," says Dr. Cron. "They've gone through all of those earlier issues, and their performance is generally good." But just when things are proceeding smoothly, the specter of retirement looms.

On the plus side: As ambition subsides, life can become easier and more fulfilling. Those who come to the realization that they never will make it to chairman (or even vice-president) can work to enjoy what they have succeeded in achieving—and work to leave something worthwhile behind.

On the minus side: It's easy to view young people as a threat. And older workers can be devastated upon retirement if they have not adequately planned for it.

We also become more realistic. And we're more serious about our work, more loyal, and less sidetracked by distractions in our social life. "On average, people get more interested in on-the-job achievements (as opposed to meteoric advancement) as they get older," explains Dr. Howard. Adds William Cron, Ph.D., associate business professor at Southern Methodist University in Dallas: "As you get more mature, you find you don't take the short-term focus. You don't have to produce something today because you want to get someplace tomorrow." Combined with your wealth of experience, such traits are invaluable to employers. But problems can surface when you find yourself in a job that doesn't utilize your unique perspective.

Make sure you're in a position that takes advantage of your strengths and weaknesses as they now exist. "Generally speaking, older people should be in jobs that utilize their judgment and thinking, not the ability to work fast and handle pressure," says Arthur Witkin, Ph.D., chief psychologist at Personnel Sciences Center, New York, and professor of industrial psychology at Queens College. His recommendation: Where possible, opt for staff positions over line operating situations in business.

If you're in a position that doesn't make use of your skills, a career counselor can help you devise a strategy for making a job move within your company. If you're at the point where you don't even know what your best assets are, career aptitude testing can point you in the right direction. (For names of career counselors who test in your city, contact the International Association of Counseling Services, 5999 Stevenson Ave., Alexandria, VA 22304.)

If you're job hunting, use the cover letter to your résumé as a place to highlight the special traits you have, suggests Dr. Witkin. In no more than two paragraphs of the letter, address the myths of older people—and how you have a great deal to offer: your experience, your know-how, your devotion to work.

2

ASSERTIVENESS

*A*ssertiveness is a word we tend to use without really understanding what it means. Here's an example. A new man transfers into your department, and the word you get from his former manager is that he is a great worker, detail oriented, and very assertive. What's the first thought that comes to your mind? "Hmmmm, I could use a go-getter like this guy. I just hope he isn't too bossy or demanding."

Upon hearing someone described as assertive, most of us would automatically assume that what's really meant is that the person is aggressive. We picture an assertive person as being contrary, stubborn, domineering, and terribly demanding.

In fact, assertiveness has nothing to do with any of those things. Truly assertive people do express their feelings, needs, and opinions in a forthright way. But they stop short of the abrasive manner that is the hallmark of the aggressive person. As we explore the differences among assertive, aggressive, and passive behavior it will become apparent that a little judicious assertiveness may be just what you need to cut through many of the interpersonal problems that spring up every day.

WHAT ASSERTIVENESS IS— AND WHAT IT ISN'T

Often, the best way to understand something is by comparison. Just as the color blue is only one of many colors aligned in a spectrum, assertiveness is only one of several kinds of behavior we may use in an effort to communicate our needs and thoughts.

At one end of the scale is nonassertive or passive behavior. If someone were smoking in the office, for example, a nonassertive person would probably not say anything about it, even though he or she was experiencing discomfort. "This kind of behavior usually arises from the belief that one's self doesn't matter—that one's feelings, rights, opinions, and ideas aren't important," says Elaina Zuker, author of *The Assertive Manager.* "Not only is there a low level of self-confidence, but nonassertive people often fear that if they speak up they will seem pushy or aggressive. So they either say nothing or make tentative statements beginning with the disclaimer, 'This is only my opinion' or 'I don't know if anyone will agree with this, but . . .'"

In addition, nonassertive behavior reflects low openness and high respect for others, according to Zuker. While nonassertive people don't communicate their feelings, at least they are not depreciating anyone else's. On the other hand, passive/aggressive behavior combines low openness with low respect for others. Everyone has run into this type of person. If you happen to be speaking a little too loudly in your office, rather than asking you to keep it down, the passive/aggressive person will slam his door hard enough for you to hear it. While he won't communicate his feelings, it is also obvious that he has no respect for yours.

Moving to the range of conduct characterized by high openness, our first stop is aggressive behavior. "This type of behavior is self-enhancing at the expense of others," says Zuker. "It is dominating and controlling. Aggressive people often sound accusing or superior, and they tend to blame or label the behaviors and attitudes of others." So while the aggressive person is able to get the message across in no uncertain terms, this type of behavior indicates absolutely no respect for anyone else. If you were talking in your office and it was annoying the aggressive person, he might come in and say, "I've never heard anyone that talks as loud as you. It's driving me up a wall. Knock it off!"

Last we come to the best possible conduct, characterized by high openness and high respect. This is assertive behavior. "Basically, assertive behavior is the expression of our needs, feelings, and opinions clearly, without violating the rights of others," says Zuker. "People usually act assertively out of a desire to be fair to themselves and to others. They wish to share control and responsibility."

Being assertive does not mean that you want to win at the other person's expense. What it does mean is that you want your fair say. You want your input to be considered in an equitable manner by the person to whom you are talking. This will happen only if you don't threaten or challenge the other person. An assertive person reacting to the noise level in your office might stop by and say, "Sometimes when you are having a conversation in your office, I have a hard time concentrating. It could be that the walls are thin and the sound carries. Would you mind keeping it down a little in the future?"

So, contrary to popular belief, the assertive person is not someone who seeks conflict and thrives on abrasiveness. Instead, he or she is a person who communicates on the best of all possible levels, where there are no losers, fools, or enemies—just two people who are mutually trying to solve their differences.

ASSERT YOURSELF TO SOLVE YOUR PROBLEMS

There are many reasons why people either don't assert themselves at all or assert themselves to the point of aggressiveness. As we mentioned before, some people are afraid of offending or appearing too demanding. Others go overboard out of a fear that they will be taken advantage of. In other words, we tend to avoid being properly assertive because we are subject to normal human frailties such as irrationality, pride, and fear.

Viewed from this perspective, the quest for a more assertive you seems like a Herculean task that would require a complete personality overhaul. On the other hand, if you look at assertiveness simply as a useful problem-solving technique, then there is every possibility that you could get up tomorrow and assert yourself straight through the day. So let's take the latter approach and begin by analyzing the typical problems you're likely to encounter in an office environment.

Most problems generally revolve around some form of argument, a clash between two conflicting views based upon the same information. In many office arguments, finding the *right* answer is not as important to the combatants as having the *winning* answer. That's where aggressiveness often comes into play. If you were to handle the situation aggressively, you would either ignore what the other person has to say or advance your own view by driving your opponent's view into the dirt.

But if you were a scientist assessing conflicting launch data for a manned space flight, you wouldn't want to satisfy your pride or stubbornness at the expense of a failed mission. Rather, you would compare your flight figures with those of your fellow scientists and make a logical decision that had the highest probability of success. If you treat an office argument in the same way, you will not only get your opinions across, you'll also be in a better position to show the other person why you think he may be wrong. And you can do it without incurring any rancor.

Here are some guidelines for arguing your case assertively.

First, assess the data. There is a set amount of information that pertains to any problem. That information, both pro and con, must be assimilated and considered. "Likewise, when dealing with another person whom you are in conflict with, you should take some initial time to listen to her side of the argument," says Filomena Warihay, Ph.D., president of Take Charge Consultants, a training and organizational development firm based in Downingtown, Pennsylvania. "Listen to it well enough that you can paraphrase it and repeat it.

"By reiterating what she is saying, you drive home the fact that you understand where she is coming from. If you remain silent and then steamroll into your own opinion, she will feel ignored and will view you as aggressive," notes Dr. Warihay. "Once she thinks you don't care about her, she will cease to care about you and you'll find yourself facing an aggressive person. So always end your listening period with a statement that begins, 'Let me see if I understand what you are saying . . . ' "

Accept the data. In an assertive argument, no opinion is without merit. "That's an axiom," says Dr. Warihay. "In an aggressive argument, on the other hand, no opinion has merit but your own."

You've shown the other person that you understand what he is saying. Now you need to make it clear that his opinion has some value. "It doesn't mean that you have to agree with him," says Dr. Warihay. "You just want to make sure that you've built up some trust before airing your own opinions."

Let the other person know that you admire the amount of work he's put into the project so far, or praise the uniqueness of his solutions.

State your own case. Having done the necessary prep work, you are now in an excellent position to voice your ideas and have them seriously considered by the other person. He is ready to listen because you've already bestowed your own attentiveness. He will even accept a measure of criticism because you have already shown some appreciation of his ideas.

"There is one more thing that you may need to do in your quest for self-assertion," says Dr. Warihay." And that's to offer the other person a little extra incentive to see things your way." Just as any conqueror knows that magnanimous terms make surrender an easier option to accept, you may want to ask if there is anything you can do to help your opponent implement your ideas. After all, while the idea is yours, you will still be depending on him for a great deal of support and input.

Done correctly, this plan of assertive action not only releases you from a common fear of disagreements (that you will be too abrasive or hurt someone's feelings), it also allows for maximum consideration of your ideas—which is why you wanted to be more assertive to begin with. It also fulfills two primary requirements of assertive behavior: that the situation be seen in a clear, unemotional light and that there be no losers.

Think "cool" thoughts. Seeing things clearly becomes even more important when you have to assert yourself in a situation where someone is doing something personally distasteful to you. "A good example is when you are in a meeting with three of your peers as well as your boss," says Dr. Warihay. "The meeting is going well until a point where your boss begins criticizing your latest work in front of the other people at the table. Naturally this would be upsetting and embarrassing to anyone. What do you do?"

"To see the situation clearly, the first thing you need to do is bring your emotional level back to room temperature," says Zuker. "Your primary reaction to the criticism will be composed of 'hot' thoughts such as 'How dare he make me look like a fool in front of everyone,' or 'What is he trying to do? Ruin me?' But before voicing your objection, you want to begin focusing on what I call 'cool' thoughts: 'Well, maybe he doesn't realize how his criticism sounds.' Or 'I guess he's only trying to solve the problem that led to the meeting in the first place.'"

Once you've taken inventory of your "hot" and "cool" thoughts, you may begin to see the difference between intent and effect. "Someone's actions may have had a harmful effect on us and may have led us to feel angry, but that might not have been the other person's intent at all," says Zuker. "Very often we attribute motives to others that they don't really have."

Since you probably aren't a mind reader, the only thing you can be sure of is your own feelings. "So when you approach your boss after the meeting to discuss the matter of public criticism, you want to be sure that you broach the subject in a way that doesn't place blame or label intent," says Dr. Warihay.

Rather than saying "You really make me mad when you criticize me in front of my peers," try this: "When you criticize me in front of my peers, I feel angry." The difference? "In the first sentence there is an implied blame placed upon the manager," says Dr. Warihay. "What you are saying is that your manager *makes* you mad. But in the second sentence there is a bit more distance between the 'I' and the 'you.' What you are saying is that there might not be anything intrinsically wrong in practice or intent with what your boss did, but your personal reaction was one of anger."

"This type of assertiveness technique is sometimes referred to as 'ownership,'" says Zuker. "It means that you and you alone are taking responsibility for the reaction you had. One advantage to this is that it allows room for the other person to see the situation differently and to speak for himself, thereby avoiding the need for defensiveness on his part. Second, by speaking only for yourself and assuming nothing concerning the other person's intent, you show yourself to have a certain self-respect and desire to keep all communications clear and accurate."

Observe, don't accuse. When you need to correct an employee's behavior, you could find yourself in a touchy situation. If (like many managers) you'd just as soon avoid conflict, things may get out of hand. Let's say an employee is having trouble processing orders on time. Rather than confronting him with the problem and possibly incurring his resentment, you let things slide and hope that the situation rectifies itself. Finally, you begin to get a little angry yourself and approach the employee: "You never seem to be able to process orders on time."

"This type of generalized statement is exactly what you want to avoid when confronting the employee," says Zuker. "Such an implied accusation leaves the other person with nowhere to go, except to get defensive and deny the accusation or retaliate in some way later. Those are exactly the things you had hoped to avoid."

Rather than generalize, try using what Zuker calls "sense statements." These are comments based entirely on what you see and hear. For example, you could say to the employee, "I see that your desk is piled high with unprocessed orders." This kind of statement is hard to argue with and allows you to broach the subject in a nonthreatening manner that will keep conflict to a minimum.

"The one thing you need to remember about sense statements is that they need to be as exact as possible," counsels Zuker, "Rather than tell someone that her phone is always ringing off the wall, mention that you heard her phone ring 15 times this morning. Ask if there is a problem. Instead of accusing an employee of laziness, bring up the fact that her output for the last week is five points below the average."

Obviously we have only scratched the surface of situations in which an assertive manner will help get you what you want. But the guidelines are clear. Make no assumptions. Give the other person a fair shake. Speak only for yourself and take responsibility for your feelings. Try to view the situation in an emotionally cool manner. In other words, discuss your emotions but don't speak emotionally.

These guidelines will go a long way toward keeping you from crossing that fine line between assertiveness and aggressiveness. What's more, they are practical problem-solving approaches that can help clear up just about any interpersonal situation.

GETTING OUT OF THE PASSIVE MODE

The previous section assumed that you have no trouble opening your mouth. But what if your problem is just the opposite? After all, many of us have a little factory in our brain that does nothing but churn out clever excuses as to why we shouldn't speak up for ourselves. "Oh, nobody listens anyway." "They'll think my ideas are too simplistic." "He'll think I'm stupid."

"The thing to keep in mind, however, is that these thoughts are not facts," says Zuker. "They are merely unfounded opinions, and you need to treat them as such. Too often we live with our fears for so long that we assume them to be true. But you can make an effort to change your beliefs."

In her book *The Assertive Manager,* Zuker suggests a four-step process for changing the way you see things and gaining a plan of action to become more assertive.

1. Identify a situation in which you are not as assertive as you'd like to be.
2. Identify the belief underlying your nonassertive behavior.
3. Visualize yourself behaving more confidently and assertively in that situation.
4. Make up one or more new beliefs that you would need to accept in order to practice the desired assertive behavior.

Let's say that your department often gets together for brainstorming meetings. But because of your current nonassertiveness, you simply sit there quietly, waiting for the meeting to end. Perhaps the belief behind this behavior is that everyone will think your ideas are stupid. Now visualize yourself speaking up, offering ideas along with everyone else. Imagine the same reaction directed toward you that the person next to you receives when he speaks up. Form a new belief that your ideas—good or bad—will be welcomed and considered in the same light as everyone else's. Your new desired behavior is to toss out at least one idea at the next meeting.

"If you are particularly timid or self-conscious, start slow," advises Dr. Warihay. "Pick a situation in which you have a large probability of succeeding. The only way that you will change your current beliefs concerning failure is if you receive conflicting data—in other words, some evidence of success."

Once you experience some minor success, target a different situation, one that's a bit more difficult. Buoyed by your recent success, you may find it a bit easier to adopt your newly made beliefs and then act on them. Tell yourself you're starting with a blank slate. You have the power to write whatever you want on it.

3

ATTITUDE

Because this *is* the United States of America, where people are just as likely to salute large sums of money as they are the flag, it gets a little tough sometimes to base your job satisfaction on factors other than the most obvious ones of cash, power, and prestige. In part you can thank mass communications for this dilemma. You can't read a newspaper without being treated to the glamorous doings of the rich and powerful. Television? Which are you more likely to see: "Crude," a series about oil tycoons who have a penchant for flexing their bank accounts, crushing honest, small-time entrepreneurs, and playing polo in their spare time; or "Good-Natured Working Guy," a moving show about a man who resoles shoes for a living. He doesn't make much money, has only seen the sights that Butte, Montana, can offer, and is saving up to buy a water purifier. But shoe resoling is a mission to him, and the artistry he brings to his job is repaid every time he sees one of his customers taking a comfortable stroll down the street.

Obviously, the networks will not be fighting over the concept for "Good-Natured Working Guy," but perhaps we can take a hint from him. Liking your job for what it is can provide you with a bigger payoff than the most overinflated salary or the biggest desk with the most toys on it. And while that may sound just trite enough to be printed on one of those posters that has seagulls flying around on it, think about this: You can sit around bemoaning the fact that you are not in the fast lane, that you're underpaid, that the corporate world is not treating you the way you like . . . but it won't do you any good. Cash, power, and prestige must be given to you. On the other hand, self-esteem, pride in a job well done, and a sense of importance are all bonuses you can give yourself. Unless you happen to be a lily of the field, you're going to have to put in 40 hours a week whether you like it or not. So you've got nothing to lose and everything to gain by learning to find enjoyment in your work.

GIVE YOURSELF PERMISSION TO LIKE YOUR JOB

Where did the notion come from, anyway, that work is a trial that mortals must endure? "Well, you have to remember that this is a nation founded by a highly religious sect," notes sociologist Saul Greenberg, Ph.D., author of *The New Jerusalem*. "The Puritans came here not only to seek religious freedom but to establish a whole new society, which would be a new Jerusalem for the world to see. Theirs was a stern, rugged sort of religion that reflected the hardships inherent in starting a new order in a wild land. Frivolity had no place in this society. Good, honest, hard labor was something that not only was necessary for survival but also purified the soul. Work was not a matter of finding a job that would interest and fulfill you. You did the same work your father before you did or you learned a different trade that the community had need of."

So much for why we often group "work" with a lot of other nasty four-letter words. But if you still hold to the Puritan viewpoint, you may want to ask yourself whether it really pertains to our twentieth-century situation. To put it mildly, "leniency" is the hallmark of today's labor options. You needn't become a blacksmith just because your father and your father's father pounded iron. And you needn't become a cobbler because that is the only trade that your community seems to have a current need for. In fact, there are thousands of possible trades and professions for you to choose from and little or nothing holding you back from making a choice, as long as you back it up with the proper training.

And yet, though we freely make our choice, we still end up resenting our job at some point or another. Why? "There are two primary reasons I can think of right off the top of my head," says Maynard Johnson, a psychologist and career counselor in New York City. "First, people resent the fact that earning a living is wasting valuable time that they could spend enjoying themselves or uncovering what they suspect to be their true talents as a novelist or artist. If my clients raise this point, I usually ask them to recall their last long vacation. Was it two weeks of complete enjoyment? More likely it was a week and a half of fun in the sun combined with another half a week of 'If I watch one more sunset I'm going to go out of my mind. Boy, I can't wait to get productive again.' "

If they don't admit to such vacation blues and their work dissatisfaction is serious, Johnson suggests that they take a three-month leave of absence if they possibly can. "I tell them to go work on their novel, enroll in a few classes, or just sit around watching TV, if that's what they want to do, and then come back to me in three months. By that point, most people will have gone out of their mind. They've lost track of the days, their self-esteem is dropping to an all-time low, and they've actually begun to get irritable. The point being that while all work and no play is not good, all play and no work is disastrous. We need to feel like we are accomplishing something. And we also need some form of order in our life."

The second and perhaps more prevalent reason that people have a hard time liking their work is that they feel trapped. "Sure, initially you have some choice in the matter of what kind of work you'd like to do," says Johnson. "But once you've been at a company for five years and have picked up a spouse, a mortgage, and a child, you have very little choice about jumping ship if things aren't turning out the way you planned. A steady paycheck can be the biggest manacle of all. And while people may not mind doing something of their own free will, they absolutely resent having to do it because they have no other choice."

If you've put in a number of years at a particular job and you find that it just isn't ringing your bell anymore, you may want to consider some of the options offered in "Career Change" on page 52. But if you simply find yourself resenting the fact that you have to take what the company dishes out because you can't afford to quit, it may be time to prepare for yourself what Johnson humorously calls a "cyanide capsule." "It's a strange analogy," he says, "but if you ever watch secret agent movies, they always have a cyanide capsule hidden somewhere on their body in case they are captured. If the torture becomes too much to bear, they can simply swallow the capsule. In other words, they have an option. And having an option somehow gives them the strength to hold on a little longer in the hope that the situation may change."

Rather than packing cyanide, your option takes the form of an up-to-date résumé, a weekly glance through the help-wanted section, and a sprinkling of visits to various industry functions where some low-key networking can take place. This is not to suggest that you simply give up and get a new job. Rather, what you are doing is providing yourself with a constant option. Keep abreast of the job market, have your personal stats immediately at hand, and develop some connections so that *if* things get unbearable where you currently work, you *could* jump ship with very little downtime. The big payoff is that you will rid yourself of that constantly recurring resentment at being bound and tied to your current position. Now, when things get a little bothersome at the office, you can secretly smile and relax, knowing full well that you could split anytime you wanted to.

"Being in this position—and at the same time remember our previous discussion of the 'all-play-and-no-work rule'—does wonders for your attitude," notes Johnson. "It actually allows you to enjoy your work since, in reality, you are only there because you want to be."

How to have a positive attitude even when you don't feel like it

While understanding that you aren't trapped and that you aren't wasting valuable pleasure time can take you partway down the road to a better work attitude, there are still a few extra things you can do to perk yourself up on a day-to-day basis.

After spending 25 years working with employees, industrial psychologist and career management consultant Richard Germann estimates that four out of five workers have something major about their jobs that they dislike. The trouble is, liking your job is essential for success. "Those who don't value what they do will never be successful at it," he explains. "Those who don't enjoy their work will ultimately fail."

At the core of adopting a positive attitude is accepting the simple notion that you must assume responsibility for your own situation. That's not to say that it's all your own fault if you seem stuck in a dead-end job. But you have more power than you realize.

"Most people feel controlled by their environment, but they really aren't," says career management consultant Diane Blumenson, who along with Germann wrote *Working and Liking It.* "They have to learn to manage that environment so they can get from it what they need." Remember, nobody—neither boss nor peer—is likely to have the time or inclination to help you overcome your career blahs. It's largely up to you to do what you can to initiate a change in attitude. Here are some ways to get started.

Dream a little . . . plan a lot. Germann often instructs his clients who are unhappy about their current jobs to kick back and fantasize about their dream job description. It's a fun exercise that gets people to focus on their workplace ideals: everything from what they would really like to be doing day in and day out to what sort of office environment they prefer. The point is to encourage folks to create their own definition of job satisfaction.

Without that definition or goal, it's easy to understand why you may be feeling a little down on work. Picture yourself sitting in a car somewhere in Kansas. You've got a sales meeting to attend in two days but no one told you whether that meeting is in New York or Los Angeles. Not knowing where you are supposed to be heading is sure to put a crimp in anybody's attitude.

But suppose you do develop your concept of the perfect job? What then? You now know the sales meeting is in L.A., but you don't have a map. In other words, you know where you're going, you just don't know how to get there.

"I ask clients to start breaking down their ultimate fantasy into the smallest possible parts," says Johnson. "If they see themselves as a junior executive working under a great boss in the marketing department, when in fact they are currently a clerk working under a tyrant in purchasing, then we start looking for little 'stepping-stone' goals that will get them from one position to the other."

In that situation, for example, the first thing you might do is see if you can't get a transfer to a different section of purchasing. This will at least get you away from the tyrant's clutches. If it can be done, why not go for a low-level position in marketing? "Then you would want to get some additional training or schooling under your belt so that you look like a good executive candidate," says Johnson. "At the very least, you should find out exactly what qualifications you would need to move up the ladder and then start researching ways to acquire those qualifications. They don't need to be big steps that you take, but they need to be well ordered and regularly executed. Developing and following your own plan of action is one of the biggest ways to improve your attitude."

Think of yourself as autonomous. In effect, this is a little mental trick that you can play on yourself. Start thinking of yourself as a small business or an independent contractor with one major client—your employer. Then allocate your time so that you not only meet the demands of your customers but you also have room to develop certain aspects of your business which *you* (not the company) see as necessary for your future growth.

"The most useful part of this concept is that it moves you from an outwardly controlled motivation of simply pleasing your boss to a more internalized one where you recognize and improve your skills for your own pleasure," notes Johnson. "This also counteracts the general ennui that overtakes the best of us and leads us to think 'Why work any harder? What I'm doing is acceptable.'"

To put all this into a more definite image, picture yourself working at some job that demands that an occasional report be written. It turns out (much to your surprise) that you can turn out some nice phrases. It may not matter to the folks upstairs that they've got a blossoming Hemingway on their hands, but *you*, in your new guise as an independent business, should realize that your writing skills may open a whole new area of sales for You-Yourself Enterprises. So rather than turning in the drivel typically expected and accepted in reports, you should take the extra time to make the words glow and thereby perfect your product for a broader market.

Separate work and play. Picture this: You invite a friend to stay over at your place for a few days and give him the guest room upstairs. After the second day, his clothes are hung over the banister outside his room. On the morning of the third day, he decides he can't live without his Saint Bernard, who proceeds to take up residence on your living room couch. On the fourth day, you can't park in your garage because his car is in there. Bit by bit, as your friend takes over the house, you find yourself holed up in your room. Are you getting annoyed?

"The same thing happens with some people and their careers," notes Johnson. "At first they might work the occasional extra hour or two in the evening. Then they start taking work home regularly to look at after dinner. Soon, Saturday morning and afternoon become nothing more than office hours where they don't have to dress up. In effect, work becomes this ill-mannered guest that takes up more and more of their space and time. Most people don't even notice it happening, but suddenly they don't have a separate life apart from work, and they resent it."

Johnson is not saying that taking work home is taboo. But doing it all the time is. "The interesting thing is that many people take work home, poke at it a little, and then go watch television. They never actually *get* any substantial work done, but on the other hand they don't enjoy their leisure because that work is sitting there tugging at their conscience. This wouldn't be so bad except that if you always have some work to do lying around, you'll never enjoy yourself during your leisure time and you'll resent your job for putting you in the predicament you're in."

If you do have a heavy workload, he suggests alternating evenings of intensive work and intensive leisure. "On Monday, Wednesday, and Friday evenings (or whatever appeals to you), do your work and try not to get sidetracked. But on your leisure nights, don't even bother taking work home if you can possibly help it. If you leave it at work, it can hardly sit on the coffee table spoiling your evening with silent reprimands."

Strive for success outside of work. This one is fast and simple. Take your hobbies and leisure activities as seriously as you do your work. This doesn't mean that you should drive yourself crazy over them, but at least strive for the same kind of proficiency and take the same kind of pride in them that you do in your work.

"The reason for this is so that you can wean yourself off the feeling that work is the only thing that matters," says Johnson. "A trap many people fall into is that they get their whole sense of identity from the office. This may be great when things are going well, but things don't always go well. If your self-esteem is a direct outcome of your work situation, you're bound to have a bad attitude when the going gets rough. But if you can tie your esteem to your outside endeavors, then you can maintain a positive attitude even if the office forecast calls for thunderstorms tomorrow."

CHANGING YOUR ATTITUDE TOWARD OTHERS

The biggest influence on job satisfaction is relationships with others, says industrial psychologist Germann. So if you dislike your job, if you dread going to work each morning, chances are it's at least partly because you're not getting along with those around you.

You don't have to like the people you work with, but at the very least you should be able to interact positively with them. "No, you don't have to have outside relationships with them, but you have to have some sort of positive relationship, some level of comfort with them," says Blumenson. Again, that's a goal that can be achieved only when you dedicate yourself to a shift in attitude.

When you smile in an elevator, your fellow passengers invariably respond with a smile. The same thing can happen in your office when you start to relate to others with sincere friendliness. "If you initiate positive interaction, you're inviting positive reaction. It's human nature to react in kind," explains Blumenson. And your superiors' image of you will improve right along with your attitude, almost magically.

Don't worry that suddenly striking up relationships with people you heretofore couldn't care less about will come across as insincerity. The fact is, you *are* being sincere in your efforts to improve work relations because you want to improve your attitude and general enjoyment of your office environment. And that sincerity will be felt by your co-workers.

Now that you're committed to the task ahead, here are some ways to get started.

Have more positive interactions. Until now you hated even *being* with co-workers, let alone engaging in conversations with them. Don't be surprised if they know how you feel. After all, you probably have lapsed into a pattern of complaining—about your job, about your boss, about the weather. Germann suggests you stop complaining and start talking to people in a more positive way. He predicts the attitude of others will change, too. "From a practical point of view, it makes a difference in how you feel about your job," he says. *Note:* You can still complain occasionally—just don't make it a constant theme.

Don't jump into it. Start out slowly, suggests Blumenson. You could walk past a person's desk tomorrow morning—a person you've generally snubbed—and say "Good morning." Next day, you could walk past and say, "Is that a picture of your daughter?" Eventually—and almost invariably— the two of you will find something in common that can be the foundation of positive interactions. (Just remember, complaining about work conditions doesn't count.)

Have more frequent interactions. Don't sit at your desk and stew about the low level of conversation or the intellectual desert in which you work. Step outside your office and join the discussion about the exploits of the new pitcher on the hometown team. If you don't know much about the background of the obscure director of the obscure film everybody's critiquing, express an interest by asking someone who does know.

Change your attitude a little and you're likely to change how people feel about you. They may actually like having you around. And you may actually start to like being around.

4

BODY LANGUAGE

Remember President Richard Nixon? They started calling him "Tricky Dick" long before the Watergate affair. One reason that the former president acquired such a bad rep without really earning it is provided by David Givens, Ph.D., a research anthropologist at the American Anthropological Association. "When he spoke with people, he would look them in the face, but he would angle his body away, telegraphing the signal that he wanted to escape," says Dr. Givens. "His 'squirming' cues gave the impression that he was unfriendly and possibly not truthful."

Nonverbal communication is a potent, natural force that reminds us of our primitive links with the rest of creation. Linguistic ability is a relatively new phenomenon, but signaling is believed to have occurred among lizards, birds, and other creatures before mammals arrived on the scene. Even now, experts say that as little as 20 percent of what we communicate is done with words. And from an evolutionary perspective, it makes a lot of sense.

THE NEXT BEST THING TO ESP

Successful people are generally quite savvy at picking up on nonverbal cues. For example, a subordinate tells his boss about an impending project, and the boss—who hasn't yet opened his mouth—starts hunching his shoulders, angling his head to one side, and compressing his lips. The subordinate senses that this body language is communicating disagreement and possibly annoyance. So he quickly thinks of something to say to test the waters: "You don't seem to be agreeing with me. Is there something wrong?" he asks. One of the marvelous benefits of our current stage of evolution is that you can use verbal language to probe the message you receive nonverbally, to see if it's true.

In general, you should place more value on what you're seeing than on what the other person is saying, Dr. Givens advises. So here are a few basic nonverbal cues that ought to register on your antennae. Keep in mind that every individual has his or her own "baseline" inclination to stand, sit, or gesture one way or the other. (Examples: Some people *never* make eye contact, not because they don't like others but because they're insecure. A person may fiddle with his wedding band simply because his finger itches, not out of tension.) Once you're aware of someone's standard body language, you can assign a learned level of importance to the following cues.

Turning away. If you're speaking with someone and he either turns away or averts his eyes—after having faced you directly and maintained good eye contact—it's almost a sure sign that he disagrees with something you said or is annoyed with you. It's virtually guaranteed that you're losing points. (Note: In Asian cultures, the same response may be a sign of respect. In the Middle East, for a man to look a woman directly in the eye is akin to attacking her physically. Remember what Barbara Walters said after interviewing Colonel Muammar al-Qaddafi? She announced how disconcerting it was that he "kept looking all over the room, but rarely at me." That wasn't necessarily an indication that he's shifty.)

Turning to face you. Generally speaking, the opposite is true. If someone begins by facing away from you and suddenly swivels his upper body towards you, aligning his shoulders and making eye contact, you're probably winning him to your side.

Slouching. When a person is sitting or standing erect and then lapses into a slump, you'd be wise to take it as a sign of disinterest.

Grasping a chair arm and locking ankles. You see it regularly on airplanes during takeoffs and landings (holding back fear). You see it when someone is forced to postpone a trip to the rest room (holding back). In a meeting, this posture may signal that the person is holding back information, a concession, or his or her true feelings.

Raising hands to the chest. When a person who is speaking to you raises his hands to chest level, a few inches in front of his body, and speaks with hands relaxed and slightly curled, you can generally take it as a sign of honesty and openness.

Clenching a fist or banging a hand against a table. These are warning signs. (You probably wouldn't be where you are today if you didn't already know that.)

Wringing hands. The person is nervous. If you want to try to make him relax, you should smile, look him in the eye, and lean slightly forward.

UNDERSTANDING DOMINANT/SUBMISSIVE SIGNALS

When one wild mammal approaches another, there's a natural instinct to reinforce the hierarchy that dictates who is dominant and who is submissive. A leader wolf, for example, will approach a subordinate wolf with his tail in the air, but the subordinate wolf will keep his tail down.

The animal kingdom—as you've probably surmised—is not much different from our corporate one.

Your boss comes up to you and pats you on the back. It's a sign of dominance. You will probably respond by pigeon-toeing your feet inward, which Dr. Givens describes as "a classic sign of submission." And the boss will toe out, which is a sign of dominance.

Dr. Givens points out that people in submissive roles tend to do a lot of self-clasping: flexing their limbs, crossing their arms, crouching. These are self-protective stances designed to make the body as small as is possible. Submissive people may also cross their legs or touch their throat.

"A dominant person picks up on this and can take advantage," explains Dr. Givens. The classic dominant gestures are more expansive and include "spreading the arms and legs and creating an air of openness."

So how do you control any tendency on your part toward submissiveness? "Take a mental note of yourself when you're with someone you like," advises Dr. Givens. "Note what your body is doing, where your feet are, how you hold your arms. Then consciously try to duplicate that stance the next time you're with a dominant person."

Note: There may be some occasions when you might want to consciously make yourself appear *more* submissive. Especially if you're a large person and your size tends to intimidate people—particularly undersized superiors. By throwing in a few submissive signals, you'll appear more properly deferential to them. Of course, at no time should you use body language that feels totally unnatural to you. People will sniff out the discomfort—and, yes, the dishonesty.

ARE YOU SAYING ONE THING WHILE YOUR BODY SAYS ANOTHER?

How many times has this happened? Your boss is finishing up giving you a new assignment and she ends the conversation with the words, "Let me know if I can be of any help." But somehow you go away thinking her last words were: "Hey, don't bother me." Are you paranoid?

No. It may have had something to do with the fact that your boss was glancing at her watch when she issued her offer of assistance. Or she may have been staring out the window. Or her arms may have been folded tightly across her chest. "If there's a mixed message, we believe what we see, not what we hear," says Germaine Knapp, founder and president of Wordsmart, a Rochester, New York–based communications consulting company.

According to Knapp, when it comes to interpreting what other people are saying, visual cues are more important than anything else. Next in importance is the voice (we can pick up commitment, enthusiasm, disinterest, skepticism, and other messages through tone alone). And least important are the words themselves.

So how do you make sure you're not sending off the wrong message with your own body language? "The way you can tell if you're giving off the wrong signals is if you're not getting what you need from other people," says Anita Brick, cofounder of Decision Dynamics, a Chicago-based consulting firm. For example, ask yourself, Do people generally decline my assistance even when I'm hoping to be of help? Observe how others generally react to you and whether they show a pattern of response opposite to what you would expect.

Basic Body Talk Tips

Want to make a solid impression? Chicago consultant Anita Brick sums up her advice in a single sentence: "Carry yourself as if you care about yourself, as if you're confident."

Germaine Knapp, founder of a Rochester, New York, communications consulting firm, suggests some specifics.

- Sit or stand erect.
- Lean slightly forward.
- Maintain eye contact.
- Unfold your arms and legs.
- Look open, pleasant, and positive.
- To emphasize agreement, nod your head occasionally and say "yes."
- To show command, sit at the head of a table or stand while others are seated.

Also pay attention to your posture and gestures. Do you cross your arms defensively when praising an employee? Do you smile when you impart serious information? Take note of such inconsistencies in your gestures. "People are put off by nonverbal inconsistency," says Brick.

BODY LANGUAGE ADVICE FOR A NEW JOB

If you've worked in an office for a while, you're bound to know how people ordinarily stand, hold their bodies, and gesture—so you'll be tuned in for nonverbal cues. But you have no such advantage when you start a new job. If that's the case, Dr. Givens suggests you hold back on making interpretations because (1) you are stressed out, and as a result, possibly a bit too paranoid, and (2) you won't know what people's baseline postures are. "After a couple of weeks, you'll know them better," he says.

As for your own body language? "Give off as little as you can. Err on the side of being nonexpressive until you know what's appropriate," Dr. Givens advises.

The Subtle Power of Gestures

Here's how to get a subordinate to finish a long-winded discussion. At some time during his talk, clasp your hands behind your back and listen, nodding in agreement with what you hear. Then, when you want to stop him, move your hands in front of you and clasp them in front. Experts say the subtle shift—physically putting something between the two of you—may signal to the talker that it's time to wrap up.

Here's how to put more power into your hand gestures. Keep your fingers together, not spread apart. Gesturing with fingers apart is said to communicate weakness. Gesturing with fingers tightly together communicates power.

5

BOSSES

When the Wyatt Company, a large consulting firm, polled 3,500 workers in all industries and at every job level, it found that 52 percent thought their bosses were good at handling problems related to work tasks. But only 39 percent thought their bosses knew how to deal with people.

That should come as no great surprise to anyone who has been on the losing end of a boss/subordinate relationship. The standard excuse for this national dearth of good, people-sensitive managers is that folks are generally promoted on the basis of their ability to make things happen—to produce successful bottom lines, for example—and not because they know how to deal with others. Moreover, a lot of the bosses in power today got their start in the days when organizations tutored upwardly mobile workers in the most rigid of management techniques, something akin to what is taught to officers in the Marine Corps. And those bosses are now managing employees who grew up in a less structured atmosphere.

Whatever the reasons, one thing is clear: As a subordinate with a problem boss, you may need to take some control of the situation before it can improve. "You have to know what your boss expects of you and other people. If you don't know it, nothing else you do know will make any difference," says Donald H. Weiss, Ph.D., a St. Louis–based management trainer and author of many books about interpersonal office skills.

But how many bosses, despite everything they've learned or read, bother to sit down with new employees and clearly spell out their needs and expectations in words that are simple and direct? Few indeed. So you have to take the matter into your own hands. Suggests Dr. Weiss: "Managing the boss may require walking into his or her office and saying, 'I'm trying to meet your needs, but I don't know what they are.' "

Dr. Weiss offers a few other tips for putting your relationship with the boss on a winning track.

Remind yourself that your boss isn't perfect. Don't expect him or her to be a parent who loves you, knows everything, and always has your best interests at heart. You're bound to be disappointed. It's amazing how many boss/subordinate problems are caused by people who overlook this simple fact of life.

Understand your boss's goals. Think about the requirements upon which his or her performance is going to be judged.

Study your boss's behavioral style. Draw up a list of your boss's values and preferences. Does she arrive at work early just to see who's in on time? Or doesn't she care how many hours you put in (as long as you get the job done)? Does she joke about the latest government scandal, or does she sit in her office and listen to Verdi on headphones? Does she solicit contradictions or does she pounce on anyone who thinks for himself? Does she value loyalty over productivity? Does she withhold praise?

Think about the climate your boss is trying to create. Is he trying to create a competitive climate? A cooperative climate? A climate in which disagreement is tolerated but conflicts aren't?

Measure your boss's tolerance for stress. Some bosses thrive on stress; others are demolished by it. If your boss likes stress, chances are that you'll have to like it, too. If your boss doesn't respond well to stress, try to anticipate his or her breaking point.

LEARN TO READ THE SITUATION THROUGH YOUR BOSS'S EYES

Think about it for a moment. Sure, your superior may seem like the nastiest S.O.B. on the planet. But consider this fact of life: The stakes often are higher at the top. More is expected of him by *his* bosses. And each time a new subordinate comes under his command, he loses another dimension of direct control over the final work result. Yet every time an employee screws up, he's held responsible. So when he assigns you to close the Henderson deal or prepare the Wisconsin market report, remember that he may be sweating a lot more than you are.

That's not to say you should forgive your boss for being such a cruel, demanding, manipulative, inconsiderate person. But by learning to read a situation through his eyes, you may go a long way toward developing smooth relations. It's actually not that difficult, explains San Diego–based management consultant Natasha Josefowitz, Ph.D., author of *You're the Boss* and coauthor of *Fitting In: How to Get a Good Start in Your New Job.* "In any relationship, at some point in time," she says, "there is going to be a difficult situation in which it would be wise for you to ask: 'If I were that person, what would I be feeling?' "

Take this example: Your boss needs a report from you so he can use it in a meeting with his superiors. You turn in the report, but it's incomplete. He takes it into his meeting and the CEO gets upset with him because of its shortcomings. So afterwards he calls you in for a talking-to.

"Normally, you'd only think about protecting your own hide," says Dr. Josefowitz. "But instead, concentrate on how bad your boss looked at his meeting." Don't get defensive. Rather, develop some compassion for what your boss is feeling—regardless of how mad he is at you. Instead of lapsing into "But you gave me this assignment with practically no time to complete it," say: "I feel terrible that you had to go to the meeting with an incomplete report."

After that, say: "Let's talk about what happened, so that it doesn't happen again." Next, explain whatever the particular problem was. ("You gave me the assignment too late," or "I didn't have the resources.") In general, says Dr. Josefowitz, "Instead of getting defensive, answer to what you know the boss is feeling."

WHAT TO DO WHEN YOU'RE AT ODDS WITH YOUR BOSS

Regardless of the kind of conflict you're having with your boss, here are some important things to consider.

Know what you want. "Until you know that, you won't know whether to fight or fly—whether it's worth staying and battling it out or whether you're in an irreconcilable situation," says Dr. Weiss. So when the boss wants you to pursue a project that you think is unworthy of your time, consider the reason you're working at your present job in the first place. Are you there only to get three years' worth of solid experience at a major insurance company? Isn't that three years up? Or maybe you're in a different kind of situation where it's worth staying and fighting, or worth staying but backing down. You really can't decide until you are clear about what you want from the job. (Possible reasons for staying: You haven't been in the job very long; you are learning important skills; it would be difficult to find a similar job in the current employment market; you need the salary.)

Get clarification of your boss's perspective. Dr. Weiss says there often are major conflicts over simple misunderstandings. It's the first possibility to check. "Maybe once you get clarification you'll realize that there is no conflict," says Dr. Weiss, "You simply didn't understand."

Express yourself. You can't expect your boss to read your mind. Ask for an opportunity to express your opinion. If it's denied, start looking for another job, suggests Dr. Weiss—unless you actually *like* working for someone who commands you with no concern about what you think. Throughout your discussion, be direct, nonthreatening, and as honest as you feel you can be.

Look for common points. Chances are that you'll agree on something that can be the basis of negotiation. Look for points that you are willing to lose—something that is important to the boss but not very significant to you.

Present your ideas in terms of benefits to the boss and the organization. Just don't give the impression that you're being manipulative.

Get a fresh perspective. If the situation is intolerable and you feel trapped, seek the advice of a qualified career counselor who can aid your search for a new job—and a new boss. Too many people stay in bad jobs with bad bosses because it's easier to endure a familiar torture than to explore the unknown. When things get unbearable, a good career counselor can do wonders.

SECOND-GUESSING YOUR BOSS

Your boss has just learned that a minor error one of your subordinates has made will cost the division a sale. It's the second time this has happened recently, and your boss calls you into the office within seconds of learning about the lost sale. He starts hollering and tossing annual reports around in a wild rage. "Fire Johnson!" he yells. "Get that guy packing by this afternoon!"

But you do not fire Johnson. Instead, you wander back to your office. You may explain to Johnson that the boss is displeased with the error. You do some calculations at your desk. A couple of hours later you calmly pay a return visit to the boss. You say: "Look, I understand you want to fire Johnson over the past two errors, but I did some calculations, and his work on the four previous sales netted us more money than the work of anyone else in the department for the same period. Also, the cost of replacing him will be at least 20 percent more than it would be to keep him on and convince him that he must mend his behavior." Your boss looks at you and says: "Fine. Let's give him another chance."

This is what's called being a useful, knowledgeable subordinate—and it illustrates a good way of saying no to your boss. The trick is not to approach your boss with an argumentative style. "If you just like to argue a lot, you won't last long," warns Robert L. MacDonald, Ph.D., a lecturer at the University of Pennsylvania's Wharton School. He lists several situations, though, in which it is a good idea to diplomatically second-guess your boss.

When your boss likes to blow off steam. We've already examined this possibility above.

When your boss drinks too much. In this situation, you could say, "Last night at dinner, there were a couple of things we talked about. You were quite specific about firing Johnson. He's been a good producer over the last five quarters. Is that what you really want to do?"

When your boss is known for changing his mind. Hastily executed orders under these circumstances could easily be regretted by both of you.

Should you ever go over your boss's head? "There are very few bosses who are going to like that," says Dr. MacDonald. "So the reasons must be extremely important." (Translation: Only if you feel the issue is worth the risk of losing your job.)

Thankfully, some of the younger industries that are built on new technologies are breaking down the hierarchical standards. In some high-tech

---

Tough Questions That a Good Boss Needs to Face

When was the last time you asked an employee about the well-being of his family—and stuck around for an answer?

When was the last time you offered an employee praise for a minor achievement?

When was the last time you solicited advice from an employee in advance of issuing him an assignment?

If you tend to sit back and create problems for people (passive/aggressive style), when was the last time you got up and helped prevent problems before they occurred?

If you find it difficult to sit back and let underlings do the work that they alone are supposed to be doing, when was the last time you forced yourself to let them work on their own? When was the last time you delegated something you really didn't want to delegate?

When was the last time you consciously forgave a subordinate for an error in judgment that did not destroy your entire department?

companies, disagreement is actually encouraged. By welcoming contributions and criticisms from virtually everyone, these companies create tremendous energy and get many extra hours of work from their employees.

A BOSS'S GUIDE TO PEACEMAKING AMONG EMPLOYEES

When two of your employees are (figuratively speaking) at each other's throats and it's wreaking havoc on your department's operations, here's a solution you can try.

Invite both of them into your office. Explain that you are going to let each person speak and that neither is to be interrupted. After each has made his case, ask if anyone can think of a way of compromising on the conflict. If they can't, tell them that you'll leave them in the office together for 1 hour (or 2, 3, or 4 hours) and that if they can't arrive at a compromise, you will come up with your own solution that they'll both have to accept—and that one of them may not like.

Sure, this sounds like something dreamed up by a second-grade teacher (actually it comes from business-relations expert Dr. Josefowitz). But it frequently fits the occasion. *Note:* Don't attempt this if there is an obvious, clear-cut solution you can suggest right at the outset.

If you need the immediate cooperation of two competing subordinates but they refuse to deal with each other, Dr. Weiss has a message for you to relay: "I know you don't get along, but this is a project we need. Do it, and we'll talk about it later." But he warns: "Do talk about it later. You cannot ever let a conflict die. It will never die. It will lie there and gasp at you, interfering with everything."

Here are some other tips on reconciliation.

Thoroughly investigate the situation to the best of your ability. Don't act on insufficient evidence. "Frequently managers will make a decision on how to handle a conflict before they see the entire picture. It only makes the conflict worse," says Dr. Weiss.

Help others solve their own problems. Don't try to solve the conflict for them, but help them do it themselves. Mediate between the conflicting parties.

Don't command unless you have to. That is, only if time and the situation demand it.

Mix up the members of warring groups. If your organization has split into two factions that exhibit unhealthy competitiveness, breaking up the groups will divide loyalties, says Dr. Josefowitz.

How to be critical
WITHOUT HURTING FEELINGS

There's a school of thought that believes you cannot be critical without inflicting some sort of a wound. And it's something to keep in mind when you prepare for the evaluation of an employee's performance, according to Dr. Josefowitz. "It's important to recognize that you might hurt the person's feelings," she says. "Through that recognition, hopefully, you'll gain some compassion. And as a result you might try to minimize the hurt."

Her first piece of advice is that you should never criticize in generalities. Your comments should always be "behavior specific." "You take unfair advantage" is too general. "You take 30 minutes for a 15-minute coffee break" is specific.

When you criticize, don't use the words *always* **or** *never.* Instead of saying "You're always late" or "You never file your reports on time," give the person actual data he can use. Say: "Your reports have been late three out of the past four times."

Don't be evaluative, be descriptive. In her book *You're the Boss,* Dr. Josefowitz says the point is not to judge. "You are lazy" is a judgment. "You work more slowly than the others" is a description.

Be sure to give sufficient praise along with criticism. It's crucial to reinforce positive kinds of behavior, explains Dr. MacDonald. But be even-handed about it. "Nobody will be fooled if you give lots of praise and just slip in the criticism," he says.

Criticize people about things they can do something about. "You cannot expect people to be smarter if they have limited intelligence or expect them to be quick if they ponder and are somewhat plodding. These are personality characteristics that probably cannot be changed," writes Dr. Josefowitz.

Adjust your critical style to meet the individual. Successful sports coaches have known for years that they need to treat different team members differently. Two players make the same mistake. The coach kicks one guy in the butt but kindly pats the other fellow on the helmet. People are not machines. Your task is to find out what method of criticism will motivate an employee to get back on the field and score. One person may need an arm around the shoulder and an understanding little chat of the "let's try to get the clients' names straight" variety. Another may respond only to a stern lecture: "Listen, you've seldom had trouble keeping the clients' names straight in the past. This sort of error is something I will not tolerate in the future."

Tell the employee what his or her behavior does to you. Instead of saying, "When you slam doors, I don't like it," explain the impact that door-slamming has on you. Say, "It startles me." As Dr. Josefowitz explains, "They can't argue with the fact that it upsets you; they can't say that it's not true."

Remember to reinforce positive behavior. One theory holds that individuals tend to slack off and make more errors shortly after they're praised for good work. We don't buy it. Tell them when they do something right, and also tell others—it will get back to them.

If you hate to criticize for fear that an employee will dislike you, think about the chain of damaging events you may be creating for the employee, for the organization, and for you if the undesirable behavior is allowed to continue.

WHEN YOUR BOSS IS *TOO* NICE

It happens. Your boss is a softy who tries his darndest not to make waves for you and your co-workers. He never utters a word of complaint or criticism about anything you do. So why not just enjoy the smooth sailing? The reason is simple: Demanding bosses get us to work our hardest, perfect our skills, and accomplish more than we ever realized was possible. When a superior is satisfied with everything we do and never pushes us toward perfection, we get stale; we seldom achieve greatness.

So here's how to break out of the doldrums and get moving again.

Solicit criticism. After you've submitted a report, for instance, read it over carefully with a sharply critical eye. Develop a list of possible problems. Then sit down with your boss, and instead of saying something vague like "What did you think of my report?" or "Did you have any problems with my report?" be specific. Say, "I thought I relied a bit too heavily on the five-year project figures. Were they overused?" Or, "In my next report, do you think it would be wise to include recommendations for the West Coast operation?" Don't be satisfied with a yes or no answer. Generate a dialogue that draws out your boss's honest assessments—anything that can help you grow in your job.

Find colleagues who will offer criticism. Hook yourself up with a star—a person whose work you value and whose work is valued by your organization. Simply explain that you respect her work and would like some objective criticism of yours.

Seek out a mentor. You're stuck with a boss who won't push you to the max. Befriend someone at her level—perhaps at corporate headquarters—who will be happy to take you under his wing and provide some direction and motivation.

6

BRAINSTORMING

It was exactly one month ago that the group VP issued a rousing call for the development of new product ideas. Since then you, as well as the other members of your department, have exhausted your creative powers without so much as a single flash of inspiration. Short of divine intervention or a corporate takeover, it looks as if nothing will save your unimaginative skins. Now is the time to call upon that vast and powerful force of nature known as—The Brainstorming Meeting.

Try to think of a brainstorming session as resembling a nuclear fusion reactor. With nuclear fusion, the idea is to take two hydrogen atoms, add 1,000,000 volts of energy, generate 300,000,000 degrees of heat, and when the two atoms combine, hopefully you get something entirely new: a helium atom. In a brainstorming meeting, two unattractive ideas from two different people may, through the transformative power of the group, be combined into one sexy little idea. But rather than 300,000,000 degrees of heat (a temperature that often causes people some mild discomfort), the only energy required in a brainstorming meeting is the mind's ability to make novel associations when given the raw material to work with.

To operate your own successful brainstorming reactor, there are certain rules and techniques that need to be applied. Using them will help you generate the raw ideas that will then power the reactor's collective group of minds to make novel associations, come up with new ideas, and save everyone's skin until the next crisis . . . which will hit just after lunch.

4 GROUND RULES FOR A SUCCESSFUL BRAINSTORMING MEETING

As Lord High Master (spell that f-a-c-i-l-i-t-a-t-o-r) of your brainstorming meeting, it is *you* who will set the tone of the proceedings. To make sure you get what you came for, here are four things not only to keep in mind personally but also to stress to the group.

1. Go for quantity over quality. "Try to get as many ideas as you can," says Jim Shields, associate program director of the Center for Creative Leadership in Greensboro, North Carolina. "Three years before baseball player Pete Rose set a record for getting the most hits, he set a less complimentary one for the most outs. But the two tend to go together. The more ideas (at-bats) you can solicit, the higher your chances will be of finding some real hits among the larger portion of rejects (outs). Additionally, you'll want as much raw idea material as possible for the fourth stage of the brainstorming cycle, cross-fertilization. Any idea, good or bad, can be useful during this stage."

Tips for the facilitator: Attach large sheets of paper to the walls around the room. Have someone with a fast hand and a large marker pen write down the ideas as quickly as they are contributed. Encourage a freewheeling, open forum where people shout out ideas as soon as they spring into their heads. Make sure everyone in the room can see the lists of ideas. Keep the pace up.

2. Suspend judgment. "You should be careful not to evaluate or critique ideas while people are generating them," warns Shields. "Not only will you slow down the pace, but some people will hold back for fear of a critical reception."

Tips for the facilitator: Make it clear to your group from the start that there is no place for evaluation at this meeting. The idea-gutting meeting will be next week (black hoods optional). Be encouraging. Let people know that *any* idea gets the stamp of approval in this room.

3. Reach for wild ideas. "I encourage people to think about ideas that might get them fired," quips Shields. "But in all seriousness, you want people to take risks, to break out of their boxes and advance ideas that they wouldn't ordinarily think about or dare submit."

Tips for the facilitator: Getting real for a moment here, taking risks is easier said than done. Everyone knows that while it takes years to build up a solid reputation, all it takes is 10 seconds and an open mouth to look like a fool. If you want some wild ideas from your group, you'll have to lead by example. Come to the meeting with a handful of outlandish ideas and present them at strategic intervals. Make them humorous if possible. People in your group will get the point, loosen up, and join in the fun. Remember that the courting of unusual ideas (or honest opinions) bears a striking resemblance to a junior high school dance. Nobody wants to be the first couple on the floor. But once a brave pair gets out there and starts to boogie, 200 others tie for second place.

4. Cross-fertilize ideas. "By this point, you've collected a lot of raw ideas," says Shields. "Now it's time to see if the group can improve on them or merge isolated ideas into new and different forms. This is where true creativity comes into play as people take diverse elements, make a string of novel associations, and give birth to an idea that normally would never have occurred to them."

Tips for the facilitator: At the cross-fertilization stage it's time to give everyone a breather. Hopefully the ideas have been flying fast and furious. Encourage people to pause and let their eyes run down the lists of ideas. Now ask your people to go Chinese: Choose an idea from column A and one from column B. Can anybody come up with a hybrid? Again, encourage the absurd. Allow your group to make any wild leap of the imagination it takes to merge two ideas into a totally new one. For example, imagine you are brainstorming for a toy company. As you look over the list of ideas on the wall, two leap out at you. One is a new soap-bubble wand, while the other is glow-in-the-dark action figures of mutant commandos from Mars. The first idea is old hat, the second . . . alien at best. But what if you could make glow-in-the-dark bubble stuff for kids to use on summer nights?

THE PROPER CARE AND FEEDING OF AN IDEA SESSION: SOME FACTORS TO CONSIDER

It's time to forget how much a brainstorming meeting is like a nuclear fusion reactor. Instead, we will now consider how much it resembles a living organism. Keep in mind that the optimal functioning of any living creature depends in part upon its environment and its mood as well as upon the maintenance of its target weight. The same goes for brainstorming meetings where setting, mood, and size can mean the difference between vitality and torpor.

Size. "Five to eight people is the optimal size for a brainstorming meeting," says Shields. "Any less than five and there won't be enough raw material generated for people to bounce off each other. Any more than eight and it's much harder to keep everyone functioning as a cohesive unit; instead you'll find subgroups forming. Additionally, with more people there is less floor space for each person to present new ideas. As a result some will decide to sit out."

While on the subject of size, Shields also stresses personnel rotation if your group will be working together for several months. "We've noticed that a brainstorming group's level of creativity will rise for a time, level off, and then actually begin to drop over an 18-month period. The best way to avoid that drop is to bring in new people from time to time."

When you invite someone to join your brainstorming group, tell them right from the start that you are running this project with a rotating schedule of participation in mind. Let them know the length of their stay. That way, when it's time for them to leave, they'll understand it's part of the plan and in no way reflects on their performance.

Environment. Where you hold your meeting can have a big effect on its outcome. "First of all, you want to find a place where you won't be interrupted by phone calls and where there aren't piles of work lying around to remind everyone of other projects that require their attention," says Shields.

This rules out your office, or for that matter, anyone's office. The conference room is okay, but you may want to go a little farther. "There are a lot of benefits in pulling people out of the office completely and putting them in a new environment," says Shields. "The surroundings may encourage people to make totally new creative connections."

If you are going to search for a new locale, keep in mind that while you want a stimulating setting, it shouldn't be *too* stimulating. You want to keep everyone's mind focused on the problem at hand. With this in mind, you may want to avoid having meetings outdoors. No matter how inviting it may look, Shields has found that it just doesn't seem to work. Instead, try hosting a meeting at your house.

Mood. To illustrate the important effect mood can have on creativity, let's look at an experiment performed by Alice M. Isen, Ph.D., professor of psychology at Cornell University's Johnson Graduate School of Management. Dr. Isen asked two groups of people to take a candle, a book of matches, a box of tacks, and a cork board attached to the wall and arrange them in a manner that would allow the candle to burn without dripping wax onto the floor. One group watched a funny movie beforehand. The other did not. When the experiment was done, more people from the movie group got the answer right than did those in the second group.

Humor, or any good mood, seems to increase creativity. According to

Howard Lieberman, M.D., a New Jersey neurosurgeon, good moods are associated with an increase in the frequency and rapidity of electrical connections in the brain. New connections can often present new ideas and new ways to look at a problem.

"In a brainstorming meeting, everyone needs to be happy and energetic," says Shields. "Humor often is a catalyst for this. As a matter of fact, the most productive sessions are those that have a tolerance for wacky and even off-color jokes."

If you don't feel that your group is made up of budding Steve Martins, you may want to get off to a laughing start by showing a short comedy video. It can be a great cartoon, a 10-minute stand-up comedy bit, or a skit from "Saturday Night Live." Having elevated the mood, get right to work. But keep the laughs coming if possible.

(For those of you who won't sleep tonight unless you know the answer to the candle question, here's how it's done: Empty out the box of tacks, tack the box to the cork board, set the candle on top of the tack box, and light the candle.)

3 WAYS TO CRACK A CREATIVE BLOCK

You've followed the four ground rules of brainstorming. You have 6.5 people in your group. You've invited them to your exquisitely decorated house and they are laughing so much that 3 have gone into cardiac arrest. But the best idea you've come up with all day is broccoli-flavored dental floss. Now what?

"When normal brainstorming procedures don't work, you need to use alternative means to get the creative connection process flowing," says Shields. "We often use the following three techniques to help guide groups into making novel associations which wouldn't normally occur to them."

1. Brainwriting. Unlike regular brainstorming, which operates on a verbal, extroverted level, brainwriting is introverted and happens on paper. After a problem is discussed and understood by everyone in the group, each person takes a piece of paper and writes down three ideas. Then everybody passes his sheet to the person on his right while simultaneously receiving one from the person on his left. At this point, each person is holding a sheet that has someone else's ideas on it. The next step is to have everyone try to either improve on these ideas or combine the ideas with their own to form new ones.

"The idea here is controlled cross-fertilization," says Shields. "And this particular technique has several advantages. First, if there are shy people in the group who are somewhat intimidated by the presence of a boss or more vocal members, writing ideas down will be easier for them to do."

Second, people will be spending more time on idea generation than on fighting for presentation space. "Third, taking two groups of the same size, one brainstorming and the other brainwriting, the brainwriting group will produce more ideas," says Shields.

2. Visual connections. This technique gives people extra raw material on which to base novel associations. The group is shown a series of three or four photographs and asked to identify and write down particularly intriguing aspects of each. These can include mood, color, objects, and even personal associations ("the house in the picture reminds me of my vacation home"). Once this phase has been completed, the group goes over each aspect listed and tries to connect it to the problem at hand. Suddenly ideas that normally wouldn't have occurred are popping up because the group is utilizing trigger words and thoughts that would not normally have been used. An example: You are brainstorming for a major health-care provider and want to expand the company's list of services. The words "vacation home" are on the photo-aspects list. Someone suggests a seaside recuperation resort for patients as a follow-up to hospital care (Recuperesort, Inc.).

3. Excursion technique. "This is where the novel association aspect of creativity gets pushed to the limit," says Shields. "The purpose of this technique is to take the group very far away from the problem and then bring them back in."

To initiate the excursion technique, the facilitator picks a word having to do with the problem at hand. Then the person to the facilitator's right free-associates another word. Going once again to the right, the next person free-associates off the last word spoken. Go once or twice around the room and write down all the words.

Pause for a moment and let each person choose a word that is of interest to her. Then ask everyone to take a minute or two (but not too long) to create a brief scenario or story having to do with this word. Make sure they title them.

Now, have everyone tell his or her story while the facilitator writes down story titles and key aspects of each plot. Finally, try to connect these titles and plot devices to the original problem. While some of the ideas will be truly ridiculous, you'll find others to be startlingly new and exciting— ideas that could not have been born in any other way but through a group process.

7

BURNOUT

Why do some people burn out? Considering our collective upbringing, a more pertinent question might be, Why doesn't everyone burn out? Think about it. In kindergarten we spent our time coloring in pictures of smiling doctors, happy firemen, and helpful police officers. Watching "Mister Rogers' Neighborhood," we were inundated by visions of radiant workers such as Mr. McFeely, the postman who couldn't wait to deliver his next letter and just loved to stop and chat about his occupation. In elementary school we were rarely handed a primer that read "See Mr. Corruthers, the leveraged buyout specialist. See him come unwound. See him drink. Drink, drink, drink." Given the information we received, we were quite justified in believing that employment would be something akin to a long ride on the "Love Boat."

Quite frankly, college also gave us an outlook on the working world which was neck and neck with "Mister Rogers' Neighborhood" in the race for reality. Nestled safely in an environment that gave an "A" for work well done, we were confident that the shape of our destiny was molded by our own two hands.

Then came graduation. The scene shifts to a confused person (insert your name) sitting behind a desk wondering why no one is smiling like Mr. McFeely. Why is it that no matter how hard you work, promotion is elusive? How come this job is not fulfilling? And damn it, why didn't anyone warn you that work was going to be . . . well . . . so much work?

What is it? why does it happen?

"Basically, burnout is a process in which a person's motivation is somehow diminished or damaged," says Beverly Potter, Ph.D., a Berkeley, California–based management consultant and workplace psychologist and author of *Beating Job Burnout: How to Transform Work Pressure into Productivity.* "And the cause can be traced directly to feelings of powerlessness or helplessness. Victims of job burnout feel that no matter what they do, they can't succeed."

In psychological terms, job burnout is a form of learned helplessness. This condition was first discovered through a rather sadistic series of experiments that animal lovers will not appreciate. A group of dogs from the same litter was divided into two groups. The first group was put into a room with an electrical grid on the floor. When the grid was turned on, the dogs began to run around the room barking frantically. Eventually they discovered a lever that, when pushed, would shut off the grid. The dogs quickly learned to make a beeline for the lever as soon as the current was activated. For these dogs, the world was something they could control.

Group two dogs were also put into a room with a grid, but there was no lever. When the current was turned on, the dogs raced around the room but could find no relief. The dogs progressed from a state of frantic anxiety to one of anger, and then, finally, they gave up. When they realized there was nothing that could be done, they just lay down and took the shock. When those dogs were later put into a room that offered escape, they didn't even bother to seek relief. They had developed a condition of learned helplessness.

The parallels between this experiment and the human working condition are not hard to find. The collegiate environment has many levers. Study hard and you'll get good grades. You'll move smoothly from freshman to senior with clockwork predictability. Maintain a moderately high level of competence and you will graduate. You are in control and your efforts seem to have a direct effect on your life. But once out in the working world, the levers of control become more nebulous. Suddenly there is corporate bureaucracy. There are people who seem to get promoted for no reason. There are times when you go unrewarded no matter how hard you work. Your job becomes monotonous and there seems to be no way to use your creativity.

"You start to realize that you are not in direct control of your environment and that there seems to be no way to gain control," says Dr. Potter. "So, like the dog in the leverless cage, you proceed from frustration to anger. Finally you give up and just stop trying."

The popular mythology of burnout has projected a picture of the classic victim as someone who's been working at the same desk, in the same cubicle, in the same company for 30 years. But given the underlying cause of burnout, the new wave of young executives may actually be more at risk than their older counterparts.

"Twenty years ago, work was something to be endured," notes Dr. Potter. "You got a job, you put in your time, earned your pay, and were happy. Nothing more was expected. But with the people hitting the job market today, not only is it a given that they will earn a lot of money, they also expect employment that has inherent importance, provides constant challenge, and guarantees upward mobility. When they finally come face to face with the working world and don't get these things no matter how they try, they burn out." Ironically, it seems that as our concepts of labor grow more civilized and humane, our burnout potential rises. Reality rarely keeps pace with our dreams.

Boredom, stress, a feeling of uselessness—these are all reasons for burnout that find their common origin in a feeling of powerlessness. "A person can even experience burnout from too much undeserved success," says Dr. Potter. "It's the poor little rich boy syndrome where no matter what he does or how he does it, he succeeds. His grades are bad, but he gets into a college that Daddy just donated two million dollars to. He goofs off in school but still gets a job as a VP in the company his father owns. Burnout is a distinct possibility in this situation as much as in others, and for the same reason. There is no real connection between personal behavior and the consequences."

But burnout is not always simply a matter of an unfair environment. Perceptions play a large role in whether or not a person will eventually undergo meltdown. "You can have two boys growing up in the ghetto," explains Dr. Potter. "One thinks, 'If I work hard, I can get out of here.' The other thinks, 'No matter what I do, the situation is hopeless.' It's the same environment, but the latter view leads to burnout while the former leads to accomplishment." And in that example lies the key to conquering job burnout.

ARE YOU ABOUT TO BURN OUT?

Before we embark on a cure, you probably want to know if you need one. How can you tell if you are fast becoming a burnout statistic? How about a simple test? The one you are about to take was developed by Herbert J. Freudenberger, Ph.D., coauthor of *Burnout: The High Cost of Achievement* and the man responsible for the discovery of the burnout syndrome. When taking this test, consider changes in your behavior over the past six months. Give yourself about 30 seconds before answering and then assign your answer a number from 1 to 5. One means little or no change, 5 means a great deal of change. While many of the questions seem to have no direct bearing on your job, keep in mind that although burnout may begin with the destruction of job performance motivation, if left unchecked it will rapidly affect other parts of your life.

1. Do you tire more easily? Feel fatigued rather than energetic?
2. Are people annoying you by telling you, "You don't look so good lately?"
3. Are you working harder and harder and accomplishing less and less?
4. Are you increasingly cynical and disenchanted?
5. Are you often invaded by a sadness you can't explain?
6. Are you forgetting appointments, deadlines, personal possessions?
7. Are you increasingly irritable? More short-tempered? More disappointed in the people around you?
8. Are you seeing close friends and family members less frequently?
9. Are you too busy to do even routine things like make phone calls or read reports or send out your Christmas cards?
10. Are you suffering from physical complaints? Aches, pains, headaches, a lingering cold?
11. Do you feel disoriented when the activity of the day comes to a halt?
12. Is joy elusive?
13. Are you unable to laugh at a joke about yourself?
14. Does sex seem like more trouble than it's worth?
15. Do you have very little to say to people?

The Burnout Scale

0–25: You're doing fine.
26–35: There are things you should be watching.
36–50: You're a candidate.
51–65: You're burning out.
Over 65: You're in a dangerous place, threatening to your physical and mental well-being.

The test above, while not exacting, will give you a good idea of where you stand. If you find yourself scoring above 50, it's probably time to break out the fire extinguisher. But the important benefit that can be gained from the test is recognition of the many warning signs that can tip you off to future burnout.

Besides the test, there is one other thing that can be taken as a danger sign of burnout. "Negative emotions are part of the whole burnout package," says Dr. Potter. "But many people will turn to substance abuse in an attempt to modulate these emotions. While the sudden use of drugs is a very apparent warning sign, many people don't notice the much subtler abuses such as an increased alcohol, coffee, tobacco, or prescription medication intake."

BEATING BURNOUT: 8 PATHS TO FOLLOW

"If the problem behind job burnout is a feeling of helplessness, then the solution is to develop what I call personal power," says Dr. Potter. The following is a virtual road map of possible paths that will lead you away from the bus stop of self-despairing helplessness to a town called *Control.*

Path 1: "Perhaps the most important path of the eight, this one deals with self-management," says Dr. Potter. "A very common cause of burnout is lack of feedback. You may be doing a good job, but you never know where you stand because your boss never lets you know. The reason this can be upsetting is that we were all raised to be managed by other people and trained to be dependent on their directive statements and feedback. It goes back to the teacher/student relationship of our school days."

Self-management requires you to become your own boss, to become a source of self-feedback. The reason you are probably reluctant to do this likewise goes back to your formative years. What if you went up to a teacher and said, "I hope you don't mind, but from now on I'll grade my own tests"? "But if you are to be a good self-manager, you must acknowledge your ability to judge your own work rather than wait for someone else to do it," says Dr. Potter.

Equally important is the ability to set your own goals. If no one else is going to give your working life direction, at least you can. "When setting goals, however, a good self-manager chooses ones within her power to accomplish that are still motivating," says Dr. Potter. "Where do you want to be in a month? In a year? To make it work, the goals must be clearly defined. Don't just say 'A year from now I want to be better off than I am now.' Instead, say 'A year from now I want to have taken responsibility for the accounting duties on two extra projects.' "

Reward yourself when you've done well. This doesn't necessarily mean going out and buying a Porsche just because you've aced a project. But at least acknowledge to yourself that you've done a good job. "Poor self-managers seldom give themselves a win," notes Dr. Potter.

So Path One asks you to set your own criteria and agenda. While they may not parallel corporate guidelines exactly, they will probably accomplish the same end results and allow you to get the feel of the driver's seat.

Path 2: "Stress management is a necessary part of alleviating burnout," says Dr. Potter. "Stress is inevitable, so there's no point in trying to eradicate it. But if you know how to handle it when it comes, then you'll feel more in control. Good stress-management techniques give you the lever you need to shut off your personal equivalent of the electric floor faced by those dogs in the learned helplessness experiment."

We all rely on some form of coping with stress. We run and hide. We take drugs. We eat our weight in Boston cream pies. Not only are these ineffectual ways of handling stress, but when they don't work we feel even more out of control. Rather than opening the fridge or medicine cabinet, turn to "Stress" on page 414 and develop your own unique way of taming it.

Path 3: Rather than accepting your job as it is handed to you (which is more or less how it was left by the last person who had it), determine how you can personalize it. The best way to approach this job management challenge is by thinking of your job as a company—your company. As its sole owner and proprietor, what would you do to streamline the production line? What are the most important products of the "company," and what can you do to increase their output? How can you arrange tasks so as to increase motivation and thereby quality? And finally, what areas of diversification should your "company" consider? Can you find ways to push the boundaries of the job to include new and exciting duties that will make your position stronger?

Path 4: "Research shows that people who have a strong family and peer support group are healthier and can stand more stress," says Dr. Potter. "So Path Four encompasses the development of a social support system. People who are burning out tend to isolate themselves as a means of evading the problem. But when you think about it, solitary confinement is considered a strong form of punishment in prisons. Why self-inflict it?"

Join associations and professional groups where you can meet your peers. Talk over your problems and see if you can't find solutions. Even if answers are elusive, the very act of searching for them is more empowering than doing nothing. Besides, it never hurts to discover that you are not the only one with problems.

Path 5: Learn. Pinpoint the skills you need to move up the ladder and then figure out how to get them. Does your company offer evening training programs that you've sidestepped in favor of theme night at the local bowl-ing alley? What about night school at a local college? You can sit there and continue to feel that your situation is hopeless with or without another degree, but you're never going to know until you've tried. And once again, the simple act of trying goes a long way toward relieving a state of help-lessness.

Path 6: Quit and get a new job. "Many times this is the first thing a burnout victim thinks of," says Dr. Potter. "But in fact, it should be the last. It's really much better to try to salvage the position you've earned after years of work rather than tossing it all aside in favor of the unknown. But some-times you do get into an impossible situation and really need to realize that a change of jobs is the only possible solution."

Path 7: Try thought control. You are what you think (unless you think you are Catherine the Great). And just as with the two-boys-in-the-ghetto example mentioned earlier, your burnout may be emanating from your own perceptions rather than from the environment. Changing the way you think is not an easy thing to do, but it makes sense to approach each task as a challenge rather than as a pain in the neck or a waste of time.

One way to start is by acknowledging that your present work situation is relatively straightforward, convenient, and clear-cut compared to the complicated nature of life in general. For example, there never seems to be enough time to clean the garage, take the kids to Disney World, go out to dinner with your significant other, and write the Great American Novel you've been meaning to write. On the other hand, at work you've got 8 hours a day to do exactly what's been put on your desk. So you've got the time to do it. And if you do the job well, there may be rewards. Clean out the garage and the only reward you'll get is a chance to clean it out again in six months.

Most important, ask yourself honestly what you would be doing if you weren't at work. Don't even bother mentioning your desire to climb Mount Everest. You know you wouldn't want to be up there sucking oxygen at 28,000 feet on a Tuesday afternoon. The point is, compared to most of life's problems, work is a piece of cake. You've got the time. You've got some incentive. And you probably wouldn't be doing anything else terribly useful anyway. So get to work. And consider it all the better when a difficult project comes along: You'll have something truly engrossing with which to while away those 8 hours.

Path 8: Adopt an attitude of detached concern. "Someone once asked Mother Teresa how she could stand working with sick children that end up dying despite her best efforts," recalls Dr. Potter. "Mother Teresa answered,

'We love them and do all we can for them while they are here. And when they die, we let them go.' This is a viewpoint difficult for most people to understand. The closest we get to detached concern is in sports, where both teams want to win more than anything but are then supposed to be good sports when they lose."

The point here is that burnout often develops when a person becomes fixated on the results and not on the effort. You may have done an outstanding job, but for one reason or another, the project collapses. You feel helpless in the face of such a setback. But in reality, you should feel empowered by the fine job you did. Maybe you can't control everything, but you can at least control what's best in you.

Alan Watts, America's most famous proponent of Zen Buddhism, probably said it best when he counseled people to be like a mirror. When you stand in front of a mirror, it reflects you exactly (the highest form of attention). But when you move away from a mirror, it doesn't hold on to your reflection. It lets the reflection go. Do your best. Take the results as they come. And then let them go.

8

CAREER CHANGE

T ake a moment and think about the chain of events that brought you into your current line of work. Did you follow a childhood dream? Unless you happen to be president of the United States, a race car driver, or the person who lights the fireworks at Disney World, it's doubtful. Well, then, are you perhaps involved in a line of work that intersects with a favorite hobby? Doubtful again. In most management posts, your skiing expertise or knowledge of pre–Civil War U.S. stamps will rarely if ever be called into play. Okay, did you at least make a sweeping study of career choices before staking out your territory? If not, don't feel bad. Most of us didn't.

The stark reality of the matter is that the majority of us working Joes and Janes fell into our professions based upon anything but strong personal interest. Oh, sure, there was that sophomore economics course that we liked well enough, but given the magnitude of career choices facing us, is one college course (or even 15) a substantial enough platform upon which to build a lifetime career path?

In a way, picking a career is like choosing a spouse. You may currently like what you see, but who really knows what the scenery will look like 5, 10, or 20 years down the road. Things change. People change. You change. And one day after working at the same desk day in and day out, you suddenly feel as if the thrill is gone. What do you do about it?

In Japan, where lifetime tenure with a single company is a matter of course, you'd grin and bear it. But in the United States, where the typical worker has had at least eight different employers by the age of 40, you just may feel inclined to jump ship. If you feel yourself getting the itch, however, there are a few things to consider first. Things like: Why are you jumping? Do you really have to jump? and Just how far do you want to jump?

BE A CAREER-CHANGE SCIENTIST

"The problem that most people run into concerning career change is that they often make it an either/or proposition," says Beverly Potter, Ph.D., a Berkeley, California–based management consultant and workplace psychologist and author of *The Way of the Ronin: Riding the Waves of Change at Work.* "They hit a depression at work and figure it's one of two things—temporary burnout, or total boredom and dissatisfaction with their career. This leaves them with one of two choices: either they make a few minor changes in their current job to provide themselves with stimulation, or they get out of their profession entirely and look for something new."

But it's not that simple. Each day at work, you face a multitude of different factors that, separately or in varying combinations, have an effect on your mood and level of job enjoyment. First there are your duties and responsibilities. Then there are the people you work with and the people you work under. There's also the corporate culture or environment to consider, as well as your ever-changing prospects for advancement. "A problem in any of these areas could be the cause of your current funk, but it doesn't necessarily warrant a total career change," notes Dr. Potter.

Here's a typical example involving a teacher named Mary who works at an inner-city high school. The school receives nowhere near the funding it requires to function properly. The textbooks are inadequate, drug use is rampant, and absenteeism is at an all-time high. Mary originally chose teaching in the hopes of helping young minds to develop. Now, instead, she simply hopes that she will get home tonight safely and with her wallet intact. She's sick and tired of the situation and is ready to bail out in search of a new career.

The problem is not teaching. The problem is the environment. If Mary stopped to think about the situation, she would probably remember with pleasure a few treasured moments when she actually connected with her students and they (much to their own surprise) learned something. So Mary is not tired of teaching. She is tired of teaching at that particular school. Rather than a career change, she simply needs a transfer.

"This is why it's so important to determine the origin of your depression before taking any drastic action," says Dr. Potter. "And the best way to get started is by applying a little scientific methodology to the situation. Before solving your problem, you need to identify it. But to identify it you need to collect data."

The first thing to do is get a notebook. In it you will jot down entries every time you start feeling depressed or negative at work. Write down your exact feeling, the circumstances, and any thoughts you may have. One tip here is to keep your entries brief and to the point. Here are some sample entries.

> **Tuesday—3:15:** Feel annoyed. Have two reports to write and don't want to do either of them. Getting sick of spending the whole day writing reports. Now I'm going to spend the whole night doing them, too.
>
> **Wednesday—9:30:** That hour-long drive through city traffic every morning leaves me feeling drained. When I finally do get to work, I can't seem to get started until around 11.

If someone at work annoys you, write it down. If your boss chews you out in front of others, write it down. If you can't stand having lunch with the other junior executives, write it down.

But make sure you don't make this strictly a gripe book. When something good happens, that also goes into the journal. And it doesn't have to be about anything as dramatic as a raise or promotion. Maybe you simply found yourself taking a lot of pleasure in doing some routine task.

"One reason for including the good things that happen at work is to see if perhaps it is your perceptions that are skewed rather than the job itself," says Dr. Potter. "It's amazing how people will often brood over the one bad thing that happened to them rather than the five good things. It could be that when you write everything down you'll find that overall, you like the job. There just seems to be one thing that is actually getting under your skin."

Dr. Potter suggests that you keep the journal for one to two weeks. Besides your section for current observations, you'll want to set up another one for memories. Call up some of the best and worst moments that your current job has provided and write them down. Take time here to really recall the details of the situation as well as your feelings.

Finally, include a section in which you simply review all your duties and responsibilities. By each one, make a note as to whether you enjoy that particular function or dread it like the plague. The reason for this section is to cover any job aspects that don't make an appearance during your journal-keeping period.

MAKING AN INTELLIGENT ASSESSMENT

You've now spent some time observing yourself in a variety of work situations. You've not only taken copious notes on your current daily behavior but also made a small study of your work history. Now it's time to assess the data.

"Look for patterns that point to a consistently recurring problem in a particular area," says Dr. Potter. "For example, your entries may depict a perfectly fine working environment, you enjoy your projects, you like the company . . . but every time your boss shows up, a black mark appears in your journal. Now you'll realize that what you thought of as a vague unpleasantness inherent in your work was in fact the effect your manager has on you. You don't need a career change. You need to get out of the department or rectify the relationship you have with your boss."

The combinations of possible conclusions you may come to are endless. It may be that according to your journal all systems are go . . . except for the fact that you don't feel as if your future is terribly bright. In a case like this, you need to realize that it's not your career that is nearing an end but simply your tenure with your current employer.

Then again, you might have an actual problem with the work itself. If that's the case, it's time to get more specific. "A corporate lawyer I know finally decided he'd had enough of his current practice," recalls Dr. Potter. "Upon reviewing the situation, however, he realized that it wasn't law that he was tired of—it was the sharklike maneuvering associated with *corporate* law."

Likewise, you may find that while you enjoy your chosen field, you may not be thrilled with the particular way you are currently applying your skills. While this type of problem may seem fairly transparent, when you're caught in the middle of it, it can be quite confusing. Consider the case of a journalist writing for a trade magazine targeted at transmission repair shops. That person may love to write, but after writing about car transmissions for ten years straight, he breaks out in hives if there happens to be pen and paper within a ½-mile radius. And that writer will think that it's writing and not car transmissions that's the problem.

"The important thing to understand is that you don't have to give up your skills to change the situation," says Dr. Potter. "Instead, you want to try to intersect those skills with something that holds interest for you. For example, that lawyer I mentioned has a strong interest in the arts. But rather than abandon law for a completely different career, he took a smaller step

Who Can Stand Their Jobs the Longest?

Barbers can, according to information compiled by the U.S. Department of Labor. After studying the work history of more than 109 million people, they found that the typical employee stays in one occupation for 6.6 years before moving on to an entirely different career. On the other hand, barbers tend to keep on clipping for a median tenure of 24.8 years. In case you are curious as to how long you're likely to last in your current line of work, check the following list and see how the rest of the world is doing.

Occupation	Median Tenure (years)
Barbers	24.8
Farmers	21.1
Dentists	15.7
Pilots	14.0
Civil engineers	13.0
Pharmacists	11.8
Chemists	11.1
Electricians	11.0
Physicians	10.7
Plumbers	10.4
Practical nurses	10.3
Lawyers	10.1
Truck drivers	10.1
Registered nurses	9.3
Managers and administrators	9.1
Personnel managers	9.0
Industrial engineers	8.9
Office supervisors	8.6
Sheriffs	8.6
Financial managers	8.4
Psychologists	8.4

and wrote a book for authors about copyright and contract law. He also acts as counsel for a variety of authors."

The big question, however, is what kind of data assessment would give you just cause to consider an entirely new career? "You might want to opt

Occupation	Median Tenure (years)
Insurance salespeople	8.1
Carpenters	8.0
Musicians	7.9
Lab technicians	7.7
Purchasing managers	7.7
Accountants	7.6
Data processing equipment repairers	7.2
Health managers	7.2
Mail carriers	7.0
Management analysts	7.0
Computer systems analysts/scientists	6.6
Actors/directors	6.3
Real estate salespeople	6.0
Reporters/editors	6.0
Teachers	5.9
Physician's assistants	5.8
Public relations personnel	5.5
Securities/financial services salespeople	5.4
Insurance adjusters and investigators	5.3
Physical therapists	5.2
Advertising salespeople	5.1
Salespeople (general)	4.9
Computer operators	4.8
Computer programmers	4.8
Underwriters	4.8
Maids/housemen	4.6
Athletes	4.4
Bartenders	3.9
Car/boat salespeople	3.7
Receptionists	3.3
File clerks	2.5
Restaurant busboys	1.7
Food counter clerks	1.5

for a more radical change if you find yourself having problems with important functions of your position or with the lifestyle that your current career dictates," says Dr. Potter. "For example, I know of a man who used to be the manager of a major U.S. international airport until he quit, moved to a rural area, and became a schoolteacher. It could be that he suddenly realized he disliked having to make hundreds of fast decisions daily, dealing with labor disputes, and living in a congested metropolitan area. Since those three things tend to be inseparable from the job, the most logical decision for him was to leave."

So there are varying degrees of change that your data may indicate you need to pursue. On the low end it might be a change of bosses, of companies, or of location (urban vs. rural). On the upper end, you might determine that the career itself has finally lost its glamour. In this case you have one of two choices: Abandon it completely, or modify it to include new areas of interest.

WHAT DO YOU WANT TO DO AND HOW DO YOU DO IT?

You've definitely decided that a change is due. But what have you got going for you? Well, for one thing, you've acquired some clear advantages since the last time you chose a career. You've matured and stabilized. You know your work habits and what you can expect from yourself. You also have several years of solid experience from which you can distill a list of your likes and dislikes. As a matter of fact, if you've been keeping a journal, it should be very apparent what they are. This is where you begin getting an idea of what you would like to do in the future.

"One mistake you want to watch for is switching careers only to find yourself facing the same problems you were trying to escape," says Dr. Potter. "If you don't like meetings, delegation, and decision making, then don't quit your job as an executive for a vacuum cleaner manufacturer only to become a vice-president for an entertainment corporation. On the other hand, if you've discovered that household appliance manufacturing is not your bag but you've got show biz in your blood, then a change of this nature may be just what you need—as long as you don't mind the typical tasks a vice-president would have to perform. That's why it's so important to keep your journal to discover what you really like and dislike about your job."

Looking at your journal, you may find that what you disliked the most about your last job was never having any contact with other people. That's a clue to keep in mind this time around. Other clues may be found in the memories section of your journal. Was there something you used to do early in your career that provided you with a lot of enjoyment? Is there some way that it might be incorporated on a larger scale into a new job?

What about hobbies? How about all those hours you spend in your basement darkroom developing photographs? There's a possible career clue.

The main point is that you've got a chance to do things right this time around. If you remember, the last time you chose a new career you may have been just out of school, anxious, and praying that you'd land a job so that you could move out of your parents' house and start a real life. Just about any job would have looked good. Now, you've got a job. It may not be ringing your chimes, but it's certainly ringing your cash register. So use this period of financial freedom to review your experience and explore your current tastes until you *know* what you'd like to be doing.

Having determined what you want to do, now it becomes a question of how. "While it may seem excitingly daring to just shoot off onto a new career path, at some point you're going to run into hard reality," says Dr. Potter. "Money is the first problem. What will you do for cash while you are making the change? Education is the second problem. Are you really prepared to go back to school or start at square one in some training program? And finally, you need to consider the competition you're going to face in your new career. You'll be going up against people who, for all their professional lives, have done what you are only beginning to do. That's why I always counsel potential career-changers to take small steps."

One way to take small steps is to intersect your current skills with your interests. A good example of that approach was displayed by the lawyer mentioned earlier. "By intersecting skills, you can make some directional headway without giving up your accumulated expertise," says Dr. Potter. Think of it as a kind of job evolution. If you were an accountant and you wanted to be a lion tamer, your first move might be to become an accountant for a circus. From there you can familiarize yourself with the terrain.

Intersecting skills also can transform you from a wet-behind-the-ears beginner in a trade to that most valued of all things: a specialist. "A research chemist from a large pharmaceutical firm came to my seminar and told me her fantasy was to chuck the research business and become a counselor," recalls Dr. Potter. "After we had engaged in various experiential and self-exploratory exercises within the workshops, she went back to her company, set up a staff meeting, and showed everybody what she had learned.

"I pointed out to her that even if she did go back to school at age 45 and get a counseling degree, she might not be able to use it. The trade is already flooded. Competition is rough to begin with and would be especially tough on a latecomer. On the other hand, I suggested, she could continue to hold informal meetings and perhaps convince her present company to make it part of her job."

As the woman develops her skills in a noncompetitive, company-subsidized environment, she might become not merely a counselor, but a counselor for chemists. After all, she is thoroughly familiar with their problems as well as the challenges and demands of their work. After she becomes confident in her counseling skills, she could offer them to the many other companies that employ research chemists.

The last example also demonstrates another way to take small steps toward career change: Get your own company to pay you while you learn. "Most large companies hire thousands of people in areas ranging from advertising to truck driving," notes Dr. Potter. "If you've been with your company for five or ten years, you've already proven yourself to be an intelligent, reliable employee. If you want to get into a new line of work in which you have little or no experience, you'll probably have a better chance of doing it with a company that knows and values you."

Rather than give up your former career entirely, you may convince your company to let you work part of the week in a new department and the rest in your old one. This will give you a chance to get your feet wet without drowning. From the company's viewpoint, as long as you can still do your job, it's always a plus to have multifaceted employees.

As you may have gathered by now, dashing feats of career change derring-do are out. But this doesn't mean you can't take some serious steps that will eventually set your feet on a new path. You just want to make sure at this point in your life that it's the right path. And that means taking it slow and steady. Remember, the word for the day is evolution, not revolution.

9

CHANGE

If there's a single skill that separates the successful executive from the great horde of also-rans, it's the mastery of change.

When confronted by sudden change—especially a change that affects our jobs—most of us react with something closer to abject fear and trembling than presidential aplomb. The departmental reorganization, the revised marketing plan, the new assignment: Our first reaction to each of these is often dread and defensiveness.

But the fact is that change lies at the very heart of successful management. It is the engine that fuels our whole economy. It's what keeps your company alive. It's what created your job. After all, as Walter Wriston, former chairman of Citibank, has said: "If wages come from work, rent from real estate, and interest from savings, where do profits come from? The answer is that profits come from risk."

And risk is spelled c-h-a-n-g-e.

The big winners in the game of business tend to have a very different attitude toward change than those who are plugging along somewhere down in the great gray middle. To them, change is not something to be feared. They don't hunker down and cover their heads when the winds of change come howling through. They relish it. They're exhilarated by it. They embrace the dance and the dazzle of it like children plunging into the sea. They're the ones who initiate change, not the ones who merely react to it. They understand that mastery of change will make them powerful, successful, and maybe even rich.

"Experience shows that successful companies are those that have initiated change in technology, marketing, or organization, and managed to keep a lead in changes over competitors," says the powerful, successful, and rich Anders Wall, president of Beijerinvest of Sweden, a consortium of companies that includes Volvo and many other enterprises.

It's a bit of business wisdom that many American managers failed to take to heart over the past few decades—and for which we're all now paying dearly. In the years after the Second World War, the U.S. economy so dominated the globe that it was almost impossible for an American company not to make money. All you had to do was keep on doing what you'd always been doing. In the flush and complacent 1950s, nobody even seemed to notice the Japanese, who first entered U.S. markets with almost laughably shoddy imitations of American products. But they were the masters of change. They paid attention, they learned, they adapted, they grew. Today, the Japanese have opened such a commanding lead in so many market segments that at times one can only gasp in awe.

Now we're entering a new era—an era in which the pace of change will accelerate at an even more dizzying rate than it did during the 1960s, 1970s, or 1980s. It's a time when managers will have to paddle even harder to keep ahead of the breaking wave of change. Today, products that were once expected to produce earnings for three to five years now last a year or even less. In the microcomputer business, new models now replace old ones in about nine months. And not only have product life cycles shortened, so has the time a company can expect to hold the technological lead. An innovative Japanese electronics company like Sony once expected to dominate the market with a new product for two or three years. Now technological leads are measured in months.

Business writer Daniel Kehrer, in his book *Doing Business Boldly,* points out something else: In contrast to the go-go postwar years, the U.S. population is now growing at only about 1 percent a year, and slowing. That means, he says, that "growth will no longer be an American economic birthright." In order to gain and keep a competitive edge, managers will have to become even more flexible, quicker to adapt to changing market conditions, more boldly willing to take calculated risks.

Flexibility, adaptiveness, intelligent risk-taking: They're the hallmarks of a businessperson who is a master of change.

What's the risk of *not* changing? Consider the case of the National Cash Register (NCR) Corporation, a dynamic, fast-growing company during the 1960s and 1970s. It was the market leader in mechanical cash registers and accounting machines, with a seemingly unbeatable lead in its market segment. Then electronic cash registers appeared on the scene. NCR's managers were reluctant to dive into this bewildering new sea of technological change, choosing instead to protect their dominance in the old, familiar world of mechanical machines. As a result, a world of opportunity simply passed them by. With astounding speed, the old world all but vanished and a completely new—electronic—world took its place. In the space of just four years, NCR lost not only most of the market it once controlled, but also the even vaster new markets that replaced it.

"Not taking action is not a risk-free situation," observes Roberta Goizueta, CEO of the Coca-Cola Company. "Remember, if you take risks, you may still fail. If you do not take risks, you will surely fail. The greatest risk of all is to do nothing."

Staying afloat in a sea of change

So what is the manager, or aspiring manager, to do in this bewildering new world of ever-accelerating change? The basic idea, put simply, is to learn to love it. Be the joyful initiator and celebrator of change, rather than the passive, fearful victim of it. Be the one who gets the ball rolling, rather than the one who gets rolled over. You might as well learn to love change, since no matter how you happen to feel about it, market conditions, interest rates, and everything else about the business climate are in a state of constant flux anyway. "Nothing endures but change," Heraclitus observed back around 500 B.C., but he might as well have said it yesterday.

More recently, best-selling business writer Robert H. Waterman, Jr., put together a team of business analysts who identified 45 high-powered and innovative companies and then studied them to figure out what they were doing right. His conclusions, laid out in his book *The Renewal Factor: How The Best Get and Keep The Competitive Edge,* may sound familiar. These companies were, in effect, past masters of change. Their managers did everything they could to continuously reinvent, restructure, reinvigorate, and renew their organizations in order to stay competitive. They went to great lengths to keep their companies from getting petrified, so they could respond quickly and creatively to changing market conditions.

"In companies that are able continuously to renew, the management system is best described as consistency with constant experimentation," Waterman writes. "Quantum change over time, as a product of tiny steps every day." At IBM, for instance, departments are reorganized so frequently that employees joke that IBM really stands for "I'll be moving."

How can you as an individual manager foster the sort of atmosphere that will help you, your department, and your company learn mastery of the process of change? Consider these suggestions.

Make change the norm. At the companies Waterman's team identified as "renewing" organizations, one thing the researchers noted was the managers' "disposition for welcoming change as the norm." "Leaders at the renewing companies often mention their acceptance of the inevitability of change," Waterman writes. "By talking about it, by treating change as normal, these leaders take away much of the fear and anxiety that surround change."

If people come to feel that the way the company has always done things is the way they'll always be done, a departmental reorganization or a new product introduction will be welcomed about as warmly as a Sherman tank crashing into the lobby. It will just *feel* like trouble. But at the most successful and innovative companies, where change is the norm, everything is *always* in process. People get used to it, and come to welcome it—because they've also seen that change is just another word for opportunity.

At the immensely successful biotech company Genentech, for instance, founder Bob Swanson has gone to great lengths to preserve the atmosphere that was present in the company during its wild and woolly early days, when the company was growing faster than capital could be found to fund the expansion. (Many early Genentech employees who took stock instead of pay are now millionaires.) "One of the things we work very hard at at Genentech is creating an atmosphere for people to take risks, to maintain the sense of creativity and excitement and innovation that got us to where we are, even as we grow bigger," Swanson says.

Too often, he maintains, companies respond to success by forgetting what made them successful in the first place. They get fat and defensive and complacent. Why aren't there more two-time Nobel Prize winners? Because it's a natural human tendency to rest on your laurels. But you're never *there*, Swanson maintains. Once you've achieved your goal, it's time for new goals. And the only way to reach new goals, and continue to grow, is to continue to change.

Keep the rules to a minimum. At Genentech, the company's overall goal is clear: to develop and market new biotechnology products. But there is tremendous flexibility about how individual employees and departments reach that goal. Says Swanson: "One of the things that we felt was most important, and we describe this in our corporate philosophy, is to have minimum guidelines and procedures, giving employees a great deal of freedom within the company to apply their skills and knowledge." After making the company's goals clear, "then you give them a lot of flexibility to use their own creativity and skills to figure out the best way to get there, including taking risks, coming up with new ideas, different ways of approaching things."

Swanson adds one more critical ingredient to this recipe for success: "We don't work on any projects we can't get somebody excited about."

Move people around. Gilbert Trigano, CEO of Club Med, believes there's magic in the idea of simply moving people around the company, from job to job, on a fairly regular basis. Change energizes people, boredom enervates. Says Trigano: "When you move, the first year you study and learn. Your productivity is 60 percent. The second year your productivity is 80 percent. The next year it is 80 to 90 percent. Afterward, it starts to decrease. After ten years, I think your productivity is 25 percent."

Trigano is not the only one to have discovered this simple truth. Fluidity of movement among employees was a characteristic Robert Waterman discovered among the 45 dynamic companies he studied. Within these companies, he found, "people move more often and with greater degrees of freedom across functions, divisions, from line to staff and vice versa. They move laterally. Some move down, but without the stigma that moving down means moving out."

Even if your current corporate commission involves managing nobody but yourself, you'd do well to heed this advice. Don't be afraid to move around in the company. Try something you've never tried before. Retrain yourself. Be bold, be daring, be different. But whatever you do, keep yourself interested, alive, and changing. Says Waterman: "When you start to get too comfortable, when there aren't many questions you can't answer, it's time for a change."

Hire for "hybrid vigor." If you sit on the hiring side of job interviews, you might consider using the energizing magic of change in another way. Consider this: At Smith & Hawken, a California-based direct marketing company, the head of data processing is an ex-seminarian who knew nothing about computers—and in fact had never even held a job in his life—at the time he was hired. But the company's cofounder, Paul Hawken, also knew that the man was a gifted pianist and composer, and guessed that his genius for music could be transferred to software. He was right. Hawken's bold, intuitive hiring decision proved to be a stroke of genius.

Energized and excited by the novelty of dramatic change, a bright person will thrive. "If the person is generally competent . . . and if the new job is suited to his or her abilities, he or she will be on a very steep learning curve," Hawken explains in his book *Growing a Business*. "The individual will see the work with new eyes and spot the conventional wisdoms that are wrong. . . . Such employees will not conform but transform. Their naïveté will often lead them to new ideas and ways of doing things a pro would have overlooked."

This process of throwing competent but untrained people head over heels into a raging torrent of change is similar to an old technique used by breeders of plants. A breeder seeking to improve a strain of, say, orchids will breed one variety with another, very different variety, in hopes that the resulting progeny will be larger or more fragrant than either one of the parents. When it happens (and it doesn't always work), the result is known as "hybrid vigor." It's a happy accident that is superior to everything that preceded it.

Says Hawken: "The best way to keep good people is to create an atmosphere of hybrid vigor throughout your business, from top to bottom. Keep people active in as many aspects of your operation as possible. Give them as many different responsibilities as possible."

Shake it up, and keep shaking. Nothing kills an innovative idea or product faster than an entrenched bureaucracy. That's why many of the most successful companies make a practice of regularly shaking up the system, breaking institutional habits, reorganizing departments. At IBM, every major unit has been reorganized at least once in the past 2½ years. "We reorganize for good business reasons," says CEO John Akers. "One of the good business reasons is that we haven't reorganized for a while."

The always-brilliant Peter Drucker says that "every three years or so, a company should be put on trial for its life—every product, process, technology, service, and market." Nothing should be shielded from the transforming hand of change. The most extreme example of this process comes from Japan, where Chiyoshi Misawa, founder of Misawa Homes, the largest home-builder in Japan, "dies" at least once every decade. He sends a memo to his company formally announcing "the death of your president." In this way, he forces his company to rethink everything, to break old habits, to reinvent itself, to be reborn out of the ashes of old assumptions, habits, and procedures.

Change a little—often. To keep your company or department from turning into a fossil, says Robert Waterman, you have to keep changing all the time—but it's best to do it with one tiny change at a time. Frequent minor changes are a lot better than infrequent, major changes, he says. Change that's too sweeping and too sudden is counterproductive, because people get scared. They tend to freeze up. They may quit on you, or stage a revolt. But a constant stream of minor revisions, alterations, adjustments—changing the way you conduct staff meetings, redesigning the company newsletter—is a good way of getting the troops used to the habit of change.

And besides, lots of little tiny changes may actually be the best way to get things done. Most of IBM's success is based not on the stunning technological breakthrough but on the incremental step. The great success of Alcoholics Anonymous can be chalked up to a similar principle—if you can't stay sober your whole life, at least you can do it for one day at a time.

Becoming a master of change may be something best learned the same way: One little change at a time.

10

CLOTHES

B asically, the American businessman should dress as though he recently lost his entire family in a tragic boat explosion.

—Dave Barry
Claw Your Way to the Top

In the annals of corporate America, it had to be the most unusual assignment yet. A West Coast–based company (whose name will remain anonymous) sent one of its brightest managers to New York, where executive image consultant (that's right, executive image consultant) Fred Knapp was instructed to give the manager an ultimatum: Stop wearing red socks in the office or watch your career grind to a halt. This, we repeat, is not fiction.

Knapp, who conducts American Management Association–endorsed seminars, tactfully conveyed to the manager that he was talented and valuable and well liked by his bosses—and that the only obstacles blocking a promising career were his trademark red socks. The manager decided that his corporate advancement was more significant than his hosiery. And soon he was out shopping on Madison Avenue with Knapp, selecting a new wardrobe of socks befitting a rising corporate star. "I think we bought him black and dark blue over-the-calf socks," Knapp recalled years later.

Silly? You bet. But this little tale illustrates a simple reality of organizational life: People who don't wear the proper uniform aren't seen as team players—and are not totally trusted.

Don't think that just because you aren't working at IBM—which is renowned almost as much for its button-down, white-shirt style as for mainframe computers—you aren't subject to a dress code. The styles may be vastly different at, say, Ben & Jerry's Ice Cream, but the rules are roughly

The "Weirdos" at Ben & Jerry's

Most everyone at the Waterbury, Vermont, headquarters of Ben & Jerry's Ice Cream is proud of the fact that, with the sole exception of production employees who must wear hair nets and the like, they are free to dress as they please.

As if to emphasize the sartorial freedom, the company holds an annual "Tacky Day," at which prizes are awarded for the funniest outfits. Past winners have worn polyester-leisure-suit-and-love-beads outfits or house-dress-and-hair-curler ensembles.

But the freewheeling dress tradition is in its own manner just as rigid as the button-down tradition at some Fortune 500 companies or the fashion-forward tradition at Madison Avenue advertising agencies.

At Ben & Jerry's, the weirdos are well known.

They include Michael Brink, the media buyer in the company's marketing department who is known for wearing conservative bow ties and sweaters (never a jacket). And Sue Elliott, who works in the company's franchise department, "looks as if she just stepped out of a Talbots catalog," reports a company spokesperson, who adds: "She's very stylish in a New England preppy sort of way, pearls and all. She appreciates fine clothes and that's great. Nobody makes fun of her. But she is seen as an oddity."

the same. "Our CEOs and upper management usually wear jeans and flannel shirts," says Elise Brown, Ben & Jerry's spokesperson. "And we can always tell when our director of sales, Rick Brown, is going out of town on business. He puts on a jacket and tie." But imagine the suspicion that would arise if he started showing up at work every day in a three-piece suit.

"They'd ask me where my job interview was," responds the sales director, adding that on those days that he must wear a suit for out-of-company meetings, "Jerry always teases me and tells me I should be wearing a Ben & Jerry's T-shirt." (For more on the Ben & Jerry's dress code, see "The 'Weirdos' at Ben & Jerry's" above.)

DISCOVERING THE UNWRITTEN DRESS CODE FOR YOUR NEW JOB

For some folks, the ability to pick up on subtle dress signals comes naturally. For others—those who are not totally convinced that appearance counts—it takes a concerted effort. And why not? Women in particular are socialized at a very early age to recognize that their dress expresses a great deal about them. (Which may be why women, and not men, generally dress up to shop for clothes.) For them, the organizational dress codes are fairly obvious. For many men, however, it's a vastly different story, partly because of the simple fact that men don't have nearly as many clothes choices to make. Even though John T. Molloy begins his classic *Dress for Success* by proclaiming, "The first rule of dress is common sense," not everybody has common sense about what to wear.

The truth, says Stanley Rosenberg, Ph.D., Dartmouth Medical School professor of psychiatry, is that "most people who will make it in organizations will be able to quickly index themselves. For instance, they'll be able to look around the room and determine if their boss favors formality, or if she's on the informal side. Their antennae are always up."

Most executive image experts suggest you dress like your boss, or at least like the people one level above you. "Learn to be observant of those people," says executive stylist Lois Fenton, author of *Dress for Excellence*. "If people at the level above you never wear blazers, don't wear blazers. If you see more than one person wearing white contrast collars, you can wear white contrast collars. If you see only the people nobody has respect for wearing certain things, I'd say that's another clue."

Why, you might ask, should you dress for the position above you, instead of for the position you already have? "When an opening for a promotion occurs, people will be looking to fill the job with someone who looks right, someone who would fit right in," Fenton explains. (Companies such as Metropolitan Life pay $2,500 a day for Fenton to provide this type of advice to fast-trackers who are sent to her Executive Wardrobe Engineering seminars. She'll take you clothes shopping for $900 a day.)

So yes, your eyes should be open to your superiors' dress habits. But to truly get your antennae up—or to "get a reading," as Knapp prefers to put it—you've got to rely also on your ears. Not that anyone will take the trouble of telling you such things directly. "In the corporate world, a great deal of extremely serious information is transmitted by means of jokes," he says. His advice: Pay attention to all those off-hand remarks and quips you hear around the water cooler. Fenton concurs: "Men are very cutting about how other men dress. You hear them say things like, 'Would you look at the tie?' Take your cues from such comments."

Now what happens when *you're* the butt of office dress jokes? Perhaps you like to indulge in expensive dress habits and your sartorial splendor is the constant target of office quips—good-natured or otherwise. Be aware that the assets you gain in trendiness may become business liabilities. For one thing, superiors, co-workers, suppliers, and a host of others may find it difficult to take you seriously as an executive if you've got a fondness for high fashion. And even your boss—the guy who only buys at Brooks Brothers and who thinks Ascot Chang is a martial arts champion—may feel threatened. If too much is made of your clothes, maybe you should tone things down. (*Note to your boss:* Ascot Chang is a well-known Hong Kong tailor, the fellow who makes President Bush's shirts.)

FINDING A UNIQUE LOOK THAT'S RIGHT FOR YOU

If this sounds like you're destined to don a corporate uniform regardless of where you work, don't despair. You still can maintain some sense of individual style within any fashion format. The trick is in being subtle.

Guys, if your organization's unwritten dress code calls for navy blue

---

This CEO Sets Her Own Style

For Maria Monet, one of the perks of being the boss is the freedom to express herself in clothes. Monet is president and chief executive officer of New York's Ogden Financial Services, a subsidiary of Ogden Corporation, and she thinks nothing of coming to the office in a suede skirt or the red leather suit she's worn twice. Monet has worn skirts above the knee. "I have the self-confidence and the position to do this," she says.

It wasn't so at the law firm where Monet worked earlier in her career. "All of the women there wore the uniform, the suit that looks like a man's. I wore conservative suits but I never did wear those [requisite] silk ties," she says, adding, "In a law firm, some people find it hard to advance unless they wear the uniform." In her next job at an investment banking firm, Monet started wearing clothes she describes as "a little more stylish, a little more feminine, a little more colorful."

Now, as the boss, she sets the fashion tone. But there's still a code. She dresses each day "according to what will be happening that day." For example, if she will be meeting with members of a company that adheres to a conservative corporate culture, Monet will dress in one of her more conservative outfits. Is there anything she'd never wear to the office? "Pants," she responds. "And anything provocative."

suits and starched-collar white shirts, why not wear some subtly patterned socks? Fenton adds a few more ideas: Wear pleated trousers with traditional suits. Wear point collars with collar pins or collar bars. Wear antique cuff links. Carry a pocket watch. Sport pocket squares (a.k.a. pocket hankies), but make sure they don't stick out too far. (This pocket square suggestion is one that is vetoed by Knapp, who says such adornments should be worn only by the man in charge and, in some cases, by the number two man.)

Ladies, one way to stand out is by wearing "noticeably well-coordinated colors," says Fenton. Or wear very bright colors but with a conservative design. Or wear quiet colors with an interesting silhouette. When it comes to handbags, shoes, and belts, don't sacrifice quality for quantity.

To sum up, don't try too hard to sport a look that you feel is stylish but that really makes you look like a clown. In order to succeed, you want to be known for your talents and energy, not for your red socks.

5 SIMPLE RULES TO ADD AUTHORITY TO THE WAY YOU LOOK

1. Wear dark colors. When the *Wall Street Journal* surveyed 351 chief executive officers for their preferred suit color, no one was surprised that 53 percent of the respondents favored blue, dark blue, or navy blue, and 39.6 percent opted for gray, charcoal, or dark gray. For both men and women, dark suits spell formality, conservatism, and authority. Dark ties, too, contribute to the image. (Puh-leeze, throw out all those yellow ties that were considered such a power look for part of 1985.) Make sure the geometric patterns on your ties are minuscule: Go for pin dots, foulards, or the small, tight patterns found in ties by Hermès.

But don't extend this dark-is-beautiful look to shirts. The general rule is that the darker the color of the suit and tie, the lighter the color of the shirt. (White was the preferred color of 53 percent of the CEOs surveyed by the *Wall Street Journal*, and blue came in second with 35 percent.) And don't feel constrained to wear those dark colors every day of the month. Vary things a bit, so you don't drive your colleagues batty with your somber appearance. Unless, of course, you're a funeral director.

2. Avoid "fashion-forward" dress. This goes both for men and women. Generally speaking, employers are more willing to trust conservative dressers than those who would shell out $1,500 for one of Bijan's fur-lined denim jackets. *Note:* This does not apply to the marvelous folks who toil daily in a few notably glitzy industries such as the music industry or, more important, the fashion industry (to the folks in the latter, we offer an apology;

we're just reporting the facts, not making the rules). In men's suits, the dull-as-dishwater, traditional soft-shouldered suits that have kept Brooks Brothers flourishing since 1818 are preferred in most industries and in most regions of the United States over sharply tailored European suits.

3. Avoid clothes made of polyester and other synthetic fibers. This is advisable even if your company manufactures synthetics. They are inferior to natural fibers in a multitude of ways. Unlike natural fibers, synthetics don't express your individual shape. Nor do they "breathe." In synthetics, you're likely to feel every escalating degree in the warmer months (and, if you perspire, your co-workers are likely to suffer, too). Better to select from the many variants of wool, cotton, linen, and silk.

4. Wear expensive shoes—and keep them shined. This sounds like stupid advice, but such things get noticed, whether we like it or not. (Just how expensive can shoes get? A pair of waxed-calf Lobb dress shoes goes for $3,000, but that's the extreme.) Too many folks think nothing of spending $800 for a suit but turn cheap when it comes to footwear, says Fenton. Ladies: For authority's sake, favor dark versions of the plain pump (closed toe and heel) over shoes of many colors or over boots, suggests John Molloy in *The Woman's Dress for Success Book.* Men: If you already wear expensive, well-maintained shoes and want to add still more authority, exchange slip-ons for lace-ups.

5. Ladies, avoid heavy doses of pastels. Fenton, who advises the success-bound of both genders, says that women can add authority by wearing less pink, baby blue, and other pastels that are equated with nurseries. She also says that there's little or no authority to be found in dangle earrings, sexy shoes, and (ugh!) ankle bracelets. You're not dressing to pick up a guy at the Roller Derby.

How to look like a million without spending it

1. Shop smart. Don't want to pay $700 for a typical Paul Stuart suit (or $2,200 for the retailer's top-of-the-line, off-the-rack cashmere-and-wool blend)? Take advantage of the burgeoning discount outlets or wait for sales at full-price stores.

Here are a few hints for discount shopping.

- Ask about the return policy, suggests Vicki Audette, author of *Dress Better for Less.* And ask even if it's posted. Some places will return your money, some will give you credit. To be safe, find out beforehand.

• Make yourself a regular at the discount store. After several repeat visits, you may discover that the Calvin Klein shirts get doubly marked down after two weeks on the shelves.

• Ask salesmen when new shipments arrive.

• Don't even think of buying an item without trying it on. (Yes, undergarments and socks are excluded.)

• Examine the garments carefully, looking for small rips and tears.

• Find out when the store is least crowded, and shop then if your schedule permits.

• Be suspicious of clothes bearing discount store labels—they could be inferior to manufacturers' overruns that are sold by the same discounter, according to *Dress for Success.*

Here are a few tips for sales.

• Get yourself on a store's mailing list for "special" customer sales.

• Delay purchases of seasonal clothes until end-of-season sales. (Typically, cold-weather items go on sale in January and February, while warm-weather items go on sale in July and August.)

• Be wary of stores that seem to have permanent "sales."

2. Look for quality workmanship. Audette, who frequently appears on national television offering advice for bargain hunters, explains what to look for.

• Straight, even stitching in colors that match the fabric.

• Good-quality linings that are not attached all around (loose linings wear better).

• Generous seams of ½ inch or more.

• Buttons that fit tightly in the buttonholes.

• Ample, even hems.

• Felt backing on wool collars to retain the shape.

3. Be well tailored. When having your pants fitted, wear the shoes you will be wearing with the pants, wear your own belt, and remove pocket change and anything else you ordinarily carry around in pockets. Remember: Suit shoulders should fit right from the start—they can't be altered. And try on your garments after the alterations are made; don't accept the purchase if it still doesn't fit properly.

4. Carry an expensive accessory to upgrade moderate-quality clothes. Specifically, Fenton suggests a fine, imported leather briefcase, wallet, or belt for men. They add class. They rarely go out of style. And, besides, you only have to pay for them once. When it comes to briefcases, Knapp says the narrower the better. Three-inch imported versions are probably the most impressive. "The general rule," says Knapp, "is the narrower the briefcase, the more important the papers."

Women should carry an expensive, well-made handbag. Fenton explains that most European women own a minimum number of purses, but that the ones they have are always of the highest quality. So instead of having a different purse to match every outfit, why not own a few well-made ones? The same goes for shoes and belts. "Fine handbags, shoes, and belts can upgrade an inexpensive outfit," she says.

5. Men: don't blink at paying $45 for a tie. Good ties last longer and will do wonders to improve the look of an average suit or shirt.

---

10 Clothing Mistakes to Avoid

For men:

1. Light blue or bright blue suits
2. Short-sleeved shirts (unless you're in tropical or subtropical climes)
3. Ties that land above or below your belt
4. White socks
5. Short socks
6. Cheap digital watches (unless your company manufactures, imports, or distributes them)
7. Tacky jewelry (wide tie clips, gold chains, bracelets of any type)
8. Headbands (unless you're a Native American)
9. Unpressed pants or jackets
10. Alligator shoes

For women:

1. Skirts that are 3 inches above the knee (the same effect can be achieved by wearing knee-length skirts)
2. Excessively tight anything
3. Indistinguishable versions of the same "uniform" (pin-striped suits and butterfly ties) day in and day out
4. Tacky jewelry

(continued)

10 Clothing Mistakes to Avoid—*Continued*

5. Nurse-white stockings
6. Cheap blouses
7. Halter tops
8. Wrinkled outfits
9. Fashion-forward hairdos (unless you're a full-time rock musician)
10. Suggestively sheer anything

11

COMPETITION

If people were competitive to the exclusion of any other thought or emotion, what would a typical day at your office be like? It might start with you not being able to find a parking space in the company lot. Why? Because everybody who arrived early parked perpendicularly—each car taking up three spaces. So you end up wasting 15 valuable minutes finding a space five blocks away. That's a 15-minute head start your co-workers have on you in the race for personal success.

A cup of coffee? Maybe not. Last week the person in the office next door laced the pot with an industrial-strength diuretic. That took seven people out of action for the day. Instead you decide to head over to your 10:00 A.M. meeting, where you plan to unveil your latest marketing brainstorm. But after sitting in an empty room for 25 minutes, you find out that someone switched the meeting to 9:00 without bothering to tell you.

Don't worry though. You get in your licks, too. In calculating the budget for a new project, your boss made a mistake which could have cost the company millions. Luckily you catch it. Your boss would have been thankful except that, instead of discussing it with him, you take it to his superior. Congratulations on your promotion.

Let's interrupt this cutthroat scenario right now and give thanks for the fact that competitiveness is *not* the single driving force in human nature. On the other hand, let's admit that neither do we exist in an angelic state of equilibrium where self-interest never rears its calculating head. But that's okay. There's nothing wrong with wanting to be number one. It's what makes people run faster, jump higher, and work harder.

A little competition is healthy, but too much is clearly harmful. Where do you draw the line? And while we're asking questions, let's not forget that competition is like a loaded gun that can be aimed in many different directions: at an opponent, yourself, or a goal. Which way should you point it?

REDIRECTING COMPETITIVENESS IN YOUR EMPLOYEES

No doubt about it. If there is a co-worker in the next office doing twice as much business as you are, it's going to push you to work harder. And as a manager, you may even want to encourage a bit of rivalry between your employees for this very reason. "For the most part, people are only going to work as hard as they feel is necessary to maintain their job," says J. T. Ruthers, an Atlanta psychologist and management consultant. "And sometimes the only way to make an employee realize that he or she needs to work harder is by letting him see that other people in the department are consistently reaching higher levels of performance."

By creating an environment where excellence is expected and achieved, you ensure that the number one performance spot in the organization becomes a coveted position.

"A point can be reached, however, where winning becomes all that matters," cautions Ruthers. "For example, one of your employees might be making sales calls in a particularly affluent neighborhood that provides a high percentage of finished sales. A second employee is currently having no luck in another locale. While the first employee's area is furnishing her with more calls than she could possibly handle, an atmosphere of high competition will keep her from sharing her area with anyone else. The result is that your company only makes a profit at the speed with which that one employee can mine the rich territory. Had it been a team effort for the greater reward of the department at large, then the first employee might have shared the territory with the second."

So how do you foster a competitive edge and at the same time make sure the edge isn't cutting anyone's throat? By redirecting it away from fellow employees and toward something entirely different. One way to view competition is to look at the relationship between a second baseman and a shortstop, says Alfonso Duarte, vice-president and partner at Korn-Ferry International, the world's largest executive recruiting firm. "Each player is competing to get a better individual batting average, but they all have to work together to make a double play that will enable their team to win."

When University of Minnesota researchers examined more than 100 studies on the topic, they found that the highest productivity was achieved where there was an atmosphere of cooperation on the inside of an organization coupled with an atmosphere of competition on the outside. "Outgroup competition stimulates ingroup cohesion," says Andrew Van de Ven, Ph.D., 3M Professor of Human Systems Management at the University of Minnesota's Carlson School of Management.

"Before you can foster an 'Us vs. Them' attitude, you have to let your troops know that there is a war to be fought," notes Ruthers. "You can start informally, perhaps with a dart board with the other company's logo on it. You might show the competing company's commercials, particularly the ones bashing the competition, during coffee breaks. Or maybe even circulate a few jokes about the other company. These things hurt no one and yet get people's spirit up for a little friendly rivalry."

From there you move to the second phase: some general discussions about how well the competition is doing and how some of their production teams are putting your company's to shame. What you are really communicating is that everyone in the room is currently in second place. Who likes to hear that?

"Finally, you've got to make it a battle with territory to be taken and spoils of war to be won," says Ruthers. "Put up a big chart by the coffee machine showing the competition's output and yours. If possible, see if you can't break down the information so that it takes on added meaning for your employees. If you are in charge of widget production for left-handed blow-dryers, for example, show your employees just how many widgets per week the competition is turning out. If you merely show them the total profit of the other company, the battle becomes meaningless because your employees have very little to do with the overall profits of your company."

In the spoils-of-war-department, figure out a target goal in comparison to the other company. Perhaps it's reasonable to expect your employees to match or beat the opposition's output. But if that's not possible, use a starting goal that is. If your department closes the production gap by 50 percent, for instance, they might be rewarded.

"And be sure you do reward," cautions Hal Angle, Ph.D., chairman of the Management Department at the University of Cincinnati. "As the old saying goes, 'What you reward is what you get.' So if you reward group effort, you get group effort."

"If war against the competition doesn't seem feasible, you can still create team competitiveness by letting your employees work against a deadline or production goal," says Ruthers. "For example, if they can turn out 2,400 widgets by the end of the month, then everybody in the department gets a day off of their choice. By doing this, personal achievement takes a back seat to group achievement because it's an everybody-works-and-everybody-gets-something situation."

On the personal level, the quest to be the best can be channeled into self-competition rather than an all's-fair-in-love-and-war approach. "The question to put to your employees is 'Do you want to win by running faster, or do you want to win by tripping up the other person?'" says Wilbert Sykes, M.D., a psychiatrist whose TriSource Group coaches executives on how to function better in their jobs and personal lives. "When we win by running faster, we can enjoy the victory. When we win by whatever means possible, we experience guilt, anxiety, and a sense of dread that there will be revenge. What we succeed in doing is diminishing our victory."

Too often, though, the cutthroat style is subtly encouraged by management. "The only way to change this is by rewarding people when they have competed successfully against *themselves*," notes Ruthers. "Come review time, manager and employee should sit down and chart the employee's output for the last year. And when I say chart, I mean exactly that. Get a piece of poster board and graph the employee's work month by month. Then agree on a percentage increase in output for the coming year. Have the employee put the poster somewhere in his office where he alone can refer to it. Make sure the employee marks the chart on a month-to-month basis so he can watch his own progress. In effect, what you will be doing is getting the employee to compete against himself."

By rewarding employees who beat their own past performance, you'll infuse them with a competitive edge that doesn't undermine the team. "Since the battle has been redirected from their fellow employees to themselves, there's no reason they can't cooperate with everyone," says Ruthers.

ARE YOU TOO COMPETITIVE?

Having directed your employees' competitive energies onto more appropriate targets than each other, the next question to be answered is whether *you* are being more competitive than is considered healthy. "Competition, like booze, sex, or drugs, can be addicting," says Dr. Sykes, who has seen more than a few executives get consumed by the cycle of competition and reward. The more competitive they are, the more rewards they reap . . . and the more they need.

"The problem with competitiveness when directed at a peer, however, is that there is always a touch of aggressiveness that goes along with it," notes Will Johnson, Ph.D., a psychologist and career counselor based in Oakland, California. "Several problems can develop from this. For example, while it is perfectly natural to be angry when you don't do well, being too competitive will also make you angry when anyone else *does* do well. Another problem is that you may be behaving badly toward others and simply rationalizing that that's what it takes to get ahead."

Ironically, that kind of behavior is what it takes to be left behind. In one famous study that contrasted the behavior of corporate executives who got derailed just before reaching the top with the behavior of executives who made it all the way, it was determined that those who never made it were the type who stepped in other people's faces on the way up. "Friends come and go, but enemies accumulate," says David Campbell, Ph.D., a psychologist and senior fellow at the Center for Creative Leadership in Greensboro, North Carolina. "When you get near the top, you suddenly realize you need a favor from someone you stuck a pin in ten years ago."

Before you end up having your co-workers take you for a long walk off a short pier, try answering the following questions as honestly as possible to see if in fact you are too competitive.

Are you out to annihilate the other guy? Do you want to be surrounded by folks whose hard work and talent motivates you to do your best? Or do you prefer to work with incompetent types, so that like Pac Man you can gobble up everyone in your path? "You know you're too competitive when you lose your perspective, when you concentrate on beating the other guy and not on improving your own performance," says Larry Iwan, a manufacturing operations manager at Eaton Corporation. "I love competition because it brings out the best in you. But you should use competition to motivate you to work harder, not to worry about winning or losing."

Do co-workers resent you? "You'll know you're being too competitive if people avoid you, if they are hostile to you, if they don't give you the information you need, and if they appear cautious and guarded in what they say to you," explains Robert A. Lefton, Ph.D., an industrial psychologist and president of Psychological Associates, a St. Louis–based consulting firm.

Does your boss resent you? Sure, some bosses would love the fact that you're doing such a good job of outpacing your peers no matter what the cost to the team's emotional well-being. But a good manager will be disturbed by an overly competitive person. The reason? You may be demoralizing others. "If one employee is happy but the other nine are unhappy, the group will be ineffective, no matter how much that one person produces," says executive recruiter Duarte.

Is your life too narrow? Do you spend substantially more time at work than your peers do? Are all of your interests closely aligned with work? (Example: You couldn't imagine attending a sporting event without taking a client.) Does a large percentage of your conversation with family and friends revolve around how you are doing at work?

Do you always keep score? Do the mistakes of your peers count as pluses in your own ledger of success? If you find yourself spending a lot of time simply trying to get facts and figures on your co-workers' achievements so that you can figure out where you stand, then you have a problem.

If you've answered one or more of these questions with a yes, the solution is not simple. But there are a few ways you can start to break out of the competition-intensive mode. "First, you might ban all talk of work from your home," suggests Dr. Johnson. "And while you're at it, try lunching away from your co-workers for a month. Normally, lunchtime is when everyone compares notes, and that's when competitive people get their dander up—when they hear all the lunchroom scuttlebutt concerning raises, promotions, and company favorites."

Dr. Johnson also suggests that you don't go rooting around for information on other people's progress. "This means no gossiping, in general, and turning a deaf ear when someone wants to chew the fat with you. The last thing you need to hear is that the guy next door just topped your production record."

Finally, take a few chances. Most competitive types play it too close to the chest at work, rarely taking a risk lest they lose their favorable position in the ratings. Forget it. "If you take a chance and it pays off, you've discovered a whole new world of adventure that should keep you far too busy for petty competitiveness," notes Dr. Johnson. "If you blow it, it's almost going to force you to take yourself out of the running for Mr. or Ms. Perfect, and to start viewing things a little less seriously."

WHEN A CO-WORKER IS TOO COMPETITIVE

You've finally done it. You've actually gotten yourself to admit that winning may not be everything. Congratulations. Now what are you going to do about the guy sitting at the desk next to yours? You know the one we're talking about. His desk looks like a cross between the Bastille and the Maginot Line, and all of his guns are pointing straight at you. He hasn't heard the news that too much competition can cause cavities. Here are a few ideas you can use in self-defense.

Offer an olive branch . . . but a little one. "My sense is that you're committing suicide if you decide to be a cooperator or an accommodator while swimming in a pool of sharks," cautions Dr. Angle of the University of Cincinnati. But he concedes that you can make certain overtures to office rivals that may get them to become less competitive. First, decide what you're willing to relinquish (some mildly helpful data, for example) and offer it to the competitor as a sign that you are eager to help him—with the tacit understanding that he reciprocate. Say, "I thought this could be helpful to you." The point, explains Dr. Angle, is to send two clear messages: (1) that you could play hardball with the information you have if you wanted to, but (2) that you choose not to.

Bring the rivalry out into the open. Eaton Corporation manager Larry Iwan believes most interoffice competitive situations work themselves into "personal grudge matches," which can be smoothed over with the right approach. "What I would say to someone is 'We've been bumping heads on this for quite a while. You've got a position; I've got a position. Let me try to understand where you're coming from and I'll explain where I'm coming from. Maybe we can break this thing down and start getting productive again.' "

Point out the rewards of cooperation. For one thing, the office could become a more pleasant place to work. You can almost take it for granted that the other person has felt the strain, too, so a change might be welcomed. Another reward of cooperation is that as you help each other advance, you'll both be in better positions to render each other favors in the future.

Understand the limits of your power. "Understand what you can and can't control," says Dr. Sykes. "Remember, you don't have dominion over the mores and behavior of others." Some people are just never going to budge. They will remain competitive until their dying breath and probably be happy that they beat you to the grave. Fine. Let them be that way. As long as you are competing only with yourself—continually seeking to better your own past performance—they can't touch you.

12

CONFIDENCE

The most revealing scenario in Lee Iacocca's first best-selling book portrays what day-to-day life was like for him during his waning months as president of Ford Motor Company.

Iacocca was the unappreciated, undercut, and professionally battered number-two man to chairman Henry Ford II. By reading Iacocca's memoirs, which describe his being out of favor with such a powerful boss, one begins to feel his dread of arriving at work each day to find yet another round of humiliations heaped upon him. How could he stand it all? How could he muster the enthusiasm to get out of bed every morning, let alone show up in the office and function as president of one of the nation's largest corporations? In retrospect, it seems that Iacocca wondered about that, too.

Somehow we're always surprised to learn that successful people do have lapses in confidence. Like Abraham Lincoln. Or Ernest Hemingway. Or former DuPont chairman Irving Shapiro, who in his first job at the company was passed over for a promotion and "thought the world had come to an end." (What did he do? He decided not to let his emotions take over. He concentrated on his work. He went for three years without getting a raise. But eventually, when he outstripped his rival, he admitted that it felt "nice.")

Amazingly, tales of career woes among the successful and famous do little to instill confidence in us, says Salvatore Didato, Ph.D., a Scarsdale, New York, psychologist and author of *Psychotechniques: Act Right, Feel Right.* ("So Abe Lincoln failed at nearly everything he did before being elected president. Big deal," you must be saying. "He never had to work for my boss.") Yes, it sometimes seems as if our jobs are battlegrounds that do nothing but destroy our self-confidence. That's when we have to work twice as hard.

How to project it— even when you don't feel it

First off, nobody's going to be impressed if you come to work looking like the downtrodden loser you feel you've become. So the initial step in regaining self-confidence in the face of any opposition (external, internal, or imagined) is to stand up straight, dress better, and try to play the part.

Pretend. Acting confident ultimately makes people appear confident. "Imagine yourself to be a confident person. Get that image in your mind and you'll act it out," advises Carol Ann Kell, whose C. A. Kell Associates in Philadelphia coaches business and community leaders in dealing with the often unfriendly media and public audiences.

When you meet people, look them in the eye. Confident people do this. People who are not confident don't.

Smile. It can be a subtle sign of confidence.

Listen. Confident people are magnanimous enough to listen to others.

Know your stuff. Of course, the simple techniques above fall into the realm of style. Your confidence can't be all a front. So Bernard Roberts, vice-president of Mills Roberts Associates, a New York City business training firm, says that while you're looking people directly in the eyes, standing straight, and otherwise acting as if the world were your oyster, you also have to know what you're doing for whatever task is at hand. "If you're prepared and sure of your facts, you've got a better chance of projecting confidence," he says.

Know ahead of time what you want to say. In other words, if you get into the habit of thinking before you speak, you'll be ahead of most people—and will start to feel it. And stay focused. "People who are confident focus on what it is they want to say and don't ramble on and on," says Kell. "They're respectful of other people's time."

Fighting unfair criticism

Let's say you're in a meeting and you've just finished making a proposal that you've slaved over for weeks.

"Joe, that's the stupidest idea I've ever heard," says one of your colleagues. "You're always coming up with stupid ideas."

You feel angry and humiliated in front of your peers. Do you: (1) snap back at the critic that he's a sniveling alcoholic and womanizer, or respond defensively in any other way? (2) accept the criticism politely by acknowledging that not everyone will agree with your proposed idea, but then emphasize its finer points and mention that it's a well-thought-out plan, adding that "personalities shouldn't enter into this"?

If you selected (1), you may be making a big mistake, says Arlene S. Hirsch, a Chicago-based psychologist and career counselor. "It takes a pretty confident person to let himself be criticized unfairly in a meeting and not let his anger take over. But hostile anger doesn't really accomplish anything in a public forum. It just invites everybody to be a spectator, while the two sides become entrenched." Also, in general, losing your cool signals to others that you can't be trusted to maintain control.

She suggests you bite your tongue and later initiate a private discussion with the person who attacked you. Explain that you don't appreciate being unjustly attacked in a meeting and would like to solve any interpersonal problems on a one-to-one basis.

If it's your boss who's doing the attacking, wait for a private moment. The calmly tell him or her that you felt bad being criticized in front of other people and would feel better if such intense criticism were delivered in private, suggests Roberts.

Sometimes people will also respond defensively if their ideas are met with only a lukewarm reception (and not downright criticism). Say you make your presentation and someone responds with the words: "That doesn't hit the mark."

New York City career strategist Adele Scheele, Ph.D., says if that's the case, you could respond by good-naturedly saying, "Thanks for noticing." She predicts that everybody will laugh—and that you should laugh, too, to ease any tension. And then you can say, "But seriously, here was the problem I was faced with and here was how I attended to it . . . " You are offering a point-by-point, objective response and explaining as nondefensively as possible the reasons you believe your proposal is good.

If you feel your proposal is being shot down by someone who is trying to steal your thunder, simply stop speaking—or go on to another topic—when you finish explaining your rationale. If you don't feel there was malice behind the criticism, you may end by asking: "What would you have done?"

But before you do anything, ask yourself a tough question: Are they right?

THE 5-STEP METHOD TO WIPE OUT WORRY

There are few people who know as much about worrying as Thomas D. Borkovec, Ph.D. (And you thought your mother was qualified.) He's a professor of psychiatry at Pennsylvania State University who has conducted much of the research on worrying and the people who indulge in it. So if you can't stop obsessing about that big presentation you have to make next week or the outcome of your next performance review, heed his advice.

1. Postpone worrying. To do this properly you have to schedule a worry period of about ½ hour. Then, as soon as you catch yourself worrying, tell yourself that you'll be available to really worry about the matter at, say, 5:00 P.M. When that golden hour rolls around, sit down with paper and pen and worry to your heart's content. Just be sure to think your problem through completely, to the point that you begin problem-solving, prudently figuring out what you'd do if catastrophe were actually to strike.

2. Be realistic about the downside. While you're sitting there with your paper and pen during your worry period, make yourself write out what you consider to be the worst thing that could happen regarding whatever it is you're worrying about. (Your proposal is met with indifference; you will lose your job if your company is taken over; you won't get that promotion.) And then force yourself to be realistic about the chances that the downside scenario will likely occur. Spell out a game plan in case the worst happens.

3. Focus on your successes. Still at your desk, compile a list of how many projects you've been involved with at work and what the outcome was for each. Chances are you'll have had more successes than failures. The trouble is, you probably have a short memory when it comes to successes. Most of us tend to focus more on the failures. But if you're like most people, you'll be able to make a dent in your self-doubts by simply writing a list of your successes over the years.

4. Take a short meditation break. Either when worry strikes or during your worry period, spend a few minutes to let the stress dissolve. It doesn't have to be Transcendental Meditation or any other formal method—although those certainly are fine. Simply sit quietly and focus on your breathing or a restful image for 10 or 20 minutes until you feel more relaxed.

5. Focus attention on the task at hand. You're crunching numbers but your mind keeps drifting to the proposal that now sits on your boss's desk or the nasty letter you just sent your colleague. As much as possible, refocus all your energy on the number crunching.

UNDERSTANDING WHAT'S WITHIN YOUR CONTROL

Some confidence-busting things, like a pending takeover of your company, obviously are beyond your control. (This does not apply to you,

T. Boone Pickens, Carl Icahn, and others of that ilk who may be reading.) When the dread of such unknown events damages your own fortitude as a manager, the best thing to do for the short term is block out the big picture and concentrate on the tasks at hand, suggests Hirsch.

"It's often the bigger things that you can't control that make you lose confidence. But you generally can control things in your immediate world, such as a meeting you have to run. So try to center yourself and focus your energy on your meeting, not on the external forces that are beyond your control," she says. Worry about any impending disaster and what you can do about it after the meeting.

Or maybe you've gotten into the habit of blaming yourself for problems that were caused by others. When there's a workplace predicament that's eroding your confidence, take a moment to step back and objectively consider that it may not be your fault. A boss may be giving you impossible tasks; a competitor may have an unfair advantage over you. Perhaps it's something else—your industry's slump, for instance—that truly is causing the grief.

"Most men find it easy to blame someone else if there are problems. It's their first trained cultural response," explains Dr. Scheele. "On the other hand, most women, when they can't perform, feel it's their own fault." Her advice: "Men must learn to ask themselves: 'What do *I* have to do to fix the situation?' and women must learn to ask: 'What do *we all* have to do to fix it?'"

So how do you take charge of things you can control? Start small, suggests Dr. Didato. A *leading task* is a small, positive step that in a subtle way can make you begin to regain confidence. Let's suppose you're sitting at your desk and an intense lack of inspiration makes you feel brain-dead. What can you do? Straighten out your desk, reorganize your files, throw out that stack of annual reports that's been cluttering your office floor. It sounds minor, but the rewards to be reaped by such simple accomplishments will be multiplied.

Having an interpersonal problem that's causing you grief? Sit down and write a letter to that person—you don't even have to send it.

In general, ask yourself what's the least you can do to break the impasse and build confidence. Then do it.

REHEARSAL: THE BEST CONFIDENCE-BUILDER

Okay. So it's absurd to imagine salesman-of-the-century Lee Iacocca sitting around his Tuscan villa, having one of his daughters videotape him

5 Things to Remember
When Doubt Strikes Suddenly

1. You're a good person. You have good intentions.
2. You *will* get through this. You've been in tough situations before and have managed to survive—and even flourish.
3. Nothing is so important in this world that you should ruin your health or relationships.
4. Life will go on regardless of the outcome of a particular meeting, project, or other hurdle.
5. You've succeeded more often than you've failed.

as he practices his speech before the World Economics Council. Some folks are natural persuaders. The rest of us need to rehearse.

Rehearsing can be as simple as writing out a speech or intended conversation and reading it before a mirror. Or making an audio tape and listening carefully for inarticulate spots or rhetorical blunders.

If you're preparing for an important interview or meeting that you'll be running, ask a friend, spouse, or anyone who has your interest at heart to videotape your little speech beforehand and to help you review the outcome. And get them to play the role of the interviewer or any adversaries you expect to have—corporate naysayers who will shoot down everything you propose in the meeting. That way you'll get some practice in responding to unexpected challenges that might occur.

And then, there's rehearsal with imagery.

Say you're trying to build up confidence for a meeting with your manager in which you will propose a new billing procedure. To tackle your underlying fear of failing, you can set aside some time in advance to *imagine* yourself succeeding. Dr. Didato explains how.

1. Sit down.
2. Close your eyes.
3. Spend about 10 minutes relaxing your muscles (this will reduce your anxiety).
4. As completely as possible, imagine yourself accomplishing the task. See yourself getting up from your desk, gathering your folders, walking down the hall, knocking on your manager's door, sitting down, making the presentation, responding to criticism.

"By working through the situation in its entirety through imagery, you are taking out the negative emotions such as fear, aggression, anger, and worry," says Dr. Didato.

CONSULT YOUR IMAGINARY MENTOR

Irving Shapiro was named chairman of DuPont in 1974 without having had any formal management training. What did he do when he got into a situation that called on executive skills he didn't necessarily have? He tried to imagine what Walter Wriston, the legendary Citicorp chairman, would do in the same situation. Then Shapiro would adapt it to his own personal style. A similar approach worked for Peter Ratican, who was named chairman of Maxicare Health Systems in 1988. When he found himself in a situation where he didn't know how to respond, he would try to imagine what Joe Conner, chairman of Price Waterhouse, and Lew Wasserman, chairman of entertainment giant MCA, would have done in the same situation. Next, he would ask himself what *he* thought was the right course of action. Then he would try to reconcile the three positions.

It's called mimicking, and experts say it can do wonders to help get you out of little slumps. And you don't even need a well-known executive to play the part of your role model. Dr. Didato once had an executive client who relied on the imagined behavior of his favorite movie star. "Mimicry is a very justifiable method of giving people confidence. We copy other people all the time," says Dr. Didato. Once you gain confidence in yourself, though, you don't need role models. When that happens, you'll start succeeding on your own. Then you'll be able to copy from yourself, from situations where you've already succeeded.

Meanwhile: Do you have an imaginary mentor to consult?

TALKING OUT YOUR WORRIES

One time-tested method for helping regain confidence is to talk out your worries with someone you trust. It could be your spouse, your co-worker, or your brother or sister. Dr. Scheele says you don't even have to solicit the confidant's advice. "Say to your friend: 'Do you have 15 minutes? I need you to just listen.' Then tell your whole problem without holding back. Tell of an earlier time when you felt the same lack of confidence. You may find yourself experiencing various emotions, which is good. It's good to discharge emotions in private with a friend," she says.

Or you could learn to talk back to your worries. Dr. Didato explains that in the face of big work projects, we're frequently guided by such negative self-talk statements as: "I'm afraid I'm going to fail." (It's something we'll tell ourselves even if we've succeeded at virtually everything else we've pursued.) Such statements are part of the "personal guiding fiction" that keeps us from achieving success. One antidote, he explains, is to sit down and say to yourself, I've been in tough situations before and I've managed to come out ahead and to do well. And for emphasis, once again make that list of your successes. This time around, spend as much time as you'd like reminiscing about those positive accomplishments. Go ahead, you deserve it.

Soon you may discover you've talked yourself into a better, more confident frame of mind.

13

CORPORATE CULTURE

T alk about contrasts. Imagine you're a computer whiz trying to decide which of two companies you want to join. On the one hand, there's IBM, also know as "Big Blue," a monolithic, East Coast corporation whose very name conjures up images of by-the-book bureaucracy and starched white shirts. On the other hand you have Apple Computer, the rebellious offspring of two California garage geniuses, where first names and free-spirited innovation are as de rigueur as blue jeans, where meeting rooms are named after the Seven Dwarfs and the seven deadly sins.

These two archrival computer corporations may represent the extremes, but they point out a basic fact of organizational life: Every workplace (even a company of two members) has its own special culture. And when you try to wedge your square peg of a personality into a corporation round hole, you're bound to get stuck—bad.

"The C-word may be a bit overused," says Richard Munro, chairman of Time Warner, "but every corporation *does* have its own culture. For example, in some organizations, competition is encouraged, and even rivalries are encouraged. Aggressive behavior is encouraged. In other cultures, teamwork is encouraged. I've often counseled young people that perhaps the first thing they should do when they enter a corporation is to determine what kind of environment they have become part of. And if they are a Type A in a Type B environment or vice versa, they had better find a new job."

Organizations operate under what are called "shared basic assumptions." While the folks who make the rules at Company X may believe the best work is done by individuals, those who call the shots at Company Y may operate under the assumption that the best work is done in groups. Or one corporate culture may adhere to the belief that truth is discovered by seeking the advice of an expert, such as a consultant. Another culture may live by the rule that truth is discovered by letting opposing viewpoints fight it out, says Edgar H. Schein, Ph.D., professor of management at Massachusetts Institute of Technology's Alfred P. Sloan School of Management, and author of *Organization Culture and Leadership.*

In addition, social scientists tell us that cultures are built upon behavioral "norms," which are defined as a set of expectations on how people will behave in a given situation—such as when the boss finds your ideas highly objectionable. These cultural norms grow and evolve over a period of time, they're generally not written down in any formal policy, and they are not usually discussed by people within the culture, explains Ralph Kilmann, Ph.D., professor of business administration and director of the program in corporate culture at the University of Pittsburgh's Joseph M. Katz Graduate School of Business.

Within any large organization there are multiple subcultures that may, in fact, operate under shared basic assumptions or behavioral norms that differ from those that govern the larger entity. "I'm sure that within IBM you'll find groups that are flamingly not part of the corporate culture," says John P. Fernandez, Ph.D., Philadelphia-based management consultant and author of *Survival in the Corporate Fishbowl.* But for members of such a divergent unit to succeed, they have to be acutely aware of the rules that exist within the bigger corporation. By way of example, Dr. Fernandez points to AT&T's headquarters personnel division, which he headed from 1983 to 1986. "We were much more of a risk-taking division. We were much more creative. We implemented things that are now part and parcel of the overall culture," he says. "You can do things in your division that are different, but you have to understand how others are different and how you can interact with them to meet your objectives. In meetings, we were very straightforward in how we gave our views," Dr. Fernandez recalls. But when his division members met with clients, such as members of different operations divisions, "we had to be less open, more circumspect, and alert to their signals," he says.

CULTURE SHOCK STARTS HERE

Only a fool would accept a job at an organization without first doing some serious anthropological investigation. But before you probe a particular corporate culture, you've got to probe within yourself, to discover your own particular workplace needs. Here's a brief look at three potential trouble spots.

Levels of autonomy. "An important thing to consider is how well your personal style matches the way the organization delegates work," says Dr. Schein. In other words, figure out whether you personally need to have a high degree of freedom in what you do or whether you prefer to depend on the organization to tell you what you should be doing. "What upsets people most is being on either too short a leash or too loose a leash," explains Dr. Schein. Some people want an employer that affords a lot of freedom; others want a company that provides a great deal of direction.

Preciseness of job descriptions. Many new firms in growing industries have made an art form out of the open-ended job. When John Scully left PepsiCo to take control of Apple Computer in 1983, he was struck by the fact that Apple didn't have regular secretaries. Instead, they had "area associates," who, as Scully later wrote, "were encouraged to do more creative tasks on their own." Again, if you're the sort who prefers a structured environment, you're not likely to flourish at a place where your subordinate won't feel the least compunction about wandering into the chief executive's office with an 80-page proposal for a new product line, without ever mentioning it to you in advance. But if you like to feel free to propose new ways of doing things—and to see your ideas get immediate, serious attention—you're not going to thrive at a place where your suggestions will get watered down by the seven bureaucratic levels from which you must receive prior approval.

Attitude toward disagreement. So you thrive in environments that permit you to express your keen critical sense? ("I'm sorry, boss, but here are 14 good reasons why we shouldn't pursue your proposed strategy . . . ") Well, in some organizations, just the slightest suggestion that your boss could possibly be wrong about something is enough to have you branded a recalcitrant baddie. And all the hard work and dedication you give to the company could wind up being ignored—your negative image would thwart any advancement. Ever. But then, too, there are organizations that actually reward disagreement and bosses who sincerely do mean it when they say, "Please, tell me your objections. I could learn something from them." Think for a moment: How comfortable would you feel voicing your honest disagreements if you grew up in a family where objections were patently discouraged?

CHECKING OUT A CORPORATE CULTURE BEFORE YOU WADE IN

Ideally, you want to get a fix on important cultural details like the ones in the previous section before you sign up. But that's rarely easy to do. For one thing, there may be a wide chasm between what any recruiter or personnel-type tells you and what really takes place. (Example: How do you truly know from the outside looking in that you'll be free to openly disagree with your boss? You don't. Even if, in your initial interview, she makes a big deal of mentioning how open she is to criticism, she may just be trying to convince herself that she is.) And as Dr. Kilmann says, a company's norms are likely to be unspoken and highly informal.

Also, the formal interview process is highly staged and not likely to put you in touch with the folks who could give you the real gritty details. "It's just like visiting Russia in the old days," Dr. Kilmann says. "They wouldn't let you off the bus, even though you needed to mix with real people in real communities to learn what life was like." So you should ask your potential employer's recruiter if you could visit one of the plants or one of the divisions and chat informally with some of the people. "If a company is reluctant to do that, it's a signal about what sort of culture they have," says Dr. Schein. "The best clue is how they deal with you when you push and probe a little bit."

Dr. Kilmann suggests that one method for getting a truer glimpse at an organization before joining is to track down fellow alumni from your alma mater who have worked for the potential employer or who work there now. (Your college's alumni office could be helpful in locating someone.) To get them to be honest with you, Dr. Kilmann says you should try to appeal to the bond of having gone to the same university. Also, try to find friends of friends. Don't hesitate to talk to people at the lower levels of the organization, people who have less of a vested interest in what is said. You could even speak with people who no longer work at the company—but weigh their comments carefully, since they may have an ax to grind. Of little help are employees who have worked at the organization for less than six months.

Like a good journalist, you should ask people the same question (or variations of it) several different ways.

First ask, "What does it take to get ahead here?"

Listen to the answer, then ask, "What does the boss really want?"

Finally, ask, "Who has been promoted recently and what were the criteria?"

The point of rephrasing the question is to try to catch discrepancies in the responses. The point of asking about the promotions, says Dr. Kilmann, is that frequently a corporate culture will reveal itself through its reward system.

"Very often the propaganda says something about 'fair, equal opportunity,'" he explains, "but experience tells us that other things come into play.

The Rules of the Game

What types of behavioral norms should you be concerned about? Here, according to business professor Dr. Ralph Kilmann, are some unspoken rules that flourish in corporations whose cultures are rooted in the past.

- Don't rock the boat.
- Don't enjoy your work.
- Don't disagree with your boss in public.
- Don't be the first to come up with a new idea (because you'll be criticized).
- Don't come to meetings on time (you're far too important to be prompt).
- Look busy, even when you're not. Don't share information with others or other groups.
- Don't be the bearer of bad news.
- Don't say anything the boss doesn't want to hear.
- Don't be associated with any failures.
- Complain.

And here are some that are common in modern, forward-thinking organizations.

- Treat everybody, that's *everybody*, with respect and as a potential source of valuable insights.
- Encourage people to suggest new ways of doing things.
- Enjoy your work.
- Speak with pride about your organization.
- Initiate changes.
- Be willing to take on responsibilities.
- Bring uncomfortable issues out in the open.
- Feel free to disagree with your superiors or others in your group.

The cultural variables may involve the mentoring system, and some mentors may have more weight than others. Or certain projects may have more weight than others. Or there may be favored areas, such as research and development marketing, or finance. Also, a culture may dictate that if you step on people's toes, or step on a certain person's toes, you will never get ahead, regardless of how well you perform and how smart you are. Or perhaps if you're not aligned with a certain network, it won't matter how hard you work, you won't get ahead."

Another thing to consider: communication protocol. "Some organizations have norms that block communication between departments. For example, they may adhere to a military protocol: You only communicate with your boss and not to members of other departments," says Judd Allen, Ph.D., a psychologist and president of Human Resources Institute, a Burlington, Vermont, company that buys small and midsized companies with "bad internal functioning," turns them around, and sells them. For his part, Dr. Allen sees the military-style protocol as being detrimental to a company's success.

14

CREATIVITY

Besides your wafer-thin, gold-monogrammed briefcase, creativity is and will always be the most valuable executive asset you possess. Creativity brings forth new products and new procedures. It can remedy conflict, open new doors of opportunity, and miraculously make something out of virtually nothing.

Now, having praised creativity so highly, there is an inevitable question to be answered: How do I get myself some? The only problem with this question is it presupposes a lack of creativity to begin with.

This is the wrong tack to take. Let's approach creativity from a different perspective. Try to remember the weirdest dream you've had in the last two weeks. Write it down. Ask yourself if Edgar Allan Poe and Steven Spielberg on a three-day bender could possibly have come up with anything as fanciful and twisted as your dream. No? Congratulations. Somewhere inside your head lurks rampant creativity. As a matter of fact, *everyone* is creative. So the whole question of creativity becomes one of training rather than acquisition. How do you find creativity? How do you train it to come when you call? And how do you encourage it in those who work for you?

INCUBATION: THE EASY ROAD TO CREATIVITY

Our first foray into the world of Creativity is Easy comes under the Has-this-ever-happened-to-you? heading. Your company has just developed a new product sure to have the competition weeping red ink. All that's needed now is a name for the product that will inflict the lust of consumption upon the buying public. Pen in hand, you sit before a large scratch pad ready for action. And you sit . . . and sit. Nothing. Three days later, desperate, you once again approach that pad with the tread of a condemned prisoner. *Miracle!* Within an hour you have not one but ten great ideas that seem to have materialized with a casual effortlessness. What happened?

According to Eugene Raudsepp, president of Princeton Creative Research, you've just experienced a form of incubation. "Incubation," says Raudsepp, "is a process in which you cease activity on one process of thought and do something else for a while so that the solution to the first problem has time to take shape and reach maturity."

While incubation is something we've all experienced from time to time strictly by chance, in recent years musicians, corporate vice-presidents, and others have begun taking a more studied interest in harnessing the process. After all, taking a break to solve your problems is a nice way of getting things done. The question is, how does it work?

"There are specialists in the field of creativity who believe that when you take a break from something you're working on, your mind continues to consider the problem . . . even when you've gone on to a totally different task," says Raudsepp. "It's a subconscious process, one we are totally unaware of while it's happening. All we see of it is that one day we have an unsolvable problem that keeps getting worse, and the next day it's solved."

The reason your subconscious mind is able to make a creative conquest that your conscious mind cannot may have something to do with memory access. Much like a library, your mind takes bits of information and stores them in memory by subject. If you were working on a chemistry problem, you would go to the science section of the library. Likewise, your mind serves up information from a particular part of your memory depending on what you are thinking about.

But occasionally, information from one section of your memory could be useful on a totally unrelated problem. A line of Shakespeare might help a company president make a personnel decision. But consciously, she doesn't remember the line because her memory is only releasing information from the business section, not the literature section.

A naturally creative person (that is, a person born with a beret attached to his or her head) is a master at freestyle memory access. He or she *would* have quickly hooked the business and literature information together and solved the problem because of an ability to cast a line over boundaries and fish for unrelated information that could help.

For those of us who aren't great at mental fishing, Raudsepp feels that incubation does the same thing. "Consciously, we rely on the left side of our brain to solve problems. Language and logic are on this side and this is where information is compartmentalized. But subconsciously we work on problems with the right side. This side provides creativity and the ability to see the cohesive whole."

When you incubate, your subconscious creatively accesses all sorts of information and assembles it into a colorful, interesting package—all while you're poolside playing volleyball.

How do you incubate? "First you have to assemble data," answers Raudsepp. "Get all the facts and information available concerning your project or problem. Then sit down and give it a good going over. At this point you're priming the pump, so to speak."

Familiarize yourself with the information but make no attempt to solve the problem yet. This part of the process could take anywhere from 20 minutes to several days, depending on the amount of information you need to look at.

"Then put it away," says Raudsepp. "Go do something else. It could be anything from a walk in the woods to spending a weekend in Bermuda. But make it unrelated to the project you're concerned with. When you come back, there's a good chance some things have fallen into place, and you're well on your way to finishing your project or solving your problem."

Of course there are major incubations and minor ones. Some musical composers work on a piece for two months and then put it away for six before finishing it. On the other hand, some problems may only need a 30-minute or two-day reprieve before the ideas start flowing. "A good way to start incubating is while you're asleep," says Raudsepp. "Think about a problem for 20 minutes before you go to bed. The next morning you may wake up with some good ideas."

What incubation can mean to you in a business environment is better ideas provided by a more economical use of your time. When you come into the office on Monday, pick three problems that need to be solved by Friday. Instead of bashing away at them day in and day out, still coming up empty-handed until Thursday at 4:30, spend an hour on each problem Monday morning and then put them all away. Take care of unrelated business until Wednesday afternoon and then haul out those problems again. What might have taken you days to solve before may now take hours once you've done some of the work in your subconscious. So start practicing this simple technique and keep a record to see just how dependable incubation is for you.

How to be creative
when you're on the spot

It's nice to know that you can count on your creative subconscious for the occasional idea or solution. But there are times when you'll want to bring the creative process to a conscious level. Moments when you'll need an idea now. Circumstances where you'll want more direct control over the course your ideas take. Again, whether you think you are creative or not, spontaneous creativity is well within your power.

The first step is to look at the problem without putting any boundaries on how it may be solved. For example, imagine that you are a landscape designer working for an eccentric millionaire who has but one desire. In his backyard he wants you to plant four trees. The only problem is that he wants each of the four trees to be exactly 15 feet away from the other three. Go ahead, knock yourself out.

There is an answer, though, and it's simple. Plant three trees in an equilateral triangle with 15-foot sides. In the middle of the triangle build a hill just tall enough so that when you plant the fourth tree on it, the distance down to each of the other trees will measure 15 feet.

Okay, the answer isn't *that* simple. And if you were one of the 99.9 percent of people who tried to solve this problem on a flat plane, the answer is pretty near impossible. But here's the point: The question never stipulated that you couldn't manipulate the shape of the land.

The problem is, we are all born assumption-makers and boundary-builders, taking unspoken rules for granted. Here's one more example—one you can embarrass your office mates with (and earn a little betting money if you're truly unscrupulous!). Using two American coins, one of which cannot be a quarter, can you make the total equal 35 cents? The answer is yes. A quarter and a dime make 35 cents. Despite what you assumed, all the challenge stated was that *one* of the coins not be a quarter. And indeed, one of them was not. It was a dime.

"Finding a creative answer to a problem frequently involves finding a creative problem-definition," says Jim Shields, associate program director of the Center for Creative Leadership in Greensboro, North Carolina. "In our classes we encourage people to really notice how they see the problem and then challenge them to come up with a long list of different ways to think about it."

A problem frequently used as an example at the center comes from the tea industry in Great Britain: In 8 hours a day, this company could produce all the tea bags it needed. The machines therefore had a spare production capacity but were sitting idle for 16 hours a day. What could be done?

"The first and most common way people look at this problem is to think of what other drinks can be put into tea bags," says Shields. "Answers usually include such things as coffee and hot chocolate. From there some people may also suggest trying different foods or spices."

But as Shields quickly points out, the question may not have anything to do with what else can be packed into a tea bag, as was originally thought. "The real question might be what can be done with all the extra bagging material that is produced? Once you've stated the problem in this way, a whole new realm of answers is born. The material could be dyed and used to make curtains or disposable clothing. Perhaps it could be made to function as mosquito netting."

Getting yourself to break out of the habitual manner in which you look at problems is sometimes not easy. It takes practice. Practice and a few tricks, that is. "At the problem-redefinition stage, there is a list of techniques that can be used to change your mind-set," says Shields. "The first is to magnify and extend the parameters of the problem. Instead of asking what other foods can be placed in tea bags, for instance, try asking what kinds of medicines and household items could be used. Or magnify the size of the tea bags. Could furniture be stored in giant tea bags?"

Next, try minimizing the problem. If you made tea bags a whole lot smaller, what could go in them? Perhaps electronic components?

"Creativity is putting together things that have not been put together before, in ways that have some pragmatic application," says Shields. "With this definition in mind, you might try using analogies from a totally different subject to help rework the problem. Colt got the idea for his revolver by watching the paddle wheel on a riverboat."

To bring this idea down to a personal level, try to find an analogy between your particular business problem and a hobby or subject that you follow in your spare time. Suppose you spend your evenings in an astronomical vein, gazing at the stars. Could tea bag material be used to clean telescopic lenses? This same analogy-finding strategy was used successfully at a mining company where a budding entomologist (one who studies insects) managed to develop a piece of extraction equipment based on how a praying mantis eats!

If these techniques still don't yank you out of your problem-redefinition rut, haul out a dictionary and let it fall open where it may. Then try to connect the first word you see to your problem. You'll be amazed at how farfetched the connection may become, but that's exactly what you want.

At a Campbell's Soup brainstorming session several years ago, the dictionary word was "handle." This in turn led to the word "utensil," which then became "fork." The only way you can eat soup with a fork is if it is chock-full of chunky meats and vegetables. This is where Campbell's highly profitable line of "Chunky" soups came from.

To practice this technique at your leisure (that is, when someone isn't actually jumping down your throat for a solution), pick two words at random and try forging a connection between them. Let's take "milk" and "violin." Milk comes from cows, and cows can be beasts of burden. Violins play music, and music hath charms to soothe the savage breast (or beast). Could music piped into barnyard stalls increase a cow's production of milk?

FINE-TUNING AN IDEA

Let's say you've come up with a brilliant idea and visions of VP suites are dancing inside your head. Now it's time to step down from the lofty heights of unbridled creativity to functional reality. To be sure your idea is not shot down before its true genius is realized, you'll want to take a few potshots at it yourself. Nothing fatal, but the more critical you can be about your idea, the less room you'll leave for others to be.

SHOULD YOU ADAPT OR INNOVATE?

"There are two creative perspectives from which all people tend to approach a problem," says Bob Burnside, manager of innovation projects at the Center for Creative Leadership. "The first is called *adaptive*. A person accepts a problem as stated, works with the tried-and-true approach, but finds a way to make it work better. By contrast, with an *innovative* approach, you reject the problem as stated, throw out the old way of doing things, and come up with a totally unique solution that does the task in a completely different manner."

All of us have some of each perspective within us, although rarely in equal balance. Likewise, some of our ideas will be innovative while others will be adaptive. The question that concerns you is whether you have an adaptive or innovative problem on your hands. Having determined this, you may be able to weed out one or two of your brainstorm results as unlikely solutions.

"As a general rule," says Burnside, "if you have a large budget and a lot of time to play with, you can lean more toward the application of an innovative solution. These solutions frequently require more start-up time and can also carry an increased risk. But if you have very little time as well as a low budget, you'll want to use an adaptive solution, one that fine-tunes what's already there."

One final question to ask yourself is whether or not the problem you've been working on is a recurring one. If so, the odds are that adaptive solutions have probably been applied in the past, have worked for a while, and then failed. In this case you definitely want an innovative breath of fresh air.

11 WAYS YOUR IDEA MIGHT BE WRONG

Having considered the adapt vs. innovate side of the situation, now it's time to get down to brass tacks. Vincent Ryan Ruggerio, author of *The Art of Thinking,* has come up with a list of common criticisms against which you should measure your idea. If you find yourself unable to defend yourself against one, start reworking that aspect of your idea.

Your solution is:

1. Impractical
2. Too expensive
3. Illegal
4. Immoral
5. Inefficient
6. Unworkable
7. Disruptive of existing procedures
8. Unaesthetic
9. Too radical
10. Unappealing to others
11. Prejudiced against one side of a dispute

ENCOURAGING CREATIVITY IN OTHERS

As a management kind of person, one of your concerns is how to coax (squeeze) the nectar of creativity from the people working for you. But due to the inherent nature of creativity you'll want to forget words such as "coax" and "squeeze." As it turns out, creativity in others is best encouraged by applying the lightest of touches on your part.

For full-blossomed creativity to occur in a person, he needs three things. "*Domain-relevant skills* is the first component required," says Theresa Amabile, Ph.D., associate professor of psychology at Brandeis University. "You have to acquire mechanical skills as well as knowledge in a particular area before you're able to produce innovations."

You also need *creativity-relevant skills.* These include the ability to take new perspectives on problems, to take risks in thinking, and to persevere in your line of thought. Assuming your employees possess these fundamentals, there is still a third factor which completes the creative triangle, a factor upon which *you* as their boss can have a positive or negative effect.

"If people do not have *intrinsic task motivation,* then they do not have that internal spark of interest that drives their domain- and creativity-relevant skills," says Dr. Amabile. "You need to have each employee become personally interested in the problem he is working on."

In a nutshell, intrinsically motivated people produce more creative work than those who are extrinsically motivated. So your job is to use a subtle hand in planting a seed of interest within your employees rather than applying the overt fist of stringent evaluation, threats, and even bribery as a means of motivation. Even though that overt fist sounds like it could only be attached to a despot's arm and not yours, you may be surprised to discover how many extrinsic thumbscrews you're already applying even in the most pleasant of manners. Just consider these three areas.

Autonomy. "I think a primary way of boosting intrinsic task motivation is by giving your employees a degree of autonomy," says Dr. Amabile. "You need to let them feel ownership of the project." One way to do this is to present the project free of any constricting parameters you may have already determined. Sit down with your employees and through discussion see if they can't figure out those parameters on their own. Not only will they immediately feel as though they've got a personal stake in the project, but they will be happier with the restrictions they created than with the very same ones you might have imposed in a seemingly arbitrary manner.

Competition. At a leadership seminar, Dr. Amabile and her colleagues divided the attending business managers into two groups. "One group was asked to solve a set of problems, keeping in mind that prizes and recognition would be awarded to the ones who did the best job. Competition was not mentioned to the second group; they were only asked to have fun with the problems. When we studied both groups' solutions, we did find a difference. The second group's solutions were more creative than those of the group working under a competitive mind-set."

While competition may give tired projects a shot in the arm and produce a flurry of results, quantity is not quality. While you may have gotten people to work harder that way, you have not won their personal interest in the project. The key difference is this: A competitive solution needs to be quickly produced and just a little better than the rest of the pack. An intrinsically motivated solution, on the other hand, is often the very best that a person has to offer.

When soliciting solutions from more than one source, make everyone feel that there is room for many in the winner's circle.

Reward. Hold on to your hat. Rewards can be detrimental to creativity. In one of several experiments on the subject, Dr. Amabile asked groups of elementary school and college students to make collages. Before the experiment began, some of the students were promised rewards for their work. It was these students that turned out the least creative projects. "A reward can often eclipse personal interest in a project," says Dr. Amabile. "If you need to make a bribe to enlist interest, then the project is probably not interesting in itself, and the reward is the only thing that is worthwhile.

"This does not mean, however, that you should do away with rewards altogether," cautions Dr. Amabile. "But rather than formally stating at the beginning of a specific project that there will be a reward, try recognizing creative effort on a regular basis." An important point to remember is to reward creative effort even when a project fails for some other reason. "If you reward those efforts as well as the commercially successful ones," she says, "people are going to know they're working in an organization that recognizes and rewards superior creative effort. I think that this feeling is a very powerful motivator for overall creativity."

15

DECISION MAKING

Okay, quickly decide:

Research tells you there's a 15 percent chance that you'll lose customers by selecting a particular vendor. Do you pick that vendor?

Research tells you there's an 85 percent chance your customers will be satisfied with a different vendor. Do you choose that vendor?

If you're like most folks, you would reject the first vendor but select the second—despite the fact that the results they promise are the same. The reason? The two choices were framed differently, and therein lies an important key to understanding how we decide, according to Daniel Kahneman, Ph.D., professor of psychology at the University of California, Berkeley, and one of the developers of the concept of *framing.* Even when we're trying to be as logical as possible, he says, we sometimes are swayed to illogical choices; it's often a matter of how the problem was posed.

If framing sounds like a simple concept, you're right. But it's one of the many considerations people overlook when they have to make up their mind. The fact is, if more people understood how they decide things, there wouldn't be nearly as many bad judgments going around.

Few skills are more important for successful managers than the ability to make good choices. But the sad truth is that most people simply don't like to have to make up their minds. The reason is that every decision we make involves a risk. So, in effect, we are putting ourselves on the line each time we have to decide on something. Nobody wants to have to prove himself constantly, but that's precisely what happens during the decision-making process.

The first step in reducing the odds of making bad decisions is to have a clear understanding of your individual decision-making style. And to keep in mind that when it comes to decisions, nobody bats a thousand. The best you can do is hope to make more good decisions than bad ones.

DECIDING HOW YOU DECIDE

So, how *do* you decide? Are you the kind who couldn't possibly make up your mind until you've got every conceivable bit of information at your fingertips? (At which point it may be too late to decide.) Or do you get overwhelmed by the facts and find yourself rushing into whatever feels right in your gut? (And realize later that if you had only listened to logic, you wouldn't have fouled up.)

Dorothy Leeds, a New York City management consultant and author of *Smart Questions: A New Strategy for Successful Managers,* divides our planet's population into four types of decision-makers:

Commanders, who are by nature impatient and whose eagerness leads them to jump into quick decisions.

Convincers, who are the persuader-promoter types. They tend to act on their emotions, deciding quickly on whatever feels good.

Carers, who decide on the basis of their feelings but are concerned with others. Since they don't want to hurt or disturb others, they'll take a long time (perhaps too long) to decide.

Calculators, who are perfectionists. They want all the information before making a decision, but as Leeds explains: "You never *can* get all the information you need to make a perfect decision."

Can you see yourself here? Leeds's advice is first to assess your own decision-making style and then to find someone with an opposite style with whom you can establish a system of checks and balances.

"If you're a Commander-type, force yourself to slow down and bring your proposed decision to a Carer, someone who would consider all the sides," she says. Likewise, if you're a Carer-type, try to set a time limit on your information-gathering stage and find a Commander type to assess your judgment. If you're a Convincer, bring it to a Calculator. If you're a Calculator, find a Convincer.

Admit to any biases or fears that may be causing you to let your emotions overshadow your better judgment. And be clear on the impact your decision may have. Leeds suggests you answer the following questions beforehand.

1. "What will it cost—in money and resources?"
2. "What impact will this decision have?"
3. "What happens if we don't do it?"

HOW TO MAINTAIN YOUR OBJECTIVITY

When we're forced to make a decision, we often convince ourselves we're doing a stellar job of gathering and evaluating all the necessary evidence. The hitch, of course, is that we seldom realize just how biased that evidence may be. A simple example: A new salesperson is faced with the task of preparing his first major sales presentation. So he asks a few colleagues for details of their own successful presentations. Impressed by the number of successes he hears about, he incorporates the suggested methods into his own presentation. How is he basing his decision on biased information? The colleagues never bothered to tell him how many times the suggested strategies *failed* to work for them, which may have been far more frequently than they succeeded.

To make better decisions, you also have to understand as fully as possible how your own biases may be tampering with logic. Here are some pointers on maintaining your objectivity.

Realize that you may be experiencing stress. Often, decisions are precipitated by stress, explains Irving Janis, Ph.D., a former Yale professor who has written extensively about decision making. It's important to understand that a high level of stress may cause you to be "hypervigilant" and to search randomly, rather than systematically, for the evidence to support your choices. And experts say that in times of stress, you are more likely to have a bias toward the first idea you hear about, without carefully exploring others. For example, feeling the panic of needing to find a new job, you'll short-cut your usual process of carefully evaluating the pros and cons of a potential offer. Instead of being thorough, you'll overlook or minimize the possible problems—and you may wind up making a decision you'll regret.

Beware of heavy emotional leaning, one way or the other. "A heavy emotional sense is not a sign of poor judgment, but it's a signal that you should at least be cautious," says Robert G. Rose, Ph.D., a Dallas-based consulting psychologist. Say you are considering hiring one of two job applicants to be your assistant. You get excited about the prospect of working with Candidate X; you are mildly interested in Candidate Y. Stop and carefully examine what it is about Candidate X that generates such enthusiasm. Then stop and consider which of Candidate Y's finer points you are overlooking simply because you have little or no emotional excitement.

Perhaps your emotions *are* telling you something you should listen to. But be aware that they may also be leading you astray—away from a logical choice.

Are you motivated by a hidden agenda? The emotion of fear can cause you to lose your better judgment. You decide to select a particular vendor primarily because you're afraid that if you don't, a competitor will drain the vendor's inventory. The emotion of anger, too, can lead to counterproductive decisions. You're angry with a subordinate, so you quickly slash the budget for a project he's completing—turning your back on weeks or months of good work that could be useful to your entire organization. Envy (not a true emotion, psychologists tell us, but a variant of anger) is another culprit in far too many bad workplace judgments. Even elation can create a bias, leading you to enthusiastically grab the first available option.

Is it wishful thinking? The self-deception of wishful thinking can cause erroneous judgments, says Jonathan Baron, Ph.D., a professor of psychology at the University of Pennsylvania and author of *Thinking and Deciding.* Here's how: You want something to be true, so you distort the evidence in its favor. For instance, you know your boss is involved in unethical behavior, but you try to convince yourself that it's untrue. When facing a tough choice, "ask yourself if you're trying to defend a belief because you want it to be true," suggests Dr. Baron.

Don't make decisions based on assumptions about what "everybody knows." Folks who are first-time managers often make this mistake. In an effort to motivate workers, they try to get approval for increased wages or bonuses for their staff. Their reasoning: "Everybody knows that money is the main motivator." But the fact is, financial rewards are pretty far down on the list of motivators. When decisions are based upon such automatic assumptions, they tend to be poor ones, says Dr. Rose. Check for the reasoning behind your choices.

Don't lose sight of the big picture. "Whenever we make decisions, we tend to think only of decisions that serve a single goal. And we forget about other goals and the fact that we may be subverting them," explains Dr. Baron. So don't opt for a decision that will solve an immediate problem at the expense of a bigger one. Maybe you're bored with your current job and feel it holds few opportunities for advancement. Then your company offers to provide you with skill training in an area that could lead to a promotion. But the training will direct you away from your area of interest—and into an entirely unrelated field that offers you little or no satisfaction. Is it worth the promotion?

Remember to check your decisions continually as you carry them out. Engineers, for instance, frequently are asked to predict how long it will take them to produce a deliverable product. But in the interest of presenting themselves as swift workers, they may almost unconsciously shave days, weeks, or months off an accurate prediction. "To calibrate yourself, take the trouble to measure how long something is taking you to accomplish as you accomplish it," suggests John R. Hayes, a psychology professor at Carnegie Mellon University in Pittsburgh and author of *The Complete Problem Solver.* Doing this will enable you to factor more realistic time predictions into the decision-making process in the future.

Seek as much good, objective advice as you can. Here's an example. You're deciding between two offers. One is a stable position in a stale but solid firm. The other is a job with room for quick advancement in a small, growing company that has an uncertain future. Don't even think of making a decision before running the pros and cons past several trustworthy sources—folks who are familiar with your concerns, your personality, the companies in question, and the industry prospects.

WHEN LOGIC SAYS ONE THING AND INSTINCT SAYS ANOTHER

Intuition has been good to Akito Morita, the president of Sony Corporation. He acted on a hunch that the Walkman would be a great success, ignoring the reasoned advice of his sales experts who predicted otherwise. Score one for intuition. Any successful person knows that there's a wealth of gold to be gleaned from your gut feelings. In fact, Donald MacGregor, Ph.D., a psychologist with Eugene, Oregon–based Decision Research, says intuitive judgments are a "richer source" of decisions than is logical analysis.

But he cautions that hunches can also be much less reliable. For every intuition-bred success à la Sony Walkman, there are hundreds of intuition-bred flops. (Perhaps it was someone's gut instinct that led to the marketing of the short-lived Nehru jacket, for instance.) "On some days your intuition isn't up to snuff, but your logical analysis is always up to snuff—whatever your level of snuff is," says Dr. MacGregor. So how do you combine the two for optimum results?

Establish guidelines for your intuitions. Let's suppose you'll be interviewing a series of candidates for an important job you need to fill. Instead of simply conducting the interviews and then relying on your intuition to help you decide, sit down beforehand and determine what attributes you're looking for in a candidate. Set up a point system for quantifying those attributes. Then be sure to evaluate each candidate based on your planned criteria. In addition to imposing a framework on your selection process, this is also a good way to get a clear reading on your own values, says Dr. MacGregor, whose nonprofit organization studies human judgment and decision making.

Examine your motivations, and be willing to admit to motivations that you don't want to admit to. You have to select a computer system for your organization. The facts indicate that you should select system A, but your instinct is that system B would be a better choice. Think for a minute: Is it because system B would be more complementary with your home computer? In general, try to be aware of any hidden factors that could be influencing your gut-level decision, suggests Robin Dawes, Ph.D., professor of social and decision sciences at Carnegie Mellon University in Pittsburgh and author of *Rational Choices in an Uncertain World.*

Fight the urge to ignore the facts. Among the major causes of bad decisions are misinformation, misperceptions, and biases on the part of the decision-maker. With so much bad information going around, it's understandable that people often prefer to act on instinct rather than assess the facts. But if you find yourself not even wanting to be bothered by all of the facts before deciding, you may be jumping into regrettable decisions at the expense of reasoning. If that's the case, own up to your bad habits. Step back and force yourself to spend some time asking for facts and examining them before deciding.

Consider who will bear the consequences of your gut decision. Research indicates that people are more likely to go with their gut if it's other people who will suffer the consequences should the decision turn out to be bad. "If you see that someone else will suffer, that's a good argument for rethinking your gut decision," says Dr. Dawes.

HOW TO GIVE YOUR DECISIONS
THE ACID TEST

A large part of what causes people to make bad decisions is a lack of confidence in themselves and in their decision-making ability. It's a condition that may worsen, not improve, over time. When we start to decide about something, an ambivalence or cognitive conflict arises as a natural reaction, says psychologist David W. Johnson, Ph.D., professor of social psychology at the University of Minnesota and author of many books, including *Reaching Out: Interpersonal Effectiveness.* Here's how to check the effectiveness of your decisions.

Find a devil's advocate. Dr. Johnson suggests you present a friend or associate with the facts and say, "Here's the problem. Here's what I want to do. Is there anything wrong with this? Do you see flaws in my thinking?" Management consultant Leeds recommends the "devil" be of an opposite decision-making type.

Pretend you're an outsider. Another method of gaining some distance on your plan is to consciously look at the situation from an outsider's point of view. To accomplish this, pretend you're giving advice to someone else who is making the decision, suggests Dr. Kahneman.

Investigate your information. If you want to minimize the risk in your decision, try to make sure the information you're basing it on is good information, recommends Leeds. "Know your people. Your experience should tell you what sources are trustworthy and whose judgment is most sound and consistent," she says. "Make sure that whatever specific information you have makes sense. Don't take for granted that the list of figures you've been handed is accurate. As much as possible, check things out yourself."

Ask yourself, How comfortable am I in explaining my decision to someone else? "If you experience a lot of discomfort when explaining your decision to a sympathetic listener, you're probably less sure of your decision than you think," says Dr. Kahneman.

Check that you're not vacillating. A little bit of cognitive dissonance is good, but you should feel fairly comfortable about your decision once

---

A Case for Making Mistakes

"You should not be afraid to make mistakes," says Robert T. O'Connell, executive vice-president of General Motors. "Mistakes place you very high on the learning curve—much higher than success does." These are words to remember when decision-anxiety strikes. Here are a few more: "Making mistakes is a signal that there's a healthy and dynamic decision-making process and that the organization is aggressive, innovative, and leading-edge," he says.

Okay, so what sorts of mistakes have been made by O'Connell, who's chief financial officer for the world's largest industrial corporation? In the area of hiring, for example, he reports having placed "too high a premium on the personal chemistry and not enough on the basic worth and capability of the individual involved."

Of course, O'Connell and other successful folks make a point of remembering to learn from their mistakes—instead of mindlessly repeating them.

you've made it. "Implement the decision with full force," suggests Dr. MacGregor, "not as if it's a decision that you haven't yet made."

MONITORING FOR SUCCESS

The process doesn't end once a decision is made. You have to establish a system for continually monitoring your judgment and the impact it is having. Robert T. O'Connell, executive vice-president and chief financial officer of General Motors, calls this "cradle-to-grave reassessing." Remember, factors that are out of your control may enter the picture to make your decision seem wrong after the fact. (We're talking about unanticipated market changes, unforeseen government regulations, an unexpected oil embargo—that sort of thing.)

Dr. MacGregor likes to look at decision making as an ongoing process. Some of the best big decisions can be made by building on small decisions—after you've monitored their success. That way you have the opportunity for your values to evolve and change. If you have a small business and are considering hiring your first employee, for example, it may be best to hire someone on a part-time basis, to determine what kind of person works best with your new organization. Later, you may want to add another part-timer; it may be that your needs will change and a person with different attributes will fit the bill.

WHEN YOU'RE LEADING A GROUP DECISION

The more voices added to the decision-making process, the greater the chances that the decision will be flawed. Dr. Johnson suggests the following six steps for achieving a clear group perspective and reaching the best decision.

1. Define the issue. It's your responsibility to be sure that group members clearly understand, from the outset, what they should be focusing on. Tell them what is expected, and if they seem confused or distracted by side issues, keep the discussion on target.

2. Gather the alternatives. Groups tend to fixate on the one or two options that initially seem to be the best thing to do, so they rarely look at other viewpoints. Also, groups often latch onto whatever the group leader first suggests—they focus on how great the idea is instead of thinking critically about it. To avoid such groupthink, make certain that all options are introduced, and that all options get a fair hearing.

3. Assign advocacy subgroups. To solicit alternative points of view, assign pairs to research and analyze the various options that are suggested. Each pair should be responsible for presenting the strongest argument for its assigned option—much as a lawyer would in court—even if its members are unconvinced of the merits. But unlike a courtroom scenario, members should operate in an atmosphere of cooperation. Remember that the group, not an impartial judge, will ultimately decide on the best option. If in its research one pair finds something that would help another pair, the information should be shared. When selecting pairs, it's important to create teams that are roughly equal in articulateness and persuasive skill.

4. Challenge and criticize. At this stage the group looks for the holes in the reasoning of each pair's presentation.

5. Reverse perspectives. The danger at this point is that advocates of one option will be locked into their own position and won't clearly see the merits of other points of view. So members now are instructed to reverse perspectives, to accurately summarize the opposing positions. By reiterating the other points of view, they make it clear that they understand them.

6. Reach a consensus. "You should work toward a group consensus, not competition on who did the best job," says Dr. Johnson. One method of deflating any lingering competitiveness is to integrate as many different views as possible into the final consensus decision.

Stand Up for Better Decisions

Having trouble making a decision? Try standing up. Researchers at the University of Southern California's Laboratory of Attention and Motor Performance determined that people think better on their feet.

"The act of standing causes a heart rate increase of about ten beats per minute and an increase in neural stimulation resulting in improved cognitive functions," says Max Vercruyssen, Ph.D., the study's principal investigator.

By standing, a person can increase his or her information-processing speed by as much as 20 percent for several tasks involving rapid decision making, according to Dr. Vercruyssen, an assistant professor of human factors. The experimental findings, he says, suggest that regular workday rest breaks and stretching sessions would help clear the way for speedier decisions.

WHEN YOU HAVE TO DECIDE NOW: THE 5-MINUTE TECHNIQUE

Ben Franklin, statesman, inventor, and friend of thunderstorms, had a strategy for making quick decisions. He would list the reasons for taking an action on one side of a sheet of paper and the reasons for not acting on the other side. Then he did whatever had more listed reasons.

When rushing to make a decision, you can apply the same simple technique, but with a twist.

Make the lists, but assign a priority to each reason. Say you're deciding whether to take a particular job. A reason in favor of the new job may be that it could be a good stepping stone to future jobs. A reason for not taking the job may be that the boss has a bad reputation. Don't assume the pros and cons hold equal status; assign a numerical weight to each reason before deciding. (If you feel the considerations mentioned are equal in weight, consultant Leeds suggests you look at other factors, such as the fact that you may have to move for the new job.)

Think about how the problem is framed. Without much time to decide, you could fall into the trap of having your judgment flawed by the way a problem is presented. So think of another way of describing the situation. If the decision was originally framed in terms of customers lost, now think of it in terms of customers retained.

Think about making a subdecision that will buy you time. Business leaders do this all the time. What can you do, for instance, if the press is beating down your door for a response to a particular controversy your organization is involved in? Instead of saying nothing (and risking bad publicity) or communicating more than you feel like sharing with the public, you could opt to buy time by explaining that the matter is under assessment. Then indicate a time when you will communicate completely.

Err on the side of caution. When GM's O'Connell must respond quickly, he consciously tries to narrow the risk he's willing to take. Five minutes won't allow you to gather—much less evaluate—all the information you need in order to make a proper decision. Without all the facts, it's wise to be more conservative.

THE PROTOCOL: A DYNAMIC NEW TECHNIQUE FOR INTELLIGENT DECISION MAKING

Some decisions, even fairly complex ones, are made by executives in a matter of minutes, even seconds. Often those decisions prove to be wise. The ability of the human brain to evaluate vast amounts of information, drawing on knowledge, practical experience, and intuition, is awesome. And, of course, we executives like to think it's especially awesome in our breed.

But sometimes, decisions come hard even to the best of our kind. Weeks or months go by, meetings are held, business plans generated, memos sent and answered, and still a rational answer proves elusive. The pluses and minuses seem locked in equal combat, with a dozen or more side issues shoving each other around at ringside.

What's a poor leader-of-mankind to do?

To help you solve this problem—and impress the hell out of colleagues when you do so—we have developed what we call the Protocol.

The Protocol is a structure that permits us to analyze and evaluate an idea, or competing ideas, and come up with a single number—from 1 to 10—that estimates its relative strength.

More important, it literally lays open the idea the way a mechanic opens a car engine, so we can see the strengths and weaknesses of the various components and how they work with one another.

Most important of all, it gives us the chance to tinker with those components, do strategic fine tuning, or even do major rebuilding.

In a minute or two, we'll show you exactly how to conduct a Protocol meeting. But first . . .

If you feel you don't need a special structure to help you make better decisions—that you've done "just fine" so far without one—think about this analogy for a minute.

As a professional executive, you get paid to make important decisions, just as a professional scientist is paid to carry out important research.

Any good scientist, though, however brilliant she may be, needs a special structure to build credibility into her work. Depending on her specialty, all manner of double-checking, control groups, cross-overs, replications, and statistical analyses are used to boost confidence in the information and "results" generated by the actual research.

The average executive, on the other hand, does little more than gather information, think about it (maybe with the help of a computer), and then reach a decision. He or she does not use any special tool to ensure that all the information, however accurate, actually 'means' what it seems to.

Computer-generated business models are frequently used to help us make decisions on complex questions involving many variables. They are great things to have because they can tell us the answer to the question, What if the following assumptions are correct?

But too often they come to be regarded as saying, This is what probably will happen.

The assumptions in such models are just that—our best guesses. Sometimes multiple models are generated so that we can see how different assumptions lead to different results three to five years from now. But there's no way to know which one comes closest to the truth. And in practice, such models are often tinkered with until they show a favorable forecast. The result can be a model with wildly optimistic projections as to sales, revenue streams, overhead, etc.

The ultimate limitation of a business plan, however, is that it has no provisions for helping us answer such questions as:

- How credible are the assumptions?
- What will the effect of this new project be on the rest of our operations?

- Is this project loaded with hidden dangers that don't show up in the mathematical model? Hidden benefits? How important are they?
- What are the secret feelings of the management team about the wisdom of this undertaking?

Such questions are all answered—or at least *asked*—in the Protocol. The result is a much more "three-dimensional" look at the idea than can be gathered from a business model. So generate your models. Study and critique them. Then use them as *part* of your decision-making toolbox.

How to use the protocol

1. First, ask yourself if you have to make the decision by yourself, or if you should involve others. Ideally, major decisions should have opinion input from those most directly responsible, and from top management, when appropriate.

   In any event, at least three out of four participants need to have significant experience with your organization and a broad knowledge of its workings. Having a few "specialists" in the group is fine, so long as they are outnumbered by people of broad vision.

2. Make sure that all parties concerned realize one thing: The procedure planned is not to "make" the decision. The individual with the highest responsibility retains the right to do that. The Protocol procedure is a way for top management to allow others to participate in the decision process without forfeiting the right or responsibility of ultimate voice. Later, top management can make the final decision by themselves. Of course if this is to be a purely group decision, the judgment can be made at the same session.

3. Information, analysis, and opinion should all be exchanged prior to the day of the Protocol meeting. Without really good information, you will never be able to intelligently score any question. Be sure assumptions in business plans are justified or explained in detail.

4. Reserve a conference room and a 90-minute block of time. About half of that time will be used to cast scores; save the rest for analysis. A brief review of information and opinion may be held before beginning. Once you begin the Protocol, though, no opinion should be openly voiced.

5. Key documents relating to the question should be brought to the meeting in case they are needed for reference purposes before or after the scoring.

6. Each participant will need a stack of small papers marked with large numbers, 1 through 7, with separate sheets for questions 6A and 6B. Each will also need *identical* pens or pencils. Have all this material on the table before the session begins. The Protocol facilitator will need two simple calculators. A large blackboard or two easels will also be needed.

7. On the blackboard or easel, you should have written beforehand the titles of all of the questions.

8. In reading the questions to the group, be sure you speak slowly, clearly, and without any special inflection or emphasis. The facilitator, whether an active scorer or not, should in no way reveal a personal bias on any question.

9. After the reading of each question, each person should write down a score, confidentially, then fold the sheet. Don't have the score sheets passed; go around the table and collect them. Clip them together and place them on a separate table or in a box. Confidentiality is essential to this process.

10. The instructions that follow are written so that they can be directly read to the group, with or without your own modifications. Portions written in brackets are for your help, but may be read to the group if appropriate.

One caution: It is far easier to understand the instructions that follow when you actually do a Protocol than when you are just reading them. So don't worry if a point here and there seems confusing. When you do the Protocol, everything will clear up.

Now let's go through the questions!

1. COMPATIBILITY WITH CORPORATE PHILOSOPHY

How well does the proposed project fit in with your organization's personality, experience, and direction, its perceived role in the marketplace and world?

A score of 10 indicates perfect compatibility, 9 indicates very strong compatibility . . . 8, strong . . . 7, moderate . . . 6, marginal . . . 5, no positive compatibility at all. A score of 1 or 2 indicates strong incompatibility.

If, for instance, your organization is a public relations agency, and the question is whether to branch out into textile manufacture, the score would probably be 0. [This example is not as silly as you may think. Owners or CEOs are sometimes people of powerful impulse. And suppose the head honcho announces that the company now has a *new* direction: manufacturing athletic wear. You, however—thanks to secret voting—may feel free to decide it's just a wild idea, not a new corporate philosophy or direction.]

If your group is a library in a firm that considers itself a leader in engineering innovation, and the question is whether to purchase a new, highly advanced information-retrieval system, the score would probably be 9 or 10. *That's regardless of cost—here we are only deciding compatibility with corporate philosophy.*

[Sometimes the compatibility question needs a lot of discussion before voting. Let's say your P.R. agency is deciding whether to build its own complete in-house sound and video studio. You must ask if the philosophy is to bring all functions under the house roof (as opposed to vending-out whenever possible). Not sure of the answer? You could also ask if the company is dedicated to the idea of having lightning-fast production capabilities. Not whether it's a neat idea, but if it's a philosophy, a corporate theme. Yes? High score. No? Probably a 3 or 4.

[If you cannot find *any* connection with corporate philosophy or direction, one of two things is true. Either (1) the question is trivial, or (2) you *have* no corporate philosophy, in which case *no* important decision can be made rationally. As the saying goes: Any port looks good to a ship that doesn't know where it's going. Decide now whether you want to wind up in Boston or Bombay.]

2. REWARD POTENTIAL

This can be viewed in terms of dollars, efficiency, or whatever the primary goal is.

Here we're not concerned with how likely it is that the idea will work. *We'll assume it will.* And then we're going to estimate the extent to which the resulting reward will outweigh the investment.

Looking into the foreseeable future, if you believe that the reward potential will barely match the investment, even if the idea succeeds, your score would be 0 or 1. If you think that the reward would about equal what you'd get from a good mutual fund over the period in question, the score might be 2 or 3. If the potential is there for rewards tremendously greater than the investment, score it 8 to 10. In the business world, where many ideas fail, and the winners have to get it all back and *then* some, reward potential must be extraordinarily high to rate the top scores. But remember to put aside for the moment any question about whether or not the idea will work.

You'll consider, of course, estimates of potential return made in business plans or other projections. But since these are based on assumptions, not facts, you can believe them or not.

3. LOSS POTENTIAL

Now let's assume the idea simply doesn't work. The new product flops . . . the new contract is abruptly rescinded and you never get to move into the big new plant . . . the new computer system is installed but you can't get the software to run.

Here, *assuming failure,* we're gauging the impact that the resulting loss will have on the total resources of your organization.

To make a rational estimate of loss potential, you need to know at least three things.

First, the actual size of the investment in dollars, time, sweat, or all three. You may feel, by the way, that the sum suggested by a business model is unrealistic. Actual investments frequently turn out to be considerably greater than shown in projections. Use your experience and intuition.

Second, you need to know what, if any, safeguards exist to limit the extent of downside momentum. Are there explicit go/no-go checks built into that major development project? Do you think they'll be followed or ignored? Will test-marketing precede full-tilt manufacturing? Is that new building going to be paid for or leased? Leased short-term or long-term? Could you sell it or sublet it if need be? Is there a performance guarantee on the new equipment? Does the vendor have the financial strength to stand behind the guarantee? The answers to such questions will have a major influence on your estimate of loss potential.

Finally, you need to know enough about your company's resources to be able to gauge the negative effect of a failure. If you don't, a top official in your group will have to provide some guidelines.

If the near-total loss of investment would barely cause a corporate blip, score it 1 or 2. If the negative effect will clearly stain your balance sheets or cause notable discomfort, the score might be in the 4-to-6 range. If the loss would be downright scary, rate it 7 to 10.

4. SUCCESS PROBABILITY

Regardless of investment, regardless of potential benefits, what is the likelihood that the idea presented will actually succeed in its mission? Will the new branch office be able to sell a million dollars' worth of advertising within three years? Will it come close? Will your new power mower capture 5 percent of the market as promised, or stall out at 2? Will your new building meet your needs for five-year expansion or be pathetically inadequate?

An easy way to score this question is as follows: If you feel the idea has a 10 percent chance of success, score it 1. For a 20 percent chance, score 2, and so on. Ideas that have a greater than 80 percent chance of success, by the way, are rare birds indeed. They are usually restricted to purely mechanical-type projects, and usually simple ones at that—largely immune to human foibles.

[You might wonder why a whole battery of questions is needed if we are asking what the chances of success are. Doesn't this one question answer it all? No—and that's exactly why we need a Protocol. If an idea earns a healthy 7 score here, but only a 4 on the Reward Potential question, and a troublesome 7 on the Constraint question that comes later, it might not be such a good idea after all. Conversely, a new product idea that only earns a 3 on the Success question but gets a 10 on Reward Potential and a 2 on Constraint might be an idea of great merit. Some very successful companies are built on a heap of 90 unsuccessful ideas, and just 10 successful—but very profitable—ones.]

5. CONSTRAINT EFFECT

Every new project requires an investment of an organization's resources to get it up and running—money, leadership, time, etc.

Here we aren't gauging the sheer amount of the investment. What we specifically want to know is to what extent implementing the idea will produce short-term *constraints* on how the organization keeps itself healthy and strong on a day-to-day basis.

If your company is making $500 million before-tax annual profits, an investment of $75 million might rate a Constraint score of only 3 or 4. But if your company needs to pay out large dividends . . . retire serious debts . . . buy back a large chunk of stock . . . renovate an obsolete plant, then the score could be considerably higher. A score of 8 or higher suggests that the project could well cause a resource crunch that would endanger important ongoing operations or prohibit essential investment in an on-line operation with already-proven potential for success.

In a smaller organization, or a corporate department, a project that will suck up all the available time of key personnel, allowing no leeway for response to emergencies or for planning, would be rated 9 or 10—even if it requires only minimal cash outlay. If the plan provides for additional staffing, the Constraint score would go down sharply—assuming the additional salaries don't create an equally great constraint.

6A. POSITIVE SIDE EFFECTS

Assuming the project is implemented with reasonable success, to what extent do you think it will open the way to advances and benefits *beyond* the stated mission? Will it gain you a solid foothold in a promising new area of business? Bring brilliant new people into your management team? Significantly improve staff morale? Enhance your corporate reputation? Improve your credit rating?

If such benefits appear scant or strictly speculative, indicate neutrality with a score of 5; if breathtaking, 9 or 10.

6B. NEGATIVE SIDE EFFECTS

Good ideas, like good medicine, occasionally produce dismaying side effects. While these are sometimes impossible to predict, we can often estimate their likelihood and severity, based on our experience and intuition.

Regardless of whether the new project succeeds or fails, how much potential does it have for producing serious confusion as to corporate direction? Lowering morale? Causing good people to leave the organization? Straining facilities to the breaking point? Producing a whole new dimension of vulnerability to legal problems? Putting doubts in the minds of your customers? Causing your stock value or credit rating to drop?

Now, *any* new idea causes a certain amount of mild anxiety or confusion in staff people. But it usually resolves itself in a few weeks. Look beyond this phenomenon for negative side effects that *won't* disappear in two weeks. They'll linger for months, maybe longer. How harmful to your organization might they be? The greater the total negative impact, the higher your score should be.

If you see no serious negative side effects, score a 5. A score of 6 or 7 means "We'll have to be very careful." A score of 8 or more is saying "Even if we *are* careful, we could still be seriously hurt."

What if you can't come up with any meaningful positive *or* negative side effects? In that case, use the "No Side Effect" option. Simply wipe this question off the Protocol, and give one added "weight factor" (explained later) to some other question.

7. PERSONAL ENTHUSIASM LEVEL

How do you rate your own level of enthusiasm and commitment to the project?

Consider everything that's been discussed—plus any other factors you're aware of. Sometimes a person with cogent objections to an idea never openly voices them, either for fear of offending someone or for fear of appearing to be a "negative thinker."

Feel free to consider any strong intuitive feelings you have, but also be fair. Don't downgrade your Enthusiasm score because of personal envy or idiosyncratic beliefs (e.g., "It's a great idea but I just don't think America needs any more condos/frozen yogurt/country & western music/whatever").

You can often get a handle on your level of enthusiasm by imagining how you'd feel about investing your own money or prestige in the project.

Here's a special note: You may believe that however good the plan under consideration may be, there is another, even better option that's mutually exclusive of the first. If this is the case, be sure to have that competing idea evaluated by your group as soon as possible (maybe today). In any case, if you feel that way, your Enthusiasm score has to be very low—even though your other scores may have been high.

A score of 9 or 10, of course, suggests great enthusiasm. If you're basically neutral or undecided, vote a 5. If you believe that the idea is notably weak, go lower. And if you believe that it's the kind of idea that's not only weak but may well cause extensive damage to the organization, go even lower.

Now that you've completed scoring the Protocol, there's a special job to do before you add up all the numbers.

Face the most senior member of the group, typically a department head or company officer, and announce, "As the senior person in our group, you have a special responsibility at this point. We need you to *weight* these questions. And we have *three* weight factors you can distribute any way you see fit. Each weight factor means the score to that question will be counted one extra time. So you could choose three different questions to each get double weight . . . or assign double weight to one and triple weight to another . . . or give *all* the added weights to just one question.

"To help you select the questions to be weighted, you might want to consider those that seem particularly important or sensitive in relation to this issue."

If the person asked is unsure, you can say the following: "In issues revolving around long-term investments, the question of Reward Potential is often given two added weights, while the third could be given to something else, like Loss Potential or Constraint Effect. If there is a controversial ethical question involved, you might give one added weight each to Compatibility, Negative Side Effects, and Personal Enthusiasm."

When the weights have been decided upon, indicate them by placing one check mark for each added weight factor next to the questions they're assigned to.

Now comes the addition. You can do this off to the side, if you wish, with a helper, while the members of the group chat or fill their coffee cups. Or, if you have a flare for drama, you can do as follows.

"Lisa and Bill, would you each take one of these calculators? I'm going to start with the first question, Compatibility, and read off the scores. I'd like both of you to add them, to be sure the arithmetic is right."

When the total is read off, ask them to divide it by the number of people participating.

Then write the quotient—let's say, 8.1—to the far right of the question. If any question has a check next to it (indicating an added weight factor), write the score twice. So the first question might appear as follows.

	Raw Score		Adjusted Score
√ 1. Compatibility	8.1	=	8.1 + 8.1

Do exactly the same for question 2.

But *not* for question 3. Questions 3, 5, and 6B, you may have noticed, are all expressions of negative feeling. But we're adding *positive* opinion. Here's how we do it. For those questions—3, 5, and 6B—write the group average score to the *immediate* right of the question. Then, to make it positive, flip-flop the number. To do that, subtract the number from 10; the remainder is the adjusted score. A 0, for instance, becomes 10, while a 7 becomes 3. Write this adjusted score in the same column as the other positive numbers, as shown below.

	Raw Score		Adjusted Score
√ 1. Compatibility	8.1	=	8.1 + 8.1
2. Reward Potential	9.1	=	9.1
③ Loss Potential	4	=	6.0

To remind us that 3, 5, and 6B need to be reversed, we draw a circle around each of those numbers.

Question 4 is treated just like questions 1 and 2. Question 5 is like Question 3.

Question 6 is unique.

First write down the score of 6A. Put down the 6B raw score to the immediate right of the question, and its flip-flop version to the far right.

Now, add 6A and 6B, divide by 2, and put the answer to their right. It'll look like this.

	Raw Score	Adjusted Score
6A. Positive Side Effects	5 = 5	
6B. Negative Side Effects	1 = 9	$= 14 \div 2 = 7$

What we now have is a single number that represents the totality of side effects, expressed in positive terms. We didn't use this one-number approach in the question phase, because it is too confusing to balance positive against negative side effects in one fell swoop.

(In the event that either 6A or 6B was given added weight, it's easy to accommodate. If 6B, for instance, is given one extra weight, add 6A + 6B + 6B and divide by 3—rather than 2—to get the final score.)

The last question, Personal Enthusiasm, completes the scores.

At this point, have your math wizards add up all the numbers in the far right column. Make sure all the extra weights are considered: *There should be ten numbers to add up.*

When both agree on the total, have them divide it by 10. That is your Protocol Score.

EVALUATING THE SCORE

The Protocol Score does not tell you if the idea is good or bad. What it tells you is the degree to which your best people (the participants) believe it is worth pursuing.

You might want to use the following as a guide in evaluating the overall score.

    10: Unrealistically high
     9: Extremely strong support
     8: Very strong support
    7.5: Strong support

> 7: Good support
> 6.5: Marginal support
> 6: Weak support
> 5: Uncertain or doubtful support
> 4: Negative consensus
> Less than 4: Negative mandate

As we said before, the top executive has the right to interpret these results as he or she sees fit. Many would want to see a score of 7 or 7.5 before feeling comfortable with a new project. But if it's something they believe in dearly, they may decide that anything over a 5 or 6 represents a good enough consensus. They should be aware, however, that while a relatively weak score in no way reflects on the intrinsic merits of the idea, their best people are saying that successfully implementing the project is likely to be extremely difficult, or perhaps not even worth the effort.

The overall score, though, is just the beginning of the evaluation process. Ultimately, whether we decide to go ahead with the idea or not, we can also search the configuration of individual question scores for clues on how to make the idea stronger.

To begin this process, go through the following descriptions and see which apply.

FUNDAMENTALS LOOK GOOD

This description probably applies if the scores for questions 2, 3, and 4 add up to 20 or more. (The scores we're referring to in all examples are the scores on the far right, where all the negative numbers have been "adjusted," i.e., flip-flopped.)

A total score of 20 or more suggests a reasonably sound relationship between what is to be gained, what could be lost, and the chances of success. While a score of 22 or more puts you into more of a "comfort zone," you may need to be satisfied with 20. This applies particularly if you're in a business where taking on long-shot projects that can pay off lavishly is normal.

FUNDAMENTALS NEED WORK

This is probably true if the total from above (questions 2, 3, and 4) is *under* 20.

There could be some close calls here. A score of 18 or less, though, clearly suggests that the reward/risk/chance-of-success ratio is not what it should be.

Later we'll suggest what might be done to improve the score.

HIDDEN STRENGTHS

This may apply if the Personal Enthusiasm score is more than 1 point greater than the overall score. This can be worth investigating, because the implementation team may be able to actively use these strengths if they know what they are (e.g., favorable new tax regulations, or the proposed designer of the new line is gaining recognition as an international trend-setter).

HIDDEN WEAKNESSES

This is possibly true if the score for Personal Enthusiasm is more than 1 point lower than the overall score. This suggests that participants have reservations about the idea that didn't show up on the other questions. The first order of business should be to discover if there are competing, mutually exclusive ideas that have not been presented. Remember, even if an idea gets a high score, an alternative may score notably higher.

If this is not the case, ask if any participants want to discuss their reservations. Don't push the point, though; you may be getting into sensitive areas.

The wise chief executive, seeing a significant Hidden Weakness, won't let it just pass. She'll quickly schedule private meetings with all participants and ask for confidential input. She may discover, for instance, that the key player in the new project has already told close friends that he's planning to take a new job. Whatever the problem, knowing it opens the way to remedial action.

WHITE KNUCKLER

This applies if the total adjusted score of questions 3 and 5 is less than 10.

What you have is an uncomfortable degree of long-term loss potential *and* immediate resource constraint.

Depending on just how much lower than 10 the score is, this may or may not be a warning. But it does tell you that your project group will need steady nerves and an extra degree of caution to implement the plan. Combined with a finding of Fundamentals Need Work, however, a White Knuckler may be a trip you want to avoid.

MINE FIELD

This designation applies if the total adjusted scores for questions 3, 5, and 6B are less than 17.

Here we not only have resource risk and constraint, but possibly significant potential for negative side effects as well.

Now if the overall score is solid, and the Fundamentals Look Good, you may well decide you need to walk through this Mine Field to reach the huge rewards on the other side.

But if you do, be sure that the leaders of the project team are well seasoned, cool-headed, very adaptive individuals. This is no place for beginners, however bright. Even if the worst never happens, fears or rumors that it's *about* to happen will drive them to distraction.

SEETHING VOLCANO

If your idea earns the Mine Field award, described above, *and* the Personal Enthusiasm score is less than 7, you're sending the troops out on a potential suicide mission. Because if the worst happens—the cash starts crunching, the negative side effects start popping—your people will have nowhere to go, no one to turn to in time of crisis: Their bosses have no stomach for the job.

If you feel you *must* do this, fine. Suicide missions have been known to save the day—and the company. But at least see if you can reduce some of the risk (details later).

OPEN ROAD

You have an Open Road if the total adjusted scores of questions 3, 5, and 6B equal 22 or more, *and* Personal Enthusiasm is at least 8.

This *doesn't* suggest an easy journey or a successful one. Rather, it suggests that although the road ahead may not be easy, at least it is relatively free of mines and snipers. Risk, constraint, and nasty side effects, as a group, seem under control. The management team likes the idea. This in turn specifically suggests that the project can be handled by individuals who, although capable, may lack seasoning. They will probably be able to concentrate their energies fully on the job at hand, without being distracted by fierce financial pressures, legal crises, or negative office politics.

USING THE PROTOCOL
TO IMPROVE YOUR IDEA

The overall score, and your score in specific areas, only reflects opinion of the idea as it presently stands.

The most valuable use of the Protocol can be to pinpoint specific areas that need improving and see how changes would affect the scoring.

You may, for instance, find that a clear area of concern is Constraint Effect. Coming in at a scary 2 (adjusted score, indicating high constraint), it throws the project into the White Knuckler category. Yet with Reward Potential at a hearty 9 and Loss Potential a reasonable 4, you want to find a way to go ahead.

Fortunately, Constraint is often one of the easier factors to modify. Ask, for instance, Can the investment be spread out over a longer time without endangering Success Probability? Can purchases be replaced by leases? Would borrowing money lessen Constraint, or is the debt position such that more borrowing would only increase Constraint? Can tax laws, investment credits, or the like be used to cut short-term pressures? If the resource to be constrained most is people, can temporary employees or even new hires take the pressure off? Can an ongoing but unrewarding project that's burning up resources be skeletonized and the resultant savings plowed into the new idea?

Here we come to one of the chief benefits of the Protocol. *Once we've identified the problem areas in the idea, we can stop wasting time worrying about the idea as a whole and concentrate our creativity in the areas that need work.*

After making changes *you must rescore the whole Protocol.* The changes in one area are bound to affect others. By improving the adjusted Constraint score from 2 to 5, for instance, you may also increase Enthusiasm from 5 to 8. Then again, the Probability of Success may go down 3 points (due to less aggressive investing). The result: The White Knuckler tag is removed, but on goes (perhaps) the Fundamentals Need Work tag.

Here is one piece of advice: Don't change your score on a particular issue, once you've cast it, simply by rethinking it. Demand that clear, substantive changes be made in the plan before you change your vote. Experience suggests (*shouts*) that unless you do this, your group will wind up with a session of wishful thinking instead of decision making and problem solving.

An example of the protocol in action

Many of the toughest business-related decisions we must make are complicated by factors that are not, strictly speaking, business matters at all. Personalities, prejudices, emotions, and other purely "human" factors often play a role of surprising importance.

The example of Protocol use we will present here has clear elements of this human factor, though it is by no means an extreme example.

Although the substance of this example is true, the particulars have had to be changed to ensure privacy.

BACKGROUND

Dan was president and board chairman of a company that had been growing and producing respectable profits for a number of years. But lately both growth and profits had flattened, even shrunken somewhat. No one could see a simple way to reverse this trend.

The company was actually a group of small businesses. The oldest, started some 40 years earlier by his now-retired father, was a large lighting-fixture store that drew customers from a 50-mile radius in the mid-Atlantic region. There was also a thriving home-remodeling business that his father had helped Dan start 15 years earlier. That had led to a small, custom home building business. Dan's latest venture, begun just 18 months earlier, was the manufacture of super-high-quality doors and door frames.

Here is how the respective annual profits, which totaled $1,050,000, shaped up.

Lighting Fixtures: $200,000
Home Remodeling: $300,000
New Construction: $500,000
Door Manufacture: $ 50,000

The lighting fixture business had declined more than 20 percent since his father retired and seemed to be slightly less profitable each quarter. Home remodeling was strong, doing just about all the business it could handle. New construction, though nicely profitable, had proven to be erratic and was now beset by a very weak real estate market; predicting its future was difficult. Finally, the high-end door business, though small, was doing much better than expected.

Certainly not a bad picture overall. But the company was owned not only by Dan but by three other family members as well. And except for him, they had all come to the point in life where they essentially lived off the annual profits of the company. The result was that after taxes there was precious little left for expansion or rejuvenation. Due to increasing costs of maintaining inventory and a fleet of vehicles, along with a poor real estate market, the company—for the first time in its history—was losing ground. The notion of borrowing money for expansion had been virtually hooted down by the board of owners.

It was from this position of impasse that Dan developed the idea of selling off the lighting fixture business and using the proceeds to expand the more dynamic parts of the family business. We will call this the Rejuvenation Plan.

In reality, Dan went through the Protocol several times. When he first received it, he immediately did an off-the-top-of-his-head version and came up with a score of 7.9.

Soon after, he called a meeting of the board and presented his idea, along with some projections prepared by the company financial officer. Although the immediate response to the idea was negative, he asked them to think about it for a week and come back for another meeting.

At the later meeting, he discussed the Protocol and made a proposition to the group. If they could come up with a score of 7, he would go ahead with the Rejuvenation Plan. If not, he'd back off. They said, No way. They didn't trust the Protocol to begin with. But they did offer to give the idea serious consideration if they could come up with a score of at least 8. They then did the Protocol but arrived at an overall score of only 6.3. (Well, the Protocol wasn't a bad idea, they told Dan; too bad it made your Rejuvenation Plan look weak!)

Three months later, a second formal Protocol meeting was held. This is how it went.

REJUVENATION PLAN PROTOCOL

The second time around, Dan did several things differently.

First, he was much better prepared. Instead of rough projections, he had meticulously detailed financial forecasts prepared by an outside consultant. He distributed them several days before the Protocol meeting. These forecasts said that:

- If the company stayed as it was, annual profits would slowly decline over five years from the present level of $1,050,000 to $850,000. By year seven, they would be $775,000.
- If the company were sold in its entirety, it would likely bring about $8 million. The interest on the net proceeds could provide ongoing income for the shareholders approximately equal to current dividends, but after five years, the effect of inflation would be felt with an ever-increasing pinch.

- If the fixture component were sold for an estimated $1.7 million, and proceeds invested in expanding the remodeling operations and door manufacture, annual profits by year five would be $2.3 million—more than twice the current level. By year seven, through investing most of the incremental profits in expansion, profits were estimated at $3 million.

Second, Dan learned at the first Protocol meeting that the other board members did not trust him completely. That is, they assumed he would be voting a 10 for every question, just to drive home the decision he wanted to make.

At the same time, Dan felt that at least two of his fellow shareholders (both over 70 years old) did not care very much about the long-term growth of the company as long as they'd be provided for during the remainder of their lives. While he could sympathize with this bias, it seemed that this precluded a decision in the best interests of the company and of the next-generation family members.

He made the following proposition. He would exclude himself from voting if the board agreed to take on, just for Protocol purposes, three additional members: a good family friend who ran his own successful business, an independent business consultant recommended by that friend, and a trusted attorney long known to the family. They agreed.

Dan made a few other changes we'll get to in the Protocol.

Weighting factors were decided prior to the vote by all present, including Dan.

1. Compatibility with Corporate Philosophy: Some voters thought it was not very compatible with company philosophy to sell off the arm of the business that had started the whole enterprise—his father's fixture business. (All this came out during a lengthy pre-Protocol review.) Dan argued that accepting a slow, inevitable decline in a business that had grown for decades was even more incompatible. The average score was 8. (We're eliminating decimal points for convenience.)

2. Reward Potential: The increased level of profitability—assuming success—was not exactly earth-shaking. However, to have the profits more than double in five years, as opposed to seeing them slide lower and lower, was thought to be fairly impressive. One member questioned how much credibility should be placed in a seven-year forecast (showing profits to be tripled). The business consultant said there was no hard-and-fast rule, but such a projection had relevance in a repositioning move. The important thing, he said, is that the long-term projection showed the company would be positioned for continued growth. He advised possibly giving the longer projection about one-quarter the weight of the shorter forecast. The average score voted was 8.

3. Loss Potential: Following the first Protocol, Dan learned that some board members had two specific fears. One, they thought that pouring a lot of money into the almost-new door business (with the hope of creating a national brand) was highly speculative, no matter how successful it had been so far.

Worse, they feared that regardless of what he said, Dan might put a big chunk of the investment into construction of new homes, on a speculation basis. They all knew builders who had gone bankrupt doing that.

This time Dan said he would sign an agreement, which would be monitored by an attorney, not to invest a penny into building "on spec" without formal consent by the board.

He also had worked up a series of four go/no-go points for the first 21 months of the expansion of the door business. Full disclosure would be made to the board at each step.

Whereas the first vote had given Loss Potential a 6, indicating a definite "scare" factor, this time it got only a 3. (Since we flip-flop this question, the adjusted score was now 7 vs. the previous 4. And since it was double-weighted, the new strategy had added 6 points to the score.)

4. Success Probability: While the first meeting had produced a score of 4 on this question, it now rated a 6, or a feeling of 60 percent certainty that the Rejuvenation Plan would at least come close to its forecast. All the changes made, plus the much more careful financial analysis, had led to this improvement.

5. Constraint Effect: Because the essence of this plan was to infuse fresh capital into the company, Constraint was voted to be 0 (adjusted score, 10).

6. Side Effects: Pre-Protocol discussion did not reveal any significant side effects. The possibility of getting a strong position in a new manufacturing business was not considered a side effect, since this was part of the basic reason for the plan and was reflected in Reward Potential. It was therefore decided to choose the "No Side Effect" option and simply remove this question from the Protocol. To do this, remember, you must double-weight another question. The group decided on double-weighting Reward Potential.

7. Personal Enthusiasm Level: The first time around, Enthusiasm came in at 5. This time it was 7, reflecting the greater confidence shown in most aspects of the plan.

The score looked as follows:

	Raw Score		Adjusted Score
1. Compatibility	8	=	8
✓✓ 2. Reward Potential	8	=	8 + 8 + 8
✓ ③ Loss Potential	3	=	7 + 7
✓ 4. Success Probability	6	=	6 + 6
⑤ Constraint Effect	0	=	10
6A. Positive Side Effects	(Question zeroed out)		
⑥Ⓑ Negative Side Effects	(Question zeroed out)		
7. Personal Enthusiasm	7	=	7
Overall Score			**75 = 7.5**

There were no markedly low scores. And the profile met the requirements for Fundamentals Look Good: The sum of the adjusted scores for Questions 2, 3, and 4 beat the required 20 by one point.

Although the overall score of 7.5 fell short of the 8 score originally demanded by the board, its members approved the Rejuvenation Plan after a brief discussion.

Dan remarked that going through the second formal Protocol was a very rewarding experience. It forced him to develop the idea more carefully. And building in the various safety factors had actually given him more confidence in the plan, just as it had the board. He also reported that the quick approval of the other family members was based not solely on "the merits of the case" but also, he learned, on their appreciation for being invited to participate in a fully active manner in the affairs of the company. For the first time, they felt like partners instead of just shareholders.

USING THE PROTOCOL
FOR PERSONAL DECISIONS

The Protocol can be used for personal as well as business decisions. Though most personal decisions are based far more on "gut feelings" than the business variety are (and rightly so), some of the major personal decisions we make are strongly intertwined with elements of finance, career opportunity, relations with family and friends, and other considerations. When such decisions seem far from easy, you can use the Protocol in the same way you've used it at work. As at work, the chief benefit is not simply to arrive at a yes/no determination, but to understand the elements of the decision better. That in turn suggests improvements to the proposed plan.

Here we'll use the example of a friend we'll call Matthew.

Matthew was faced with making a decision that would, for better or worse, change the shape of his life and career. A 29-year-old marketing executive in a multinational firm, he had been offered the chance to join two former colleagues in a new, independent business venture. As many of you who have faced similar decisions know, such a decision can be excruciatingly difficult. After three or four days of obsessive thinking, Matthew decided to run the decision through the Protocol. He chose to do two Protocols—one for staying put (Plan A), the other for striking out on his own (Plan B).

LOOKING AT PLAN A

1. Compatibility: Matthew asked himself how psychologically satisfied he felt with his current position. Answer: He was happy, though not ecstatic. Was the position compatible with his short-term goals? Yes . . . but. Though he had a good job in a firm with an excellent reputation, he felt that unless he was given an important promotion within a year or two, he'd be spinning his wheels, and he would begin looking elsewhere. He rated his Compatibility for Plan A as 7.5—between moderate and strong.

2. Reward Potential: What could he expect to gain over the next few years by staying put? Valuable experience? Not that much, he decided, unless he got his promotion. On the other hand, he had a good salary, and his position seemed to be secure. And he had just begun to come to the attention of some of the top managers in the regional headquarters of his organization. He gave Reward Potential a 7.

3. Loss Potential: What were the chances that remaining in his current position would give his career a serious setback or cause him to lose his savings or anything else of vital importance? Extremely low, he thought, and he rated this question with a 1.

4. Success Probability: Deciding what "likelihood of success" means in a situation that is already proceeding as well as can be expected was a little tricky. But Matthew thought that it should be considered. He defined success as the chance that he would get the promotion he was hoping for within two years. He thought his chances were a little better than 50–50, so he rated this question with a 6.

5. Constraint Effect: To what extent would staying there put pressure on his available time, energy, or personal financial resources? Only to a small degree, equal to what any demanding job requires, Matthew thought. He rated this question with a 3.

6A. Positive Side Effects: The fact that he was secure and not forced to work ungodly hours was already accounted for under the Constraint question. Relevant positive side effects, Matthew decided, would be whatever benefits accrue to one's résumé simply by working for an acknowledged leader in the industry, as well as the fact that the company's generous insurance program would soon come in handy when his pregnant wife delivered their first child. He rated 6A as a 7.

6B. Negative Side Effects: Matthew could not think of particular negative side effects—with one exception. What if the chance to join his friends in a new business would be a one-of-a-kind opportunity? An opportunity he would miss by staying where he was? There was no way to judge this accurately, but Matthew guessed there was only a 20 percent chance this was true. So he rated 6B as 2.

7. Enthusiasm: Matthew felt comfortable though not excited about staying put, so he scored his enthusiasm for Plan A as a 7.

Here is Matthew's scorecard, then, for Plan A. He gave the three double-weight factors to the questions checked.

"Plan A" Scorecard

	Raw Score	Adjusted Score
1. Compatibility	7.5	= 7.5
✓ 2. Reward Potential	7	= 7 + 7
③ Loss Potential	1	= 9
✓ 4. Success Probability	6	= 6 + 6
✓ ⑤ Constraint Effect	3	= 7 + 7
6A. Positive Side Effects	7	= 7 ⎫
⑥B Negative Side Effects	2	= 8 ⎬ = 15 ÷ 2 = 7.5
7. Enthusiasm	7	= 7 ⎭
Overall Score		**71 = 7.1**

LOOKING AT PLAN B

1. Compatibility: The excitement of helping to launch a company in which he'd be a significant partner, Matthew considered, was exactly what he'd always wanted. He backed off from the top score, though, because he had to admit the risk of the venture was not his idea of the perfect situation. Score: 9.

2. Reward Potential: As a partner, Matthew would reap relatively enormous rewards if the new company succeeded. Score: 10.

3. Loss Potential: To become a partner, Matthew would not only have to resign his present position, but also put up over half of his modest savings to help launch the company. If it failed, his loss would be nearly total. On the other hand, being young and having good experience, he'd be able to get back on his feet again before too long. So he rated his Loss Potential as 8.

4. Success Probability: In his gut, Matthew felt the new business couldn't miss. But he was smart enough to realize that every new entrepreneur feels the same way. Objectively, he had to admit that most new ventures fail. Imagining himself to be a coldly practical outside investor, he decided the venture had about a 40 percent chance of succeeding. Score: 4.

5. Constraint Effect: The short-term effects of Plan B, even if it eventually proved successful, would strain Matthew's personal finances, energy, and mental health to the maximum. He could see himself routinely working 12-hour days, six days a week; cutting back on little luxuries; and putting aside plans to purchase a house in the near future. Score: 10.

6A. Positive Side Effects: The experience of launching a new venture—regardless of how difficult, or how it turned out—would be very valuable to him in his future career, Matthew thought. Score: 9.

6B. Negative Side Effects: Launching a new business while he and his wife were simultaneously launching a family would be a tricky undertaking at best, Matthew had to admit. At worst, it could be a nightmare leading to deep regrets and possible divorce. Score: 10.

7. Enthusiasm: It was difficult for Matthew to come up with a number here—that was the real reason he'd decided to use the Protocol. On one hand, great excitement, great rewards. On the other hand, back-breaking work, high risk, and high stress. Averaging these two feelings (something you can do mathematically even if not psychologically), he scored his Enthusiasm as a 7.

"Plan B" Scorecard

	Raw Score	Adjusted Score
1. Compatibility	9	= 9
✓ 2. Reward Potential	10	= 10 + 10
③ Loss Potential	8	= 2
✓ 4. Success Probability	4	= 4 + 4
✓ ⑤ Constraint Effect	10	= 0 + 0
6A. Positive Side Effects	9	= 9 ⎫
		⎬ = 9 ÷ 2 = 4.5
⑥B Negative Side Effects	10	= 0 ⎭
7. Enthusiasm	7	= 7
Overall Score		**50.5 = 5.05**

Analyzing matthew's protocol

Plan B, with a score of 5.05, can be described as having "uncertain or doubtful support" according to our guidelines. The Plan A scenario (staying put), with an overall score of 7.2, may be said to have "good support." A difference of over 2 points is usually quite significant. But let's look closer.

Fundamentals Need Work is a weak point of Plan B since the scores of questions 2, 3, and 4 didn't add up to 20 or more (10 + 2 + 4 = 16). The real problem area is Loss Potential. If Matthew didn't have to give up the better part of his life savings to help launch the new company, that paltry 2 would have risen to a 3 or 4, he thought. But that would still leave him shy of 20. Could the score of 4 for Success Probability be increased another few points? Probably yes—if his future partners had several large accounts already lined up. But they didn't. In fact, it would be Matthew's job to get those accounts.

Plan B is also qualified as a White Knuckler because the combined total of questions 3 and 5 is far less than 10 (2 + 0 = 2!). Worse, Plan B gets a mere 2 when a total of 17 is needed on questions 3, 5, and 6B to escape the Mine Field designation.

Plan A has none of these negative designations. While Matthew's current position is not heaven on earth, it is no Mine Field, either.

There are times when a person may feel the urge to cross a Mine Field. With a baby on the way, Matthew didn't think it was a great idea. He decided to wish his friends well and stay put for the time being.

COMMENT

You may think from this example that the Protocol, like Hamlet's Conscience, "doth make cowards of us all." Is there no time, no justification, for throwing caution to the wind?

Of course there is: when every fiber of your being says *"Do it!"* In Matthew's case, the fibers turned out to have mixed feelings. Under different circumstances—perhaps to come later in his life—the decision might be different.

The Protocol, remember, is not for every decision in personal or business life. It's only for help in making a choice when an overwhelming sense of intuition or cold logic does not point to the obvious answer. In these cases, which can have us hung up for months or even years, we need all the help we can muster to clear our minds and agendas of paralyzing conflict. While there is no way of knowing if the resolution we reach is the wisest possible one, we will at least feel that we are able to make decisions, to choose our own path and follow it. That confidence is one of the best resources we have for a successful future.

16

DELEGATION

The delicate art of delegating is one of the most difficult skills to learn and use. In fact, if you're like most managers, the thought of entrusting important work to others may actually turn you off.

Why would you be so loath to assign some of your tasks and responsibilities to others? Well, for one thing, you probably like to view yourself as a hands-on, take-charge type. And you enjoy the tangible reward that comes with completing a simple task. Moreover, you frequently feel it's far easier just to do the job at hand than to explain to someone how to do it.

Sometimes you simply don't want to burden your subordinates. But when you delegate, you aren't necessarily imposing on others. You're teaching them self-sufficiency and the skills associated with whatever task you're giving them. By coaching them, you develop them for their own career advancement. And you also develop your own ability to create strong boss/subordinate relationships.

But there's likely to be another, perhaps more important, reason for your resistance to delegating: You don't always trust your subordinates as much as you probably should.

First, you don't trust them to do a good job. "When you delegate, you feel that things are out of control. You worry that 'other people are going to be making the sales calls. Are they going to be doing it right?' " says Stephen Strasser, Ph.D., associate professor of hospital and health services administration at Ohio State University and author of *Working It Out: Sanity and Success in the Workplace.* But he explains that while you may feel as if you're losing control, the opposite is really true. "When you delegate, you actually are *more* in control because you have a greater effect on the outcome," he says.

Another crisis of trust: You don't trust your employees to remain satisfied with their own level of advancement. In your paranoia, you figure that once they get a taste of those delegated tasks, they'll start assuming all your responsibilities, be better at the work than you are, and wind up taking over your job.

Actually, turning over your job is something to aspire to, something for which you should plan. As you delegate your tasks to others, and as the added responsibilities and powers bolster their skills and confidence, you are ultimately grooming possible successors. Many organizations, in fact, won't promote managers *until* they've developed qualified people to fill their place, according to Charles D. Pringle, Ph.D., head of the management department at James Madison University's College of Business in Harrisonburg, Virginia.

By building a team of competent subordinates via delegation, you hone your own management prowess. "The real measuring stick of a manager is how well the people below him or her do their work," says assistant professor of management Philip DuBose, Ph.D., also at James Madison University. When you delegate, you free yourself to take over new assignments from your boss. Delegating is how you save your company money (a subordinate's time is less costly than yours). It's how you advance up the organizational ladder. (The option to delegating? Staying stuck where you are.) So you're doing what's most important for yourself, your employees, and your organization. If delegation is handled properly, you can't lose.

But for the brand-new manager, all this may be easier said than done. As Dr. Strasser explains, the newly promoted supervisor often has to unlearn the very behaviors and attitudes that proved to be so helpful when he was a subordinate. "When you're a subordinate, especially in American business, you're expected to be a doer. But as a manager, you can't do everybody's work. You've got to stop seeing yourself as a doer and start seeing yourself as a delegator."

PICKING THE RIGHT PERSON FOR THE RIGHT JOB

Make a list. When Minneapolis-based organizational psychologist and consultant Nicki Davidson, Ph.D., runs up against managers who are "underdelegators," she instructs them to draw up a series of lists. First she has them indicate the individual strengths and developmental needs for each of their subordinates. "It forces them to see where the talents lie," she explains. Then she has the manager list each task that can be delegated. (Some, like performance reviews, simply cannot.) Next she directs the process of matching the task with the appropriate subordinate.

This method may sound so elementary that it hardly requires drawing up a formal list. But the process of writing is a tangible step in the right direction for almost anyone beset by a problem. In this case it gets the underdelegating manager to see the positive possibilities in delegating, and it gets him started.

Imagine a particular assignment that requires a person who can interface well with other departments. The manager looks down his list for someone with interpersonal skills who may need more organizational exposure. Or there's a task that requires careful attention to detail and the ability to plan. For that, he finds someone who's a good administrator but who may not have done much formal planning—someone who will benefit from the experience. The point is, whenever possible, not only to match task needs to talents but also to concentrate on delegating to people who need to learn new skills.

Look for complementary skills. In some cases, primarily when you are trying to round out a person's base of experience for her own career growth, you should be looking for projects that teach complementary skills. For example, when your detail person has perfected the art of planning, you'll want to delegate an assignment that requires her to work with people.

Be prepared to supervise. Think about how closely you're going to have to keep tabs on the project and on the person. All projects require regular monitoring—especially in the beginning stages. So do all employees. But some projects require more scrutiny than others and some employees demand more direction. Here, too, it's a matter of matching the task with the person. "You don't want to give a person who needs a lot of direction a task that really shouldn't require it," says Dr. Davidson.

Test the waters. If you're not sure whether a person is ready to take on the assignment you need to delegate, have a discussion with her in which you ask how she would solve a theoretical problem related to the task. ("Let's say we had to reevaluate our need to retain so many lawyers. How would you start the process?") Use her response as a basis for deciding whether or not to give her the project.

Plan ahead. Keep a tally of which upcoming projects you'll have to assign and who will be available to complete them. Likewise, keep track of who will be advancing to the point where they will be able to take on new work.

Consider how much the person can handle. One reason managers fear to delegate is the nagging suspicion that the subordinate will fail. And given the fact that so few organizations allow much room for failure, *you're* likely to suffer the consequences if your subordinate botches something you delegate. So when you select a person for a task, make sure he can do it—or that it's something he can botch up without detonating the entire organization.

What if an employee has an idea of how to tackle something that may or may not prove successful? "You've got to know the risks," says Dr. Strasser. "If he does it his way and it blows up in his face, it's a damn good lesson that he'll remember. But you've got to know how much failure the department can handle." Suggests Dr. DuBose, "Start with the small things at first, things that won't turn workers off but will give them the chance to prove themselves."

Know who's doing what. Keep track in writing of who is doing what so you neither overassign nor underassign. And don't fall into the trap of becoming too dependent on a few superior performers. Delegation at its best is getting those superstars to train inferior performers.

In the case of a particularly odious assignment, find someone who might actually like that particular style of busywork. What if it's something so routine and basic it's not likely to develop any new skills for anybody (except perhaps the ability to keep awake amid drudgery)? Ask yourself, If I'm the kind of person who hates this, who in my organization likes it? Or identify the person who despises it the least.

Note: The process also works another way. Your boss is likely to have routine tasks that *he* hates doing, tasks that he may not be delegating. Why not volunteer to relieve him of something he despises if it's something you don't mind doing?

WHEN TO DELEGATE
AND WHEN TO DO IT YOURSELF

Many routine tasks should always be delegated—even if you could do them more quickly yourself. The point is to create time for you to do more important things. So when you're faced with writing up that meeting report, or some other time-consuming and uninspiring task, ask yourself, Is this a valuable use of my time? Is there someone else who could be doing this?

A rule of thumb, says career management consultant Diane Blumenson, is that you should delegate tasks you are less motivated to perform yourself, since those will be the ones that are not likely to draw out your best efforts.

"If you delegate those jobs you are less motivated to perform yourself, you'll wind up being a high achiever," she says. Here's an example of what she means. Let's say you're a creative type who likes to invent things (a new system for marketing your company's product, a new method of getting publicity for your organization). You're inspired by the creative process and don't like to give it up. But you hate the maintenance phase—the process of monitoring whatever you create. So you could develop a procedure for monitoring the progress of your new systems and then delegate that maintenance function to someone else.

Whatever tasks you ultimately decide to delegate, just be sure that you really are delegating. In an article entitled "Seven Reasons Why Managers Don't Delegate," Dr. Pringle wrote of a purchasing manager who delegated to his assistant the task of purchasing a certain line of items. But the manager vetoed each purchase plan made by the assistant until the purchase plans conformed to the way the manager would have done it in the first place.

Even though the manager was genuinely convinced that he was delegating, he was not, according to Dr. Pringle, who encourages supervisors to distinguish between real and "nominal" delegation. "Under nominal delegation, the manager ensures that the employee makes the decision precisely as the manager would. The manager's behavior signals to the subordinate that the decision is actually too important to delegate," writes Dr. Pringle. Don't fall into that trap. Subordinates have to learn how to make decisions. So train them. Step back, and let them stretch their skills.

SETTING DEADLINES YOUR EMPLOYEES WILL MEET

The process of setting realistic deadlines for delegated assignments is essentially a form of negotiation. Each party has to walk away feeling it's made a personal gain.

It makes sense that an employee be given some input into a project's timetable. If he sets the deadline, the responsibility is up to him to complete the assignment in the time he felt it required. So Dr. Davidson, who works with the firm of Martin McAllister Consulting Psychologists, suggests you sit down and ask the employee how long it will take. But before you do, "you should have it in your mind how long you want it to take," she explains.

If your employee estimates that the project will take longer than you think it should, you can break down the assignment into its various stages and assign interim deadlines for each. Alternately, you could set up check-points, saying, "Let's see how far you get by this time."

In the event that your subordinate feels he can finish the task in much less time than you believe it will take, express cautious optimism—but still set up a timetable of agreed-upon checkpoints so you can monitor the progress.

If it's the first time a subordinate will be tackling a particular assignment, or if you have your doubts about the employee's abilities, give the person an opportunity to explain how he would go about doing the work. It could help head off unpleasant surprises, such as missed deadlines. Make sure he completely understands what is expected of him and that you understand what he will be doing. "For some subordinates, you can just say 'do it' and all will be fine. But for most subordinates, it's a dangerous statement," says Dr. Strasser. "You must be clear about what is expected, without sounding like Attila the Hun."

OVERDELEGATION—ARE YOU LOSING CONTROL OF YOUR OWN EMPLOYEES?

Just as your boss will see the effects of your underdelegation (you'll be needlessly overloaded and behind schedule), she can tell if you *over* delegate. She'll inquire about various projects, and you won't know their status. And when your subordinates report the results of their work, you'll wind up being more surprised than pleased. ("What? You drew up a schedule for coordinating regional data and we won't get to break out our national figures for three fiscal quarters?") Either they'll do the unexpected or they'll do the unacceptable. In the first case, you've lost control of the monitoring process. In the second case, you've probably given them too much to do.

Delegate, don't abdicate. Remember, even though you are turning over various tasks to subordinates, you aren't relinquishing your responsibility as overseer. So make it clear that while the subordinate is to complete the assignment (or perhaps handle it on an ongoing basis—taking charge of the ethics committee, for instance), you aren't going to be far from the scene.

Set up a system of monitoring. When you sit down with an employee and say, "From now on, I want to make this your responsibility . . . ," you also should establish a reporting structure. Explain that you'll be expecting written or verbal progress reports twice a week. After he gets familiar with the task—and after you feel confident of his abilities—you can reduce the frequency of the briefings to once a week or less.

How to turn a task you're tired of into a challenge for your employees

When there's tedious but necessary work to be done, you are not beyond your bounds in delegating such drudgery to others—as long as you're even-handed about it.

Pair grunt work with challenging work. You can assign the less inspiring task at the same time you turn over responsibility for a more challenging assignment that will enable the person to show his true talents. Academics call this "task variety."

Assign "plum" projects as a reward for those who succeed in unchallenging ones. And make it known among your entire staff that there is a link between the two.

Set limits. You can set a time limit on how long you wish to have the person perform the unexciting work. ("Look, I'd like you to take on the scheduling function for six months.") And keep to your promise. "A known end is always helpful," says Dr. Strasser. In general, he suggests you try to minimize the time a person has to work on a boring project.

Ask employees if they can develop a better way of doing it. Tell the person, "Look, I know it's tedious filing these clippings, but I'm open to suggestions for a new way of ensuring that we have a complete record of all published mentions of our company's product." The subordinate may track down a computer data bank that will eliminate the need for all the clipping and filing.

17

DIFFICULT
PEOPLE

The easiest way to deal with difficult people is to stay as far away from them as you can," suggests Robert Bramson, Ph.D., an Oakland, California, organizational psychologist and management consultant with Bramson, Gill Associates, and author of *Coping with Difficult People.*

Great advice. And for those who work by themselves at home, it's a workable option. But the vast majority of success-bound people can't avoid interactions with a wide range of personality types, including some who are inconsiderate, inane, incorrigible, inappeasable, intransigent, indecent . . . or even downright sleazy. In fact, success sometimes depends on your ability to work well with all of the above.

WHEN DO YOU IGNORE?
WHEN DO YOU CONFRONT?

"If you avoid dealing with a touchy interpersonal problem, it's not going to go away. In all probability, the avoidance will make things worse," says Peter Wylie, Ph.D., a Washington-based organizational psychologist and management consultant who is coauthor of *Problem Employees: How to Improve Their Performance.*

A manager who avoids conflicts sets an organization on a calamitous course. Let's say you're hesitant to confront a chronically tardy worker. Not only will you be reinforcing his unfavorable work habits, you'll begin to lose the respect of everyone else who works for you. Those troopers who are pulling more than their weight to cover for the tardy employee will start grumbling, and their eventual demoralization could permeate the organization.

When the impact of your artful dodging is felt by *your* boss, one thing's fairly certain: Chances are *he* won't avoid confronting you.

On the other hand, you can't go around confronting everyone and everything. Chewing out a worker who arrives late for the first time in his life may do nothing but earn you a reputation as the office tyrant.

Fortunately, there are a few simple rules for when to make your move.

1. When an employee's performance impedes your organization's goals. If a person's disruptive behavior is affecting the group's work, it's time to take action. When a worker's lack of preparation for a meeting delays completion of a group project, for example, you have to confront him about it, says Bernard Rosenbaum, president of MOHR Development, a Stamford, Connecticut, business training firm, and author of *How to Motivate Today's Worker.*

2. When you determine that a person's actions will impede your own success. The fact that you're being bullied by one of your peers may have absolutely no impact on the rest of your organization. But the bully's actions may succeed in derailing your advancement. When a co-worker does something that may cause you harm, ask yourself, Can I afford to ignore this?

3. When a problem keeps sticking its head up and causing you anxiety every time you see it. Perhaps one of your subordinates is overly demanding of one of his assistants. You want to sit down with your subordinate and discuss the problem, but the prospect of having that discussion makes you nervous. You worry that it could open up a Pandora's box of other problems, that your subordinate will resent you, complain about you, or even respond by quitting. Just remember that by doing nothing, you'll probably only make things worse.

But before confronting a problem individual, it's crucial that you at least consider that you may be contributing to the trouble. "If a person 'drives me crazy,' he may be doing something inappropriate. But I have to ask myself why I'm having difficulty coping with that person's behavior. I have to understand my 50 percent of the deal," says Gisele Richardson, president of Montreal-based Richardson Management Associates.

LEARNING WHAT TO SAY
AND HOW TO SAY IT

Whether it's the abusive manager who chews you out in front of others or the vengeful employee whose laziness demoralizes your entire unit, the keys to getting anyone to change are what you say and how you say it. Here are some points to consider.

Remember that they can't read your mind. It's important that you state very clearly how you see the situation, stresses Richardson. You may even need to do this more than once. Don't assume that the person knows how you feel.

Don't be condescending. Your tone should be firm and direct, but you should never talk down to the person. "People listen better if they don't feel put down," says Dr. Bramson. Instead, concentrate on disclosing the effects that the person's behavior has on you. For someone who is a relentless excuse-maker, try saying, "What happens to me when you come in and make excuses all the time is that I stop listening."

State the facts succinctly. Once you've stated those facts ("I've noticed that in the last month you've been late 10 percent of the time"), don't dwell on them. There's no point in getting entangled in a lengthy recitation; the person is likely to start tuning you out. So quickly move on to the effects of his or her behavior: "It's concerning me. It's frustrating me. And I need to talk to you about how we can get a change here." Also, discuss the impact the person's behavior is having on other members of your organization: "We all suffer when one person doesn't contribute a fair share."

Frame your concerns in a positive way. Don't concentrate on the difficult person's erroneous behavior. Instead, focus on how he can improve. Don't say, "You're always alienating your co-workers." Say, "You need to be more cooperative." Instead of "You never get to work on time," try "You need to improve your attendance."

Consider the other person's self-esteem. "The single most important motivating factor for all of us is self-esteem," says Rosenbaum. He suggests that whenever you confront a difficult person, you ask yourself how the discussion may be eroding that person's esteem. "By understanding how it has been eroded, you can begin to reverse the effects," he says.

Have a clear game plan in mind. After you've explained your problem to the difficult person and told her exactly what you want from her, tell her how you're prepared to help, and spell out the time frame in which change has to occur. You might end by saying something on the order of: "And here are the consequences—If you do what I ask, we will have a good relationship. If you don't do what I ask, you won't work well with me."

3 THINGS TO AVOID WHEN CONFRONTING A DIFFICULT PERSON

1. Overreacting. We're not even going to elaborate on the physical consequences of mercilessly lashing out at someone: the epinephrine that starts pumping through your body, the risk of ulcers, high blood pressure,

When to Drop Good Manners

Under most circumstances, Patricia M. Carrigan, Ph.D., could be a contender for Miss Congeniality. She's the well-mannered former plant manager of General Motors' huge Bay City, Michigan, operation—the only female to run a major GM plant. She's also a trained clinical psychologist and is now president of Pat Carrigan Associates, a management consulting firm. But on at least one occasion she faced a situation that challenged her good manners.

The plant was in the midst of a serious cost-cutting campaign that required the cooperation of every member of her staff. A subordinate came into her office and elaborately proposed an unnecessary new project that would have cost the operation a great deal of money.

Dr. Carrigan stood up at her desk and relentlessly shrieked at the manager.

"No, I don't make a practice of screaming like a fish wife at employees. But in this case I needed to do something that would get his attention," she says. "And it worked." The employee had never seen Dr. Carrigan act that way and knew that whatever she was saying (or, to be more precise, screaming) had to be important. The message was transmitted.

Assuming you ordinarily operate with proper managerial manners, it may make good sense occasionally to rant, rave, and otherwise behave unpredictably to prove your point. Two things to keep in mind: You should be fairly certain beforehand that your actions will have the desired effect, and you should avoid getting carried away.

"The trick is to stop yelling at them once you've gotten their attention," says management consultant Dr. Robert Bramson. "After that, hollering only stops them from listening. They will begin to react emotionally, which prevents them from understanding." He suggests that after you've stopped yelling, calmly explain why you're angry.

Remember: This is a strategy to employ only if absolutely nothing else will work. "If you yell and scream too frequently, such behavior will lose its impact," says Dr. Carrigan.

And *never* yell at a person in front of others.

and other ill effects. Let's concentrate instead on the organizational problems that will result.

First off, it may seem like a great temporary release of frustration to haul off and holler at a subordinate. But any positive on-the-job results are likely to be merely short-term, says Dr. Wylie. "Someone may do what you want right away because he's scared, but that doesn't last long. Eventually, he'll find a way to get back at you."

Moreover, workers who are afraid of you may wind up doing only what you say—and no more. You could create a creativity-stifled troop of yes-people. "For the sake of your own credibility and respect, you simply can't afford the mistake of overreacting," explains Dr. Wylie.

2. Complaining. First, let's draw a distinction between complaining and venting. "There's nothing wrong with occasionally venting your frustrations to a friend and then working to solve the problem," says Dr. Wylie. "But complaining is chronic venting. By doing it, you'll accomplish nothing." Endlessly complaining to a friend about someone else's behavior, for example, overlooks the obvious: You're talking to the wrong person. Also you're creating the illusion that you're doing something, when you really aren't.

By complaining to others, you may divide an organization. Folks will find themselves choosing up sides—behind you or behind the person you're complaining about. And by gaining the reputation as a complainer, you'll find yourself losing credibility, Dr. Wylie warns.

And remember this: One of the quickest ways for a boss to gain the mistrust and resentment of his subordinates is to complain to one of them about one of their peers.

3. Lecturing. By age 37, the average person has spent about 100,000 hours on the wrong end of lectures from parents, teachers, and others who purport to know what's best. Somewhere along the line, the message starts to get lost in the medium. So remember that nothing will turn off a co-worker quicker than being talked down to, lecture-style.

COOLING OFF AN ANGRY CO-WORKER

First of all, never utter the words "Don't be angry." Rosenbaum suggests you instead encourage the individual to tell you all about what's angering him. "Without interrupting, without judging, and without taking a position, you listen and reflect back to him how he's feeling and why he's feeling that way." By empathizing, by letting the other person know you've heard him, you may lead him to a nonangry state.

At that point, explain in as much detail as possible why you think his unsatisfactory condition exists. Get his ideas on how to cope with the situation, and then offer your own ideas. Discuss ways to keep him from getting angry about similar matters in the future, adds Rosenbaum.

When trying to work with hostile colleagues, keep in mind that their self-esteem may be in the dumps. Compliment them whenever possible. Avoid arguing with them, even though that's often what they want.

Sometimes the challenge is preventing an exchange from *escalating* into anger. Here's a real-life workplace story. A fellow we'll call Sam is bragging to co-workers that he was able to sniff out the details of a colleague's raise in salary. Sam was able to do it because he made a point of becoming friendly with the person in charge of confidential personnel information.

As Sam tells you the story, it suddenly dawns on you that he would think nothing of snooping around in *your* confidential personnel files—in fact, he probably has.

What do you do?

You talk directly to Sam, suggests Dr. Bramson. In a nonconfrontational manner, you register your disapproval. "Sam," you could say, "my thought is that those records were confidential, and I would never want you to look in mine. My expectation is that you will only do that if you have my permission. I would be offended if I found you trying to check out my salary."

SAFE HANDLING OF THE DANGEROUS TWO-FACED CO-WORKER

You discover your office "friend" has been bad-mouthing you to others. Here's what you should do.

Resist the urge to haul off and slug her. Instead, march into her office,

---

Before Yelling at Someone, Try These Alternatives

1. Go for a solitary walk in the woods and yell. "Sometimes it clears the way for more constructive thinking," says management consultant Gisele Richardson.
2. Write an angry letter that you're never going to send. It gets the hostility out of your system so you can later address the individual in person without emotion.
3. Write a second, more carefully reasoned letter, and deliver it. Say, "Would you read this and then we'll talk about it." The act of writing the letter enables you to carefully choose the words you're using. "It's not a time to be spontaneous," says management consultant Dr. Robert Bramson.

and in your best no-nonsense tone of voice say, "I'm very much aware you're saying negative things to other people about me.

"We have to think of a way of making this stop. If you've got a problem with me, deal with me directly."

At this point, predicts Dr. Wylie, the co-worker will probably disavow any wrong-doing and spew forth a stream of utter nonsense (although "nonsense" isn't the word Dr. Wylie used).

Stand there and listen to the denial and the nonsense. Let it subside. Say, "I've heard what you've said, but . . . " And at this point you repeat your message, as firmly as you issued it the first time.

"You may have to listen to another round of denials, but keep repeating your message until it finally sinks in," says Dr. Wylie.

So what if it happens again?

March up to her and say that once again you know she's said negative things about you. Look her in the eye, even point a finger, and say, "I want you to stop!" The point is to be as intimidating as possible.

"What two-faced people hate is to be caught," says Dr. Wylie. "They're also pretty intelligent. So if you keep confronting them, they may eventually decide you're too much of a hassle to pick on—and they'll find some other victim."

18

EDUCATION

A New York financial consultant is intentionally stranded in a remote region of Baja California, forced to rely on her wits—and not a heck of lot more—for survival. She survives, all right. And boosted by the new-found respect she's gained for her own instincts and smarts, she flies back to Manhattan with enough vigor and spirit to rise to the top of her profession.

A Philadelphia television reporter attends a conference in Oklahoma on video storytelling and returns to her job with so many new ideas and skills that her new reports suddenly attract increasing acclaim from all corners of her viewing region.

A Canadian insurance executive on a mountain-climbing expedition in Banff National Park suddenly discovers that you have to learn to trust others before you can hope to convert a group of individuals into a cohesive, productive team. And when he gets back to Montreal, he . . .

Okay, let's pause for a minute. The act of reading example after example about the benefits of training experience is a lot like listening to your parents go on and on about the importance of education. We're willing to concede that training sessions are more fun for the participant than for the casual listener who only gets to hear the details later. But we're not inclined to stop stressing the crucial role that such sessions and other forms of continued learning can play in your success.

Training has become a multi-billion-dollar-a-year growth industry, according to the American Society of Training and Development (ASTD). That should be great news for you. Although Outward Bound–type wilderness programs fashioned for execs get a lot of the press, they represent a mere fraction of the training available. The American Management Association (AMA) alone offers 290 training programs a year ranging from its 3-day "Fundamentals of Finance and Accounting," which is designed for nonfinancial types, to its "Top Management Briefings," a 3½-day CEOs-only affair.

Under the rubric of training, there are courses that teach you how to make effective speeches, how to manage problem employees, how to better utilize computers, and how to tap into your creative juices. So-called sensitivity training sessions that made such a splash in the 1960s and 1970s are currently out of vogue, says ASTD vice-president Edward Schroer, adding that today "about the worst that happens is you have to hold hands, close your eyes, and think positive thoughts—which can be very beneficial, by the way."

Taking control of your education

Don't sit around waiting for your company to send you for training. And don't expect your boss to wander into your office and say something like: "Oh, by the way, if you're not doing anything special for the next two years, why don't you enroll in the executive MBA weekend program at the state university and we'll reimburse you." Yes, companies sometimes seek out employees for training that will help them advance professionally (sometimes they even offer such courses as a perk). But that shouldn't stop you from taking the initiative and seeking out learning opportunities wherever they exist. When you find something appealing, you should formulate a strong, logical case for being included.

A single example: The television reporter mentioned at the beginning of this chapter applied to attend the video-storytelling conference despite the fact that it was supposed to be exclusively for news *photographers*—not reporters. Her boss wasn't eager to send her, but a middle-management type who recognized the potential payoff to the news operation interceded on her behalf. True, supervisors may not be willing—or able—to spare you for even a two-day seminar, particularly if they don't believe they'll get much back in the way of added skills. But education rarely is easy to attain.

What if your organization makes it absolutely clear there's no training in your future? Perhaps you should start looking for a company with a more favorable attitude.

8 THINGS TO DO BEFORE YOU GO

1. Know why you're going and what's in it for you. Have a clear understanding of your supervisor's expectations for the training. Make sure you know the point of it all: why you're going, what skills you will be improving, and what will be expected of you when you return.

2. Check out the program's merits. If it's a classroom-style course, get a copy of the outline in advance and determine if it's appropriate to your needs, suggests Richard Kalbian, who develops curriculum for the AMA management courses. If it's an experimental training program and you're a bit wary of baring your emotions to a group, get a description of the program's intent and its format.

3. Call some prior participants. If you want to assess the value of any program you're considering (or one you've been assigned to attend), track down a few people who have participated and ask them some frank questions. Your organization's personnel department may help in locating such people. Or simply phone the trainers and ask for several names.

4. Get some background on the course leader. If it's a course within your company, ask the training department for the background of the instructor. Look especially for the individual to have experience as a trainer in the subject or to have direct experience in the field itself. Ed Schroer of the ASTD suggests you call up the instructor and chat about any questions or concerns you may have.

5. Do some prep work. If you can get a head start on any reading that will be required, you'll be that much better prepared to absorb the course material—and you'll be a more efficient learner.

6. Avoid going alone. If you're the only one from your company attending a particular course, you're less likely to get reinforcement for what you learn once you return to work. If possible, find a colleague to participate with you.

7. Psych yourself up for it. "One way to help motivate yourself is to find out what benefits will accrue to you afterwards—possible promotions or better assignments," says Philip C. Grant, Ph.D., a human resources management consultant in Bangor, Maine.

8. Find the time that's best for you. If you have a choice of when to participate, pick a time when there won't be many distractions, suggests Dr. Grant. "It makes very little sense to get into training if you have a lot of other problems to grapple with," he says. The best time is when everything else is relatively in order: when your in-basket isn't approaching record heights, and during a week when you're *not* expecting the delivery of your first child.

Ideally, try to schedule sessions when there's some honest-to-goodness slack time.

5 THINGS TO DO WHILE YOU'RE THERE

1. Try as best you can to block out the rest of the world. You need to concentrate on what you're being taught.

2. Take notes, if appropriate. AMA's Kalbian cites the statistic that most people retain only 50 percent of what they hear—regardless of how bright they are.

3. Engage in a Socratic dialogue. Here's a variant to the Socratic Method that really helps you learn: As you're reading material or listening to a lecture, keep formulating questions about the material and answering them in your head. For example, if your instructor says, "Here are five reasons for being ethical," ask yourself, What is a good example in my life of each reason for being ethical? Then answer yourself.

4. Make friendly professional contacts that could pay off in the future. Do this not only with other participants, but with the instructor, too. Why waste such an opportunity?

5. Keep reminding yourself of the skills you're supposed to be developing. And when you prepare to leave, formulate a task list based on what you've learned—a list of the actions you'll be taking in the next week, the next month, and the next year.

MAINTAINING THAT AFTERGLOW

It happens all the time. Folks return from training sessions all charged up and ready to conquer the planet. But their bosses shoot them down. There's a sad and confounding secret about corporate training: "Most companies, even though they're paying for the training, discourage people from applying what they've learned," says Kalbian. One reason, speculates St. Louis–based management trainer Donald H. Weiss, Ph.D., is that supervisors frequently exhibit a disdain for anything that isn't learned on the job. Here are some ways to get around all that.

Draw up a contract. Dr. Weiss says that if you've had such a letdown in the past, you may want to consider drawing up an agreement among you, your supervisor, and your program's trainer before embarking on a future training program. It should spell out what the training will provide and how what you learn will be carried out on the job. "It's a good idea *if* you have

An Amazing Success Story

Lawrence O. Kitchen made it to the top of the huge Lockheed Corporation despite the fact that he never got a college degree. In fact, he never even enrolled as a full-time student. How did he do it? Part of his strategy involved taking every conceivable continuing-education course he could find—whether it was a night class offered at a local community college or a corporate-sponsored training seminar. Kitchen's official corporate biography even boasts about his unusual educational background: "While it is true that Kitchen did not receive a college degree, during his career he has probably taken enough courses in night school, in management development programs, and in executive training institutes to qualify for a couple of degrees in management and associated disciplines."

No, Kitchen—who retired in 1989—did not plan it all this way. He was the oldest of six children in depression-plagued Selby, North Carolina. His parents worked in the textile mills, and after high school, so did he. After Pearl Harbor he joined the Marine Corps, where he was trained in engineering and aviation. When the war ended, he took a job as a clerk-typist with the Naval Bureau of Aeronautics.

"It was obvious to me that I had to have a lot more education if I were to advance in the field of aviation. So that's what I did," he explains. Thus began his seemingly endless succession of courses. And it worked. Over the next 12 years he advanced from clerk-typist to a GS-13 aeronautical engineer. When Lockheed offered him a job setting up a logistics organization for the Polaris missile program in 1958, he turned his back on his civil service retirement benefits and joined the private sector—all the while keeping up with the continuing-education classes.

In 1975 he was named Lockheed's president and chief operating officer; by 1986 he was chairman and chief executive officer. (*Important note:* He reports that somewhere around the middle-manager level, people stopped asking him where he went to school.)

While Kitchen concedes that it's far easier to get a degree *before* embarking on a career, he still highly endorses after-hours studies. "It's worth the extra effort never to stop educating yourself," he says.

a good supervisor," cautions ASTD's Schroer, "but if you have a jerk for a boss, it isn't going to work."

Debrief with your boss. Soon after you return from training, sit down with your supervisor and give him or her an oral debriefing of what you learned. And explain what you want to do that may be new or different.

Keep yourself charged up. Often, it's not the company's fault that you lose your training "high." Instead, the passing of time and the lack of reinforcement simply lull you back into the same bad habits your training was supposed to fix. Keep yourself recharged by staying in touch with other participants. Or talk to management about your problem. "Ask them to support your desire to apply what you've learned," says Dr. Grant, "recognizing that there may be risks in doing some of the things you've learned."

19

ENEMIES

You love your job and are generally fond of your co-workers, especially the guy in the next cubicle, the same guy you go jogging with every Monday, Wednesday, and Friday before lunch. He's someone you would trust with your life—even with the keys to your brand new Honda. You're sure he doesn't want to steal your job—or even make a bid for the one you're shooting for. What's more, he's even told you he's not the most ambitious guy in the universe.

Now let's suppose your company just happens to pit the two of you against one another. You're told that you and your jogging buddy are in direct competition for the job heading up a special new department. It's a dream job. But imagine the nightmare that may unfold: If he's like one particular breed of colleague, he may be bent on thwarting your career in order to advance his own (and he assumes you are planning the same).

At first you make vague, hopeful references to "friendly competition." Then one of you starts to cancel your workouts for flimsy and undocumented reasons. Then one of you makes a dramatic shift in lunching routine (let's say he suddenly begins ingesting his calories with unrecognizable folks of higher salary level in alien departments). Next, the morning chatter about the previous night's TV fare is condensed into a meager few sentences. Then it drops off altogether.

Depending upon how devious he is, he may just start bragging to the higher-ups that *he* gave you the idea for that latest project. Or in any number of other ways, he could routinely take credit for some of the good work you've been performing. Worse yet, through subtle schmoozing with your co-workers—sprinkled liberally with lies—he may even be able to get the entire department to think you're an incompetent, spouse-abusing, church-collection-plate-thieving bum of the worst sort. . . .

All right, maybe we are getting a bit carried away. The adversary scenario could just end at the "friendly competition" level. But it would be a disservice not to reflect for a moment on that most wonderful of clichés: Just because you're paranoid doesn't mean people aren't out to get you. "Develop a realistic, and I emphasize *realistic,* skepticism of others," advises Nicki Davidson, Ph.D., an organizational psychologist with Martin McAllister Consulting Psychologists in Minneapolis.

Dr. Davidson points out that, sad to say, sometimes people first have to be burned before they develop this realistic skepticism. Others "have the insight instinctively and don't need to be burned to develop it," she says.

Regardless, it's important always to remember a few key points. First, personality clashes exist virtually everywhere. Second, people's ambitions to succeed usually are far stronger than their ambitions to help co-workers succeed. And, third, even the most forward-thinking organizations contribute to an environment where success can come to those who consciously thwart the career of the person on the other side of the room divider.

And another thing. "A lot of people—and it's mostly women—who suddenly find themselves in a workplace conflict situation have a tendency to ask themselves, 'What am I doing wrong?' " explains Leslie Rose, founder of Career Confidence, a career consulting firm based in New York City. "The fact is, unless you've played team sports, you don't realize that it's the other person's *job* to tackle you."

How to tell an enemy
from just another ambitious person

Listen to your superiors. Be particularly alert for the innuendo. Say you're vying with a co-worker for a specific job. And, in a discussion with the superior who will eventually make the selection, you are asked: "By the way, how did you get the idea for the such-and-such project?" or "Was it really your idea to do that?" Career counselor Beth Wilson of Philadelphia-based Options, Inc., cautions, "Your boss may be implying through those queries that the other person is trying to take ownership of your idea or accomplishments."

Listen to your colleagues. Another sign: People are constantly bad-mouthing this person to you. It may indicate that they think you know the other person is your enemy. Keep in mind that people ordinarily won't freely criticize a third party unless they feel they have your permission to do so.

Observe. Is the other person doing more things socially with the decision-maker, but trying to give you the impression that he isn't? Does he (among many other obvious things you may be overlooking) make a habit of freely interrupting you in staff meetings or shooting down your ideas?

HOW TO LIVE WITH AN ENEMY
UNTIL SOMETHING BETTER COMES ALONG

Career counselor Rose recently was visited by a distraught client. The woman, an advertising account executive, had been at a group meeting in which her boss soundly criticized her in front of important advertising clients—over a matter that the boss had praised her for just days earlier. The woman bemoaned the fact that she "didn't deserve" such treatment, that she was "leaving anyway," and that she didn't think she could continue working for a boss who turned out to be—and let's not mince words—an enemy.

Rose asked her what she ultimately wanted for herself. The answer: to improve her writing skills to the point where she could earn a living from the creative side of the industry.

Rose asked her what she wanted from her present employer. The answer: a paycheck for six months, while she hunted for another job.

Rose asked her what the minimum was that she would have to do to keep her job for the next six months. The answer: keep the important customers happy and not confront her boss.

There's a simple lesson here. If you're like many people, you get caught up in trying to win the current battle and thus lose sight of your own agenda. "Your whole world gets narrowed to you and that enemy, so you lose your long-range perspective," says Rose. By focusing on your own long-term goals and aspirations, you'll be better prepared to endure any minor setbacks (as difficult as it is to believe that a back-biting boss is only a minor setback). You'll see such obstacles for what they really are: only temporary.

GIVE YOUR ENEMIES AN ALTERNATIVE
TO DIRECT CONFLICT

When you feel caught in a battle against an enemy, often the most effective offense is to remove yourself to a more peaceful realm (and take your enemy with you). There are several steps involved, but Rose suggests you start by viewing yourself as an entity of which work is but one part.

"Realize you're a whole human being with a variety of interests, and that work is simply what you're currently being paid to do," she suggests. It will help you gain the perspective you need to defuse the battle.

Recognize (or even pretend) that it isn't personal. "Try to step outside of the 'you' that's in the conflict," she advises. Once you do, you may be able to see the issues more objectively.

Deal with your own anger yourself, away from the other person. You don't have much of a chance at circumventing direct conflict if you're operating out of anger. So before the next time you interact with your nemesis, go home and beat up on a pillow or punching bag. Or go for a jog. Defuse the emotional charge that comes with your anger.

Recognize that you've chosen to be here. That's right, nobody's putting a gun to your head. You've made a choice to be here, as part of this organization. And if you don't like it, you can motivate yourself to move on. "It's very important not to limit your agenda to what can happen at that particular company," explains Rose.

Look beyond the immediate conflict. Think about your long-range agenda. Then think about the other person's agenda. "See if there are any similarities," suggests Rose. "If there are, try to get the other person to assist in achieving what you both want." It may be possible.

Disarm your adversary by finding ways of supporting what he's doing. "It sounds really difficult but if you can make that person look good, you may make it embarrassing for him to act out of hostility. Once you've recognized that you may be helping yourself by helping your enemy, you can say things to him that let him know you support him.

Finally, focus your energies on getting results in your job. It's the essence of professionalism: putting work-oriented results ahead of interpersonal conflicts.

What to do first
in response to a threat

In a meeting you point out the flaws in a colleague's proposal. Afterwards the person corners you in the hallway with fighting words: "I'm going to make your life miserable!"

Do you: (1) Practice the front-snap karate kick on him that you just perfected? (2) Say, "You picked the wrong person to threaten, buddy"? (3) Say, "Listen, I'm sorry I criticized you; it won't happen again"? (4) Not react, but let the person explain the problem he has with you?

There are instances in which each of these responses would probably be justified: (1) if it was your karate instructor who issued the threat, (2) if you're a supervisor of preadolescent newspaper carriers and it was one of them who issued the threat, (3) if it was the chief executive officer of your company who issued the threat, (4) if it was just about anyone else.

No, we aren't of the wimpy-is-beautiful persuasion. Actually, by actively listening to the person's criticism, analyzing it carefully, and responding in a calm, straightforward manner, you may be taking the most assertive approach to a direct threat.

Think of what you accomplish: You relay the crucial message that direct threats don't work on you. You let the person know you have enough sense, maturity, and class to listen to him or her before responding. You give him or her the opportunity to let off steam. You have the chance yourself—even if for only 90 seconds—to analyze the situation.

By listening, you may find out just how deep the problem lies. "You may learn from listening and analyzing that there's an even bigger issue than the fact that you've criticized the person," says career counselor Wilson. "You may determine, for instance, that you're involved in a turf war that you hadn't known about." If that's the case, you might require the assistance of a supervisor to draw distinct boundaries for the two of you.

Lyn Malone, a personal power and communication consultant based in New York City, suggests you go one step further by using the threat as an opportunity to open up a positive interchange. She says, "Coming from an inner attitude of respect, you could simply say, 'What's happened between us?' That way you're reframing the conflict from the vantage point that both you and the other individual are worthwhile human beings."

It's worth a try. (And you won't destroy your toes, as you could with a front-snap kick.)

WHEN SOMEONE ELSE TAKES CREDIT FOR YOUR WORK

There are two rules for confronting other people who take credit for work you do. Rule one: Give them a chance to explain themselves. Rule two: Make every attempt to communicate your displeasure clearly.

Let's imagine that you pick up the corporate employee newspaper and run across a story in which your colleague is quoted as exaggerating her role in a project for which you did an abundance of hard work. (*Note:* Across America, that type of scenario was probably played out about 1,000 times during the time it took you to read that last sentence.)

David Behrend, a Philadelphia-area career counselor, suggests you start off by giving the offending party the benefit of the doubt. Say something like: "Mary, we've got a great team here and I feel there should be credit

Shooting for Victory in a Lose-Lose Situation

The folks who run organizations rarely think twice about pitting two colleagues against each other for a particular promotion. But it could result in trouble down the road.

Let's say you've gone head-to-head against an enemy and have come out ahead. You're promoted to manager. But he remains in your department. Suddenly, you are your enemy's boss.

Don't rub your hands together and devise ways of making his life miserable. He may already have a head start in attempting to prove you're incompetent. How? By working to align the staff against you, for one thing.

As uncomfortable as it may be, the best strategy often is to directly confront your enemy and sincerely try to bury the hatchet. Philadelphia career counselor Beth Wilson says you can begin the conversation by saying, "I know you wanted this position. I know you're unhappy with the outcome. But you and I are going to have to work together." Show the person you don't hold a grudge and impress upon him the need to work together.

What if you lose the competition for promotion and your enemy is now your boss? First, find out if there's another person on your staff—who knows both of you—from whom you can solicit advice. Your goal should be to assess if it's best to talk to the enemy directly about burying the hatchet. But he may be uncomfortable with you on his staff. If your objective assessment tells you that your enemy is probably incapable of becoming a fair manager (now that the direct competition is over), perhaps it's time to redirect your career. But don't act too hastily. "I would encourage the person to give the enemy a chance," says Wilson.

given for the entire team . . . " If you use stronger language, you run the risk of putting the person on the defensive and making a new, real enemy (as opposed to an imaginary one). Consider the real possibility that the person simply did not recognize she was stealing the credit. (Sure, it's possible. It's also possible that she was misquoted.) If she knows that you're not going to let her take all the credit, she'll likely think twice before doing it again.

But what if it does happen again? If it's a colleague with whom you have a reasonable working relationship, Behrend recommends you approach her with the offending evidence (it may even be word-of-mouth evidence) and say, "You've claimed again that you did all the work on this project. We both know that's not the case."

Again, give her a chance to answer for herself. Respond by saying, "I don't intend to let this happen again." Depending upon the circumstances and your organization's culture, you may even want to mention the episode to your boss—and then include *that* bit of information in your discussion with the real, new enemy.

Some cautions are in order here. Peter Wylie, Ph.D., a consultant with Washington-based Performance Improvement Associates, and coauthor of *Problem Bosses: Who They Are and How to Deal with Them,* says you should remember that if it's a boss who is stealing your thunder, you've got to be more careful than you would with a colleague.

"The best thing to do is to say how you feel," he says. Dr. Wylie recommends a "describe and disclose" strategy. Sample script: "When you claimed credit for the report I wrote, I felt surprised, disappointed, amazed, and angry because I put in the lion's share of the work. I wanted to let you know how I felt."

Then look the boss in the eye and wait for a response.

Dr. Wylie explains that you should let the person finish. Then, regardless of the response, you should repeat yourself with the preface: "I heard everything you've said, but I want to be clear about what I said, so you can understand how I feel." Hold the person accountable.

20

ENERGY

Let's face facts for a moment. Five days a week most of us are required to perform some type of labor for periods of 8 hours or longer. On the plus side, this provides us with 8 hours each day that we won't be sitting home watching TV game shows, we won't be answering the phone only to find a computer on the other end hell-bent on selling us real estate in Wyoming, and we won't be mowing the lawn. Small advantages, but we'll take them. The downside, however, can be summed up even more quickly and highlights an important problem: The only thing humans can easily do for 8 hours a day is sleep.

This unrealistic demand on our powers of attention becomes readily apparent right around the magic hour of 3 in the afternoon. Up until then we are models of efficiency, our posture is that of a cadet on parade, and our energy is boundless. But at the stroke of 3:00 we begin to resemble Superman after a dose of Kryptonite. Shoulders droop, eyes begin to glaze over, and our will is broken. (We also tend to be crushed under any buildings we're currently lifting with one hand.)

However, while Superman can blame *his* blues on a mutated chunk of his home world, we seldom get away with the same excuse. For humans, the matter of fatigue is a bit more complex and has as much to do with the mind as it does with the body. Fortunately, there are ways around fatigue, natural ways of infusing yourself with additional energy with which you can finish out the day in style. And you won't have to lurk around your local health club at dusk to purchase mysterious protein packages made by smiling people on the beach somewhere in California.

AVOID THESE 6 ENERGY THIEVES

In the quest for more energy, the first thing to learn is how not to sabotage the natural supply you already have. Look over the following list of criminals to see if you might be an unwitting accomplice to self-energy thievery.

Disorganization. Nothing puts a damper on your power plant faster than an unruly mob of "Things that Need to Get Done Today." Problems get jumbled in your head, solutions are sporadically lost and found, and it's hard to tell if you're making any headway. "To avoid that tiring feeling of too much to do with no recognizable starting or ending point, begin each day with a definite plan of action," says fatigue specialist David Sheridan, M.D., of the University of South Carolina School of Medicine. "In an orderly fashion, chart short-term goals for the day that are within your abilities to accomplish."

To understand the energy difference that this simple technique can make, picture yourself running a marathon. You've been running full tilt for about an hour, and just when you think you can't go on, you see a sign up ahead: "1 Mile to Finish Line." With victory in sight, you suddenly experience a burst of energy that carries you across the line. But suppose a sadistic person with a bad sense of humor changed that sign to read "10 Miles to Finish Line." There is little doubt that you would crumple into a pathetic mass of fatigue.

In this case, preserving energy becomes an exercise in mind over matter. If you create a list of things to do each day and follow it, by three o'clock your list should be looking pretty small, in effect saying to you "1 Mile to Finish Line." You can handle it, no sweat. Those last 2 hours will whiz by in a burst of energy. But if you have no list, who knows? It could be 1 mile, or it could be 10. Might as well call it a day right now.

Smoking. This one is fast and simple: Don't smoke. A cigarette is the quickest way to cut down oxygen delivery to your tissues. Less oxygen means less energy. If you do quit, keep in mind that you may initially feel even more tired. Because nicotine acts like a stimulant, your body will miss it for a little while. But the feeling will pass, and you'll wind up a winner.

Ruts. Getting yourself into a rut is yet another insidious way to lose energy. The problem is that you rarely even notice when you are in one. Suddenly one day you realize you've eaten lunch at the same place for the better part of a decade. Or it occurs to you that the precision with which you take your 10:30 and 2:45 coffee breaks could be used to reset atomic clocks.

Break it up, suggests Rick Ricer, M.D., a fatigue expert at the Ohio State University College of Medicine. Even the smallest of changes can make a difference in the amount of vitality you feel. By doing things exactly the same every day, you've been giving your brain a chance to shut down and go on automatic pilot. No wonder you're feeling a little groggy.

Start anew by driving a different route to work. Try that strange Jamaican-Canadian bistro for lunch. And for heaven's sake, take down the duck print that's been hanging on your wall since the Civil War; maybe toss up a Matisse print instead. In the field of sociology, there is a famous phenomenon known as the Hawthorne Effect: Over and over it's been observed that tiny changes in the workplace environment cause higher employee productivity on a short-term basis. Put this effect to your advantage. When the newness of the change wears off, make another.

Overweight. Find out from your physician what your ideal weight should be. If you're 20 percent over that target, you may have found the culprit behind your fatigue. While you're at the doctor's office, find out about a sensible diet and exercise program to drop your weight and raise your energy.

Too much sleep. Everyone knows that skipping sleep can stop you in your tracks. But few are aware of a threat from the opposite direction. In fact there are two ideas concerning sleep that are so firmly etched in the public psyche that they make the Ten Commandments look like fly-by-night guidelines: (1) Everyone should get 8 hours of sleep a night, and (2) The more sleep you can get, the better. But following these rules may be another reason you're lagging. "Usually, 6 to 8 hours of sleep per night is enough for most people," says William Fink, an exercise physiologist at Ball State University in Muncie, Indiana. "If you oversleep, you're going to be groggy all day."

As you grow older, your sleep requirements change. If you've stuck to the tried-and-true 8 hours a night for the past ten years, you may want to try an experiment to see if your body craves a different schedule. Try going five days with only 7 hours of sleep a night. If you feel even more tired, go back to 8. But if you feel better, try 6½ hours a night. Keep cutting back gradually until you find what's best for you. Just be careful not to experiment your way into serious fatigue and possible illness.

Coffee. A cup of joe to make you go in the morning may be why you're gone in the afternoon. Coffee triggers an insulin reaction that may leave you with a mild case of low blood sugar at the end of a manic, energy-packed hour. Additionally, coffee can play havoc with your body's circadian rhythms. These rhythms are a type of physical clock that raises and lowers blood pressure, temperature, and countless chemical levels throughout your body. The monkey wrench that an ill-timed cup of coffee throws into this cycle could be causing your fatigue.

If you do need a daily cup of coffee, try it between 3:30 and 5:00 P.M. At this point the caffeine won't interfere so much with your circadian rhythms, and it will give you a boost just when you need it most.

5 NATURAL STIMULANTS FOR LATE-NIGHT WORK SESSIONS

You're facing a deadline tomorrow at 8:00 A.M. and it's time for a do-or-die effort. The only problem is that your body has already voted for the die option. Try one of the following solutions to power up fast when your generator has conked out.

Walking. Rather than reaching for a candy bar the next time you're experiencing an energy shortage, reach for your walking shoes. According to research performed at California State University, a brisk 10-minute walk should provide you with a significantly better energy boost than any candy bar. And the best part is that unlike a candy bar, walking won't make you a fatigue victim an hour later.

The chemistry behind this minor miracle is simple. Candy will raise your blood sugar too high too fast, thereby setting you up for a fall. A 10-minute walk, however, elevates blood sugar at a comfortable pace that can leave you energized for as much as 2 hours. Best of all, walking has been shown to cause cavities in only 1 out of 235,000,000 people.

A shower. It's midnight. Your work is spread all over the living room floor. And as a clock ticks in the background, your eyelids are getting heavier and heavier. It's time to hit the showers. But there's no need to perform icy self-tortures upon yourself. Hot, warm, or cold, it's the falling water that gives you a kick. The special magic it works comes to you by way of negative ions, molecules that adopt an extra electron due to the water rushing through the air. According to research, higher concentrations of negative ions in the air will lower levels of a brain chemical called serotonin. This in turn makes us more cheerful and energetic.

Deep breathing. Breathing in general is a good idea. In fact, it's rather habit-forming. But *how* you breathe is important. While concentrating, many people tend to breathe in a shallow manner. Less oxygen intake means less energy. To tell if you are a shallow breather, ask yourself this question: When you finally look up from your work, do you generally take a deep breath and let it out like a sigh? If so, you have probably been robbing yourself of oxygen while concentrating. In a case like this, you should take a 2-minute break once every 45 minutes and do a little deep breathing. But don't exaggerate or prolong your little exercise or you'll find yourself getting light-headed.

Music. Anything that can whip a tribe of aborigines into a fighting frenzy or turn mild-mannered teenagers into whirling, pelvis-thrusting dervishes certainly ought to be able to lift you out of a momentary fatigue. Make a home cassette of your favorite upbeat tunes and keep it at work with an inexpensive Walkman. When things start getting a little cloudy, pop on those headphones and rock out for 5 minutes. The ensuing adrenaline rush should carry you through the next hour. Repeat this prescription as needed. If you really want to double your fun, do some jumping jacks in time to the music.

Meditation. Moving 180 degrees away from the rock-and-roll technique brings us to meditation, the pause that refreshes. Researchers at Harvard asked a group of test subjects to sit in a relaxed position and shut off distracting thoughts by repeating a word over and over again. Not only did this technique reduce the body's response to stress, but the achieved state, one of "restful alertness," yielded optimal mental functioning on the part of the participants.

To do it yourself, remain in your chair and let your body go limp. Close your eyes and mentally repeat a word that has little personal meaning to you. Continue repeating the word to the exclusion of all other thoughts. If you find your mind wandering, don't get upset. It happens to all of us. Gently return your mind to the word you've chosen. Even 15 minutes of this technique can yield amazing results.

POWER LUNCHES: HOW TO EAT FOR ENERGY

Voodoo practitioners in Haiti are said to turn their hapless victims into zombies by administering a chemical mixture of plant and insect extracts. Up here in the United States, we do it to ourselves by way of our lunchtime eating habits. In her book, *Managing Your Mind and Mood through Food,* Judith Wurtman, Ph.D., of MIT writes that the foods you eat can either enhance your mental alertness or dull your mind and slow down your reactions. To ensure that tomorrow's lunch will work in your favor, here are a few guidelines to follow.

1. Choose proteins over carbohydrates. The reason for this rule has to do with certain chemicals in your brain called neurotransmitters. Two of these, dopamine and norepinephrine, are released in reaction to a substance

Sleepless Nights, Mindless Daze

If you find yourself counting sheep all night and welcoming the dawn without a bit of shut-eye, you can also count on having only half of your mental powers to carry you through the next day, according to research from Great Britain. Tests conducted by Dr. James A. Horne, a psychophysiologist, seem to show that spontaneity, flexibility, and originality in our thought processes can be seriously undermined by as little as one sleepless night.

Why? Dr. Horne believes that one of the primary functions of sleep is to repair the brain's cerebral cortex from the wear and tear of consciousness.

But while these creative abilities, known by psychologists as divergent thinking, are lost after a sleepless night, we can still count on our powers of convergent thinking. Convergent thinking, the opposite of creativity, is used in rote situations such as drawing up balance sheets, dealing with familiar and well-defined situations, or taking a simple true-or-false test. But even these abilities start to decline if you happen to go two sleepless nights in a row.

The tip? If you did spend last night watching TV test patterns, rearrange your work today to avoid any kind of creative challenges. Instead, use the time to dispense with various busywork that's been piling up lately. And be sure to get some sleep tonight.

found in proteins. Both of these brain chemicals cause the mind to power up for action. On the other hand, serotonin, a neurotransmitter that causes the brain to relax and slow down, is produced in higher quantities when carbohydrates are eaten.

All you need to remember is to favor things such as lean meat, poultry, or fish. Eggs are okay, too. What you want to stay away from at lunch are potatoes, corn, bagels, muffins, bean-based foods, pasta, and doughnuts. Also, you want to avoid high-fat foods such as pizza. While the cheese in pizza might afford you some protein, the high fat content will slow down and dilute the protein's desired effect.

2. **If you do eat some carbohydrates, make sure you eat a good portion of your proteins first.** Make it halfway through the proteins on your plate and then you can eat some carbohydrates with relative impunity. By the time you're ready to start on your potato or side of pasta, the collected proteins in your body will block the production of serotonin in your brain.

3. Limit your caloric intake. This means eating only about 500 to 600 calories at lunch. The more calories you have to digest, the less alert you're going to be. Try 4 to 6 ounces of seafood or poultry, a side vegetable, and maybe a clear soup. This kind of menu should ensure an energy-packed afternoon of achievement.

21

ETIQUETTE

Right now, etiquette books are outselling cookbooks," says Marjabelle Young Stewart, an author of books on manners. With 17 such titles on bookstore and library shelves and a reported three-year waiting list for her seminars, Stewart is a veritable Betty Crocker of manners. A lot of the advice on the market seems to be aimed at scaring the readers, implying that anyone who would be gauche enough to grab for the wrong water glass (properly on the right) or salad plate (on the left) at an important company function will swiftly be banished to the West Podunk office.

Even though life is a great deal more casual than the strict proponents of etiquette would have us believe, it never hurts to show some polished manners—especially in the field of business. On the surface, manners are supposed to reflect one's upbringing. For instance, when you're introducing your boss to your new assistant and you correctly "present" the subordinate to a superior by saying "Mr. (Superior), I'd like you to meet Ms. (Subordinate)," you're ostensibly indicating that you've been properly raised—the implication being that you've got an inbred ability to handle any situation life thrusts upon you. But is the appearance of being well-bred a requirement for success? We're not convinced that it is, and we think Letitia Baldrige, author of *Complete Guide to Executive Manners*, is overstating it a bit when she says, "Good manners is the most important asset an executive can have."

But Protocol 101, on the other hand, should be a required course. And just in case the folks who determine your career fate happen to be sticklers for proper manners, it might be wise to know the ground rules. Thanks to the guidebooks and etiquette seminars that proliferate, virtually anyone can adopt the manners of the properly bred. "It's just one more skill, one more arrow in your quiver," says Linda Phillips, who with her husband, Wayne, runs the Executive Etiquette Company in Taunton, Massachusetts. "Learning business etiquette is like learning how to write a memorandum," she explains. "No one is born knowing how to write a memorandum, but it doesn't take much time to learn."

10 TOP ETIQUETTE TIPS

1. Know when to use someone's first name. The general rule is that you always defer to authority by using an honorific (Mr., Ms., Dr.) until you are given permission to use a first name. It is inappropriate to call prospective clients by a first name until they grant you permission to do so, says Linda Phillips, who is coauthor of *The Concise Guide to Executive Etiquette: Absolutely Everything You Need to Know About Business Protocol.* Also, if you're on a first-name basis with your boss and you are introducing someone to him or her, always introduce your boss as Mr., Ms., or whatever, and include his or her title ("This is Mrs. Renquist, senior vice-president of marketing"). At that point, the boss will probably tell the person to "call me Sarah."

2. Don't give your boss a gift. Unless you have a personal relationship with your boss, don't give him or her a gift for holidays or birthdays. "It's inappropriate, can be seen as apple polishing, and puts the employer in an awkward situation," explains Phillips. An option: Use the occasion to write a letter of thanks. Thank the employer for providing you with opportunities—and be specific. In general, try to downplay the need for exchanging personal gifts in your office. One idea is to create a sunshine fund for purchasing birthday flowers for employees or for taking them to lunch.

3. Don't get drunk at business-related social functions. It's the biggest out-of-office blunder made today, says Baldrige. So what do you do if you made a fool of yourself last night? "Apologize," says Baldrige, "and go on the record. Write a note to the hostess, explaining to her that 'it has been brought to my attention that my behavior last night was anything but exemplary. . . .' And send flowers along—it helps."

4. Know how to use small talk to fill an awkward moment. You are meeting a potential client or employer for the first time at a business lunch. You arrive at the restaurant and are immediately shown to a table. An uncomfortable silence fills the space between you. Break the ice by talking about where you are—physically. You could mention how beautifully appointed the room is. You could say what you've heard about the restaurant.

Don't Become the Office Clown

Some people do it out of nervousness. Some do it merely because they want to be liked—and because it achieved that end in the past. But Marjabelle Young Stewart and other etiquette experts warn against gaining a reputation as the office jokester. The reasoning is simple: "People are less likely to take you and your ideas seriously," Stewart warns. If such advice contradicts your naturally jovial personality, here's an option: Maintain both a 9-to-5, low-key persona and a less-serious, after-hours persona.

On the other hand, if you're meeting your company's chairman for the first time, even though it's in a social setting, mere small talk wouldn't be appropriate. You should say something that borders (but not by much) on business talk—and something that reflects that you're up on your organization's happenings. For example: "I've just seen the design for the new Cleveland office, and I think it's excellent."

5. To avoid sexual harassment, err on the side of caution. Some men still feel an obligation to tell a female colleague or client how nice she looks since she cut her hair or how attractive a particular outfit looks on her. But such comments denigrate your business relationship. Save such compliments for personal friends.

6. Don't correct your boss in public. "You can do it in private," says Baldrige. An exception: If you're in a meeting and the boss makes a ghastly error in his statements, you can pipe up gently with something like "Come to think of it, it's five million, not ten million, Bill."

7. Know what to talk about with the boss's spouse. You're bound to meet him or her at a business-social function. If the spouse is a woman, don't make the blunder of assuming that she's engaged only in traditional female activities. Nor should you make the assumption that the spouse knows little about the workings of the company. If he or she begins by talking about the company, pick up on the cue. Or pick up on other interests he or she may have. Ideally, you will know in advance where his or her interests lie. So your homework will pay off when you say, "I understand that you were the chief judge of the art center's photo competition this year. That must have been quite an undertaking."

8. Don't draw attention to your tardiness (and other minor blunders). You're late for a big meeting. Don't start rattling off about how the 6:02 was

---

I Want That !#$*% Report on My Desk by Tomorrow!

Normally considered a football field–sized breach of etiquette, profanity is used "selectively and consciously" by eight of ten company presidents, according to a survey conducted by management consultant Debra Benton. Benton counsels that profanity should only be used for impact and aimed at projects, issues, or situations, *never* at people.

---

stranded by a broken signal. Nor should you go overboard in apologizing. Simply say, "Excuse me," or "Pardon my tardiness," and slip into your seat. Later you can explain to your boss about how you were closing the Murphy deal.

9. Recognize that chivalry (not courtesy) is dead. Any woman who waits for a man to open the door in a business situation deserves to remain stranded. Unless, of course, she's carrying two huge bundles, or unless she's recently had open-heart surgery. According to today's business etiquette, whoever gets to the door first does the opening—unless either party is encumbered.

10. Rise and shake hands when business introductions are made. Scarlett O'Hara, forget what your mama taught you. In a business situation, when anyone enters the room and is being introduced, stand and shake hands. No, it doesn't matter who puts his hand out first. And Phillips says when you're waiting in a conference room for a superior to arrive at the meeting, remain standing until she arrives—and let her take the best seat.

MIND YOUR MEALTIME MANNERS

The power lunch (or breakfast) is designed to accomplish a number of things besides the mere ingesting of calories. For one thing, it's a way of removing the two or more participants from the ringing telephones and other workplace interruptions for one or two hours of undisturbed business. For another, it's a quasi-social setting that can help cement a relationship—or enable potential business partners to size each other up. In any event, the meal itself is a prelude to the work that will take place.

The person who does the inviting is the host and should immediately and clearly establish himself or herself as such, advises Phillips. Start when you call with the lunch invitation. Give the person a choice of dates ("How about next week? Tuesday or Friday?"); a choice of restaurants ("Le Grand Oeuvre, or Scrimshaw Inn?"); a choice of times ("Would you prefer noon or 1:00?"). Arrive 10 minutes early to greet your guest. When the maître d' pulls out a chair, make sure your guest gets it—yes, even if you're a woman and he's a man.

Never start discussing business until after you've given your guest the chance to order. In fact, it's a good idea to wait until the major part of the meal is over before bringing up the business topic at hand. That way you're not chewing food or buttering rolls while trying to make your best pitch for a more lucrative contract.

Etiquette authority Stewart suggests the following approaches to bringing up business: "Well, shall we talk about the new contract?" "Well, what do you think of the proposed merger?" "While it's on my mind, I've been meaning to ask you about the new product line."

When it's time to take care of the check, the rule is simple: The host pays. Some dyed-in-the-wool Southern gents would rather subdivide their family plantations than let a woman pay. That's why smart women in the South and elsewhere prearrange with the maître d' to pay the bill away from the male lunch partner's embarrassed gaze. They either pay in advance or on their return trip from the ladies' room.

If you'll be dining at carriage-trade restaurants and clubs with much regularity, by all means take the hour or so required to learn about such dining esoterica as the fish knife. "Most business occurs in social settings," says Phillips, "so why be intimidated by those settings?" Her *Concise Guide to Executive Etiquette* devotes an entire chapter to utensils. (The fish knife, by the way, was introduced in the days of Queen Victoria as a means of deboning fish that were brought, head and all, to the table. To use the knife, simply hold it like a pencil and use it to push fish onto your fork.)

Avoid these snags in foreign relations

Some of the biggest etiquette blunders occur when cultures clash. Imagine the American businessman who, in trying to work his way into the good graces of a Japanese potential client, offers the fellow a gift of pierced earrings for his wife. (The Japanese view the act of poking holes through one's ears as mutilation.) Or perhaps he delivers a gift set of four ceramic plates. (The Japanese have a phobia about things that come in sets of four, basically because their word for four, *shi,* is also the word for death.) Or picture the visitor to the Moslem world who proudly presents a gift—a nicely framed painting of a hunting dog set against a green background. The trouble is, Moslems are offended by anything depicting dogs or pigs. And because they consider green to be the color of God, it is reserved for only the most respectful of items. (You *could* deliver a nice emerald brooch, for instance.)

Pity the poor businessperson who wades into foreign waters without first checking out the protocol. Here are some major points.

In most parts of the Middle East, the left hand is reserved for personal hygiene. So your potential client is likely to be highly offended if you pass him the contract with your left hand. (But probably not as offended as he'd feel if you passed him the rice with your left hand.)

In Latin America, business and social activities are strictly segregated. So you should never take someone out to lunch hoping to negotiate a deal.

Few cultures, in fact, develop business relationships or rush into business deals as quickly as Americans do. By contrast, the Japanese seem to take forever to act. For Americans hoping to do business in Japan, it's crucial to have a flexible timetable and to understand that the negotiating won't even start until the Japanese party feels that a suitable relationship has been established.

Don't make the mistake of one American CEO who thought that since Argentinians are such big beef-eaters, a set of expensive steak knives would be a swell business gift. It was a major mistake, recalls Lydia Klatsky, co-owner of Corporate American Gifts in Farmington, Connecticut. The reason? In Latin America, knives and scissors symbolize the cutting off of a relationship.

Never take a French woman a gift of perfume or red roses. It's considered far too intimate a gesture, warns Klatsky.

In the Middle East, you're expected to *try* a taste of everything on your plate. (A thought to remember: The sheep's eyeballs are reserved for special guests.) In Europe, you're expected to *clean* your plate.

Don't wrap a Japan-bound gift in white (it's the color of mourning). Also remember that in Japan the wrapping is almost as important as the gift itself. Don't give anything that's unwrapped or poorly wrapped—and don't expect the recipient to open the gift in front of you, says Klatsky.

In Britain, don't flash the V-for-victory sign with your palm facing you. (It's considered obscene.) For the same reason, avoid the thumbs-up sign in Australia and West Africa, and the thumb-to-forefinger "okay" sign in Brazil.

22

FAILURE

Oscar Wilde once wrote that "Experience is the name everyone gives to his mistakes." While his observation contains a hidden barb intimating that people can always find an excuse for what they've done, it also points out a truism that in essence says, "To fail is to learn a valuable lesson."

So valuable a lesson, in fact, that failure—while hardly something to wish for—can be viewed as virtually a necessity for both career and character growth.

Before perfecting the incandescent light bulb, Thomas Edison developed more than 200 prototypes that failed miserably. When he did finally succeed, a reporter asked him how he felt about all those failures. Edison smiled and said that they weren't failures at all, because without the information he learned from them, he never would have succeeded. To Edison, failure was a loaded word that shouldn't even be applied to what he saw as logical steps toward success. Now *there's* a way to look at a mistake.

You might be inclined to acknowledge Edison's spirit but still be a trifle skeptical about the value of failure in a business setting. After all, in the land of the bottom line, you either win or you lose, right? Not necessarily. When the Center for Creative Leadership (CCL) interviewed a group of successful Fortune 500 executives about their careers, 66 percent admitted to contributing to a business failure, being exiled to a poor position, having major conflicts with their company's bigwigs, missing promotions, or simply being overwhelmed by their job.

Granted, there are also many executives who failed and permanently derailed, but the difference between that group and the Fortune 500 alumni is how they dealt with failure. According to the CCL, those who derailed typically tried to hide their mistakes or shovel them onto someone else's shoulders. But those who won in the end had met their mistakes head-on, called attention to them in the hopes of finding some effective means of damage control, and—most important—learned a valuable lesson, which they applied the next time a similar situation arose.

Can it be argued that these executives might not be where they are today without the failures they experienced? Perhaps. But one thing can be said for sure: Sooner or later we all bungle something. So a lesson in damage control is hardly out of line.

THE 4 WAYS MANAGERS DEAL WITH FAILURE

To a large extent, how you deal with failure depends on what kind of ego resilience you have. Does your sense of self-worth bounce back after defeat, or is it crushed like a tulip under the wheels of a bulldozer?

In his book, *Office Hours: A Guide to the Managerial Life,* Walter Kiechel III has divided managers into four types, based upon their response to setbacks. The first type is what he calls *the bulletproof.* Essentially, these are people who have an ego as large as an office building and as impermeable as a marble desktop. While failure doesn't even come close to destroying them internally, it also never teaches them a lesson. This type of person either doesn't admit a mistake ever occurred or covers it up when possible. Bulletproofs are doomed to repeat their mistakes again and again, since they never accepted them in the first place.

Better prepared are *the rebounders,* who, Kiechel notes, score the highest in ego resilience. They learn from their setbacks and even find a measure of confidence in themselves from the manner in which they deal with those setbacks. People in this category are less likely than others to "go down with the ship" because their pride is tempered enough to admit to a mistake. They can start taking steps to rectify a bad situation as early as possible rather than stubbornly persevering in an attempt to save face.

Setbacks hit *the changers* a bit harder than the rebounders. Since their egos are more fragile, when failure strikes, changers retire into a period of self-examination during which they review their strengths, weaknesses, and career opportunities. As Kiechel notes, this can be a gut-wrenching experience, but one that may provide them with a more realistic sense of themselves. Should they survive the ordeal, changers often come away as better people-managers, since they've gained a measure of insight into what their employees experience when they've blown it.

Finally, there are *the broken.* They have "brittle, eggshell egos," writes Kiechel. These people are crushed by defeat and never operate effectively again. These are the people most likely to fall prey to what psychologists call "learned helplessness": the idea that failing can create an expectation of unquestionable future defeat that indeed prevents such victims from ever trying for success again.

Interestingly enough, learned helplessness can actually strike those with strong egos as well as the weak—but in a slightly different manner. Psychologists John Klien and Arden Miller of Southwest Missouri State University conducted an experiment in which college students were first divided into groups classified as having high, medium, or low ego values and then given a matching-figures test that was impossible to solve. Having tasted failure, the students were then given 15 jumbled words to unscramble. While the test was the same for everyone, some of the students were told that the problems were extremely hard, while the problems were described as only moderately hard to the rest.

The results showed that while students in the high-ego group were willing to persist if they thought the task was extremely difficult, they were equally willing to give up quickly when they were told the problems were relatively easy to solve. The most probable explanation for this is that even if they failed to solve what were considered difficult tasks, they would still be able to salvage some part of their ego. After all, there's little shame in failing what may be a next-to-impossible problem. But their egos, still somewhat bruised by their initial failure, feared the possibility of failure with respect to something considered easy to accomplish.

On the other hand, the low-ego group performed in the exact opposite manner. When told the problems were extremely difficult, they gave up easily. Yet when told that the problems were not so hard, they were more apt than the high-ego group to make an extended effort.

WHY DO PEOPLE STICK TO A FAILING COURSE OF ACTION?

We've all experienced this or at least watched it happen to someone else: A project is launched in a flurry of flying memos, widespread approval, and a general hurrah rising from the corporate peanut gallery. But things take a turn for the worse. Some outside influence—a production problem or any one of a dozen other factors—suddenly arises to turn what once was a Rolls Royce of a project into an Edsel. It's apparent to everyone witnessing this turn of events that it's time to jettison—apparent to everyone, that is, except the person running the project. He has suddenly gained a strange glint in his eye and lost most of his hearing when it comes to discussing defeat. Why?

One reason may be the project parameters themselves. Some projects by their very nature demand high up-front expenditures with long-delayed benefits. In such cases, it's not always easy to tell when failure is actually occurring, so a manager used to handling this kind of project is willing to wait patiently for the payoff—perhaps a bit too patiently if he has never failed before.

Additionally, it must be confessed that there are some projects that end up being an all-or-nothing proposition. Halfway through building an airport, the project may start shaping up to be a real dog. But what are you going to do with half an airport? Sure, when completed, the thing is going to take a loss. But will it be as big a loss as dumping the project now? Mankind has yet to find many uses for half an airport.

But project parameters are only the most obvious reason that people continue to persevere in the face of obvious failure, according to psychologists Barry M. Staw, Ph.D., and Jerry Ross, Ph.D. The subtler elements, the ones we must really be on our guard against, fall within the psychological and social realms.

Amazingly, reinforcement is number one on the hit parade of psychological factors. Amazing because typical reinforcement theory dictates that a manager should withdraw when faced with negative reinforcement in the same manner that a person would quickly remove his or her hand from a hot stove top because it hurts. But as Dr. Staw and Dr. Ross point out, many managers have experienced success in the past by ignoring negative feedback and riding out, for example, a period of slow sales until the tide turns. So what happens is that the past positive reinforcement overrides the current negative one. The problem is that the manager with a successful track record begins to have a hard time seeing the difference between a temporary low point and a bona fide nosedive. It's rather akin to gambling fever, where a player is always convincing himself that the next hand will be the one that changes his luck.

Another psychological factor that Dr. Staw and Dr. Ross target is the biased-data phenomenon. If a manager believes a project will ultimately succeed, she may slant cost estimates or potential payoffs to reflect her optimism. Let's face it, when your soul is afire with the anticipation of victory, it's not too hard to convince yourself that you can actually draw up a production schedule that demands a 100 percent increase over last year's output and that will run without a hitch for a 12-month period. Likewise, when production costs are beginning to spell out the word DANGER in 10-foot neon letters, the now trapped but still success-hungry manager may seize upon ambiguous marketing information and come to a favorably biased product-sales projection that she would have laughed at in a more lucid moment.

The most obvious social influence for persistence in the face of failure is the desire not to lose face with one's peers. No one likes to be branded a loser, and in an attempt to justify an original course of action, a manager may go to any lengths and invest additional time and resources in a failing project just to prove he was right. One almost gets an image of the manager as a mad scientist, cackling to himself in some dark Gothic castle: "Call *me* mad will they? I'll show them. I'll show them all . . . " Of course the more realistic side of this dilemma is that as a project begins to fail, invariably the manager in charge finds his name ever more closely linked with the imminent disaster: "The Janson contract? Oh, yes. Ron's carrying the ball on that one. Yes sir, Ron's the man behind that deal." Admittedly, being lassoed with responsibility in this way could drive anyone to a desperate attempt to turn things around or die trying.

Another potential lure for the unwary manager is the mantle of determined leadership that society likes to bestow on those plucky diehards who stick it out in the face of overwhelming odds. As Dr. Staw and Dr. Ross point out, if you happen to win out in the end, à la Winston Churchill or Lee Iacocca, the rewards are twice as sweet as those garnered if the situation hadn't been so chancy. This socially instituted belief that leadership is born of persistence has unfortunately led many managers to continue a failing endeavor, rather than disengage and cut their losses, lest they look like quitters.

The real question is, however, How do we guard ourselves against the potentially disastrous effects of what can only be called human pride and vanity? Dr. Staw and Dr. Ross offer two options. For a manager, the first option is to encourage an environment where accurate information is accepted and valued even if it is the harbinger of doom. If employees are not afraid to be the bearers of bad news, the manager can be somewhat assured that his attention will be called to potential danger signs. Dr. Staw and Dr. Ross go so far as to suggest the institution of a type of "quality circle" where key project people regularly meet to assess problems and chances of success. To keep it honest, executives somewhat removed from the project could be invited occasionally and asked for their unbiased opinions.

The second option is to separate the initial decision-making process from the ongoing one that will continue throughout the project. In other words, while one group may make the original decisions and plot the proposed course of action, a second group, one without quite so much personal investment in the original plan, would then ride herd over the completion of the project.

9 SURE-FIRE WAYS TO FAIL

Knowing nine ways to fail means knowing nine things that you probably won't want to try—unless you always felt that the life of a kamikaze pilot offered a world of opportunity.

The following picks are provided courtesy of Mortimer Feinberg, Ph.D., chairman of BFS Psychological Associates, a New York City management consulting firm.

1. Refuse to share your power. Insist on exclusive control and don't bother to solicit opinions, so that any flops are entirely to your discredit. "You won't survive long as an autocrat," says Dr. Feinberg. He cites the blunder of a young executive in a food distributing company who was so enamored of a new nut-and-yogurt product that he didn't consult his sales staff before ordering boxcar-loads. Then he discovered that his salespeople hated the stuff and would have gladly told him so if he'd asked. "He and his family were eating the yogurt for years," Dr. Feinberg says.

The converse of this is the survival strategy of David Dubinsky, the former head of the International Ladies' Garment Workers Union. "When things go right, I make the decisions," Dubinsky said. "When things go wrong, I look for a partner."

2. Organize the opposition. When you beat out a colleague for a promotion, make sure he stays an opponent. If you lose, hold a grudge. Never join forces with your rivals.

Lyndon Johnson was savvy enough to avoid this blunder, says Dr. Feinberg. "If he lost to an adversary, he sought reconciliation. That's why after challenging Kennedy for the presidential nomination, he could take second place on the ticket and go on to be president himself. And whenever he won, he was wise enough to bring the defeated rival into his camp."

As former baseball manager Leo Durocher once said, "I never let the four guys who hate me get together with the five that are undecided."

3. Be arrogant and treat your staff like hired hands. You'll quickly demotivate people, cripple their effectiveness, and turn potential friends into enemies. "Charles Revson of Revlon had a deserved reputation for a dictatorial attitude," says Dr. Feinberg. "He had a large security staff because he was afraid competitors would find a way to steal his product secrets. One time a security guard asked him for his pass and he instantly fired her. He said, 'She should have known who I am.' "

Adds Dr. Feinberg: "One of the executives at Estée Lauder claimed he staffed the Lauder company with refugees. 'From Germany?' someone asked. 'No, from Revlon,' he said."

4. Once you've made it to the top, disregard the people who put you there. Dr. Feinberg interviewed one executive with a strong record of achievements who tended to keep his board of directors waiting rather than interrupt his own tasks. His healthy bottom line didn't save him from getting booted in the end.

"Ignoring those who helped you rather than staying in loyal contact with them builds a lot of animosity," notes Dr. Feinberg. "This turns out to be one of the most common errors of those who failed."

5. Defer all painful judgments regarding personnel. Wait until disaster strikes to make the inevitable decision to fire that nice incompetent person on your staff.

6. Take big financial risks for relatively small rewards. "When you get carried away by your own grandiosity, you can forget the risk-to-reward ratio," says Dr. Feinberg. He gives the example of a manager who's devoted a lot of his company's resources to cut into a small, competitive market with a new product. "Even if the product succeeds, his company isn't going to make much, and if it flops, there's going to be a big loss."

7. Cling to a product or service beyond its heyday. Insist that your product, your baby, is immune to the market's life cycles. Dr. Feinberg points to the American automobile industry in the 1970s producing outmoded gas-guzzlers while a squadron of Japanese compacts whizzed by in the fast lane.

8. Release a product or service before it's ready. If your idea is so hot it's practically radioactive, why let those drones in market research and production hold things up with their boring calculations? Go for broke—literally. One computer company announced an improved model, prematurely causing customers to pass up the current version and wait for the better one, says Dr. Feinberg. But the new model hit production snags and wasn't ready on time. Cash flow dribbled to a stop and the company went belly-up.

9. Ignore your competitors. If your business is on a roll, don't keep looking over your shoulder at the other guys. Just coast. "The Swiss were shown some of the early digital watch designs, but they didn't want to make them. They said, 'It's not a watch—it doesn't have springs and gears.' They didn't think digital watches would put a dent in their market."

Note: You may not be in a position to pull blunders of the same magnitude as those mentioned above. But when you think about it, the lessons learned by others' mistakes can have a personal application as well. Just because you are currently the departmental star, for example, doesn't mean that you shouldn't keep an eye on what others in the department are doing. It could be that while you are basking in the sunshine of your own glory, the needs of the department are changing and others are making sure they answer those needs.

"Release a product or service before it's ready," can easily be transformed into a more personal prescription for failure: "Offer up a proposal before you've had a chance to iron out the bugs." Sure it's tough to keep a lid on true genius, but until you've gotten the idea up to warp speed, premature presentation will only increase your chances of getting shot down.

WHAT TO DO WHEN THE BOTTOM HAS FALLEN OUT

When the big mistake inevitably occurs, as hard as it may sound, you need to possess a certain degree of grace under pressure if you ever want to make it to the top, say Jimmy Calano and Jeff Salzman, president and vice-president of CareerTrack, a Colorado business seminar company. This is not an easy thing to do if you are sitting there with the walls closing in, waiting for dawn like some condemned prisoner. After all, who can sit passively with total calm as the world seemingly falls apart? In a nutshell, the secret to grace under pressure in these circumstances is *action*. Engage in some form of damage control and you will be so busy fighting the good fight that you just won't be able to pencil in a block of time in which you can fall to pieces.

Calano and Salzman suggest that the first thing you may want to do is to ask yourself the big question: What's the worst thing that could happen? This sets some definite parameters on the amount of destruction that may occur. Believe it or not, knowing just how bad it really is can be a lot more comforting than facing some nebulous doom that can grow as big as your imagination. Additionally, what normally ends up happening is that the mistake is rarely as bad as you thought it was. There's a good chance that at this point in your career, the decisions you need to make don't carry so much weight that if you blow one you'll level the company.

Of course, they may carry enough weight to level your career. So the next thing you need to ask yourself is, In five years will this matter to me personally? In other words, will this be a temporary career setback? Or a permanent derailment? Needless to say, there are very few bad decisions or mistakes that will totally ruin your life. If you're really worried, it may not be a bad idea to ask your manager whether you have a reason to be. At least you'll know.

Having counted the dead, so to speak, it's time to act. You may have blown it, but that doesn't mean that what's occurred is irreversible. Calano and Salzman, being the optimists they are, feel that every mistake comes with a gift in the form of a lesson or opportunity. "When the two of us missed a deadline for mailing brochures in a direct-mail campaign, we were left with a couple of truckloads of worthless brochures. The event we were promoting was three weeks away, and the post office needed *at least* two weeks to deliver the brochures. We made ourselves look for the opportunity, but what could it be? A brochure bonfire and wiener roast? A colorful landfill?"

The solution that Calano finally hit upon was to insert the brochures into the newspaper and have them delivered the next day. While it didn't work as well as if things had proceeded correctly in the first place, they did make a small profit and avoided losing a great deal of money. The lesson is never to assume a mistake is not correctable. Make yourself look for an opportunity. Face it: It's a far better way to spend your time than cashing unemployment checks. What have you got to lose?

Equally important to remember is that when failure strikes, and a solution is not immediately apparent, you should do something—no matter how minor. But many people become immobilized. They lose confidence in their own ability to do something right. At this point, they are not only out of the game, they aren't even sitting in their car in the parking lot outside the stadium. The best thing you can do for yourself is to target some minor aspect of damage control and act upon it. It may seem trivial but it will put you back on the field of play.

There are a few other things to remember when the hard times hit.

One: Don't try to hide the mistake. Problems have a way of compounding over time, and you'll be better off reporting a newborn mistake than you will reporting a six-month-old one that's had time to put on some weight. Of course, you may reason with yourself that perhaps you can rectify the situation before it ever comes to anyone's attention. Forget it. Better to face the very real possibility that the problem can't be solved completely. But what's so wrong with reporting it and *then* trying to solve it? Sure, you may take some grief for making a mistake, but on the other hand you may also get the chance to impress the boss with your dazzling damage-control abilities.

Two: Unless the cause of your problem was so far out of your control that you were in fact the mythical helpless victim of events, don't try to save yourself with excuses. Your mistake will be fairly apparent to everyone around you, and equally apparent will be the reason for the mistake. People will be much more inclined to respect you if you take responsibility for the problem. People will also be much more inclined to dislike you if you are an excuse-maker. Additionally, what many excuse-makers don't realize is that their excuses sometimes end up being veiled self-accusations. For example, a manager gets called onto the boards for a production problem in his department. His excuse is that his assistant manager made a mistake in his calculations. What happens? The manager gets chewed out anyway because he was not doing his job in overseeing the assistant manager.

Three: Calano and Salzman feel it is of the utmost importance to show some remorse when you've botched something. In an attempt to trivialize the extent of their mistake, many people will take an "Oh well, it's not *that* bad" attitude. This may be fine to keep in mind as a personal outlook; but if you voice it aloud, others will think that you don't care about your mistake, don't take things as seriously as you should, and have no desire to improve. Let them know you are sorry.

In closing, let's remember one of the thoughts we discussed at the beginning of this chapter: You can't experience great success without first experiencing great failure. This may sound somewhat Pollyannaish, but you can always consider mistakes as part of the entrance fee to fame and fortune. Besides, where did you ever get the gall to think that you were perfect?

23

FIRING

In cartoonland, the typical termination scenario plays itself out as follows: The boss, all of 3 feet tall and smoking a cigar, calls in one of his quivering employees and begins the conversation by blowing smoke into the person's eyes. After working himself up into a red-faced rage (complete with steam blowing out both ears), he jumps on top of his desk and yells "Yoooooooooooou'rrrre fired!" at the top of his lungs. With malicious glee the boss then reaches for a secret lever, and the hapless employee drops through a trapdoor into the waiting mouths of some hungry crocodiles. *Gusto* is a pale word to describe the sense of enjoyment a cartoon boss derives from a good canning.

But in the real world, everyone dreads firing time, employee and employer alike. For the employee, dread is an understandable emotion. Eating and paying the mortgage are habits most of us are loath to give up. But for the employer, firing brings up a more complex range of emotions. *Guilt.* A manager may wonder if he is at fault for an employee's failure and may have a deep-seated suspicion that an innocent person is being sent to the slaughter on his behalf. *Resentment.* Maybe the employee is a great person going through a bad time. He has to be fired, but the manager may hate the fact that this unpleasant duty falls on his shoulders. After all, the manager was hired to produce widgets, not ruin other people's lives. And then there's *sympathy.* The kind of sympathy that hurts long after quitting time. The manager knows that the firee has three kids and is struggling to make ends meet. Even though the guy has not been working up to snuff, a manager can't help but feel bad about the situation.

While these feelings cannot be eradicated entirely, the stress caused by the firing of an employee can be minimized. And in the process, by following certain procedures, you as a manager will also be giving your employees fairer treatment and a less devastating termination.

Fair firing: how to remain guilt-free and above reproach

To fire fairly and without inviting reproach, you have to be prepared. And preparation does not mean a simple review of the situation the week before termination. As strange as it may seem, preparing to fire an employee should begin almost as soon as an employee is hired.

This rather enigmatic statement does not suggest that you should be sharpening the ax 10 minutes after you hire someone. It is suggesting, however, that to fire a person fairly, you need to constantly monitor that person's work and maintain records that show beyond a shadow of a doubt that there is a problem. You also need to be able to prove that you as a manager did your level best to help the employee understand what was required of him and to show him how to rectify the problem. In other words, the secret to firing fairly is a strong reviewing process.

"To put it in a positive way, anyone with the power to hire and fire should also know that they are in a position where they are expected to plan the work of their employees, to motivate their employees, and to evaluate those employees on a regular basis," says Mary Jean Parson, consultant and author of *An Executive's Coaching Handbook*. "The best advice I can give on firing is don't do it in a hurry, don't do it emotionally, and don't do it without records. This is why a thorough and regular reviewing process is so important."

As a rule, most companies hire people for a trial period of 30, 60, or 90 days, at the end of which is a review. "At this point you check to make sure the employee understands what the position requires and the level of work you expect from him," says Parson. "Then at the end of six months you can see if the employee and the position are a good marriage. By then you've also had more time to observe the employee and make your first really comprehensive evaluation of his performance. As you set further goals, give constructive criticism, and discuss additional requirements of the position, you need to get the employee involved. Make sure that he understands what is expected and can indeed accomplish the things agreed upon. This means going so far as to write down the requirements and have the employee sign the paper."

It is enormously important to make sure that the employee understands and agrees to the requirements you've set, in case the relationship ends in termination. If the employee never really understood what you were asking of him, then in reality you may be firing him because *you* did not communicate *your* needs clearly. But having him sign off on the agreement is proof positive that the employee understood and promised to deliver. You can hardly be faulted if you must fire someone who does not honor a business agreement.

After the six-month review, employees are typically evaluated once a year. "Many managers will bring in an employee, go through a little checklist of items, and have them out the door in 10 minutes with their 7 percent raise," notes Parson. "This is better than nothing, but it's not what the reviewing process should really be. That checklist is only a starting point that the manager should use to get the employee more on track, keep him on track, and motivate him to overachieve. If a manager doesn't take the opportunity provided by a review to fine-tune the direction of his or her employees, then it really isn't fair to fire them for slipping off the path."

Besides review data, a good manager should be constantly monitoring employee performance and keeping records of accomplishments and failures, which will be added to the files. As these files grow, you will gain a

Why People Get Fired

It's not hard to guess that incompetence is the number one reason to fire an employee. But what a survey by Robert Half International has found is that *other* key factors are responsible for six out of ten firings. When asked, "Which is the single greatest reason for firing an employee?" vice-presidents of 100 of the top corporations gave the following answers.

- Incompetence—39 percent
- Inability to get along with others—17 percent
- Dishonesty or lying—12 percent
- Negative attitude—10 percent
- Lack of motivation—7 percent
- Failure or refusal to follow instructions—7 percent
- All other reasons—8 percent

With "inability to get along with others" racking up a surprising 17 percent, it may be time for you to start smiling at the person in the next cubicle a bit more often.

resource that serves two purposes. Not only will it help you promote employees when promotion is deserved, but well-maintained records can take the emotion out of a firing decision, which is equally important.

"Suddenly, your decision becomes a matter of data assessment rather than a seemingly arbitrary call," says Parson. "The records show that the employee understood what was expected and did not meet those expectations. The records show where he failed. And the records will show that you had in fact discussed the problems and agreed upon a new course of action which the employee chose not to follow. Since most of your records will have the employee's own signature at the bottom, he can hardly dispute your fairness in the situation. But even more important, should you personally doubt your decision, good records can be passed along to your supervisor for additional assessment and support."

When it becomes apparent that you *do* have a problem with an employee that has not been remedied during the reviewing process, it's time to move on to the warning system. "If the employee is not living up to expectations, you have a meeting and you document what was talked about and the course of action agreed upon," says Parson. "Be sure that you both sign the new agreement. A first warning is given and a period of time is set for the employee to make the necessary improvements."

Corporate warning policies vary, but many companies will terminate an employee after one warning. "I feel that this is somewhat precipitous," says Parson. "Better you should do a first warning and then have a review in one to two months. If things have not changed, then you give a second warning. Allow the employee a few more months to turn things around, but if there is still no improvement, at the third meeting you fire him."

Remember that you want to maintain your emotional cool when you give a warning. Don't chew the employee out. Simply state the case, reiterate the points of the agreement, and then let the employee know that the question of his termination is in his own hands. If he wishes to avoid being fired, then he needs to make the required improvements; otherwise the outcome is certain. "And when you say that you will have to fire someone, you should make sure you follow through," advises Parson. "Idle threats lose their potency after awhile."

Face-to-face: when it's time
to give the bad news

It's never easy. But if you've followed the review and warning process, at least the actual termination will not be a totally unexpected surprise to the employee. Of course, there may be times when you have to fire someone rather quickly due to downsizing or a merger. In this case, the news *will* be a surprise (to say the least). But either way, the same rules of conduct apply.

1. Be prepared for firing day. "You should have already dealt with Personnel to make sure all the records and necessities are up to date," says Parson. "You should also contact payroll and have the employee's severance check in your desk ready to hand over. Additionally, you will want to telephone the human relations/benefits department and make sure that whatever benefits the employee is entitled to are in place."

2. Tell the employee the bad news immediately. Bring him in and lay it on the table. "The person is nervous enough as it is, so don't beat around the bush and prolong the torture," says Parson. "Of course this doesn't mean that you should start off by saying 'Well, you screwed up and I'm gonna have to can you. Get out and we'll be in touch.' Instead, remind the employee of the agreement the two of you made at the last warning session. Things just haven't worked out, and now, as was mentioned previously, you have no choice but to let the employee go."

3. Move on to the good news . . . quickly. "Before the person has time to have a heart attack, follow up with the things you are going to do for him," suggests Parson. " 'Here's your severance check which includes an extra four weeks' pay [depending on your company policy]. We have engaged a firm to do some outplacement work and help you find a job. We will provide for your insurance benefits for six more months.' "

Let the employee down easy via the benefits package, and be sure to have details of the package printed out on a sheet that the employee can take home. Also take a moment to discuss what you will say should a potential employer contact you for a reference. Reassure your ex-employee that you will not be an albatross around his job-seeking neck.

The only additional way to make firing more humane is to conduct the meeting either early in the morning before the employee has started his work, or late in the day when he can go home immediately without facing his colleagues.

THE SURE-FIRE ALTERNATIVE TO FIRING

Utilizing proper review and termination techniques can go a long way toward alleviating stress on the part of both parties involved. But there just might be a better way to achieve the same end. What if the employee simply quit? Fat chance, you say? An understandable answer in light of the horror stories you may have heard concerning fired employees who continued to come to work until they were forcibly removed by security personnel. How-

T.G.I.F.?

You may not be so willing to thank God it's Friday when you learn that more people get fired on Friday afternoon than at any other time during the week. In a survey conducted by Accountemps, an accounting and bookkeeping temporary personnel service, vice-presidents and personnel directors of 100 top corporations were interviewed to find out when they preferred to do their firing. Of those expressing a preference, most (31 percent of the total sampling) favored Friday.

The next largest number, 7 percent, preferred to fire on Monday, while 2 percent named Tuesday and 2 percent selected Wednesday. Only 1 percent chose Thursday. For those of you who would prefer that your fate bore a less predictable face, you'll be happy to know that 40 percent of all the executives interviewed said that they did not make it a practice to fire on any particular day.

As far as precise timing goes, 21 percent of the respondents said they were more likely to fire in the late afternoon, 17 percent chose early afternoon, 18 percent opted for midmorning, 11 percent favored early morning, 3 percent picked noon, and 1 percent named early evening. Another 13 percent said they had no specific time of the day for firing.

So instead of rejoicing when Friday rolls around, any employee in his or her right mind would be better off saying, "Thank God it's Thursday, early evening!"

ever, if done correctly, offering an honorable way out for a wayward employee might be a smart option.

"Assuming you've had the requisite discussions with the employee concerning his areas of nonperformance, and he is crystal clear on the areas in which he is falling short, you are ready to initiate Step One of a process we've developed to persuade employees to make their own decision to quit," says Filomena Warihay, Ph.D., president of Take Charge Consultants, a training and organizational development firm based in Downingtown, Pennsylvania.

Step One: Ask yourself the "3-P" question: Does what the employee is doing or not doing adversely affect productivity, people, or profit? If the answer is yes on any of the three counts, then it's time to move on to Step Two. "But if the answer is no, then you have to ask yourself why you are so eager to part company with this person," suggests Dr. Warihay. "You'll probably discover that while the problem has something to do with personality clashes or basic value differences, it's nothing that you could call a real reason for letting a performing employee go. Step One lets you pause and differentiate between a personal problem and a situation that is costing the company."

Step Two: Do a merciless self-audit. "This is the point," says Dr. Warihay, "where you look at yourself in the mirror and say, 'Okay, I've determined that this person is costing us. Was I crystal clear with the employee concerning her behavior? Did I tell her exactly what she needed to do to improve her performance, or was I vague?'"

The next question you need to ask yourself is whether you supported the employee in making those suggested changes. "Very often a manager will say, 'I want you to get back up to par in six weeks,' and then walk away, ignoring any subtle or overt pleas for help on the part of the employee," notes Dr. Warihay. "So you have to be truthful with yourself as to whether you were a help or a hindrance to the employee's resurrection."

The third question to ask yourself in this self-audit is whether you gave the employee enough time to turn around her behavior. Two or three weeks just isn't enough. Even a Maserati can't hit 100 mph right out of the gate.

Step Three: Communicate up. Make the history of the situation known to your boss as well as to the personnel department. Let them know what's occurred and the action you've taken to date. Emphasize the possibility that the employee in question will not be working here much longer. "Very often, if you don't communicate, the person with whom you are having difficulty may complain over your head before you've had a chance to state your case," notes Dr. Warihay. "When this happens, the whole process becomes disorderly, as your superior strives to sort out conflicting stories."

Besides heading off possible confusion, communicating upward allows you to seek consensus on your decision before you do anything irreversible. Of course there is also the possibility that although a particular employee may not be working out in your department, your boss may have alternative plans for this particular person—perhaps a different job more suited to the employee's unique talents and temperament. In short, the planned dismissal of any employee should be made known to your superior as soon as possible so that the way is clear for you to take action when the time is right.

Up to this point, the procedure suggested by Dr. Warihay makes sense no matter what the firing situation may be. By following the first three steps, you'll not only make some sort of peace with yourself concerning the fairness of your termination decision, but you'll also know where you stand with your boss on the situation. In the next two steps, we begin to explore a unique variation on the typical termination scenario.

Step Four: Sit down with the individual, review the history of the problem, and then ask, "What do you think the consequences will be if your work doesn't improve?" Once you've laid out the question, clam up. "It may get a little uncomfortable, but the silence will ultimately get the words you want to hear out of the employee's mouth," says Dr. Warihay.

Naturally, the words you want to hear are "I guess you'll have to fire me." But why do you need to draw those words out of the employee's mouth rather than stating the simple fact yourself? "Because the disbelief regarding firing is phenomenal," says Dr. Warihay. "People have incredible defense systems that often keep them from realizing that something awful can really happen to them. I've found that by coaxing employees to come to their own conclusion concerning the situation, they gain a realistic acceptance of the consequences. What's more, if you get them to reach the same conclusion as you, they can scarcely argue about the legitimacy of your decision."

Once you've acknowledged the probability of the employee's conclusion, you are ready to move on to the next step.

Step Five: Tell the employee that you would like to give her a paid career-development day. "I like to have these conversations on Friday afternoon and tell employees to take Monday off at company expense," says Dr. Warihay. "And I ask them to think about whether they'd like to try to do the job as required or if they want me to help them find employment elsewhere. By giving them Monday off, I am in reality giving them three days to consider their decision rather than one. You can bet that they are already thinking about it on their way home Friday evening and will continue to review their position throughout the weekend."

Once you've offered the employee a paid career-development day, you need to make sure that she is clear about the choice that's being offered. "I tell employees that if they come to me on Tuesday morning with a decision to stay, and they can meet the work requirements that I have set, then their employment records will be wiped clean of any black marks," says Dr. Warihay. "At this point I make it very clear what is expected of them, the criteria by which the work will be judged, and the time frame in which the changes must take place."

On the other hand, the employee should also be told that if she decides to bail out, you are prepared to discuss an equitable severance package and that you will not blackball her if a potential employer calls you as a reference. Having done this, you can now send the employee home with a clear and fair choice to consider. Since neither option is any more threatening than the other, the person can make an intelligent decision rather than one based on avoiding the unpleasant.

And now the important question: Does this technique work? Like a charm, according to Emrika Padus, executive editor of *Prevention* magazine. "I had an employee who looked wonderful during the hiring process but just never seemed to get the hang of the job," she says. "During reviews we discussed her problems and possible solutions, but nothing changed. When termination seemed to be the only solution, I turned to this technique and asked her to take Friday off as a paid career-development day. I expected her answer on Monday, but she actually called from her home Friday morning to tell me that she would be leaving."

"In 20 years of management, I've only had to actually fire one person," adds Dr. Warihay. "While there will be the occasional employee who decides to stay on, most will take the opportunity to leave with grace and honor. For the ones who do opt to continue working, this technique serves as a mild reprimand that should get them remotivated. It drives home the fact that this is their last chance to make good. There's no such thing as a second paid career-development day."

How to Tell if *Your* Job Is in Jeopardy

Up until now we've discussed the art of termination from the perspective of the person in the driver's seat. But let us never forget that we, too, are but humble employees who may one day feel the breeze of a swinging ax. However, simple physics dictates that an ax cannot fall until it's been raised. And if you can see it being raised, you can move your head before it falls.

The danger signs of possible termination are many; but according to Accountemps, the world's largest accounting and data-processing personnel service, these are some of the primary ones you want to look out for.

- Your subordinates have been receiving promotions and raises; you have not.
- Choice special projects are no longer given to you.
- Your opinion is being solicited less and less frequently.
- The company retains a management consultant who asks you detailed questions about your job responsibilities and specific activities. While this may be an attempt to improve productivity and efficiency, it could also be one way of gathering information to be passed on to your imminent replacement.

- The corporation is forced to make across-the-board pay cuts, but a larger-than-average slice is taken out of your check.
- You are making more money than others doing similar work. Employees who are overpaid may be among the first to go during a business downturn. Rather than cut such a person's salary and end up with a disgruntled employee, many companies may opt to fire instead.
- Your desk is unusually clear because you're being given little new work to do. And the steady flow of interoffice memos directed to your attention inexplicably slows to a trickle.
- Your boss suddenly becomes overly critical of your work. Negative memos about your performance could be preparation for your firing. Or, conversely, management stops being the least bit critical. You may not receive any constructive criticism because you aren't expected to be on the payroll long enough to benefit from it.

Taken individually, any one of these warning signs could easily be a false alarm. The time to sit up and take notice is when you see three or more of these scenarios occurring simultaneously.

24

GOALS

A goal," says Harvey Mackay, "is just a dream with a deadline." He can't trace the source of that quote, but let's forgive Mackay this one. Fact is, this is one fellow who knows how to pursue goals. He was the owner of a $35-million-in-sales envelope company in St. Paul, Minnesota, in 1987, when he decided he wanted to write a book. Before writing word one, he interviewed several hundred writers, agents, booksellers—anyone who could offer him advice. Then, as he explains, he decided to make it a best-seller. "My goal was to get on the *New York Times* best-seller list for one week," he recalls. He knew the odds. Each year some 750,000 manuscripts make their way to publishers, and only about 55,000 of them make it into print. Of those, only a handful get to be best-sellers.

He wanted to write a business book, and he had a subtitle in mind: *Outsell, Outmanage, Outmotivate and Outnegotiate Your Competition.* Beyond that, though, he knew he needed a twist of some sort if the book were to attract serious attention. "It was my opinion that for 40 or 50 years nothing had changed in business books," he says. Most business books were about corporations, and they bore dust-jacket endorsements from corporate chairmen. "I thought, why not do a business book that could apply to life?"

So he wrote *Swim with the Sharks without Being Eaten Alive* (yes, with his planned subtitle). To inspire himself during the year-long writing process, he posted on his wall a copy of the *New York Times* best-seller list, into which his secretary had typed *Swim with the Sharks* for number five.

Mackay realized that to market the book successfully—who outside of the Twin Cities had ever heard his name?—he would have to attract endorsements from well-known people. His goal, he determined, was to generate blurbs from a uniquely diverse mix of celebrities. "I wanted to show that a variety of people who probably couldn't agree on anything else in life could agree on the value of this book," he explains.

How did a mere envelope-maker manage to gather endorsements from the likes of Robert Redford, Mario Cuomo, Gloria Steinem, Billy Graham, Abigail Van Buren, Gerald Ford, and the many other celebrities who lent their name to his project? A hyper-networker, Mackay maintains a Rolodex consisting of more than 5,000 individuals (and including countless details about each). For example, Ted Koppel spoke in St. Paul a few years back and Mackay introduced him. And kept in touch. He met Abigail Van Buren during one of her trips to Minneapolis, and he entered her on his Rolodex. As a local civic leader, he had dinner with Gerald Ford a few times over the years and took note of the corporate boards on which the former president sat. Then, when he needed an endorsement, he simply cross-referenced his Rolodex for folks who sat on the same boards and wrote to them, asking if they'd mind sending a copy of his book to Ford.

It all paid off. *Swim with The Sharks* sold 2.3 million copies and has been translated into 16 languages. It was on the *New York Times* best-seller list not for 1 week but for 54 weeks. As a result of the book's phenomenal success, Mackay became one of the nation's most sought-after public speakers; his speeches earn him about $1.4 million a year. His second book, *Beware the Naked Man Who Offers You His Shirt: Do What You Love, Love What You Do, and Deliver More Than You Promise*, leaped to number four on the *New York Times* best-seller list of how-to books just five days after it arrived in bookstores.

Mackay is a big booster of the goal-setting process. A few years ago, a goal helped him train for and successfully complete the New York Marathon (at age 55, after six months of training). More recently a goal helped him to find a major company to acquire. "If you have a clear, concise goal, the probability of success goes up dramatically," he says. "This is true at any stage of your life. And it's fun. Don't you think it's fun to continually improve yourself?"

HOW TO SET GOALS

Goals provide you with a feeling of control, a sense that you are calling the shots in your life, which can be particularly important when it comes to your career. "People who blow with the wind usually end up living lives of quiet desperation. They get to be 60 years old and wish they could do it all over again. But by that point it's too late," says Dallas career consultant

Taunee Besson. "Choosing not to set career goals allows other people and events to make choices for you." Establishing goals, on the other hand, furnishes you with a clear-cut destination, and gives you a yardstick to help measure your advancement. Here's how to do it:

Determine what you want to accomplish. The first step in establishing a goal is the one that generally causes us to stumble: We have to figure out exactly what it is we want to accomplish. Then we have to determine which smaller steps will get us there. (This advice from kindergarten still holds: The best way to pursue a big goal is to break it up into smaller ones.) Then, of course, we have to impose a deadline on our aims.

Establish a time frame. On the one hand, there are day-to-day goals ("I will contact one new potential employer each day") and short-term goals ("I will read all of Peter Drucker's management books"). Generally speaking, these shorter-term goals keep us moving in the right direction. On the other hand, midterm goals ("I will earn my MBA in three years of night school") and long-range goals ("I will find funding and launch a newsletter for personnel recruiters in the electronics field within five years") provide us with a strong sense of our individual purpose.

"You time your goals either on external needs or on what your past experience has been," explains Edwin A. Locke, Ph.D., professor of business and management at the University of Maryland and coauthor of *Goal Setting: A Motivational Technique That Works!* If you don't have a contract or a deadline staring you in the face—providing you with a calendar for your goals whether you want one or not—decide what you can realistically accomplish in a given period, and then push yourself for a little more. If you know you can make 4 sales calls a day, try for 22 calls a week. When it comes to long-term objectives, provide regular checkpoints to gauge your progress.

Be flexible. Neither your goals nor the time frame should be inflexible. You change. Conditions change. There's no reason why you shouldn't be able to alter your goals. After all, your goals of owning your own ten-room home by age 28 may turn out to be folly if mortgage interest rates and the real estate market conspire to make home ownership a bad financial move.

Whether you are establishing your own career and personal goals or helping your employees set performance targets, Mackay suggests you remember that goals should have three basic components.

1. Goals should be measurable. Example: "I want to achieve $50,000 worth of sales a month."

2. Goals should be easily identified. "I want to improve my negotiating and communication skills to the point where I am promoted to assistant department manager."
3. Goals should be written down. "Pale ink is infinitely better than the most attentive memory," says Mackay. Besson concurs: "Seeing it in black and white gives it more validity. It makes your goals more real."

Besson suggests you enlist friends to help you monitor your progress—basically as a way of backing yourself into a corner. "The prospect of disappointing someone else may keep you on track," she says.

SETTING GOALS WITH YOUR BOSS

There are a number of reasons that you should both articulate your goals to your boss and enlist her cooperation in helping you set them up. For one thing, it shows your boss that you are actively and aggressively seeking what you want, which is a good image to project. For another, it indicates that you have faith in yourself. Also, says Besson, by working together with your boss on establishing your objectives, you set a self-fulfilling prophecy into motion. The collaborative effort of setting a goal puts you and your boss on the same team. Because your boss has helped you formulate those goals, she will feel she has a stake in your success. "Since she's helped you set those goals, she's more likely to help create the environment that fosters them," explains Besson. Also, your boss now knows exactly where you are headed. And as you meet each of the targets along the way, your progress becomes that much clearer to her.

SETTING GOALS WITH YOUR EMPLOYEES

As a manager, you've got your organizational goals to achieve. Your employee has his personal goals he wants to attain. In the majority of cases, the two shouldn't be mutually exclusive. In most well-run workplaces, the boss asks the subordinate to explain his long-term goals, then he shows the subordinate exactly what it's going to take to meet them. In effect, you help articulate the steps in the goal-reaching process. Sometimes it may sound as formidable as this: "You want to be vice-president? First you've got to have three years of successful experience in finance. Then you need a couple of years working in human resources. Of course, you'll have to run a plant for a year. And, by the way, you'll probably need to get some training in public speaking . . . "

Performance targets, which are continual, shorter-term workplace goals, are different. To begin the process of establishing performance targets for your employees, ask them for their input on what they feel they can accomplish and how quickly they can do it. Discuss with them their past performance and any potential obstacles you envision, and then draw on your own instincts. Make it clear that the targets are guidelines that can be altered. Says Dr. Locke, "If the performance expectation proves to be preposterous, then revise the goals accordingly."

He adds that you should never use the goal as a club with which you mercilessly beat an employee, making him or her feel totally inadequate. For example, you may have insisted that members of your sales force achieve a 30 percent increase in performance over the course of the year, and stressed that absolutely nothing less than 30 percent will do. But by midyear, someone may have posted only a 2 percent increase. At this point, harping on the (seemingly) unachievable target could be counterproductive. "He or she may just give up, without even trying to do better," warns Dr. Locke. "Or that employee could be tempted to cheat by falsifying data." Instead of punishing an employee who doesn't meet goals, make an effort to understand why the goals are not being met. Then, if necessary, lower the goals.

WHEN YOU FALL SHORT OF YOUR GOALS

Figure out what went wrong. Derailment happens to everybody, and the best thing to do to get back on track is to make an honest effort to figure out what knocked you off in the first place. Was your bid for success far too unrealistic? Were there roadblocks you never could have anticipated? Were your estimates of the time needed to reach your targets based on erroneous information? Have you simply lost interest? The next step: Determine how (or even *if*) you can avoid whatever it was that threw you off.

Develop a support system. Another thing that can help is an honest-to-goodness support system—friendly folks with whom you can discuss your failure and solicit advice on where you went astray and how to proceed. Suggests Besson: "Get together with people who know you and like you, and brainstorm with them."

Don't call it a catastrophe if it isn't. "When failure happens, we often blow it out of proportion," says Besson. "It helps to step back and try to be objective. First, ask yourself, what's the real likelihood that you're doomed forever? Then try to envision the worst-case scenario that might result from your failure to achieve your desired goals. Draw up a strategy, a list of possible options for that unlikely outcome. "This takes the bite out the situation and helps you look at things a bit more realistically," explains Besson. "If you have a strategy for dealing with the worst case, you'll most certainly be able to deal with any less-than-worst case."

Revise your goals. Accept the fact that your goals are a bit too ambitious, and set about revising them. Break down your bigger aims into smaller ones that will be easier to achieve.

Don't give up. Don't make the self-defeating mistake of simply abandoning your goals. Remember the words that Babe Ruth once told a reporter: "Every time I miss the ball I get excited. It means I'm just one swing closer to my next home run."

25

HEALTH

Considering the fact that there are more parts to your body than there are nasty rumors flying around your office, there is little chance that we can cover the entire subject of health in one slim chapter. What we can do, however, is home in on those "little" health problems which, by rearing their inconvenient heads in the workplace, can subtly sabotage your career.

Whether or not the earth will eventually fall away from the sun and plunge itself into another ice age does not hinge on your dandruff problem. On the other hand, you should realize that a little thing such as dandruff flakes garnishing the shoulders of your navy blue dress suit *is* going to affect your business associates' opinion of you. Negatively, that is.

What happens is this. You're presenting an idea to the senior VP at an informal lunch meeting. The idea is really good. The VP thinks you're one sharp executive. But as his eyes keep wandering back to your shoulders, he finds himself wondering why such an effective, intelligent person can't take care of such a minor problem. Unconsciously, there is something that will continue to bother him about you.

Or perhaps you suffer from another minor problem, halitosis. No matter how brilliant your ideas are, if your breath is anything less then frankin-cense-and-myrrh-sweet, it's not going to be enjoyable for other people to listen to your ideas. Instead they will try to avoid talking with you.

None of the body's more embarrassing shortcomings are likely get you fired. But they can slow you up in a way you barely notice. And the worst part is that no one will ever come out and tell you that you have a problem or that it bothers him.

But enough about social embarrassment. A judicious application of the following tips will help put all of that to rest. You'll also find advice for handling vitality-sapping factors that can interfere with your optimal functioning in the workplace. The prescription drugs you take, the chair you sit on, and the computer screen you look at can all conspire to throw your body (and therefore your mind) out of kilter. Let's look at these

The 10 Top Ways to Quit Smoking

Each day it seems as if yet another major corporation jumps on the no-smoking bandwagon. As it becomes increasingly taboo to light up in the office, smokers have one of two alternatives. The first is to go outside 15 times a day (not a pleasant prospect during the monsoon season). The second is to quit.

If you're hoping to give your monogrammed cigarette case a ceremonial burial, you may want to consider the relative success rates of the various smoking-cessation methods before choosing a plan of action. According to *Review and Evaluation of Smoking Cessation Methods,* by Jerome L. Schwartz, Ph.D., here are the top 10.

Method	Success Rate (%)
1. Smokenders	40
2. Rapid smoking (smoking many cigarettes very fast, under a doctor's care, to almost cause illness)	34
3. Cold turkey	33
4. Audio or video tapes (e.g., "In Control" offered by the American Lung Association)	30
5. Fresh Start (offered by the American Cancer Society)	30
6. Nicotine chewing gum	23
7. Graduated filters (e.g., Teledyne WaterPik's One Step at a Time)	22
8. Hypnosis	18
9. Acupuncture	16
10. Nicotine fading (progressively switching to lower-nicotine brands)	10

problems one at a time to discover the path to a healthier, more comfortable work experience.

BACK PROBLEMS

Did you know that sitting can put 40 percent more pressure on your spinal disks than standing does? With this in mind, it becomes apparent that back problems are not the exclusive domain of construction workers. As an executive seat warmer, the chair you sit in and how you sit in it can give you problems unmatched by merely carrying around a 50-pound sack of concrete.

Your office chair should be low enough that your feet are planted firmly on the floor and your knees are at the same height as your thighs when you sit, says Robert Arndt, Ph.D., of the Department of Preventive Medicine, University of Wisconsin. Sitting positions where your knees are higher than your thighs (chair too low) or your legs are dangling (chair too high) can cause aches in your back, bottom, and legs. If your chair won't adjust as low as it should, use a footrest.

Things to look for in an office chair:

- Armrests so that your arms can help support the load of sitting.
- A waterfall or scroll edge on the chair's bottom cushion to keep the circulation from being cut off to your legs.
- A five-blade pedestal for better stability.

COLDS AND FLU

The object most likely to give you a cold is the human hand, says Jack Gwaltney, M.D., head of epidemiology and virology at the University of Virginia School of Medicine. Rhinoviruses, the nasty little bugs that cause all the misery, are particularly well suited to sticking to hands. Cold sufferers who do have the virus on their hands (after a hearty sneeze) can infect you. With all the hand shaking that goes on at work, the big tip is to wash your hands frequently during the cold and flu season.

While colds and flu are inherently different diseases, they do have one thing in common. Both produce the most physical symptoms in the morning and cause the greatest mental impairment in the afternoon. So if you've got a cold or the flu, you'll be better off taking care of more demanding thinking tasks in the morning even though you may feel at your worst.

Got an important presentation to give, and want to keep the hacking down to a minimum? Try eating something that contains a healthy dose of chili pepper. This centuries-old medicine for bronchitis contains a chemical called capsaicin, which thins mucus and decreases coughing.

DANDRUFF

While dandruff is often a consequence of scalp bacteria, hormone production, and oil gland malfunction, it can also result from inorganic causes such as infrequent shampooing, improper rinsing, overconditioning, and even sunburn.

Besides using a dandruff shampoo, try to spend some time in direct sunlight. Half an hour or less of ultraviolet exposure per day may have an anti-inflammatory effect on a scaly skin condition.

If you do use a dandruff shampoo, keep in mind that it will probably lose its effectiveness in about three months no matter how well it works initially. Your skin may develop a temporary resistance to the active ingredient in any dandruff shampoo. For continued effective treatment, plan to switch your brand every few months.

FLATULENCE

We won't even go into the ways this little problem can quickly sabatoge the most meticulously planned presentation or meeting. Instead let's cut to the chase with these six ways to curb a potentially embarrassing reaction.

- Eat meals slowly and chew food thoroughly.
- Avoid chewing gum or sucking on hard candies.
- Eliminate carbonated beverages like beer and soda from your diet.
- If necessary, temporarily cut back on these high-octane gas-makers: cauliflower, brussels sprouts, dried beans, broccoli, cabbage, and bran.
- Briefly eliminate milk and milk products from your diet to see if symptoms disappear. If they do, you could have a lactose intolerance problem. But check with your doctor to be certain.

HALITOSIS

A fast way to tell if you have bad breath: Lick the back of your hand, wait a minute or two, and then smell the results.

Oftentimes halitosis is a result of air being blown over something that doesn't smell too good . . . such as inflamed gums. To whip ailing gums into shape, brush thoroughly and often, and don't forget to floss.

While you're brushing your teeth, don't forget your tongue. In a study by Joseph Tonzetich, Ph.D., a Canadian professor of dentistry, toothbrushing produced a 25 percent reduction in offensive "morning mouth," while tongue brushing provided a 75 percent reduction. Combining the two would yield an 85 percent reduction. In Dr. Tonzetich's opinion, tongue brushing is the single most effective method of decreasing breath odor.

Even if your big meeting is two days away, be careful how much onion, garlic, and spicy smoked meat you have for dinner tonight. Because they contain compounds that actually enter the bloodstream, these foods can turn your mouth into a war zone for up to 72 hours while they exit the body—particularly through the lungs.

Believe it or not, overuse of mouthwashes may be the reason for your bad breath. Too much of a good thing can irritate your gums, scientists say. Try a breath mint instead.

HANGOVERS

You had one too many last night and now you're facing the new day with a head that could probably find more company in your vegetable garden than at your place of business. What do you do? Reach for some fruit. Research shows that fructose (the sugar naturally occurring in fruit) can speed up your body's ability to burn alcohol.

HEADACHES

Here are 19 food items that can trigger a migraine headache in susceptible individuals: alcohol, avocados, bacon, bananas, broad beans, canned figs, cheese, chicken livers, chocolate, citrus fruits, coffee, herring, hot dogs, monosodium glutamate (MSG), nuts, onions, sausage, tea, and yogurt.

To get rid of a headache, try using acupressure, the needle-less form of acupuncture. Find a point between the outer corner of your eye and the outer end of your eyebrow. Your finger should be on a ridge of bone, the outer edge of the eye socket. Now move a finger's width toward your ear and you'll find a small hollow. (If you're as far back as the large hollow of the temple, you've gone too far.) Find the spot on both sides of your head, then using only the tips of your fingers, press in a circular motion for 15 to 20 seconds.

HICCUPS

While hardly fatal, an ill-timed bout of the hiccups can almost cause death by embarrassment. The trick to stopping hiccups is to either increase carbon dioxide levels in the blood or overwhelm the nerve impulses causing the hiccups. Here are a few remedies frequently applied by doctors and laymen alike.

- Try filling a glass of water, bending over forward, and drinking upside down from the opposite side of the glass.
- Swallow a teaspoon of sugar dry.
- Hold your breath as long as possible and swallow at the same time that you feel the hiccup sensation coming.
- Blow in and breathe out of a brown paper bag repeatedly. Make sure the bag forms a good seal around your mouth.

Bosses Live Longer Than Subordinates

Along with more money, prestige, and responsibility, those successful in their climb up the corporate ladder can expect an even better job benefit: more years of life.

Executives and managers live an average of five years longer than their subordinates, says John H. Howard, Ph.D., a professor and management psychologist at the University of Western Ontario.

"A number of studies have shown that job satisfaction is the best predictor of longevity—maybe even better than regularly seeing your family doctor," says Dr. Howard. "And the people in management positions are generally more satisfied with their jobs. Even if the job is demanding, as long as they enjoy their work, they tend to live longer than people in a less stressful job that's lower on the company ladder."

Call it the power of power. "The higher up you go in the company, the more control or power you have. And power is very therapeutic when it comes to stress," notes Dr. Howard. "By comparison, perhaps the biggest stressor in most people's lives is a feeling of helplessness. Someone with a high-demand, high-control job is actually under less stress than someone with a low-demand, low-control job because there isn't that feeling of helplessness, of not being able to control one's own destiny."

PRESCRIPTION DRUG REACTIONS

Normally, if we're taking a prescription medicine, we only think of it once every 4 hours or so when we have to choke it down. And then we forget about it, confident that it is smoothly conducting its healing business in some mysterious part of our body. What we don't realize is that many prescription drugs have side effects that allow them to set up a branch office in the brain. Once there, their ensuing effects are varied, to say the least. Some drugs will instill you with a mild euphoria, while others can cause paranoid thinking, concentration impairment, and a host of other less-than-welcome side effects.

Rarely do we ever consider a prescription drug as the possible source of a workplace problem, unless a physician alerts us at the time he or she is prescribing the medicine. But it could be that your sudden inability to concentrate has nothing to do with your lack of sleep or a new love interest and everything to do with the cold medication you're taking. Likewise, you should be on the alert for sudden mood swings in your boss. Maybe you *have* fallen out of favor with her. On the other hand, it could be the new prescription she got filled yesterday.

Below is a list of drugs that can cause mental side effects. Keep in mind, however, that these reactions are not written in stone. A drug that may send one person straight up a wall may not do a single unpleasant thing to you. Use the list as a starting point, but talk to your doctor to get the whole story.

DRUGS REPORTED TO IMPAIR CONCENTRATION AND/OR MEMORY

Antihistamines
Barbiturates
Benzodiazepines
Isoniazid
Monoamine oxidase (MAO)
  inhibitor drugs

Phenytoin
Primidone
Scopolamine

DRUGS REPORTED TO CAUSE CONFUSION, DELIRIUM, OR DISORIENTATION

Acetazolamide
Aminophylline
Antidepressants
Antihistamines
Atropine-like drugs

Barbiturates
Benzodiazepines
Bromides
Carbamazepine
Chloroquine

Cimetidine
Cortisone-like drugs
Cycloserine
Digitalis
Digitoxin
Digoxin
Disulfiram
Ethchlorvynol
Ethinamate
Fenfluramine
Glutethimide
Isoniazid

Levodopa
Meprobamate
Para-aminosalicylic acid
Phenelzine
Phenothiazines
Phenytoin
Piperazine
Primidone
Propranolol
Reserpine
Scopolamine

DRUGS REPORTED TO CAUSE PARANOID THINKING

Bromides
Cortisone-like drugs
Diphenhydramine

Disulfiram
Isoniazid
Levodopa

DRUGS REPORTED TO CAUSE NERVOUSNESS (ANXIETY AND IRRITABILITY)

Amantadine
Amphetamine-like drugs
  (appetite suppressants)
Antihistamines
Caffeine
Chlophenesin
Cortisone-like drugs
Ephedrine
Epinephrine
Isoproterenol
Levodopa

Liothyronine (in excessive
  dosage)
Methylphenidate
Methysergide
Monoamine oxidase (MAO)
  inhibitor drugs
Nylidrin
Oral contraceptives
Theophylline
Thyroid (in excessive dosage)
Thyroxine (in excessive dosage)

DRUGS REPORTED TO CAUSE EMOTIONAL DEPRESSION

Amantadine
Amphetamine (on withdrawal)
Benzodiazepines
Carbamazepine
Chloramphenicol
Cortisone-like drugs
Cycloserine

Digitalis
Digitoxin
Digoxin
Diphenoxylate
Estrogen
Ethionamide
Fenfluramine (on withdrawal)

Fluphenazine
Guanethidine
Haloperidol
Indomethacin
Isoniazid
Levodopa
Methsuximide
Methyldopa
Methysergide

Metoprolol
Oral contraceptives
Phenylbutazone
Procainamide
Progesterones
Propranolol
Reserpine
Sulfonamides

DRUGS REPORTED TO CAUSE EUPHORIA

Amantadine
Aminophylline
Amphetamines
Antihistamines (some)
Antispasmodics, synthetic
Aspirin
Barbiturates
Benzphetamine
Chloral hydrate
Clorazepate
Codeine
Cortisone-like drugs
Diethylpropion
Diphenoxylate

Ethosuximide
Flurazepam
Haloperidol
Levodopa
Meprobamate
Methysergide
Monoamine oxidase (MAO)
    inhibitor drugs
Pargyline
Pentazocine
Phenmetrazine
Propoxyphene
Scopolamine
Tybamate

DRUGS REPORTED TO CAUSE EXCITEMENT

Acetazolamide
Amantadine
Amphetamine-like drugs
Antidepressants
Antihistamines
Atropine-like drugs
Barbiturates (paradoxical
    response)
Benzodiazepines (paradoxical
    response)
Cortisone-like drugs
Cycloserine

Diethylpropion
Digitalis
Ephedrine
Epinephrine
Ethinamate (paradoxical
    response)
Ethionamide
Glutethimide (paradoxical
    response)
Isoniazid
Isoproterenol
Levodopa

Meperidine and monoamine
oxidase (MAO) inhibitor
drugs
Methyldopa and monoamine
oxidase (MAO) inhibitor
drugs

Methyprylon (paradoxical
response)
Nalidixic acid
Orphenadrine
Quinine
Scopolamine

VISION PROBLEMS

Tight shirt collars (½ inch too small) can put a significant squeeze on the finer workings of the retina by restricting blood flow to the head, according to Cornell University researcher Susan Wilkins. The resulting vision impairment could adversely affect your work, especially if your job involves long hours in front of a video display terminal (VDT).

In trying to assimilate all the information that scrolls by on a VDT, or computer screen, your eyes shift into overdrive and do not blink as much. Make an effort to blink more and you'll give the cornea (the lens portion of the eye) the lubrication it needs to work well. This technique will help decrease eyestrain and fatigue significantly, according to ophthalmologist Frank J. Weinstock, M.D.

More on beating VDT-induced eyestrain: Try using *New York Times* computer columnist Peter Lewis's 20–20 rule when working for long hours in front of a screen. Make sure your eyes are no closer than 20 inches from the screen, and give yourself a break every 20 minutes. The break needn't be anything more elaborate than focusing on an object 20 feet or more away for a few minutes. Try looking at a tree outside your office window.

26

HIRING

In a way, the hiring process resembles nothing so much as it does a scene from "The Dating Game." On one side of a wall is you with your handful of questions and your good judgment. On the other side are several eager contestants, each hoping to be the chosen one. Within a brief span of time you have to decide, based upon the cleverness of their answers, which one gets to spend a weekend in Mexico with you.

Granted, in an interview situation, you normally get to see your choices before deciding. Additionally, you will rarely find yourself asking questions such as "Bachelor or Bachelorette No. 1, if we were a couple of duck-billed platypuses, what is the mating call you would use to attract me?" But the bottom line is that you are still required to pick a total stranger and put him or her in a position of trust.

This means that you need to gather as much job-related information as possible in the shortest amount of time. Right there you have a large task on your hands, because work-related information not only includes details such as whether or not the applicant has ever operated a Mark 7000 graphics computer (or even seen a picture of one) but additionally encompasses a broad range of personal characteristics such as creativity, ability to work under stress, and integrity.

Clouding the whole issue is the fact that the applicant is nervous, has read the same five books on interviewing that you have, and will say just about anything to get this position. He will gladly reinterpret his entire job history in a way that will make you think you are speaking to the patron saint of work.

Fortunately, there are ways to get the information you need by falling back on some simple techniques that bring focus to the process, create a stress-free environment, and get at the strengths and weaknesses a candidate has to offer your company.

CREATING THE PERFECT INTERVIEWING ENVIRONMENT

It used to be a widely held belief that the best way to test an applicant's mettle was to create a pressure-filled interview environment. After all, if she can hold up under the Spanish Inquisition, she can hold up under anything. "But what you really want to do is put the applicant at ease," says David Arnold, Ph.D., vice-president of research and general counsel for Reid Psychological Systems. "Keep in mind that once the applicant is hired and trained, except for brief, intermittent periods of stress, she will feel at ease and familiar with the job. You want to find out how she performs when she is comfortable."

To do this, the first thing you may want to consider is the seating arrangement. "There's nothing wrong with the standard face-to-face-from-across-a-desk situation," notes Dr. Arnold. "As a matter of fact, most applicants expect and are prepared for this type of arrangement. But when you run into particularly uneasy applicant, try moving a chair over to the other side of the desk and sitting next to her. This can alleviate a hierarchical situation where you are the interviewer, she is the interviewee, and never the twain shall meet." One further note on this topic: If there will be more than one interviewer, avoid the firing-squad effect, where the applicant finds herself facing three people sitting in a row behind a table. Instead, arrange the seating beforehand so that a more sociable circle is achieved.

Once everyone is more or less comfortable, start off with the easiest questions first. "Let the applicant talk a little bit about what she knows best, such as her work history," suggests Dr. Arnold. "Once she's settled in, you can move on to more probing questions that may require some fast thinking, analysis, and creativity. By using this technique, one frequently incorporated into intelligence tests, you allow the applicant to build up enough initial confidence to provide you with better answers on the more difficult questions."

"Equally important in putting an applicant at ease is to make sure you provide a lot of verbal and nonverbal feedback while he is speaking," says Roger Flax, Ph.D., president of Motivational Systems, a publicly owned consulting firm in West Orange, New Jersey. "You need to show that you are genuinely interested in what he is saying." Nod your head, and occasionally say "good" or "that's fine." Remember, the applicant is going to be looking for a reaction on your part. You may think he is wonderful, but if you don't show it, he is not going to know it and will start to lose confidence.

WHAT SHOULD YOU ASK?

Asking truly penetrating questions is a science. And as with any science, there are a variety of techniques that can be applied. One technique you want to avoid, though, is developing overly subtle tests of the applicant's character. A famous example was retailing wizard J. C. Penney's penchant for inviting applicants to breakfast and serving eggs. If the person put salt and pepper on the eggs before tasting them, Mr. Penney did not make a job offer. The reasoning behind this was that the person made decisions without sufficient information. Penney's hypothesis may have been correct, but there is no way of being sure without giving the same test to thousands of people and then following their decision-making history for several years. The bottom line: Don't ask an applicant hazy questions in an amateurish attempt to psychoanalyze him.

Simplicity and directness are best. In your most simple and direct manner, the first thing you want to do is make out a question sheet in advance. "The primary reason for doing this is to avoid having to think up questions during the interview," says Dr. Flax. "If the applicant is answering the question you just asked, and you are phrasing the question you're about to ask, you're probably going to miss some important information."

"Another good reason for a prepared question list is that it brings standardization to the interviewing process," points out Dr. Arnold. "If you're interviewing ten applicants and haven't written down the questions, chances are you won't be asking everyone the same ones. When it comes time to compare results, it will be like trying to academically rate students who all took different tests." Naturally there will be a few questions that might differ depending on an applicant's experience, but you do want the general core of your interviews to remain the same.

In planning the questions you want to ask, you first need to consider what the job requires. What kinds of skills should the candidate possess? What personality traits? What sort of knowledge? What will he be responsible for? Additionally, when questioning the candidate about what he has accomplished, you'll want to gauge his potential. Hopefully you're hiring some promotable material, so ask a few questions to test the applicant's judgment outside the sphere of expertise required by the current position.

Among the areas you want to probe are the person's intelligence, judgment, background, personality, skills, and knowledge of the field. To do all that, you'll need to rely on a smorgasbord of questions, each having a different effect.

To GAUGE JUDGMENT

To determine the applicant's ability to think fast and use good judgment, Dr. Flax suggests these questions.

- "What would you do if you learned that your manager was embezzling thousands of dollars from your company?"
- "If I were to ask your current boss to evaluate you, what would he say?"
- "How would you rate me as an interviewer?"

All three questions require tact on the part of the applicant. The first one lets you see how effectively he can deal with a potentially embarrassing problem. The second requires a sincere understanding of his own strengths and weaknesses. (You'll also be able to see to what degree he candy-coats himself.) The third question reveals how diplomatic he can be without fawning.

"When rating responses, keep in mind that hesitation will sometimes signify a lack of sincerity," says Dr. Flax. "Nervousness in the voice may represent a lack of confidence and an inability to think under pressure. In general, the answer you want will be calm and articulate, radiating confidence and an underlying sincerity."

To GAUGE EXPERIENCE

No matter how charming, diplomatic, and fast-thinking an applicant is, keep in mind that you are looking for specific expertise. In an attempt to cover a lot of ground and fill out a general portrait of the applicant, many interviewers neglect skill-related questions that get down to the nitty-gritty of what the person actually knows and has accomplished. Recruitment expert Robert Half, in his book *Robert Half on Hiring*, counsels that you need to get specific. "If you are not conversant in the technical requirements of the offered position, make sure you have someone there who is," he stresses. "Pump interviewees for detailed examples of how they fit the requirements, and look for instances where they successfully utilized the skills you are looking for."

Half recommends asking some of the following questions as a way to get detailed information on experience and skill.

1. "What did you do yesterday—in detail?"
2. "How would you solve this problem?" (Refer to a situation that occurs frequently in the position being offered.)
3. "What particular strengths did you bring to your last position?"
4. "What are some of the things your company might have done to be more successful?"

Question one is the perfect alternative to the ubiquitous and rather bland "Tell me a little bit about what you do." First of all it gives the applicant a concise direction in which to move. Second, it brooks no vague job descriptions such as "Well, I manage the product development department and work closely with my people on creating new ways to utilize dental floss." Using this question will pinpoint to an atom what this person's actual contributions are to his department.

Question two gives you a fast idea of the applicant's experience. Has he run into this problem before? If not, does his accumulated knowledge allow him to synthesize a solution quickly? Couple this question with one that is not so problem-oriented. You want to make sure he can also work well when the sky is not falling.

Question three determines if the applicant has any clue as to what the most important factors of his job are. It's nice to be a slow, methodical perfectionist, for example, but not if what the job really requires is the ability to make snap decisions under pressure. People often value personal attributes that may not be worth a dime in certain situations.

Finally, question four goes for broad scope. Was the applicant in a high enough position to get a good overview of the company? (This is a good way to check for inflated job descriptions.) If so, does he have enough creativity and business knowledge to make some insightful suggestions? As a bonus, you may also uncover a little nest of dissatisfaction with a previous job if the applicant's assessment is a little too vitriolic.

To gauge leadership potential

Next you want to explore the applicant's capacity to lead. How does he get along with other people? What's his style? Is he the kind of person who will work hard, bloom creatively, and make the best of any situation? Dr. Flax likes to begin with a few action-oriented questions.

1. "What would you do if an employee came to you with a personal family problem?"
2. "How would you handle a productive employee who complains about petty issues?"

3. "How would you motivate an employee who is suffering from job burnout?"

Aimed at applicants looking for a management position, these questions cover a lot of ground. The first question looks for empathy and efficiency in dealing with a touchy situation. It's also interesting to see whether the applicant knows where to draw the line and suggest that the employee seek professional help. Question two reveals how the applicant will deal with a troublesome employee who is still of great value to the company. Can the person be straightened out without being antagonized? Question three looks for one of the most valuable managerial assets—the ability to motivate and even inspire employees.

To gauge personal strengths and weaknesses

On the subject of personality, Robert Half suggests a few questions that can be applied in just about any situation.

1. "What was the biggest failure you've had in business?"
2. "What risks did you take in your last two jobs, and what were the results?"
3. "Describe the best boss you ever had."
4. "Tell me about your hobbies and interests."
5. "What do you think might differentiate you from other applicants?"
6. "Why do you think we should hire you?"

Question one lets you see how well the applicant knows himself and how comfortable (and honest) he is about revealing a weakness. If the applicant has any savvy whatsoever, he will make sure to tell you what he learned from a particular failure.

On the average, successful people take more calculated risks. Question two lets you see if your applicant is a risk-taker and with what degree of success he has managed those risks. Keep in mind that he probably won't tell you about risks that backfired. So if he can't think of any examples, you can assume either that he is *not* a risk-taker or that he is a poor one at best.

Question three allows you to determine the kind of management or supervision structure under which the applicant most desires to work. If he mentions a boss who allowed a lot of freedom, you can bet that he will not appreciate close supervision.

By asking about hobbies and interests, you will accomplish two things. First, you find out whether you're talking to a creative, lively, and active person . . . or a sponge. Intelligent people have active minds and are constantly exercising them in their spare time. Second, you want to make sure that the applicant doesn't have a hobby that will interfere with his work. Think twice before hiring a person who plays in a rock band four nights a week and doesn't get home until 3:00 in the morning.

The last two questions serve a double purpose. Open-ended questions such as these not only give the applicant an all-out opening to sell himself as best he can, they also let you see how well he can conduct himself orally. Does he speak persuasively and with intelligence? Is he aware of what makes him unique, and more important, what makes him uniquely suited to the job?

PICKING A WINNER

You've asked all the right questions and the applicants have done their level best in answering them. Now it's back to you for the big decision. This is where the decision-making process can bog down or go astray in the face of overwhelming amounts of data.

"You'll want to make sure you took some good notes during the interview," says Dr. Arnold. "But don't do it so extensively that you miss something the applicant is saying. Either come up with a concise way of scoring answers and jotting down highlights or have someone else present to take more in-depth notes."

Not only will your notes become invaluable when making comparisons among a dozen applicants, but they may also bring to light a candidate who scored high yet didn't exactly ring your bell during the interview. "It isn't uncommon to get off on the wrong foot in an interview, form a negative opinion, and maintain it throughout the entire meeting," says Dr. Arnold. "Without good notes you are likely to remember only the negativity and completely ignore what may have been a whole series of beautifully answered questions coupled with flawless credentials."

After each interview, take an additional 10 minutes to write down personal feelings about the applicant and to expand on some of the interview notes. Do this while it's fresh in your mind.

Understanding which questions are the most important and which answers are the ones you're looking for comes largely from a complete understanding of the job being offered. Everyone wants a winner, and it's hard not to admire a high-spirited, fast-thinking, and creative person. But you need to be honest about what situation you are going to put him in. If the potential manager he will have is the kind who likes to keep everything under tight control, then you probably don't want *too* much spirit. If the job requires 5 percent innovation and 95 percent by-the-book procedure, do you really want someone all that creative? Hire a wonderful person for the wrong job and you'll be back at the interviewing desk in a very short time.

To get a feel for how the perfect candidate will answer your questions, why not try them out on the person who currently holds the position (if he or she is not being fired and isn't quitting after just six months). If that's not possible, find someone who is doing well in the company with a similar job and do a mock interview. Assume that the answers you get are top-notch and then compare the applicants' answers to those.

Once you've started taking interview notes, maintain a file on everyone who is ultimately hired. When you have picked several winners, haul out your notes and look for common patterns in their interviews. If people are fired or leave after a brief period, look through their interview notes, too, for a common thread. Using the information you find to reassess the relative importance of your interview questions will bring additional precision to your scoring process in the future.

But until you have some records to work with, try talking to other managers in your division to find out why some promising new hires quit or were fired. It may be that since your home office is in Littletown, Nebraska, the five people you hired from New York City and Los Angeles left after a year because they were never able to make the transition. In that case, home in on the relocation issue during the interview. Don't just ask the applicants if it bothers them. Stress the fact that they'll be living in a totally different environment. The people you scare away would probably have left anyway.

By talking to other managers you may find out that three people who were fired had become bitter because the job was tedious and didn't offer more opportunities. "In a case like that, you want to make sure you ask applicants what they want in a job before you give them an exact job description," says Dr. Flax. "If you give them the information first and then ask what they want, they'll just repeat the description. Keep in mind that what they want more than anything at that point is a job, any job." For example, if you work for a magazine publishing company and are looking for a research assistant, ask the applicant what he expects out of the job before describing it. You may find out that he sees it as a stepping-stone to get into writing. If you're looking for someone to stay in research and be satisfied with the position, this person is not for you. But he might have slipped by if you had reversed the question/description order.

In general, keep in mind that it isn't that hard to find great people. But finding people who are great for the job you're offering is an exacting science. So why not borrow the same procedures that scientists use to discover the one chemical compound out of a thousand that will have the desired characteristics? First, know what you are looking for. Second, provide a controlled environment in which to conduct standardized tests. Third, take copious notes. Fourth, combine past research with new information to discover trends as well as to bring more precision to the testing process. Approach hiring in this way and the only thing you may have to worry about is what to do with your engineering or accounting degree when your company decides to make you vice-president in charge of personnel.

Hiring? The Color of Your Bait Needn't Be Green

Nothing is worse than finding the perfect candidate and then losing him because the offer wasn't right. Short of being a mind reader, it's tough to tell what people want these days. At least money is always a safe bet, right? Well, believe it or not, personal recognition is preferred over a salary boost by a four-to-one margin as the most essential requirement among executives seeking new jobs, says a survey by the Challenger, Gray and Christmas outplacement firm. Besides a pat on the back, job independence and a chance to contribute to company goals are top priorities among new hires.

27

HOME

To one degree or another, our work life permeates our home.

For some of us, home is where we toil 8 hours a day, each and every working day. Or it's a place where we set up shop part-time or arrange to complete our employers' assignments on a project-by-project basis. More likely, it's the place where we bring the unfinished office business of the day. At the very least, it's where we try to shake off (often with little success) the worries of the 9-to-5 part of our lives.

There's a good news/bad news element to the business of working at home on a regular basis. At its best, you get to wear jeans and a sweatshirt instead of a suit and tie. You commute from one floor to the next (instead of from one county to another). You set a schedule and a pace that suit your biorhythms. You can take a 20-minute break to watch "Sesame Street" with your kids. And you can switch on the telephone answering machine when you want to be left undisturbed.

At its worst, working at home is a nightmare of interruptions by attention-seeking kids, feelings of claustrophobia, disrupting midday jaunts to the copier store or the post office, and isolation from office politics and water-cooler socializing.

The benefits surely must outweigh the drawbacks, though, because people in record numbers are jumping at the chance to take part in this latest craze. An estimated 26.6 million Americans work from home at least part of the time, according to LINK Resources Corporation, a market research firm. That's 23 percent of the total labor force.

More than anything else, the work-from-home phenomenon can be traced to the profusion of personal computers (they're in place in 21 percent of American households) and such indispensable gadgetry as modems and fax machines. Add to that two more factors—the proliferation of women in the workplace who choose to be near their children for at least part of the work week, and the boom in small businesses that folks are starting in their homes—and you get a genuine trend. But it's not for everybody.

THINKING OF WORKING FULL-TIME AT HOME? READ THIS FIRST

So you want to join the estimated 1.8 million additional Americans who will enter the home-based work force this year? Sure, you'd do anything to get out from under the full-time gaze of your boss. But think for a minute how you'd feel about giving up the office camaraderie. If you're honest about it, when you add it all up, you probably spend almost an hour each day kibitzing with co-workers. Would you miss it? Would you miss the lunchtime shopping trips, the lunchtime visits to the gym, the after-work drinks, the compliments on your latest project, and all the other little pleasures you can get only from working with others? If you're a social animal, working from home probably isn't for you.

Think, too, for a moment about your capacity for self-discipline. When you work in an office, your superiors continually stack your desk with piles of work that must be tended to—and they watch and wait for you to finish. At home, you have the option of becoming a "Hollywood Squares" junkie, raking leaves, raiding the refrigerator—anything but working. You're going to have to be incredibly disciplined, or you simply won't make it. (One friend motivates himself by posting his mortgage bill directly above his computer terminal.) Are you the type who can leap out of bed at 6:00 A.M.—even when you know you *could* linger as long as you wish—and hit the job as if a boss were staring over your shoulder? If not, don't even think about looking homeward.

THE OUT-OF-SIGHT, OUT-OF-MIND SYNDROME

When you work from home for someone else, you give up two significant career-management tools: visibility and direct access to office communication. The sacrifice is nothing to sneeze at because, in the fitting words of Richard Germann, vice-president for the career management consulting firm of Right Associates, "If you're not there, people forget you exist."

So if you're toiling outside the framework of the organization, you have to work doubly hard to stay visible and to keep up with as much of the day-to-day communication as possible. Here are some suggestions.

Let your bosses know exactly what you're doing. Chances are your superiors aren't going to be ecstatic if you phone them on an hourly—or even daily—basis with updates on your marvelous achievements. So send little informal notes to report on your progress. Call them at regular but sensibly spaced intervals. And arrange for occasional trips to the office. "Don't assume anybody thinks you're doing anything useful without being told," says Germann. "Report your progress as often as is humanly possible. Otherwise they'll think you're doing nothing."

Keep up with the office grapevine. Working at home shouldn't stop you from scheduling a regular squash game with the most plugged-in person from your office. And you can still invite colleagues over for dinner.

Give feedback to others. From your communications, you'll learn what's happening with the folks in your home office. Don't hesitate to get on the phone or jot a note to congratulate a colleague for a promotion or the successful completion of a project.

CREATING THE PERFECT OFFICE AT HOME

Privacy is the key. First of all, try to set up an office that's separate from your living space. "It's important to create a work environment that keeps you away from distractions that cause you to physically or mentally deviate from your work goals," says Paul Edwards, a consultant, broadcaster, and author. Edwards and his wife, Sarah, wrote *Working from Home,* a guide for what he calls "open-collar" workers. It's wonderful to close the door on one world at the end of the day and open it on another.

Of course for those who live in Greater New York City and other real estate markets where space is at a premium, separating work space from living space is easier said than done. If you're in cramped quarters, Edwards suggests putting your desk in the living room and not in the bedroom. "There are a variety of clever things you can do with screens, platforms, and bookcases to physically separate your work space from your living space," he says. The room-divider advice is doubly important for those who live and work in a studio apartment.

Here are some additional factors to consider.

Equipment. Don't rush out and buy the latest electronic office devices before you establish a need for them. Don't spend $1,000 for a fax machine, for example, until you get to the point where the costs of traveling to a fax service and paying a per-page fax fee start to justify the purchase. The same goes for a photocopier. A good telephone answering machine, on the other hand, is a high-priority item right from the start, since it virtually eliminates the need for a secretary. A good choice for those who are frequently out of the office: an answering machine with a toll-saver feature (you can access your messages from any pay phone; if there are none, you don't have to pay for the call).

Telephone tips. Call-waiting, as annoying as it may sometimes be to the person on the other end, is a must. If you're single, a separate business line is probably unnecessary. But if you share your household with a mate, it's a smart idea. "A separate line is particularly important if you have kids," says Edwards. "You don't want your four-year-old picking up the phone when your most important potential client is on the other end. And when your child gets older, there could be even more competition for the phone." Edwards also swears by cordless telephones and telephone headsets.

A good office chair. This is one area where you shouldn't scrimp. A good chair will help avoid neck and back strain so you can work more efficiently.

Proper lighting. The point is to avoid either harsh glare or too little light. A telltale sign of bad lighting: frequent headaches.

An acceptable level of noise. Some folks like to work with a radio—tuned to a talk show—softly playing in the background, to imitate the murmurings of co-workers and to stave off loneliness. Other people shut the windows, close the drapes, turn on the air conditioning, and pray that the streets department won't start digging up the street outside. Experiment with different levels of background noise until you see what suits you, productivity-wise. For some at-home workers, there's nothing nicer—and more conducive to concentration—than to hear kids playing half a block away.

The proper color for your office. Light colors are usually a good bet for creating a beneficial work atmosphere, says Edwards. It's been found that yellow increases productivity. Red perks up the energy of low-productivity types but stresses out all others. Find out what works best for you.

The home-office deduction. Generally speaking, taxpayers who maintain an office at home are eligible to write off the cost of the office from their taxable income. *But beware:* Since the home office deduction lends itself to potential abuse, if you take it, you're more likely than most to wind up being audited. An audit should be no problem, however, if you keep meticulous records, including canceled checks and receipts verifying office expenses.

You may have to prove that the office is not used for any purpose other than work. If you're not self-employed, you may be asked to provide a statement from your employer explaining that you are required to provide an office in your home.

5 TIPS TO BOOST YOUR AT-HOME EFFECTIVENESS

1. Don't waste time running needless errands. Cluster them at the end of the day or do them during your lunch hour.

2. Set up a productive ritual. Read the newspaper first thing in the morning. Or open your mail. Or draw up your list of things to do. Anything, suggest Edwards, that gets you started.

3. Prioritize. Set daily goals for yourself. Do your most important tasks early in the day—right after your beginning ritual, if possible.

4. Take an exercise break. When the afternoon slump hits, go out for a walk around the block or spend 15 minutes doing calisthenics.

5. Don't ignore social contacts. The isolation that comes from working alone may lead to depression for some people, says Edwards. For others, it may lead to a loss of social skills. To keep yourself well-rounded (and, as a result, probably more productive), take the initiative to meet with others away from home. Schedule a lunch get-together twice a week or join a so-called networking club. (Says Edwards, "Think of yourself as working *from* home, not *at* home." The subtle distinction is that your home is your base—like a satellite office—not a place in which you're stuck.)

HOW TO KEEP YOUR WORK *OUT* OF YOUR HOME

Whether you commute via modem or via MetroNorth, you'll probably find that life becomes a lot more enjoyable when you clearly separate your work time and your personal time. It's rarely easy, but here are some tips to help.

Gripe about work for a maximum of 11 minutes. Everybody's had a bad day. To try to keep it from invading your evening at home, complain about work (to your spouse or any other sympathetic party) for no more than 11 minutes after the day has ended. Return the favor by listening to the other person's gripes, then start the evening activities.

Write down loose ends. To keep your mind off work, jot down any office-related matters as soon as possible after arriving home. "Remember to phone Jones, re: contract renewal." Then forget about it until the next morning.

Take 20 minutes to do something to clear your mind. Meditate, jog, shoot baskets, knit, watch "Wheel of Fortune," take your baby out for a stroll . . . anything to help you ease the transition from work to home. Yes, even if you're just commuting from one room to the next.

And if you *must* do some homework . . .

Set up a private work space. If you ordinarily bring work home from the office, try to set up a work space that keeps you far from your spouse and family—and behind a closed door. Family members should be asked to respect your work privacy and to hold off on interruptions. *Warning:* Unless you're a television news director, TV critic, or the like, don't install a television in your home office. And don't get into the habit of hiding out in your office with a magazine, book, or any other nonwork diversion.

Schedule your work time at home. If a crucial deadline forces you to take work home on a regular basis (a seasonal way of life for accountants), try to set up a regular work period *after* you've had a chance to (for instance) go for a short run, shower, eat dinner, play with the kids.

Don't make it a regular thing. You'd be surprised at how much brought-home work could actually be taken care of at the office. Unless you actually enjoy the rugged routine, don't get into the habit of putting off work during office hours simply because you know you can always take it home.

28

INTERVIEWS

In a way, the interviewing process poses the same problem for the eager job applicant as Thornton Wilder's characters faced in *Our Town* (slightly modified, of course). The problem is this: In a world teeming with millions of bright-eyed, accomplished, and polite individuals, what can you do to stand out from the rest? The chair you are sitting in is still warm from the last applicant who: (1) really wants the job, (2) is really motivated, (3) is really sure that he or she will be a *big* asset to the company, (4) was president of the college student council, and (5) had a 3.999 grade point average. And that person's genetic duplicates are sitting outside the office door waiting for you to finish your interview so that they can have their turn.

So there you are, nervously sitting across the desk from an interviewer who has already seen 20 other people today who vaguely resembled you, and who is now waiting to hear how well you can sum up the net worth of your existence on this planet. How do you convince this person to forget the rest and hire the best (meaning you)?

To make a long story short, it comes down to three factors: preparation, a general understanding of the conduct expected in an interview situation, and most important, a smattering of creativity. To make a short story long, here's what to do.

PLANNING YOUR MISSION IN ADVANCE

You are about to do battle. As any general worth his weight in artillery will tell you, both offense and defense play an important part in winning the war. On the defensive side, you've got to be prepared to cover your job-seeking rear end on every subject the interviewer decides to probe. This means having an answer that not only shows no weaknesses but actually asserts your strengths in that sector. If you just wander into an interview without taking some time to consider questions the interviewer is obviously going to ask, you are going to be mowed down before you even reach the front lines.

"Essentially, there are three concerns that are foremost in the mind of any interviewer," says Robert Half, president of Robert Half International and author of *The Robert Half Way to Get Hired in Today's Job Market.* "Can you do the job? Will you do the job? Do you fit in with the company's style? Additionally, there is a fourth concern on the part of the interviewer: What does he or she have to gain or lose by hiring you or by recommending that you be hired?"

So your mission is to somehow convey one of three things every time you open your mouth in an interview: Yes, I can do the job; yes, I will work hard; and yes, I can fit in. The exact questions may vary and so may your answers. But when you distill a successful interview down to its purest elements, it boils down to the interviewer asking those three questions and you answering yes to them in as many clever ways as you know how.

Up until the point when you walk through the doorway, the only things an interviewer knows about you have been picked up from your résumé. "Therefore," says Amanda Squadrilli, a New York City–based career counselor, "the first order of preparation is being able to answer any questions which might arise directly from your résumé. Two-line job descriptions on your résumé tell the interviewer what positions you've held but not how well you did in them. Take some time to go back over your job history and reacquaint yourself with the highlights of each position you handled. What did you learn? What did you accomplish? Be specific when you talk about what you accomplished."

Robert Half points out that credentials are a large part of what gets you a job. What you've done is a good indicator of what you will do in the future. So you want to make the most of your credentials. The fact that you've spent five years selling ad space for a regional magazine is a credential that you and several hundred other applicants may share. On the other hand, the fact that you boosted ad revenues by 50 percent puts you in a class by yourself. That's a credential! And that's why you should be specific about your accomplishments.

"Study your résumé for weak spots," continues Squadrilli. "Are there any gaps in your work history? You can be sure they will be noticed and discussed. Be prepared to present those gaps in a positive light." Saying you took a little time off to follow the Grateful Dead around the country is not going to go a long way toward assuring your interviewer that you are willing to work. Instead you might say you wanted to see America and satisfy your wanderlust before getting down to some serious career tracking.

"Another thing you want to be aware of is whether your work history shows a lot of movement. When an interviewer sees on a résumé that a person has held ten jobs in two years, it sets off warning bells," points out Squadrilli. Here is where you might need some creativity to show that your leap-frogging had a specific goal. Maybe you were trying for a broad overview of the industry. Or perhaps you could explain that the positions looked good initially but turned out to be dead ends once you were inside. As a last resort you could focus on the fact that not only has your diverse background weeded out any uncertainty on your part as to what you are looking for now, but your wide range of experience makes you perfect for this position.

Subtle ways to sell yourself

To better understand how to give the interviewer the three yeses he wants to hear, you need to realize that a great deal hinges on whether you have the personality traits that inspire confidence. (Well, of course you have them, but you've got to let the interviewer know that.)

"Basically, any interviewer is going to want to know that the person she hires is dependable, stable, honest, loyal, responsible, and has drive," says Half. "But you can't walk in and simply say you are all of the above. You'll sound like a Boy Scout. You've got to imply those things through your responses."

"When a potential employer asks you about a former boss, for example, you don't say that he made the Marquis de Sade look like a Sunday school teacher," counsels Squadrilli. "By never saying anything bad about former employers, you are showing a fair degree of loyalty. Or at least tact. There are some interviewers who will go so far as to say 'Oh, you worked for so and so? Wasn't he a jerk?' In a case like that you might simply say that you and he had your differences but it never seemed to get in the way of business." Even if interviewers know you are piling it high and deep, they still have to be satisfied that you won't do a hatchet job on their company when you leave (or while you are there).

"Responsibility is a rare trait and not easily displayed indirectly in an interview," says Half. "But one way to do it is by not making a lot of excuses for your mistakes. If you blew it in the past, admit it. It's not wonderful to have to do this, but it will go much further toward impressing the interviewer than if you sit there coming up with lame excuses. No one likes an excuse-maker."

Then there's dependability. To illustrate its importance, Half likes to tell the story of a man who showed up for an interview despite the fact that the worst rainstorm in years—practically a hurricane—was raging outside. When the employer asked the man why he decided to come in such bad weather, the man answered, "I said I would be here." He got the job.

Let nothing get in the way of being on time for your interview, even if it means making a dry run to the location the day before so you won't get lost. Even if it means arriving a half hour early and listening to the radio while you wait in your car.

Dependability also means that you can and will get the job done. If you had a work situation in the past where you were the one who constantly delivered when all else failed, say so. Make no bones about presenting examples in which you came through not only on a routine basis, but in a pinch.

It's also important in the eyes of most interviewers that the person they are about to hire has drive. "Many job applicants will at some point say, 'Oh yes, I've got a great deal of ambition and I am very motivated,'" notes Half. "This does not cut it. You have to *show* drive."

This is where we move from defense to offense. Naturally if your résumé shows that you have been cleaning the elephant cage at the city zoo for the past eight years, you are going to have some trouble convincing anyone that you've got drive. But if you have a typical work history with decent advancement, then the next thing you should do is show the interviewer that you are driven to get this job.

You can demonstrate your drive by getting as much advance information as possible concerning the company you are applying to. Although this advice is so old that it's probably being needlepointed into pillows, the number of applicants who don't follow it is staggering. But remember: Driven people don't just want something and wish they could have it. They want something and take active measures to achieve it.

According to Half's research, not knowing about the company they are applying to hurts as many as 75 percent of job seekers. Don't be one of them. If it's a large company, check the library for back issues of *Fortune, Forbes, Business Week,* and other periodicals that track the business community. Also read up on the industry in general. If it's a small local company, find someone who works there and talk. If you don't know anyone, try calling someone in the division you are applying to, a middle manager perhaps, and invite him or her out to lunch. Even if word of your meeting gets back to the person who is hiring, it can't hurt. It'll show your interest.

Once you have some information, look for trends. What are the company's current policies? What seems to be in its future? Where can you fit with what you have to offer? Being highly motivated and extremely interested in the job doesn't even compare to the fact that the company wants to move into canned fruit marketing and you have just helped your last company do exactly that. If you can't seem to spot any trends, at least have a couple questions ready which are phrased in a manner that lets the interviewer know you've done your homework.

THE QUESTIONS THEY'RE BOUND TO ASK

Okay. We know what interviewers want. Now it becomes a question of being prepared for the specific ways they are going to be probing you. There are common questions that seem to turn up in every interview. These are questions that not only will get at specifics but will also require you to quickly sum up your experience and potential in a concise manner. Needless to say, you don't want to wait until you are sitting in the interview to compose your thoughts. That would be like diving into a pool and considering as you hit the water the possibility of some swimming lessons. In "Hiring" on page 218, you can find some questions that experts say are useful if you are sitting in the interviewer's chair. Study them, as well as their underlying purposes. Here are some additional questions to be prepared for.

"Can you tell me a little about yourself?" "This is a good icebreaker that gives the interviewer a general feel for you," says Half. "It also points out very quickly whether you are an articulate person. If you can't speak well about yourself, you're not going to be very articulate about anything. Keep your answer down to about 2 or 3 minutes and stress positive features about yourself that somehow key in on the qualifications necessary for the job." Don't wander off about your pet boa constrictor or the singles sessions you are currently attending. This isn't therapy. Figure out the two or three things that make you stand out as an applicant and make them your opening barrage.

"What is it about this job that interests you most?" "It pays the kind of money I need to buy a BMW," although truthful, is probably not the sort of answer that will win you a job. Actually, this question is your opening to show the interviewer how much homework you've done: You are excited about the future of this company. Knowing what you do about the job, you feel that your experience can help the division grow along the lines planned by upper-level management. The company philosophy fits with yours. But the fact that the job cuts ten minutes off your driving time in the morning is not something to bring up.

"What do you consider your major strengths?" The first thing to consider is what major strengths the position calls for. If it's attention to detail, then by coincidence that is going to be one of your major strengths. The one caveat here is this: Be able to back up your major strengths with major examples of those strengths in action.

"What do you consider to be your major weaknesses?" No need to give away the store on this one. Pick weaknesses that in a way are concealed strengths: You don't know when to call it quits. You sometimes get so excited about a project that you turn into a workaholic.

"Why do you want to leave your present job?" Remember, cast no aspersions. You enjoyed working for your present employer but there comes a time when you have to look for a better opportunity.

"What are your best achievements?" Keep in mind the three questions you want to answer and the several personality traits you want to possess. Then add to that a time factor. Your greatest achievements should be recent, should make you look like a motivated, can-do person, and should say "I did this; I can do anything you want me to do."

"Do you have any questions?" An interviewer will often ask this question to catch you off guard, according to Kathryn and Ross Petras, coauthors of *The Only Job Hunting Guide You'll Ever Need.* It aims to circumvent exactly the kind of canned responses that you are currently practicing. It also allows the interviewer to give you the initiative and then receive a better idea of your primary interests based upon the questions you ask. The Petrases advise you never to answer this question with a question concerning salary, benefits, or personnel policies. You want to show how career-oriented you are, not how much you like money (after all, that's a given). Instead, ask questions that display your knowledge of the industry or company. If you don't possess that knowledge, at least ask questions having to do with current operations or planned expansions of the company. Get the interviewer to talk about what he knows best and then contribute to the conversation with some intelligent observations based upon your experience. This doesn't mean that you should in any way imply that you could run the place better than the current management.

There are hundreds of questions that you may be asked at an interview, and there is no way for you to prepare for them all. But here are just a few more which Robert Half suggests you consider.

- "What motivates you?"
- "What are your long-term goals?"
- "How would you rate yourself as a leader?"
- "How much of a self-starter are you?"
- "How long do you think you would be happy in this job before you started thinking about a promotion?"

- "How sensitive are you to criticism?"
- "What are you doing now to improve yourself?"

Answer these questions as you would the previous ones. Don't just state your attributes, give examples. Additionally, and this cannot be stressed enough, say nothing that doesn't directly apply toward your goal of answering yes to the interviewer's three primary questions. It's strange, but even though applicants know they are trying to land a job, 20 minutes into the interview they are suddenly saying things which either have nothing to do with that purpose or are actually detrimental. Maybe it's part of our nature as human beings that after 20 minutes of conversation with anyone, a certain familiarity is born. This is not the case, however, with interviewers. You can bet that they will be all business even if you are not. So when asked what you are doing to improve yourself, don't tell them about the astrology class you are currently attending.

When practicing your responses, one of the best things you can do is work with a tape recorder. By taping your answers and then playing them back, you can put yourself in the interviewer's shoes. Would you give the person on the tape a job? Is that voice full of confidence? Are those the words of an articulate person? Are you impressed with the credentials of this applicant? No? Then try again. Rerecord your answers until they are so fine-tuned that they hum. Now you are ready.

STAYING COOL IN THE HOT SEAT

Don't pull out a hamburger and use the interviewer's desk for a dining table. Don't challenge the interviewer to an arm wrestling contest. And don't wear a Walkman during the interview (even if you have assured the interviewer that you can listen to him *and* music at the same time).

Believe it or not, applicants have actually committed all of the faux pas mentioned above. One person even used the interviewer's phone to call his therapist for some fast advice on how to answer a particularly tricky question. Another simply fell asleep and started snoring.

While "try not to snore" is certainly a piece of advice at least one person might have found pertinent, the rest of us could use a few tips that are, well, a little less exotic. The first one is this: Most interviewers are not professionals. In other words, they do not conduct interviews for a living. Typically, they are managers who will end up working directly with the people they hire. As such they are probably almost as uncomfortable in an interview situation as you are. They don't know any psychological tricks to make you spill your guts and they have not been sharpened to an interrogator's razor edge by years of experience. Most of them have an honest need for a good worker and are genuinely interested in determining if you are that person. So there is no need for you to get all worked up and nervous.

This doesn't mean that you should not be on your best behavior. "Decline anything to eat or drink," says Squadrilli. "This holds true even if the interviewer happens to be having a danish himself. First of all, food is distracting in a situation where you want to minimize any distractions. Second, if you are nervous, it may show in a shaking hand holding a coffee cup. Third, you may spill something. And even though it's an easily forgiven accident, you don't want the interviewer to remember you because of the stain on his office floor." You also don't want to be caught with a mouth full of prune danish right when the interviewer asks for your opinion on the meaning of life.

A corollary to the "danish rule" is *don't smoke.* "Even if the interviewer is smoking, there is a chance that you are being tested," warns Squadrilli. "If the company has a no-smoking policy, the fact that you are a smoker will not win you any points. And if you are applying for a sales job or any client-related position, smoking is going to make you look very undesirable."

Another rule of thumb is to maintain a relaxed, animated, and confident exterior. "Body language has a lot to do with it," says Squadrilli. "Maintain good posture, but try not to have your arms and legs tying themselves up in knots. To engage the listener, lean slightly forward when speaking. But most important, don't lose your cool if something less than advantageous should happen. I had one man tell me that during an interview one hot day he put his hand on the interviewer's black lacquer desktop. When he took his hand away, the perspiration left a very noticeable handprint. Afterward, he was sure that he wouldn't get the job because of this handprint. Actually, the handprint is irrelevant. But the fact that he lost confidence probably showed in his interview performance."

Keeping up your spirits in the face of adversity is especially important when it seems that the interviewer is not warming up to you. Many applicants take this personally and throw in the towel before the battle is finished. But you need to remember that interviewers have the same kinds of problems that we all do.

Studies have shown that what happens to interviewers just before the interview is going to affect their judgment during the interview. In one case, 71 people were asked to play the role of personnel managers interviewing someone for a job. Before the interview researchers influenced their moods by giving them a test and then providing either positive or negative feedback on their performance. The results showed that interviewers who were given positive reinforcement previous to the interview gave applicants a much more favorable rating than those who had received negative feedback. As a matter of fact, the interviewers in the positive-feedback group were much more likely to offer the applicants a job and rate them as highly motivated. These results occurred despite the fact that every applicant gave exactly the same responses during the interview.

So the noticeable chill in your interviewer's bearing may have more to do with the fender bender he got into that morning than it does with you. There's nothing you can do about how his mood will affect his judgment, so you should simply play it out as best you can and not crumple into a mass of self-recriminations.

"Try not to let the conversation become one-sided," counsels Half. "This means that neither you nor the interviewer should do the bulk of the talking." Make your answers brief and try not to get sidetracked on some long-winded story that illustrates a minor point. Let the interviewer talk as much as he wants, but make sure you get in your main points.

"Speaking of conversation, make sure you let no more than 3 to 5 seconds pass between the interviewer's question and your response," adds Squadrilli. What this really means is that you shouldn't give birth to any pregnant pauses. "If you don't have the answer to the question immediately, say 'let me think about that for a moment,' or 'that's a tough one, could we come back to it?'"

Then, of course, there is always the dreaded lunchtime interview. This situation is a veritable mine field of possible problems. "Try to order last so that you know the price range you are working in," says Squadrilli. "And when you do order, make it as simple a food to eat as possible. Finger foods are definitely out, as well as anything that requires a nutcracker. You want the interviewer to focus on your qualifications, not the titanic struggle you're having with a king crab leg." Additionally, you want to remember that you're there to talk. So stay away from anything with garlic.

There is one more thing to keep in mind. "The most serious mistake that I've seen is that many applicants don't show enough enthusiasm for the job at hand," says Squadrilli. "When it comes right down to it, most applicants don't really ask for the job," agrees Half. "The mere fact that you are there for the interview is not enough. Say you want the job. And more important, wrap it up with the five words that every interviewer wants to hear: "I won't let you down.""

29

INTUITION

Bring up the subject of intuition in conversation and you can bet that you'll hear stories best accompanied by the theme music from "The Twilight Zone." Tales of almost eerie precognition in which people somehow perceive information that they couldn't possibly have known by ordinary means. In the past, if you were interested in the subject of intuition you had to peruse books with titles such as *ESP: Awakening the Limitless Powers of the Mind in Five Minutes a Day*. Yet in a curious leap from the Ouija board to the boardroom, you would now be more likely to find information on the subject in the venerable stacks of the Wharton or Harvard Business School library. Meanwhile, top-level executives around the country are making it their business to develop their intuitive talents and put them to use on a daily basis.

One of the people who is helping execs become more intuitive at organizations such as Tenneco, Walt Disney, and even the National Security Agency is Weston Agor, Ph.D., professor of public administration at the University of Texas, El Paso, and author of *Intuition in Organizations: Leading and Managing Productively*. To Dr. Agor, intuition is the key to success in business. But what exactly is it? "Basically, I define intuition as knowing something for certain without knowing it for sure," he says.

What Dr. Agor is referring to is that gut-level feeling we've all experienced, which, when it happens, delivers up an answer or decision that we somehow *know* is correct. What is particularly amazing is that the intuitive decision often seems more correct than many thoroughly weighed and analyzed decisions. In other words, we seem to be certain it is right even though we have no hard data to prove it for certain. "And while some people would see that as paranormal," says Dr. Agor, "it is in fact partly a product of experience, training, and education over the years combined with skills on the feeling side."

While that definition may seem sensible enough, if you're a newcomer to intuition, you might still have some reservations. Sure you've had your momentary flashes and gut hunches. But admittedly those moments are as unpredictable as tornadoes, and some of them didn't turn out to be the flashes of true genius they originally seemed to be.

So the questions that need to be answered concerning intuition are the same as for any good business tool: Is it trustworthy? Can I use it? The answer to both is yes.

INTUITION: MAGIC OR AN EXECUTIVE'S MOST USEFUL TOOL?

Demystifying intuition is not the easiest thing to do. After all, what is more magical than suddenly being provided with all the answers and all the correct decisions you could use? One of the best stories of business intuition involves Conrad Hilton, founder of the hotel chain. When he was bidding for the old Stevens Hotel in Chicago, a number suddenly popped into his head, seemingly out of nowhere. Hilton used the figure and with it purchased the world's largest hotel with a bid that won by a mere $200.

Magic? In a case like this, maybe it was. But for a moment let's adhere to one theory of intuition that argues that the flash or hunch only surfaces after the subconscious mind completes a process very much like conscious reasoning. Within Hilton's mind was stored varying data all relating to some aspect of the Stevens Hotel sale. Naturally there would be the run-of-the-mill information such as the assessed value of the hotel, how much he could afford to pay, and what he foresaw the hotel eventually being worth to him. But there was other information that was also being compiled. Details concerning the other bidders: how liquid their companies currently were, how much they coveted the hotel. Possibly he had met some of the other bidders in the past. Their personalities were figured into the equation. Maybe from walking around town he had gotten a feel for the financial health of Chicago in general and his subconscious factored that in also. Once everything fell into place, *bingo* . . . out popped a figure that his conscious mind picked up.

This hypothesized scenario of Hilton's inner workings demonstrates what Phillip Goldberg, author of *The Intuitive Edge*, feels to be the advantage of intuitional decision making: "Intuition . . . can work with information that is not consciously available, that may have been stored in the past or acquired through subliminal or other sensory means. Rational thinking has to work with whatever the mind is aware of at the time." In other words, when you rely on intuition, you're working with more informational horsepower.

On the other hand, intuition expert Frances E. Vaughan, Ph.D., author of *Awakening Intuition*, feels that intuition originates just below the conscious level and is a form of direct knowing—a way to tap into some core of truth. Either way, it pans out as a tool that no good executive should be without.

As a matter of fact, it appears that no good executive is without a high degree of intuition. When Dr. Agor tested several thousand executives in such diverse areas as state health bureaus, private sector corporations, the military, and state legislatures, his findings were dramatic. Without exception, top managers in every sector differed significantly from middle and lower level managers in their ability to utilize their decision-making intuition on the job.

In a way this should come as no surprise, given the management situations where intuition is the most useful. "Basically, intuition works best when there is a high level of uncertainty, there is little precedent, and variables are often not scientifically predictable," says Dr. Agor. "Add to this the times when facts are limited and don't make clear which way to go, time is limited, and there are several plausible alternatives from which to choose, and you've basically described what any executive runs into every day."

THE PROPER CARE AND FEEDING OF YOUR INTUITION

Now that you've got some idea of what intuition is, how it works, and what it's good for, there's still one question left to be answered. How do you get it to work for you? You would think that your subconscious mind is always on duty, that your core of truth, like Dunkin' Donuts, is open 24 hours a day, serving up freshly baked hunches. Yet somehow your flow of intuitional thoughts has about as much regularity as an Outer Mongolian railroad schedule. Does your intuition take days off?

"I think that your intuitive decision-making ability is always working," says Michael Ray, instructor in creativity at Stanford University's Graduate School of Business and coauthor of *Creativity in Business*. "The problem is that most of us have a hard time hearing the decision that's been made."

According to Ray, your "essence," the core from which intuition originates, makes decisions with incredible speed. You already possess the answer to your problem. In his creativity course at Stanford, Ray has developed a whole series of one-line maxims that can be followed to achieve a better utilization of creativity in the business environment. One of those maxims is "Recognize your decision now."

This is easier said than done, however. Interfering with your ability to hear your true decision is what Ray calls the "voice of judgment" (VOJ). "We all develop a voice of blame that tells us what we are doing is all wrong, that we will make a mistake," he explains. "The voice is built up over years of hearing parents, teachers, and friends instill all the normal fears of society in you. Besides a personal fear of failure and inadequacy, you are also working against a societal VOJ which comes from your colleagues at work. This VOJ says, 'Things are just not done this way,' 'your approach is too radical,' 'the boss isn't going to like this.' "

Basically, the VOJ generates so much static that it's hard to tune in to that true decision you've already made. You are also up against what Dr. Agor considers to be the opposite of intuition: projection. "This is where you rearrange facts into what you would like them to be rather than the way they really are." For example, you may have begun your career in a certain section of a company which is now doing poorly. Now the department needs to be axed, but you've got a soft spot for it and tend to accentuate any small positive factors you can find concerning its problems. Meanwhile, the negatives are overwhelming. In your heart (intuition), you know the section has got to go. But you don't let yourself hear your true decision because of your personal involvement.

TURN DOWN THE MENTAL CHATTER

Intuition is unemotional, Ray says. It doesn't succumb to egotistical involvement, intimidation, or anger. But to hear what obviously is the best in you speaking, you've got to listen. Wayne Silby, chairman of the Calvert Group of Funds, went so far as to enter an isolation tank in an attempt to hear his inner voice when his $2 billion company was facing its stiffest competition ever. In the past his company had thrived on the fact that it could offer its investors a 13 percent or 14 percent return while banks could only offer 5 percent. But his competitive advantage was in danger of being destroyed when legislation enabling banks to offer money-market deposit accounts was about to be enacted. In looking for a solution, Silby—who had previously conducted brainstorming meetings flat on his back in order to reach a more meditative state—decided he needed to focus even more intently on his intuitive essence. So he entered the isolation tank, a dark cocoon of a tub where he could float free of all outside stimuli. "You need to have a space where your mind chatter and all judgments and all the loudspeakers in your mind about who you are and what you are doing are turned down," said Silby in an interview with Michael Ray for *Leaders* magazine. "When that happens, you can get in touch with a deeper part of yourself that can start revealing patterns that are pretty awesome."

The idea Silby came up with in the tank actually allowed Calvert to funnel customer funds into the 15 banks with the highest-yielding market-rate deposit accounts and collect fees from the banks for Calvert's servicing of the accounts. Additionally, Calvert's customers were now F.D.I.C.-insured and could invest in excess of the respective banks' separate limits since the money was being spread around. Silby's isolation-tank idea resulted in $800 million in maintained and increased business.

Granted, part of Silby's problem-solving response was pure creativity. But intuition comes into play as a guide for the direction in which the creativity moves. Intuition becomes an unerring compass constantly pointing toward true north despite the critical and confounding interference thrown up by the VOJ.

If you want to get more intimate (maybe $800 million more intimate) with your intuition, you've got to start by finding a relaxation technique that works for you. It can be one of the more classic techniques such as biofeedback, isolation tank therapy, or straight meditation. But there are other ways of doing it. Stanford's Ray suggests that you try concentrating intensely on one activity that is unrelated to the problem. For Ted Nierenberg, president of houseware product company Dansk Limited, gardening does the trick. Andrew Carnegie carried around a deck of cards and played solitaire to calm his mind. Whatever you do, the main point is to focus completely on the activity to the exclusion of all else. "Don't expect anything to happen," counsels Ray. "Just see how it goes, especially when you get back to your decision problem. You might be surprised."

Don't ignore these feelings

There are ways of coaxing your intuition out of hiding that are more direct. "Flip a coin," suggests Ray. "Most decisions basically boil down to a yes-or-no, this-or-that situation. Pretend to yourself for a moment that whichever way the coin falls will determine your answer. Then see what your reaction to the result is." Do you feel good about the outcome? If so, you've got your answer. In other words, the coin's "decision" echoes what you already felt in your heart. If you find yourself wanting to go for two out of three, you've also got your answer: the opposite of what came up. Listen carefully to your inner response to the coin toss and you will feel something.

By the way, we are not talking about the word "feel" in a metaphoric sense. True intuitional flashes can often be separated from general smoke-blowing by actual physical and mental sensations. "Highly intuitive managers often describe their feeling cues in terms of 'a growing excitement in the pit of my stomach' or 'warmth and confidence,'" says Dr. Agor. "When a situation is going against the better judgment of your intuition, you might feel queasy and anxious and begin to sweat."

Everyone has his or her own special intuitive signal. For one marketing executive in Ray's class, it's salivation. Over the years she realized that her mouth actually watered when she was getting an intuitive flash. Now when her mouth waters, she pays particular attention to the decision she just made.

If you're thinking of using your body as an intuition detector, the first thing you need to do is start a little diary of physical sensations which seem to accompany or herald the development of an idea or decision. You may begin to notice, for example, that your right eye twitches when you make certain decisions. If so, write it down along with the thoughts you were having at that particular moment. Then check on the outcome.

When you've got a dozen or so entries, start looking for patterns. You may find that you always get an idea just before eating. Could it be that the feeling in your stomach is not a sign of hunger, but of intuition in full bloom? Perhaps your deepest insight comes in the shower, or when you wake up in the morning. In that case, cultivate your natural advantage. Pay particular attention to your thoughts in the shower, or sleep on particularly difficult problems and see what the morning brings. As mentioned earlier, the VOJ is your biggest enemy. Insecurity can lay waste to intuition. So the most important thing you can do is exercise, test, and act upon your intuition. One way many executives check to see if their intuitive heart is behind their latest idea is to sound out colleagues about it and then watch their own reaction to criticism. Even if everyone around them is shooting down the idea, do they still support it? That's a powerful gut feeling that many execs value over all the analytical reasoning in the world. But if you're not quite ready to bring up an intuitive thought at the next management meeting, at least write it down. Put it in a memo. Then see if you can get an intuitive yes or no as to whether to send it.

Most important—practice. All your decisions are not a matter of life and death, executive or executed. So take some chances. Try getting purposely lost and feel your way home. Next time you're at a supermarket, make a gut call as to which checkout line will move the fastest. Order the first unusual thing that hits you at a new restaurant. The point is not to deliberate. Listen and hear that instantaneous decision you've already made. Act on it immediately and see what happens. As you get on more intimate terms with your intuition, bring it to work and put it to work on a problem of minor importance. As your confidence grows, you'll find it easier to access your intuition. There'll be less static created by insecurity. Everyone has intuitive ability. What separates lower management from upper management is whether or not they use it.

30

LEADERSHIP

What makes people want to follow a particular leader? There's never been much of a mystery about it. People want to be guided by those they respect and by those who have a clear sense of direction. This is as true today as it was when Moses led his people to the promised land. And those job qualifications for leadership aren't likely to change in the foreseeable future. In fact, when Korn-Ferry International, an executive search company, polled 1,500 senior executives about the personal traits and management styles that would be most important for chief executives in the year 2000, the respondents said they wanted leaders who were, above all, "ethical" and who "convey a strong vision of the future."

To be an effective leader, your people have to trust you and they have to be sold on your vision. To get people to develop such confidence in your leadership ability, you have to help them reach their own goals, and you have to possess an energy and positive attitude that's contagious.

You should also stop thinking of leadership as something that one person does to another. Instead, consider it a reciprocal process that occurs between two or more people, suggests Barry Z. Posner, Ph.D., a professor of business at Santa Clara University and coauthor of *The Leadership Challenge: How to Get Extraordinary Things Done in Organizations.* According to Dr. Posner, it's the followers, not the leaders, who determine what constitutes successful leadership. Think about it: All bets are off if a follower is uninspired by his leader, if a follower doesn't trust his leader, or if a follower lacks confidence in his leader's ability. So to become successful, we have to convince our followers—not ourselves or our superiors—that we are credible leaders who are worthy of being followed.

GREAT MANAGER VS. GREAT LEADER

There's a whale of a difference between a great manager and a great leader. "Managers are people who do things right, while leaders are people who do the right thing," says Warren Bennis, Ph.D., author of *On Becoming a Leader* and coauthor of *Leaders.* Dr. Bennis, a professor of business administration at the University of Southern California, explains that leaders tend to be more interested in goal direction and to have a vision for the long range. Managers, on the other hand, are more concerned with attending to details, with getting things done today that need to be done. "Leaders are interested in the 'why' and 'what,' " he says, "whereas managers are interested in the 'how-to.' " The key difference, it seems, is that leaders work hard to develop a strong sense of direction. They are guided by a clear vision of the future, and not by a need to simply achieve today's goals.

GETTING YOUR EMPLOYEES TO SUPPORT YOU

This is such an essential leadership ingredient that it's almost embarrassing to have to mention. Sadly, you can have the most impressive credentials and a brilliant vision for your organization, but without the rock-solid support of those below you, chances are you'll wither on the vine, professionally speaking. Here's some advice.

Be someone whom your followers trust. "Trust is the lubrication that makes it possible for organizations to work," says Dr. Bennis. You gain the trust of others by keeping your word, by doing what you say you'll do. It's also important to stand up for your beliefs instead of shifting direction every time there's a change in the wind. "People like to trust those they can count on, even when they disagree with their viewpoints, more than people they agree with but who shift positions frequently," explains Dr. Bennis. Another way to get others to trust you is to display trust in *them.*

Convince people that you can meet their needs. You begin by becoming a good listener. And by learning what their needs are. And by taking those needs seriously. Dr. Posner suggests, "Be empathetic, and do something that convinces them that you have their interest at heart." For example, if your workers want you to upgrade their manufacturing facility, but you can't afford to do it all at once, set in motion (and share with them) a step-by-step schedule for doing so. There's always a place to start, so start somewhere. "People have to feel that you're concerned about them," explains Marvin Karlins, Ph.D., a professor of management at the University of South Florida and author of *Making the Workplace a Worthplace*. Express enthusiasm and support for their own career goals. And back up your words. Promote from within your organization.

Know your people. How many executives know what their workers like to do in their free time? Make it a point to be close to your subordinates. "Show some concern for the things that are important in their lives," advises Dr. Posner. Know their hobbies, their spouse's and kids' names, and how long they've worked in the organization. Express a genuine interest in their lives and treat them as individuals.

Treat your employees right. You wouldn't want to work for a boss who treated you with disrespect, or who held you in about as much esteem as he reserved for his favorite car-washing rag. So why should you expect your employees to settle for less? Remember, it's your employees who will be pushing you up the organizational pole. Treat them as you'd like to be treated yourself.

PROVING YOUR COMPETENCE

The surest way to prove competence is to be consistently right. Obviously, that's not always going to be the case. Since you can't exert total control over your track record, at least try this: Be clear about what you know and what you don't know. Don't pretend you've got all the answers, or that you have power over factors which you can't control. Also, continually work to improve yourself. Continue your own education through training programs, by reading, and by talking to industry people outside your company.

Set a good example. "Example is not the main thing in influencing others," said Albert Schweitzer, "it is the *only* thing." Try to imagine how far that legendary humanitarian would have gotten if he had merely sat back and instructed others to do his famous work, instead of setting an example through his tireless dedication. Don't expect your workers to willingly and enthusiastically put in extra hours if you're the type who leaves at precisely 4:59 P.M. Don't expect your employees to exhibit much in the way of initiative if you're the type who's satisfied with the status quo. Be prepared to do whatever it is you'd like your workers to do. Be willing to take the first actions yourself. "You prove your credibility as a leader by making yourself an example," says Dr. Posner. "Remember, leaders have to go first."

The Top 10 Characteristics of a Leader

In four years of executive seminars conducted by Santa Clara University and the Tom Peters Group/Learnings systems, more than 5,200 senior managers were asked to describe the characteristics they most admire in a leader. Here are the top ten characteristics, as reported in *Management Review* magazine.

1. Honest
2. Competent
3. Forward-looking
4. Inspiring
5. Intelligent
6. Fair-minded
7. Broad-minded
8. Courageous
9. Straightforward
10. Imaginative

DEVELOPING A VISION

Picture what it must have been like for piano player turned milkshake-mixer salesman Ray Kroc to deliver eight machines to Richard and Maurice McDonald's San Bernardino restaurant in 1952, to discover the line of customers waiting for hamburgers, and to come to the sudden realization that he could probably make a fortune franchising the McDonald brothers' drive-in restaurant. (During the next five years Kroc organized a chain of 228 McDonald's restaurants. The rest, as we all know, is history.)

"The first basic ingredient of leadership is a guiding vision," writes Dr. Bennis in *On Becoming a Leader.* Visionaries are able to focus sharply on a future that's filled with creative, fresh ideas. Visionaries are not afraid to explore the uncharted, to draw deeply on their experience, and to broaden that experience tirelessly. They learn by shifting perspective and by educating themselves.

"Leaders reach for any opportunities to change, grow, and improve. And out of that reaching, they develop a vision for what needs to be done," explains Dr. Posner. Here's the advice he and coauthor James M. Kouzes suggest.

Find something that's not broken and fix it before it breaks. Assume that someday your company's practices or products will be all wrong, and before that time arrives, figure out a way to improve or replace them.

Treat every job as a turnaround effort. It will help bring out the visionary in you.

THE DELICATE ART OF INSPIRING YOUR EMPLOYEES

Dr. Posner points out that the word *inspire* literally means "to breathe life into." But we can't even hope to do that, he explains, "unless we have some life ourselves."

Be passionate. Dr. Karlins talks about the "trickle-down effect" that occurs in organizations when a leader expresses great enthusiasm about a project. So if you don't communicate excitement, if you aren't solidly dedicated to a project, how can you expect your subordinates to get worked up about it? "I always tell managers to be committed to the work they're doing; otherwise, it's unfair to those below them," he says. So speak and act with passion. Would you want to follow a leader who is lukewarm in his or her ideas?

Get your employees involved in decision making. "People carry out decisions that they have participated in making much more enthusiastically than they carry out orders from the boss," writes Fred A. Manske, Jr., a Federal Express senior vice-president, in *Secrets of Effective Leadership.* So solicit their advice. Help them contribute to your organization's policies. Tell them you value their opinions. Listen to their ideas and incorporate them when it makes sense to do so. What happens when their suggestions are wrong? Dr. Posner advises you to listen carefully and then say, "Well, I appreciate that suggestion, but we're not going to be able to do it. It doesn't fit in right now."

Have confidence in yourself (and in others). "Followers don't want to see their leaders lacking self-confidence," says Dr. Posner. So believe in yourself. Trust your instincts. Stand up for your convictions. (But, again, listen to others' ideas and integrate them when appropriate.) "Know thyself" was a good enough statement to be carved above the Oracle at Delphi. And such advice is imperative for today's successful leader. Know your strengths and play to them. Know your weaknesses and strive to improve. Followers are inspired by leaders who understand themselves and exude an honest sense of self-confidence.

Show appreciation for your employees. What's the best way to prove that you are sincere in your appreciation? Be very specific when you tell someone you value their hard work or good ideas. Example: "If you hadn't come up with the notion of selling to nursing homes, we never would have made our monthly sales target. That market accounted for more than 30 percent of last month's billings." Also, when an employee performs particularly well, let your superiors know. Either praise the person in the presence of your boss, or send the worker a memo that expresses your appreciation—and send a copy to your boss. Nothing inspires better than the feeling of being appreciated.

WHEN SOMEONE CHALLENGES YOUR LEADERSHIP

It's bound to happen sooner or later: A little discontent will rise up through your organization. First one, then two, then a multitude of sour notes will be sounded in your symphony. Don't expect the bad vibes to silence themselves; you've got to take action as quickly as possible. "Go back and try to figure out what they're responding to—content or process," advises Dr. Posner. "Often, the situation is that they aren't necessarily having trouble with what you want them to do, but they're challenging the process because they weren't consulted on it."

If that's the case, ask those involved for their suggestions. "Start listening intently to what's going on. Be ready to change in order to develop a trusting relationship," suggests Dr. Bennis. You should have the self-confidence to admit if your ideas are wrong. You should be open to their proposals. Not only will your workers be more committed to a change of policy or practice they help initiate, but they'll be more motivated to work to see it succeed. (And face it: Sometimes they'll contribute ideas that are better than those you generate.) So you owe it to your employees to consider the validity of their dissent.

As a boss, you have more power than any one of your employees, but a mini-revolution could undermine your ability to lead—to say nothing of your health. An uprising often begins with one dissatisfied party. And when you're faced with a single dissenter, it feels a lot like it does to be trapped in a marriage that just isn't working. The first step is to openly discuss your troubled situation with the employee who is challenging your leadership. Be willing to listen and repair the relationship. But bad chemistry is something that isn't always possible to fix. "At a certain point, it doesn't make sense to throw good money after bad," says Dr. Karlins. If you can't develop a healthy, working relationship with the subordinate, help him find another job within your organization—or, if it's really bad, encourage him to leave.

Meanwhile, keep Dr. Bennis's words in mind: "Good leaders don't allow mutinies to happen."

How to be a leader who's not a threat to your manager

Your boss most likely won't be threatened by your leadership prowess as long as you make a point of boosting her. You give her information, skills, help, anything that will aid in *her* career advancement, advises Dr. Karlins. And the payback comes when your boss is promoted. Since you were such a crucial element in her success, she probably will help you climb with her.

That, of course, is the ideal. Too frequently, bosses suffer from what Dr. Karlins refers to as the "Green Face Syndrome." That is, they get jealous of subordinates who present themselves as being equal. Or they feel threatened by an underling who's the least bit precocious. One way you can work to prevent that reaction is by being extremely conscious of the way you present yourself. Sure, it sometimes seems that to sell your ideas you have to come across as possessing the self-assurance of Donald Trump. But you can't afford to be brazen in the way you represent your achievements and skills. Here's how to walk that tightrope: Be respectful of your boss. Ask for his advice. Occasionally, when you have an idea, solicit his comments on it. Make it clear that he's the mentor and you're the student. And that you value his opinion.

Obviously, you're not going to always agree with your boss. A non-threatening method for disagreeing with him is to explain the facts (just the facts) in the least challenging (unemotional) manner possible, and to give him time to think about what you said. Your boss may come back with a change of heart.

31

LEISURE

Anyone who even begins to suspect that a chapter on leisure activities would constitute lightweight material need only look as far as the office drone. (It's not you, is it?) He's the guy who comes in at 8:30, leaves at 5:30—sure, he accomplishes something in those hours—then heads home to a warm TV. Meanwhile, his counterparts are training to represent the office in an industry-wide 10-K race, or they're perfecting their pirouettes in an after-work mother-and-daughter ballet class, or they're accompanying the boss to see *Il Travatore*, or they're recharging their psychic and physical batteries at T'ai Chi class. Get the picture?

How after-work pastimes energize

Yes, sometimes it seems as if it's all we can do to work 8 hours, commute home, ingest a few calories, then collapse into bed. And for brief periods of our life (when we have a newborn in tow, for example), that's about all we can accomplish. The mere thought of pumping energy into an extracurricular pastime is more than we can muster. But for most of our lives, leisure activities (and you've no doubt gathered by now that we are affording them a broad definition) are a virtual necessity to keep us from degenerating into one-dimensional slugs.

"If you stick with one thing over and over again, you don't bring the kind of fresh insights to your work that you could get from other activities," says Salvatore Maddi, Ph.D., professor of psychology at University of California, Irvine, and coauthor of *The Hardy Executive: Health under Stress.* Outside activities, as anyone who engages in them will attest, pump you up with energy. The output, in fact, often exceeds the input. They have a nice regenerative effect.

One way that after-work pastimes help keep us out of ruts is by providing new challenges. When we find ourselves successfully meeting those challenges in after-work pursuits, we begin to generate the confidence needed to attack on-the-job challenges we may have been avoiding. (Example: "If I could earn my karate black belt, perhaps I could do anything—even put together that proposal for a new job description.") There's another spillover effect from our avocational endeavors. The creative juices that our hobbies generate continue to flow when we're back on the job.

That's not to ignore some of the other benefits. Sometimes the thought of attending tonight's massage workshop or book discussion group is all we need to help pull us through a particularly rough workday. Then there's the sheer relaxation that's derived from a squash game, a rehearsal with a choral group, or a date with a potter's wheel. Even a nightly crossword puzzle can be a powerful stress-buster. (Yes, so can an occasional evening with a warm TV. Our problem with that option is that it can be so dreadfully routine— and uninspiring, when you consider the alternatives. Face it: Wouldn't you prefer to get to know the person who leads rock-climbing expeditions, plays in a string quartet, and volunteers at a homeless shelter rather than the person who lives to watch "Roseanne" and "Cheers"?)

Our hobbies help us to feel that we're interesting people. And they help advance our workplace image. "You don't become a Johnny One-Note," says Dr. Maddi, who is president of Hardiness Institute, a psychological consulting firm specializing in stress management. By participating in outside activities, "you become more interesting and other people perceive you that way," he says. A study by psychologists at Arizona State University went so far as to suggest that one can get the image one wants simply by taking up the right sport. The research determined that skiers are viewed as the most sensual and attractive, that bowlers are down-to-earth, and that tennis players are cultured and full of sex appeal.

IS YOUR LEISURE ACTIVITY RIGHT FOR YOU?

With all of the benefits to be derived from extracurricular activities, it's no surprise that some people go a bit overboard. When that happens, you slowly find yourself disliking so many of the things you do that your life becomes full of tension. If your leisure activities become too frustrating on a continual basis, it's a sure sign that something's wrong. Also, "if you can't

Achievement on and off the Job

In 1961, when Benjamin Jones was the 38-year-old head of national sales for Monarch Capital, a Springfield, Massachusetts–based insurance company, he started running in marathons.

In 1971, after he had become the company's president, Jones took up shito-ryu karate, a form of the martial art that is heavy on defensive techniques. After seven years of training for a minimum of two nights a week, he earned his black belt.

And in 1982, after Monarch's board had tapped him to be the company's chairman, he began studying, first to become an emergency medical technician and later to become a paramedic. It takes two years of grueling classroom studies and homework to become a paramedic, and Jones endured the first of those years at the same time he ran his company. He also spent nights volunteering with an ambulance crew—a fact that few at Monarch Capital knew. When a photo of him helping some injured drivers appeared in the local paper, it came as a surprise to many of his employees.

Jones is a marvelous contrast to the vast majority of working Americans, those whose greatest after-work challenges lie in the sipping of wine or the watching of television. Yet he is unassuming and not the least bit boastful about his extracurricular accomplishments. When contrasting himself with others, he tends to say things like, "A lot of people just don't know there's a martial art that people over 35 can do."

Jones points to the intensity of the training and the concentration that karate requires. "It's terrific for coping with a lot of business stress. It's the greatest mind-clearer I know of. When you're at the dojo [the training center], nothing else exists." He also praises the activity's aerobic benefits. "It tends to keep the physical plant in excellent shape."

The emergency medical work, he says, "is a terrific opportunity to make a contribution on a one-to-one basis." Since his retirement in 1987, the former Monarch chairman has been working part-time as a paid paramedic in the Springfield area. (What's part-time? He worked for 18 hours, making nine emergency calls, the night before we interviewed him.)

As a corporate executive, whenever Jones was faced with hiring or promotion decisions, he often was swayed by a candidate's outside activities. "I always saw challenging activities as a plus. Subconsciously I was looking for the person who was an avid skier or an avid anything. It makes the individual far more attractive, and probably a better performer. Achievers achieve, you know," he says.

follow through on very many things, you're doing too much," says Dr. Maddi.

Figure out what you get from each activity. If you're overdoing it, use some analysis to weed out the less beneficial of your various enterprises. Sit down and carefully reflect on just what it is you're getting from each. Some may relax you, some may challenge you, some may be making a contribution to your community. Figure out what exactly it is you're looking for in a pastime. At least for the time being, drop the ones that don't give you what you need.

If possible, try to select hobbies that give you what you aren't getting at work. Some examples: You spend 8 or more hours a day toiling in the middle of a frenetic, overpopulated office. Do you really want to work out in a health club that seems as noisy and populous as Grand Central Station? Maybe a small yoga group would make better sense. Or you enjoy doing woodwork but hate the cleanup stage—it's too much like cleaning up after performing experiments in the laboratory where you work. Find a craft that creates less of a mess. Maybe you work with staid grown-ups all day. Volunteer to coach a Little League team. You work alone, at home? Volunteer to work evenings on a political campaign. You sit at a desk all day? Join a basketball league.

GOLF AND OTHER WAYS TO NETWORK

A few years ago, when the *Wall Street Journal* polled 351 corporate chief executive officers on the subject, it learned that 59.3 percent had played golf within the past year (making it the most popular CEO leisure activity), but only 6 percent named it as one of their two favorite pastimes. The message is clear: Golf is a *must* activity for those seeking exposure in the business world.

Question: Does golf (or squash or tennis or any other sport you take up partly for office political reasons) constitute an outside interest?

Answer: Probably not.

"If you're golfing because it's good exposure and good for networking, you should consider it as part of your work activity," says Dr. Maddi, "that is, unless you also happen to enjoy it." The act of going 18 holes with your boss may well help advance your career. (You'll have his uninterrupted attention for several hours, although golf etiquette discourages heavy-sell work conversations on the links.) But don't make the mistake of thinking you're relaxing. It's easy for an ambitious person to spend a month of weekend afternoons trying to perfect her backhand in anticipation of the office tennis showdown. But the same person may wonder why—if she's getting so much good exercise—she still feels so tense.

A Vacation That Does What It's Supposed to Do

How many times have you come back to the office from one of those week-long traveling, eating, tanning, and late-night partying binges so fondly called a vacation only to need more rest and relaxation than when you left? Considering the way we mistreat ourselves in an attempt to crowd a year's worth of leisure into seven days, it's no wonder that most of us end up overstuffed, sunburned, and deep in debt . . . yet no more relaxed than the day we left. To keep this from happening to you, take a few tips from Steven Shapiro, Ph.D., psychotherapist and author.

1. When to go: "When the daily grind is *starting* to wear you down, that's the time to take a break," says Dr. Shapiro. "Many people put it off, leaving for that much-needed vacation only after they've dug themselves deep into a hole of depression and fatigue. By the time they do pack their bags, they find that they can't leave their troubles at home and can't enjoy being anywhere else." To avoid this, schedule your two or three major vacations at regular intervals during the year and break up the four- to six-month intervals with a few long weekends. This will keep you from going vacationless for too long a time.

2. What to do: "People often get into ruts where they keep taking the same vacation over and over, even though what once was enjoyable no longer rests and regenerates them," says Dr. Shapiro. "While we are a very work-oriented society, we are also terribly undereducated concerning our leisure options. And what happens to many people is that the security of tradition combines with an innate fear of the unknown to keep them from finding a new vacation place or activity which they might truly enjoy."

Dr. Shapiro suggests two remedies. First, use your long weekends to try experimenting with different kinds of vacation options. If you spend every summer at the shore, try a Friday, Saturday, and Sunday in the mountains. If you don't like it, you haven't blown a big stretch of vacation time. If you *do* enjoy yourself, you've got a new vacation option for next year.

Second, if you find yourself falling into the same old routine each year, try adding two new activities to your things-to-do-list for your next vacation. Perhaps you go to Cape Cod every year but never go whale watching. Try it. But only add *two* new activities, lest you end up with the "too much to do and too little time to do it" syndrome.

3. When to come home: This one is short and sweet. Give yourself a one-day buffer before going back to work. "People tend to think that they can just shift gears instantly, which isn't the case at all," says Dr. Shapiro. "If you go back to work right at the end of your vacation, you may find that your mind and body are still in vacation mode. This can result in some disorientation and confusion, and could account for that low feeling you sometimes get your first couple of days back on the job."

No, there's nothing wrong with developing interests that will put you in touch with the office higher-ups, but don't try to convince yourself you're having fun if you're not.

On the other hand, you may wind up liking whatever it is that puts you in contact (and gives you a common interest) with the boss. Your boss is an opera fanatic? You may just pick up a copy of *Opera Plots Made Easy* and a couple of recordings and suddenly find yourself hooked.

32

LISTENING
SKILLS

Q*uestion:* If talk is cheap, why do we always find ourselves paying such a dear price for not listening?

Answer: Because we've obviously undervalued the true worth of conversation—an easy thing to do since there is such a large quantity of talk in our lives and its quality runs the gamut from time-wasting to life-changing. For example, there was the conversation you had last week with Mrs. Johnson, the widow next door. You made the mistake of asking her how she was doing and let yourself in for a 45-minute reminiscence about how life was better when we had to take our clothes down by the stream and beat them clean with rocks. That time may have been better spent building a replica of the White House out of Wheat Chex. But then again, there was that 3-minute conversation you had with your boss yesterday that changed your life. The one where you found out about your transfer to Anchorage, Alaska.

Simplification is a dangerous thing. From the above examples, it may seem that the difference between an important and an inconsequential conversation is readily apparent. But that isn't necessarily the case. Unfortunately, we tend to make snap judgments concerning the impact of another person's words and then allocate our attention accordingly. The problem with this is that language is at best a rather ineffectual means of communication. Your boss may be saying something of seemingly little import and yet behind the words is a host of other information that may be of vast importance. For example, *why* is she telling you this? How does she personally feel about this information? What is she actually saying without actually spelling it out?

You may be thinking, "I'm not a mind reader. I'll never know the secret messages behind words. Talking is still better than waving semaphore flags at each other. So why not just leave it at that?" Well, the fact of the matter is, you can become a better listener and you can begin to grasp the hidden messages behind conversation.

At this point, you might expect us to proceed to a long list of simple and easy listening techniques all centered around the injunction "pay more attention." But paying more attention, while an oft-repeated piece of advice, is of little help if you don't know what to pay attention to.

So instead we are going to spend a little time with the theories of Gerald Goodman, Ph.D., associate professor of psychology at UCLA and author of *The Talk Book.* Dr. Goodman believes that by understanding the use of several key elements of everyday talk—what he calls "talk tools"—we can begin to discover the real meaning behind what people say.

DISCLOSURES: RISKS THAT BUILD TRUST

Nothing too difficult to start with here. A disclosure is exactly what you would think it is—a personal bit of information revealed by the speaker. "I like to think of disclosures as the dramatists of conversation," says Dr. Goodman. "In the drama of human relationships, disclosures routinely bring people closer together or drive them apart."

Of course there are big and little disclosures. For example, you might say to someone that you regret the fact that you gave up on your xylophone lessons. Nothing too serious there. On the other hand, if you were to say to someone that you feel totally inadequate during lovemaking . . . well, that would be what Dr. Goodman calls a risky disclosure. "I call them this simply because they put the discloser at risk," he says. "But it is this emotional risk-taking that is a key ingredient for creating interpersonal trust."

As listeners, it's safe to say that we all normally recognize really risky disclosures when we hear them. The problem is when we run across disclosures of minor risk and don't see them for what they are. For example, an employee mentions to you that he is a little worried about his future at the company. Perhaps you respond automatically in an encouraging yet off-handed sort of way.

But whenever someone comes to you with a piece of information that falls outside the normal daily exchange, it should sound a little alarm for you to consider the risk the speaker is taking in making his disclosure. In the case of the worried employee, his risk is that you (as his boss) may consider him to be lacking in self-esteem, constantly needing approval, and hardly having the kind of winning attitude that gets people ahead. Considering the risk the employee is taking, your response should be anything but flip.

By listening to, recognizing, and analyzing the magnitude of a disclosure, you can also get some idea as to the amount of trust a person puts in you. Indeed, if we look at disclosures as a bestowal of trust by the speaker upon the listener, then it behooves the listener to respond accordingly. We will talk about empathic response in the next section, but for now attention and respect are suitable responses.

Of course this sometimes gets a little difficult when you run into the bane of every listener: the flooded disclosure. "Flooded disclosure occurs when the 'need to talk about it' dominates the conversation," says Dr. Goodman. "As the discloser becomes preoccupied with reliving, problem solving, complaining, or justifying, everything else concerning the conversation gets pushed to the background, including the listener."

A flooded disclosure might occur when your boss suddenly veers off in the midst of a project planning session to rant for 25 minutes about how upper-level management has set far too high a production quota for him to meet. "The problem with habitual flooders is that they inspire anger," notes Dr. Goodman. "Their overwhelmed victims feel crowded out, bored, or insulted by the self-absorbed, repetitious, obsessive talk marathons."

How should you respond? First you've got to consider that flooders tend to be lonely people. You may be the only person your boss can do this with. So it pays you to play the gracious listener if for no other reason than that you may need the favor returned someday. Second, allowing yourself to be drafted as privy minister to your boss's thoughts will build a relationship of trust that can only do you some good. Third, if you listen, you just might learn something. "To my ear, the language and spontaneous discoveries of flooded disclosures bear close resemblance to the language and discoveries of patients in psychotherapy," notes Dr. Goodman. "In both there is an obsessive, preoccupied, lost-in-thought process that provides avenues for insight and invention."

Of course, disclosure is a two-way street. You may have to take some risks yourself. "I call it disclosure matching," says Dr. Goodman. "And it is a phenomenon that is the bedrock stuff in the making of any long-term association."

Let's go back to the employee worried about his future with the company. You could sit there impassively and listen to his worries, reassure him, and send him on his way. Or you might do a little disclosure matching. Relate the fact that a year or two ago you had similar doubts about your own future. Tell how you dealt with them and what eventually happened. If you give a little, your employee may open up even further. Many managers complain that employees don't come to them with their problems. It may be because the managers seem more like brick walls than people.

REFLECTIONS: ACTS OF EMPATHY

Have you ever been in a room where someone is talking on the phone and all you hear is "yeah . . . uh-huh . . . right . . . yeah"? What that person is actually saying to whoever is on the other end is "I agree, I'm still listening, I haven't laid down the phone and gone into the kitchen to make a sandwich." Basically a reflection says all those things. It also says something else of the utmost importance: *"I understand what you're saying and how you must feel."*

"The term reflection is used because these statements mirror back the heart of another's message," says Dr. Goodman. "They re-present the message, usually in a condensed form. A reflection doesn't try to understand the other person's thoughts or feelings better than he does. It doesn't try to solve the other person's problems, and it doesn't try to add new meaning or analyze the message. Reflections simply show that meaning has been registered. They reveal an act of empathy."

If you consider good listening to be a means of getting the most information you can from a speaker, then reflections could be considered one of your most powerful talk tools. We will see why in the following example from *The Talk Book.* This conversation is one that actually occurred when co-author Glenn Esterly was assigned to conduct an interview with actor John Forsythe for *TV Guide.* At one point they are discussing Forsythe's quadruple heart-bypass surgery. We'll pick up the conversation about 40 minutes into the interview:

FORSYTHE: I had noticed it on the tennis court a couple of times— not feeling quite right. And when I traveled, the jet lag hit me like it never had before. But being like most red-blooded, overly macho American guys, I never did much about it.

ESTERLY: Your body was sending you signals.

FORSYTHE: Right. When I finally went in for tests, lo and behold, they came up with a heart problem.

ESTERLY: There had never been a heart attack?

FORSYTHE: No, but there was a pending possibility. Turned out I had congenitally small coronary arteries, so they had to bypass some clogged arteries.

ESTERLY: Do people die in that kind of surgery?

FORSYTHE: Yes, they do. It's immensely serious surgery—six, seven hours, although they've got it down now where the risks are considerably less these days. It's not exactly a picnic, in any event. The choice was there for me to go either way, to not do it if I didn't want to. I could have gone without it, but it would have meant compromises in the way I lived. Just being careful all the time, always cautious about any exercise and work. That wasn't appealing to me.

ESTERLY: So, even with the surgery risks, you weren't able to settle for a life of restrictions. [Notice how Esterly takes Forsythe's disclosure and boils it down into a perfect one-sentence reflection. It neither puts additional meaning on what Forsythe had just related nor does it comment. It simply reflects. "Yet by showing that he understands, Esterly encourages even more emotion and openness from Forsythe," notes Dr. Goodman.]

FORSYTHE: Oh, *that* would have been devastating for me. There was no bravado in having the surgery. There was almost no alternative. Without it, I faced the prospect of living very tentatively, always the chance that after a hard set of tennis or a hard day at work the heart could fold on me. I couldn't live under that shadow. I'm a vigorous guy.

The reason reflections are so useful and necessary is that we often have a hard time simply saying "I understand" or "I feel for you." Reflections not only reassure the speaker in a subtle manner, but they do so without seriously breaking up the rhythm of a conversation.

Reflections can also be used to guide the speaker when he digresses or moves off a subject before you feel you've heard enough. For example, your boss starts off talking about a new project, its parameters, and how it will be carried out. He moves on to a few of his doubts, one of which is whether or not the company has enough cash to implement the plan. From there he quickly moves on to the people he may assign to handle the project. You, on the other hand, would like to hear a bit more concerning his doubts, since it will be your neck on the line if funds run out. So as the conversation is wrapping up you might say, "Then in your opinion the major problem we face is lack of cash?" This may encourage him to go into more depth.

An interesting phenomenon can occur if you make reflections that are not hitting the mark. "Rather than encouraging the speaker to elaborate, you may find the speaker repeating the same message with a little different twist," says Dr. Goodman. "When understanding seems to come unstuck, as is manifested by your off-the-mark reflections, the person speaking may change the messages several times in an attempt to more accurately portray his thoughts and bring you back on the empathic boat, so to speak." So when practicing reflections in conversation, you may want to keep an ear out for the repeater effect. It could be a sign that you are not homing in on the speaker's meaning even though you thought you were.

INTERPRETATIONS: RESHAPING THE MESSAGE

"The interpretation talk tool is a cousin of reflection," Dr. Goodman notes. "The difference is that the interpretation is as aggressive as the reflection is restrained. The reflection follows the other's message, avoiding attempts at adding new meaning. But the interpretation can take the same message and remanufacture it, classify it, and deliver it as a piece of news."

"Car dealers are all crooked" is an interpretation. "The people aren't as friendly here as they are at home" is an interpretation. "Those marketing boys really know what they are doing" is also an interpretation. Basically whenever you or anyone else takes information and forms an opinion, whether it be in the shape of a solution to a problem, an insult, advice, a character analysis, or a criticism, you've got an interpretation.

"Given sincerely, interpretations try to tell something that isn't known to the listener," says Dr. Goodman. "Unfortunately, the new knowledge offered is often speculation, even though it's presented as the whole truth and nothing but the truth."

As a listener in a business setting, you may want to focus on the intent behind interpretations before acting on the information they relay. For example, if your assistant manager came into your office and said, "John has been an hour late to work eight times in the last two weeks," you might want to act immediately. Assuming the assistant manager is honest, this specific data portrays a problem that must be attended to. On the other hand, if that same assistant manager came in and said, "John is always late," that is probably an interpretation. You may first want to think about the relationship between John and the assistant manager before taking action. You may also want to find out the exact tardiness stats. It could be that a personality clash has magnified two late arrivals into "always late."

If it isn't a fact, it's an interpretation. Thinking about this difference can affect the way you listen to people. For example, you go to your manager with a great new idea but he tells you that the VP isn't interested in change. It may seem like a fact, but do you know that for sure? You may want to dig deeper. The fact may be that the department can't afford to implement any changes right now. If that's the case, your manager probably won't mind explaining it to you. On the other hand it may be that the VP has turned down the manager's last five ideas because they weren't good. It may seem like the VP doesn't want change, but in fact that's only your manager's interpretation. The VP may welcome your hot new idea.

"One important area where you have to keep your ear tuned to interpretation is in novel and new situations," notes Dr. Goodman. "Especially ones where there is the potential for embarrassment, confusion, and possible loss of face. In these types of cases we search for comfort by searching for sense. We want to form a cohesive picture of the environment we are operating in and we want to form it fast."

This is the kind of syndrome you occasionally see when a foreigner comes to this country and after two days says, "You crazy Americans are always rushing around. You never take any time to relax." Some of us rush around, others don't. Obviously, the statement is not completely true, but being a stranger in a very strange land, the foreigner wants some solid ground to stand on. And that ground is his general interpretation of how Americans behave.

In the office, new employees, newly promoted employees, and people at the beginning of projects often fall into the same trap. They are subject to generalized interpretations which either save face during a problem or support feelings of pessimism or optimism. For example, "those marketing people just aren't playing ball with us on this one" may be true. But then again it may be that your marketing liaison isn't giving them what they need because they've become picky and antagonistic in their requests.

So when it comes to interpretations, the key is to listen for phrasing. One tip: In business, words that often are danger signs of an interpretation have absolute characteristics—always, never, impossible, everyone, nobody, nothing.

QUESTIONS: THE INNOCENT AND THE WICKED

"Questions are what I consider to be the most popular piece of language," says Dr. Goodman. "We use them for reasons that are plain and veiled, innocent and wicked, protective and generous, loving and spiteful. The spoken question is used for a wider range of motives than any other talk tool."

The most interesting thing about questions is not so much what they are asking as what they are telling. For example, your boss walks in and says, "Isn't it about time for you to clean up your office?" He doesn't expect an answer such as "No, it isn't time yet, but it will be in exactly 3½ days." He's not *asking* you anything. He's *telling* you to clean your office. This is what would be called a loaded question, one in which the message is more important than the question asked.

Around the office we are constantly running into loaded and even insidious questions. When someone offers an interpretation within a question, he or she is obviously looking for a particular answer for a particular reason. "Don't you think the way we do things in this department is outmoded?" Depending on who is asking the question, you may want to be guarded in your response. It may be the manager is looking for popular support for change. It could be the office snitch is looking for a malcontent to offer as a human sacrifice to the manager. So when you listen to a loaded question, ask yourself why it wasn't phrased more neutrally (e.g., "Do you think we're handling production as best we can or could we make some changes?") "Loaded questions aren't difficult to spot in a conversation," notes Dr. Goodman. "They often start with phrases such as 'wouldn't it be better if,' 'why don't you,' 'shouldn't we try to,' 'aren't you being,' and 'doesn't that make you.' "

Semi-innocent questions are looking for a particular response, but they don't necessarily manipulate the listener to make that response. "What do you think of my proposal?" could be an innocent question made to a superior who is going to have the final say and probably has criticism as well as praise to give. But if the speaker is a co-worker asking you (who has no more or less experience and no more or less power), then the odds are he's looking for praise. He really doesn't want to hear criticism. Closed questions are asked when a brief answer is wanted. "But brief doesn't mean trivial," says Dr. Goodman. "Answers to closed questions can be vital. We recognize these often-demanding talk tools by their context and especially by their music. We tend to put an upward inflection on the end. We almost sing closed questions with a voice that sounds eager or impatient, wanting a speedy, cogent answer."

A closed question might be "Can you finish this by the end of the day?" The speaker wants a yes or no answer, not an explanation of the scheduling involved. Recognizing closed questions for what they are can keep you from running off at the mouth when someone asks you something simple.

On the other hand, you want to make sure not to use a closed question when you want someone to elaborate on a particular topic. You could ask your boss, "Has my work been up to par?" and he may say "yes," and that's that. But if you want elaboration, you might ask "In which areas have I been doing well and in which have I been losing ground?" "Open questions typically have no upward inflection at the end," notes Dr. Goodman. "They invite longer, unrushed answers. The one thing to keep in mind is that a great deal of conversational frustration originates because people don't use open and closed questions properly. The result is that you get answers which either are not full enough to be satisfying or are four times longer than what you were looking for."

Another interesting variation is the disclosing question. "An example of this," says Dr. Goodman, "would be when a teenage boy takes his car to the shop and asks the mechanic, 'Do you think the carburetor's too lean, or does the fuel pump sound weak, or could it be a clogged gas line?' Basically what the young man is telling the mechanic is that he's no dummy about these things. And indeed, one use of disclosing questions is to display knowledge or even to brag."

In the office you may run into this kind of question in several forms. It could be a co-worker asking you whether or not he should take this great promotion that was just offered to him. Well, think about it: Why does anyone need to ask whether he should take a *great* promotion? He's not asking you anything; he's bragging. Or have you ever had someone ask you a question that is so detailed, well informed, and conclusive that your answer is superfluous? Again, that person is not asking you anything. He's telling you that he is, in fact, well informed.

What we have covered in this chapter merely scratches the surface of Dr. Goodman's fascinating analysis. But this much is certain: In business, what's said and how it's said are at least as important as any paper-bound fact or figure. Thinking about talk tools and how they are used can sharpen your listening focus. At some point you may find yourself utilizing a reflection or uncovering a disclosure. And when that happens you'll know you're doing what all those other books and experts simplistically encourage you to do (without ever telling you how): You're paying more attention.

33

MANAGEMENT

It's a marvelous moment when somebody calls you into an office and announces that as a result of your hard work, you've been selected to ascend to the ranks of management. There's reason for celebration, of course. But it's also a time to prepare yourself for some serious changes.

The truth is, some of the skills that helped propel your career as a "doer" will backfire on you as a supervisor. And many a good worker turns into a disappointed manager by instinctively clinging to what worked in the past.

Here's just one example: As a new manager, you've got the choice of chastising (and hopefully remotivating) a poorly performing employee who's jeopardized the timely completion of an important revenues projection, or you could crunch the numbers yourself. You know you can do the work properly and swiftly, so you go ahead and do it. But by failing to confront the problem employee, you've just sidestepped one of your principal managerial duties. "When you become a manager you suddenly have to deal with messy things—like people," says Dick Pearson, the senior vice-president for corporate planning and development at Farm Bureau Insurance in Indianapolis.

Becoming a manager means fighting the urge to do better yourself what you are supposed to get others to do. It means becoming comfortable with the paradox that you will be giving credit to others for your department's successes but personally accepting the blame for failures. It means understanding completely how your end of the organization operates, and making sure it operates effectively—while you simultaneously look for ways to upgrade that operation.

Becoming a manager means learning to expect the unexpected, knowing how to keep yourself well-informed, learning to trust your intuition, understanding that you'll have to accept compromises, and realizing that sometimes, a little vagueness goes a long way. Above all it means *allowing* yourself to become a manager, and making yourself comfortable with the new role. None of this comes easily. But it starts with a bit of self-management.

FINDING OUT WHAT'S EXPECTED

Amazing as it seems, many folks take on management positions without first gaining a clear understanding of what's expected of them. (This is more common with new managers who are promoted from within a company than with those who are hired from the outside.) Pearson, who is an adjunct professor at the Indiana University School of Business, suggests the first thing you do after becoming a supervisor is sit down with your superior and ask:

- "What am I expected to do?"
- "What are the objectives of my group?"
- "What constitutes a good job?"
- "What kinds of authority do I have?"
- "What kinds of limitations do I have?"

Don't assume anything. If you have questions, now is the time to ask them. As astoundingly simple and crucial as this process sounds, it is often ignored.

ACCEPTING THE CHALLENGE

There's a commitment you have to make to your new role as manager, and it's no different from the commitment you make when you wed or produce a child. It begins by psychologically accepting your new role and by becoming open to learning the new responsibilities that role requires. Too many people fall victim to what Eric G. Flamholtz, Ph.D., coauthor of *The Inner Game of Management: How to Make the Transition to a Managerial Role,* refers to as the "Doer Syndrome." These folks continue to think and act like doers or technicians rather than like managers, often merely to avoid failure in the new job. "Their concept of the role is not correct," he says.

Why do they do it? Basically, there are three possible reasons. Their self-esteem is still tied to their performance as a doer instead of their performance as a manager. Or they can't let go of their strong need to exert direct control over results. Or they have not accepted the fact that in their role as manager, not everybody is going to like them. Dr. Flamholtz, who is a professor of management at UCLA's Graduate School of Management and president of Los Angeles–based Management Systems Consulting Group, offers this advice.

Manage your self-esteem so that it's tied more to your performance as a manager than to your performance as a doer. That's easier said than done if you feel a rush of anxiety every time you have to appraise an employee's performance or issue a directive. You'll need to change your frame of reference. "First you have to understand how a manager actually spends his or her time. Then look where you are now and where you need to be relevant to your role in the organization," he says. Next, understand why you're spending so much time as a doer. Is it because you like it better than managing? (Then perhaps you should change jobs.) Is it because the organization is telling you that you have to? (Then you should consider trying to change the organization or change organizations.) Is it because you don't have the skills? (Then get some training. Ask your employer to enroll you in a management development program, one that will teach you skills that will enable you to be comfortable performing your new role.)

Manage your need to exert direct control over people and results. As a manager, you'll be expected to accomplish your department's goals *indirectly*, through the work of your employees. Here's a relatively painless method for letting go. List ten things that your employees do that you feel a strong inclination to do yourself. Divide those tasks or functions into the following three categories: (A) I Must Control These, (B) I Probably Could Control These, But I Don't Have to; and (C) I Certainly Don't Need to Worry About These. "Give away all of your C items and some of the B items and see what happens," suggests Dr. Flamholtz. "Then, as you feel comfortable with the concept of giving up control, give up the rest of the B's and then the A's." Accept the fact that not everything will go as you planned, and that some efforts will be miserable failures. The process of trial and error will enable you to know when you're relinquishing enough control.

Learn to accept the fact that as a manager, not everybody is going to like you. A lot people are ineffective managers because they want everybody to like them. But there is a toughening process that takes place each time you are able to give an order (even though you could do the task yourself) or criticize an employee without wrenching inside. When you do enough of it, you slowly become comfortable with the reality that you'll make some people unhappy. So tell yourself it's part of your job—if you want to be an effective manager. But remember: Don't go overboard. Don't

Management Do's and Don'ts

Do trust your intuition. "Trust yourself. You know more than you think you do." Those are the opening words of Dr. Benjamin Spock's book *Baby and Child Care*. They apply to new managers as well as to new parents. So respect your hunches—for many executives, they're what beget successes.

Do appreciate good work in subordinates and compliment it. Nothing destroys morale like unappreciated hard work. And remember this: When complimenting, do it publicly. When criticizing, do it privately.

Don't take credit for the good work of subordinates. Superiors understand that your subordinates' good work is a reflection on your ability to lead, delegate, and make sound management decisions. There's no need to draw any additional attention to your own role.

Do make yourself familiar with employees and their work by paying regular informal visits to their work stations. *In Search of Excellence* authors Thomas J. Peters and Robert H. Waterman, Jr., popularized this concept as "Management by Wandering Around." It's not an idle exercise designed to stretch your legs and get you out of your office. As you make your rounds, ask people about their jobs and solicit their suggestions for changes.

Don't be inaccessible. Make yourself available to your employees. If your workday is so tightly structured that there's little time to listen completely to their problems, schedule regular office hours—even if they have to be after official work hours—much as college professors do.

Do tackle problems as soon as they occur. Don't let them fester. Problems have a way of multiplying if they're not dealt with promptly, predictably, and dispassionately. So don't let them get any worse.

make the mistake of assuming that nobody will like you, and that since nobody will like you, you can be as demanding and overbearing as you'd like. Strike a balance.

LEARNING HOW TO GIVE ORDERS

Beverly Potter, Ph.D., a Berkeley, California–based management consultant and workplace psychologist, doesn't like the word "orders." She prefers the word "directives," citing *Megatrends* author John Naisbitt's theory

Don't be afraid to be a little vague about your plans. No, we're not proposing dishonesty. But in some instances, by being a bit imprecise about your intentions, you leave yourself some room to change your strategy or position before it turns out to be wrong. No, you don't have to put all of your cards on the table. But *never* lie.

Do treat your employees fairly. In most cases, they will respond in kind. "You have to treat people forcefully, but fairly. If you do, they will respect you," says Joan Iaconetti, psychotherapist and coauthor of *First-Time Manager.*

Do behave in a manner that will make your subordinates trust you. Start by making it clear that you trust your employees.

Don't underestimate the destructive power of disgruntled subordinates. They will undermine you the first chance they get, which will be sooner than you think.

Do accept the fact that you need the support of the people below you in order to move ahead yourself. It's one of the first lessons learned by officers when they lead soldiers into battle.

Do be predictable. By acting otherwise, you are unfairly changing the rules for your staff in the middle of the game. If you're the type who has to have everything in writing, for example, *say so* and don't change that policy, suggests Iaconetti. You have nothing to gain by confusing your subordinates.

Don't ignore your insecurities about being a manager. Face up to them. Accept that fact that you may sometimes need to seek advice from others. Seek that advice and listen.

Don't lose sight of long-range goals. Iaconetti suggests you spend 10 minutes each day thinking first about your short-run goals (such as how you'd like to improve your department's operations). Then spend 10 minutes focusing on the long term. "Stand back and ask yourself what you're aiming for, personally and professionally," she advises. (This is a useful way to fill commuting time.)

that the new leader is a "facilitator," not an order-giver. Regardless, she has devised a four-step process that can help anyone who feels uncomfortable urging subordinates to do something for them. She calls her process DAD-Check (Describe, Ask, Direct, Check Out).

Describe the situation. Instead of just saying "Please type this paper by two o'clock," be very objective in explaining the task in terms of your company's needs. "The boss is coming in unexpectedly this afternoon and we need to make a good impression on him by having our budget report ready." Remember, people are more willing to perform tasks if they have a frame of reference.

Select a Style That Works for You

Okay, so the guy you succeeded ascended from mailroom to executive suite in record time, fueled by a blunt, autocratic style that made him nothing short of a legend. It worked for him, but it may not work for you. If you try to adapt a style that doesn't fit, it just won't succeed. You won't feel comfortable and neither will others. One option: Psychotherapist and author Joan Iaconetti suggests you spend time thinking about the five best managers you ever had. Try to analyze the personality traits, skills, and circumstances that made them so good. Then try to emulate what you can. Likewise, think of the five worst managers, to give you an idea of what you'd like to avoid.

Ask for clarification or suggestions. Say "What's it going to take to get this out by two o'clock?" Or "How do you suggest we get it done?" By asking questions, you're engaging the employee in the problem-solving effort, explains Dr. Potter. The secretary, for example, while explaining that she is busy doing other urgent assignments, may suggest bringing in a temporary worker to do the typing.

Give the directive in a clear, simple sentence. You do this once you've asked enough questions that the two of you have arrived at a suitable solution. Your directive is a summary of the suggestions: "Okay, you'll call in a temp who will be able to complete this by two o'clock."

Check it out. Say "How does that sound to you?" It's a way of confirming that the other person understands the assignment and has made a commitment to it.

Dr. Potter suggests that you avoid using qualifying prefaces that make you sound weak. If you start out by saying "This may be a silly idea, but . . . ," people will stop listening, she says. Ditto if you begin with "Perhaps I'm wrong, but . . . " You're putting a possible rebuttal in the other person's mouth, explains Dr. Potter, who is author of *Turning Around: Keys to Motivation and Productivity.*

ACCEPTING RESPONSIBILITY FOR EMPLOYEES' MISTAKES

Your subordinates' performance is a reflection on your management prowess. So if you constantly complain to your boss that your employees

Three Types of Bad Managers

During his career in the petrochemical industry, Paul Oman has seen his share of bad managers. Now the president of Protec, a Houston-based marketing consulting firm, he reports on three distinct categories. Do any of these seem familiar?

The I'm-Far-Too-Important-to-Have-to-Put-Up-with-You Manager

Prime candidates: Entrepreneurs and sales people who become managers.

Character traits: They surround themselves with "yes-people" who will do nothing but feed their egos.

How to tell if you're one: People are afraid of you. They never come forward to suggest changes or offer opinions that may differ from your own.

The Big-Chief Manager

Prime candidates: Relentless corporate climbers.

Character traits: They have to keep their fingers in everything. They're so wrapped up in their own success that they don't respect others. They're engrossed only in the procedures with which they themselves are familiar.

How to tell if you're one: You find yourself saying, "Here's how we used to do it; here's how it should be done," or in any other way constantly harping back to when *you* had the subordinate's job. You never look for changes and don't even want to listen to ways of upgrading the operation you manage.

The I'm-the-Only-One-Who-Can-Do-Anything-around-Here Manager

Prime candidates: Anyone with an inclination toward perfectionism.

Character traits: Inability to relinquish tasks that they can do better.

How to tell if you're one: You are constantly redoing the work of others. You are constantly talking about how incompetent everybody is. You express generalized dissatisfaction with your staff. You work endless extra hours while your subordinates have little to do. Meanwhile, you know something is wrong but don't want to consider yourself a factor in the problem.

are screwing up, her instinct is to wonder how you let them do that in the first place. But things *occasionally* go wrong in all jobs, and you should be prepared for facing your superiors when such setbacks occur. That means taking the blame for those problems. "You don't have to take the blame in a way that you look bad. Take it in a way that communicates that you have acted to solve the problem," says Dr. Potter. Here's how.

State the facts. Rather than apologizing for the error, it's smart to start out with the simple facts. ("The layout was not in on time." "He failed to meet his sales projection.") If you offer a reason ("There was a miscommunication." "He overestimated the market."), make sure it is factual, and not a diatribe on the person's traits ("He's lazy." "He's unrealistic.") This is not the time to evaluate an employee's general performance.

Express your concern. To communicate that you are not minimizing the error, use an "affect" statement, something that explains how the situation has affected you. ("I'm distressed about this." Or "This is of concern to me.")

Make a problem-solving statement. Explain how the error will be corrected (if possible) and what steps you'll take to prevent a similar mistake from happening again. ("I'll be meeting with him several times a week instead of only once a week." "I'm working with him to set benchmarks.") Remember, you can't make up for the past; but by acknowledging the mistake and focusing squarely on solving the problem, you'll look strong in your supervisor's eyes.

34

MAVERICKS

Mav-er-ick. *n* (After S. Maverick, 19th-century Texan whose cattle had no brand.) 1. an unbranded animal, esp. a lost calf. 2. [Colloq.] a person who acts independently of any organization, political party, etc.

Hey, hot stuff.

How does it feel to be the house trailblazer? The radical young firebrand with the sizzle and the savvy to skyrocket along at supersonic speed? Zipping up the ladder in record time, zapping down anyone foolish enough to get in your way. Pulling crazy new ideas out of your ear and getting people excited about them! It must feel:

Terrific. There's no energy like that of an unleashed, uninhibited, youthful revolutionary. It's a pleasure to mastermind great things, to challenge the status quo and be taken seriously despite your lack of decades, to be such a source of energy and fresh thinking and fun for others. It must feel:

Lonely. Inevitably, others in the herd will start to move away. ("Just who does he think he is? And why didn't he ask me my opinion first?") It must feel:

Scary. Basking in the spotlight at 23, you just might be at the pinnacle, staring ahead at a rest-of-your-life anticlimax, saying, No, it doesn't get any better than this (translation: It may get a lot worse). Or you may be fearful, in some remote corner of your mind, that you're going to trample one step too far in the wrong direction. Or that those in the herd will suddenly decide to organize a stampede that will run you into the mud.

It's complicated, this business of being a maverick. People who trade in their sensible wingtips for a pair of in-your-face sneakers sometimes find that they have to tread amazingly lightly. Organizations put up with mavericks only to the extent that their contributions are not offset by the drawbacks, which are many. They alienate those around them, they cause friction within their units, they frustrate their managers. No small wonder, then, that workplaces don't go overboard in fostering such personalities. "Most organizations couldn't handle it if everybody challenged the status quo," says William Alper, Ph.D., a New York City organizational psychologist and consultant. "Somebody has to be the soldier."

But the trouble is, just as they confuse and offend others, mavericks may be the office's best source of creativity. And if an organization doesn't find a way to accommodate the brilliant rabble-rouser today, it's a sure bet he's the kind of smarty who will prance out the door and start his own competing firm tomorrow. So managers of mavericks, just like the mavericks themselves, must strike a delicate balance—encouraging highly independent behavior when it leads to high output, discouraging it when it becomes counterproductive.

WHEN A MAVERICK ALIENATES PEERS

This is probably the most common problem facing the breed. Since they rarely exhibit stellar (or even middling) social skills, mavericks tend to turn people off. They're not good listeners. They're not good team players. They are impatient and intolerant. Their very autonomy and vitality threaten others. And they don't care. "The peer structure around them can become not only negative, but hostile," says Bruce Ogilvie, Ph.D., a psychologist and professor emeritus at San Jose State University who has studied high-performance men and women. "They don't reach out to those around them. Most people can't communicate with them, and therefore feel devalued in their presence. And mavericks tend to be just not conscious of all this; they tend to be oblivious of the effect they're having on people."

If you're a bit of a maverick yourself, here's how to tell if you're going overboard. In meetings, people don't argue with your ideas, but they don't support them, either. No one ever comes into your office. No one is terribly interested in what happens in your personal life. Office cliques form and you're not included. People begin to withhold information and support—reports get to you two days late. People don't want to work on projects with you. They don't even want to engage in conversations with you. "A lot of mavericks are so darn bright that you can't win an argument with them, so others try to shorten their dialogue with them," says Dr. Alper.

Advice for mavericks. Since the odds are that you aren't proficient at recognizing social signals, start learning to develop your internal radar *now.* Check your co-workers' body language. First, the obvious things. Do people move away from you and try to get out of conversations? Then the more subtle stuff. Are eyebrows slightly raised and eyes rolled when you say things? Solicit feedback. Learn to go to management and simply ask, "How'm I doing?" Then press for specifics: "What am I doing well? Fine, I'm coming up with useful ideas, but how about my style and office behavior?" Says Dr. Alper, "As managers, we love it when people ask such questions. And more of us should be fostering an environment that encourages people to ask."

Make it a priority to engage socially with co-workers. And control any urges to bill yourself to them as the house smarty. Addressing fast-trackers in her book *Whiz Kids: Success at an Early Age,* organizational psychologist Marilyn Machlowitz, Ph.D., advises, "Don't come on like gangbusters. When people build themselves up too much, there is a tendency for others to try to knock them off their pedestals. Fit in before you stand out. . . . The first step is to gain acceptance, not to show how outstanding you are. Save that for later."

Mavericks should strive to be "reverently disrespectful" when they are challenging the organization or its leaders, says Terrence Deal, Ph.D., a Vanderbilt University professor of education and human development and coauthor of *Corporate Cultures: The Rites and Rituals of Corporate Life.* (Translation: Anything that can be perceived as an attack should be delivered as good-naturedly as possible.) "That way you won't come off as being mean," he says.

Advice for managers. "If I'm the manager of a gifted maverick, first I'd want to know whether that person eventually wants to become a manager and run an organization where people would be under his guidance," says Dr. Alper. "Some high achievers don't have any management aspirations, but it's the only way to get ahead in many organizations. So I would work to deal with any negative behaviors by giving the person constant feedback, by putting him into training programs that teach him such things as listening skills. I would also give him temporary assignments in task forces. It may drive him nuts initially, but it may give him exposure without necessarily dampening this creativity.

"If he doesn't want to become a leader, I would fight for him to be put in situations that carry more responsibility, prestige, and income—so he won't leave. I'd try to reward him by putting him to work in special positions, in small groups, or on temporary assignments as a way of accommodating him."

Dr. Ogilvie adds: "I'd ask the person to reflect on how important the people around him are and in what ways he needs them. I'd have him step outside of himself and begin to examine what it takes to build a support staff—even though it may mean relinquishing some of his autonomy. I'd ask him to determine what about his behavior he could change without negating his positive qualities."

AVOIDING 3 VERSIONS
OF THE FLASH-IN-THE-PAN SYNDROME

1. The self-destructing maverick. It's almost a cliché: A creative upstart is taken seriously by his organization at the initial stages of his career, but his self-confidence becomes so strong that it fuels his own destruction. When you become so brazenly focused on your wonderful talents and your value to the organization, you make yourself blind to events that could work to limit your advancement. ("What? Our division is getting a new general manager? I'm sure she'll like my crazy style and unrelenting openness as much as her predecessor did.")

Solution for mavericks: Control your self-assurance enough that you can be open to changes in philosophy, personnel, or strategy that would affect the organization's tolerance for your style of behavior. Understand the impact of your personality on others, and develop a clear, objective sense of what you can and cannot get away with. Your immediate supervisor may have no problem with the fact that you stroll in at noon and work until midnight. But *her* boss may get angry when, for the fifth time in a row, she's unable to get some information from you at 11:15 A.M. Another attitude that turns people off, especially co-workers who may be at the pinnacle of their careers after years of hard work: The I'm-just-passing-through frame of mind. Delete it from your repertoire.

Solution for managers: Understand your level of tolerance for the maverick's audacious style—know precisely what you're willing to accept in exchange for the person's high-energy output. Then be clear with the maverick on what is and what is not expected of him, and on when his style is inappropriate. You walk a thin line, because you don't want to be needlessly discouraging. Be honest with yourself when you feel threatened by the maverick and develop a strategy for shoring up your self-esteem.

2. The failing-to-grow maverick. Overconfidence may be the problem here, too. You fail to keep one eye focused on the future, and you suddenly wind up becoming part of the past. If you dwell on your current success and the skills that contribute to it without giving much thought to what may happen down the line, two major problems can result: You're liable to get so competent that you are bored. Or you may find yourself becoming obsolete if your environment changes.

Solution for mavericks: To avoid making yourself either bored or obsolete, force yourself to expand your professional horizons. Ask management for training in skills that are unrelated to your present position. Volunteer for task forces or projects in different areas of the organization. Don't be afraid to grow.

Solution for managers: Anticipate the time when the maverick, like most folks, will tire of his or her current assignment. Mix up responsibilities. Don't become too dependent on the person for any one set of skills. Encourage a diversity of experiences.

3. The growing-too-fast maverick. An organization pegs you as having high potential, as being the type of individual it likes to shove forcefully up the corporate pole. Beware. In its enthusiasm over your talent and quick advancement, it may fail to give you enough hard-core training. You'll grow too fast for anybody's good. "Some companies take people with high potential, those who look right and sound right (whether or not they're mavericks), and promote them every fifteen to eighteen months," says Dr. Alper. The problem with such a timetable, he explains, is that the fast-tracker will not be in any one position long enough to learn how to fix the mistakes he or she will inevitably make. Moreover, he adds, "When an organization promotes someone at such a fast rate, they don't have the time to adequately judge the person's performance."

Solution for mavericks: You're only shortchanging yourself if you assume that since you'll quickly be rotated out of a particular assignment, you don't have to develop a firm grasp on its demands. If your organization believes that you've mastered a special skill—but *you're* not quite convinced—be honest with yourself and with management about your feelings. It's better to spend an extra three months in a lower-level assignment than to let your inadequacies surface in a higher-level one.

Solution for managers: "Think intelligently about the types of assignments you give to mavericks," advises Dr. Alper. "Broaden their skills and experiences, but don't promote them so quickly that you can't honestly judge their performance. You may be toying with disaster."

A FEW FINAL THOUGHTS FOR MAVERICKS OR WOULD-BE MAVERICKS

Can you develop the qualities of a maverick if they don't come naturally to you? Don't count on it. True, you may gain an entirely new and beneficial perspective if you start challenging the status quo. And if you throw off the shackles of convention, there's a high chance you'll free yourself to think and act at least a bit more creatively than before. But an honest-to-goodness, full-tilt revolutionary is more likely to be born, not made.

On the flip side, if you're a dyed-in-the-wool rabble-rouser, you're unlikely to experience much success in the clutches of an organization that doesn't value your style. You've got to remember above all that style takes a back seat to substance. Smart mavericks are well aware that they have to back up their audacity and impatience by working hard and smart—in fact, they may have to work even harder and smarter than ordinary people.

35

MEETINGS

If the notion of reading a chapter about meetings makes your eyes glaze over, you have lots of company. Meetings have had a bad reputation ever since the time when Adam called in Eve to discuss the hazards of serpents and fruit. Oh, a few innovative folks throughout the ages have tried to improve upon this often time-wasting method of sharing information. Southern Californians, for example, started taking their meetings in hot tubs—until soggy documents began shorting out their fax machines. New Yorkers favored the "Power Breakfast" ritual, and then "Business Teas" came into vogue. Those lasted until a certain real estate magnate realized how quickly his negotiating power (not to mention his image) diminished each time he wrapped his fingers around a tidy crustless sandwich. Even the plethora of high-tech alternatives that promised to antiquate the traditional person-to-person business assembly hasn't made much of a dent: Hey, who *wants* to talk via satellite to some "co-participator" from St. Louis while looking at his image on a TV monitor the size of France?

Despite all the exasperation, though, meetings in some form or another are here to stay. So let's take a lesson from Alcoholics Anonymous and try to understand what we can't change and try to change what we can.

Is THIS MEETING NECESSARY?

When the Wharton Center for Applied Research studied the matter for 3M Corporation in 1987 and 1988, it discovered that senior executives spent 23 hours a week in meetings *not counting* preparation time. Yet the executives reported that only 52 percent of the meetings were effective and that 22 percent could have been handled more easily through memos or phone calls.

Anyone old enough to recall the gas rationing days of World War II remembers automobile dashboards decorated with the words "Is This Trip Necessary?" So next time you order daily-planning calendars, maybe you should arrange to have the query "Is This Meeting Necessary?" printed across the top of each page.

If you've got something to tackle and your initial instinct is to call a meeting, stop and think for a moment about why you really want to meet. Is it just because that's how you've always done it? Perhaps you are mindlessly devoted to meetings because they afford you the only opportunity for Public Displays of Articulation. Or because they're the only available occasion to publicly humiliate an office competitor. (Hey, it's been known to happen.) Before proceeding, ask yourself these two additional questions.

Would a memo suffice? If the purpose of your meeting is only to disseminate information, send a memo, suggests David Lindo, Ph.D., former chief financial officer of Planning Systems, a McLean, Virginia, software developer, and author of *Supervision Can Be Easy.* You can send a memo and solicit opinions, too. When Dr. Lindo gets an inspiration at midnight—or any time he can't easily phone up others for their views of his

---

Could You Have Saved This Meeting?

"If you ever walked out of a meeting thinking 'This was a lousy meeting,' but you didn't say anything or try to do anything about it while you were in the room, I'd say you're part of the problem, not part of the solution," says Richard E. Byrd, Ph.D., a Minneapolis-based management consultant and author of *Guide to Personal Risk Taking.* When it comes to ensuring meeting efficiency, the responsibility shouldn't always rest on the shoulders of the person who chairs the meeting; unless she's told otherwise, she may just assume that her gathering is running productively.

Let's say you've been in session for an hour and a half and have barely made any headway on the first order of business. Why not just come right out and say *without a trace of criticism in your voice*, "I'm feeling that we're not moving along fast enough. Do you think we should reverse priority, Madam Chairperson, and talk about computers first?" Dr. Byrd points out that if such statements are made with candor and backed up with suggested options, they won't take a judgmental tone.

idea—he types out a memo and has it distributed to people whose judgments he values. He asks recipients to write back with their response. "It allows you to stack up those responses, read them, and then rewrite and resend the memo," he says. Sometimes Dr. Lindo prepares a "mini-paper" on the topic, explaining why he did or didn't act on particular responses to his original memo.

Can you tackle the problem on a one-to-one basis? Why not simply talk with the one or two people you really need to talk with, instead of dragging in others whom you routinely include. Be especially wary of routine, regularly scheduled meetings. It may seem like a productive idea to meet with your entire staff every Monday morning at 9:00 A.M. (and sure, it's a terrific way of getting them into the office on time). But when the meetings start to lack a well-defined purpose, they quickly degenerate into wasted time.

DOUBLE YOUR EFFICIENCY:
CUT MEETING TIME IN HALF

You'll be amazed at how much tedium you can take out of your next meeting by following these simple pointers.

Don't waste time sharing information that can be distributed in advance. By studying the data ahead of time, participants will come prepared for action. Instead of examining the information and forming opinions *during* the meeting, they'll have done it beforehand.

If possible, also distribute an agenda in advance. Or post it on a bulletin board. It may inspire participants to do their homework.

Scrutinize your guest list. The more people involved in a meeting, the more opinions to hear and the more time you'll be trapped. So before calling a meeting, go over your list of participants and weed out any who may not be needed. Organizational dynamics expert Dr. Lindo estimates that the most effective meetings occur with five participants. When 13 or more are gathered, he says, the meeting becomes a conference, which minimizes the effectiveness of decision making. Each time you add another person to a meeting, you increase your opportunity for disagreement and misunderstanding," he says. "It's better to have fewer people and—if you need—additional meetings."

Eliminate distractions. When possible, avoid holding meetings in your office (or anyone else's office). By limiting gatherings to a neutral conference room, you eliminate the subtle feeling among participants that they are socializing with you. Minutes won't be wiled away with idle questions about the Oriental print hanging on your wall or the vacation photograph sitting on your desk.

Don't encourage idle chitchat. Sure, everybody likes to giggle over the love-life ups and downs of the accounting department Casanova. But while your meeting should never be a humorless event, remember that casual conversation can eat up valuable time.

Make people stand. This sounds a bit cruel, but if you have to call a handful of people into your office for an impromptu, one- or two-issue meeting, try to ensure that a stack of legal documents occupies any seating space you may have. The point: By denying them comfort, you help ensure that participants won't linger over the issues. They'll probably come to a decision relatively quickly and then leave.

Tape-record your meetings. If you want people to think before they respond, try taping your meetings. When participants are aware that they are being taped, they tend not to ramble on relentlessly, says Dr. Lindo.

ORCHESTRATING AND CONDUCTING A HARMONIOUS MEETING

Great, productive meetings don't just happen. They're carefully crafted. Here are some tips to remember.

Know the agenda you want to cover. It's amazing how many meetings fail for the simple reason that there's no clear agenda.

Know the participants and as much as you can about their opinions on agenda topics. If possible, survey the people beforehand for their views. That way you can anticipate problems and gauge the level of support you'll be getting, suggests Waldron Berry, Ph.D., former management professor at University of Central Florida. (Note: This is different from loading the meeting in your favor.)

Try to defuse conflicts beforehand. If you know there will be a strong disagreement between various participants or groups of participants, try to head off any time-wasting opposition beforehand by meeting with opponents separately. "Try to work out some compromise they both may accept," suggests Dr. Berry.

Don't surprise participants with undisclosed meeting topics. They'll come to dread all meetings (and start to distrust you).

Arrive early, if possible. It's a chance to quickly survey other early arrivers' opinions on agenda items.

If time is a factor, set limits. Before the meeting, establish an approximate time limit for each agenda item. Keep track of the time. (And keep the meeting on track.) Explain to participants that because you don't want the meeting to exceed a certain time limit, you may interrupt the discussion when it veers off-target.

Make clear-cut assignments. If participants are expected to make presentations or prepare information to share in the meeting, make sure they understand exactly what is expected. If possible, check with them a few days prior to the meeting to determine how prepared they are. It will reinforce the importance of their homework.

Set a positive tone. You're not likely to accomplish much if the meeting turns into a laugh-fest. But nothing turns off participants quicker than a dead-serious meeting with no place for levity.

Be supportive. In the meeting itself, if someone offers a suggestion that you don't want to accept, look for at least a part of the suggestion that you can support.

Don't be afraid to compromise when you disagree with someone. It sends a powerful, positive message to others.

Schedule breaks—even 5-minute breaks—every hour. Purely for the regenerative effects.

Know when you've reached the point of diminishing returns. Are the suggestions getting more and more unworkable? Has the discussion mysteriously circled back to where it began? Are participants looking more and more sluggish by the second? Do you see yawning? Don't be so wrapped up in orchestrating the meeting that you fail to notice that the entire percussion section has gone to lunch.

Look for opportunities to summarize. It will help participants to get the most out of the meeting.

Assign an implementation strategy for any decisions made during the meeting. And follow up on it.

How to solicit honest opinions

Corporate culture, more than anything else, dictates the extent to which honesty is the best policy in business meetings. After all, if your organization responds negatively to anyone with the slightest propensity for free-thinking, why would anyone *want* to give an honest opinion?

So if you're having trouble getting people to respond with honest appraisal, keep in mind that your organization's unwritten code may be working against you.

Don't expect honest opinions in a meeting that includes many supervisory levels. Ever notice how little gets accomplished in sessions which involve many levels of management? The reason is simple, according to Lynn Oppenheim, Ph.D., a management consultant and vice-president of the Wharton Center for Applied Research. Bosses know it's counterproductive to criticize a subordinate in front of *his* subordinates. As a result, multilevel meetings are too "nice" to accomplish much; that's why many organizations never hold them, says Dr. Oppenheim.

Try to create a safe environment. Unless you make it safe for people to speak the truth, you're not going to get the truth, warns Dr. Oppenheim. So through your behavior, make it clear that subordinates can freely criticize your ideas and opinions—without fear of retribution—and that you don't have any sacred cows.

Ask for it directly. Say, "I want your thoughts on this matter. Don't hesitate to be critical. I'm open to any and all suggestions." And mean it.

Don't criticize participants for the suggestions they offer in meetings. It could send a powerful negative message to the entire group.

Encourage the quiet ones. "Sometimes the people who represent the best source of ideas in a meeting are the quiet people," says Dr. Berry. He suggests you simply ask them for their opinions ("Harriet, what do *you* think?"). Most people will respond.

Diplomatically discourage the aggressive participants who have bad ideas. There are bound to be a few individuals who never shut up—and who never have any worthy ideas. For them, you can simply interrupt and say something like "Let Bill talk for a while . . . "

And don't argue relentlessly with opinions you don't agree with. Simply register your disagreement, and the reasons why you think differently. But diplomatically thank the person for his or her suggestion.

Ask open-ended questions. Avoid questions that would elicit a yes/no response and nothing more. Ask questions such as: "What do you see as our department's role in contributing to the problem?" and "How do you suggest we change our strategy?"

Solicit opinions on a one-to-one basis before the meeting. Then when you discuss those honest opinions in a group setting, it may spur others to respond with equal candor.

In the meeting, ask for written views that will be shared anonymously. Participants may be more willing to offer opinions in writing than to open themselves up to personal attack by doing it orally. So solicit written views, tell folks not to sign their names, and then select a responsible person (someone who's not a handwriting expert) to read the responses aloud.

Want honest views? Be honest yourself. Let's say you want to solicit candid views on workplace dissatisfaction. Learn a lesson from one strategy that backfired. A manager instructed her subordinates to write out two lists:

one indicating what they liked best about their job, the other about what they liked the least. She also told them not to sign their names. After she collected the papers, she ignored the "positive" lists and read only the "negative" lists aloud in order to generate discussion. The trouble was, the subordinates felt manipulated and clammed up.

Don't invite a crowd. As a rule, the more participants a meeting has, the fewer the number who are willing to risk making fools of themselves by offering candid opinions. "If a group numbers about 20 people or more, you'll find fewer people willing to talk," says Dr. Lindo. If you're looking for honest feedback, keep your meeting small; if you just want to disseminate information and don't *want* feedback, invite as many as you like.

WHEN YOU WANT TO STAND OUT

On the bright side, meetings are terrific opportunities for visibility. Sure, your boss may already know how brilliant you are. But the higher-echelon types probably don't, and one method for maximizing exposure to them is to take full advantage of meetings you both attend.

Of course that doesn't mean you should expose yourself as a fool. Since there are so few opportunities for higher-ups to take notice, "you can blow it all by saying something totally wrong," says Dr. Oppenheim. "Careers are made and lost by how information is presented in meetings."

It's one thing to do your homework; it's another to know what to say and when it's appropriate to speak up. "More than simply getting your facts right, you need to have some sense of the needs of the people there and of the problems that need to be addressed," she says. So don't be an overanxious, I'm-so-darn-smart type. Instead, develop good listening skills and only jump in if (1) it's appropriate and (2) you've got something worth saying.

Arrive at the meeting with notes that detail anything you plan to contribute. And take notes during the meeting so you can clarify what transpired and keep track of the responses elicited by various suggestions. (If you feel you need a second meeting just to understand what happened in the first, something's wrong.)

A terrific way of gaining exposure is to volunteer during the meeting to follow up on things—even things that weren't your suggestions. It's a strategy for leveraging yourself that often succeeds (principally because most people are more than happy to have others to do work for them.)

After a meeting, sit down and objectively assess your contribution (and, yes, performance). Determine what message you'd like to get across in your next meeting, and devise a strategy for accomplishing it.

36

MEMORY

Don't you hate it when you run into someone at a conference who greets you by name and you can't remember his? Slyly you glance at his name tag, but as fate would have it a rainy day has transformed the letters into a runny mess that seems to read Blit Zuzgorb. As the conversation lengthens and you have still not used his name, Blit suspects that you don't know who he is and begins to nurture a mild resentment. At some time in the future, when you need to do business with him, Blit will make it a point not to remember you.

For any executive, a good memory is not just a minor asset—it's a necessity. In the first place, business associates take more kindly to you if they believe that you feel they're important enough to remember. Second, a good memory makes you look well informed, competent, and on top of the situation. On the other hand, a poor memory for such things as facts and figures can make even the chiefest of executives (including Ronald Reagan, who was well known for his press-conference information gaffes) look just a tad inept.

The question is, how do you get your memory to work better? Considering the fact that it would take a 100-foot-tall computer the size of Texas to hold as much information as is storable in the human brain, it would seem that we all have the *potential* to memorize the combined telephone directories of several small Baltic republics. Why, then, are there people with good memories and others who forget their home address on a daily basis?

It all comes down to the effort we put into memorizing a piece of information, explains Robin West, Ph.D., a University of Florida psychologist and author of *Memory Fitness Over 40.* Sloppy memory techniques will provide you with a sloppy memory. "Conversely, if you practice good memory techniques, there's no reason why you can't improve your memory by 50 percent," says Dr. West.

THE BIGGEST MEMORY SECRET OF ALL TIME

Believe it or not, the biggest memory secret ever was penned about 200 years ago by English writer Samuel Johnson: "The art of memory is the art of attention."

Basically there is nothing wrong with your memory. It's just sitting there waiting for you to feed it some information that it can keep safe and dry for years to come. But if you are not initially paying enough attention to that information, be it a name, place, fact, or figure, it will never be properly fed into your memory to begin with. It's rather like expecting a computer to remember a sheet of figures that you waved past its viewscreen but never punched in via keyboard.

Easy as it sounds, however, paying attention is one of the most difficult things in the world to do. Need convincing? Then just try to answer this simple question: What is depicted on the back of a $20 bill? While you've probably seen the flip side of an Andy Jackson hundreds of times, you probably never paid it enough attention to register it in your memory.

We automatically pay attention to the special, the unique, and the unusual (which is why people get bent out of shape when you don't remember them—it's as if you're implying they are none of the above). But when names, faces, facts, and figures are so numerous as to become commonplace, then an additional effort has to be made on your part. That effort is called observation.

There is a big difference between *seeing* and *observing.* Seeing something allows for a momentary and featureless experience. Observing something means paying attention to detail, setting the object apart from other things in your mind and memory. "By noticing special properties or features of commonplace items, you will have a better chance of committing them to memory,"says Dr. West.

Let's start our attention and observation training with those all important business introductions. Over lunch, you make the acquaintance of John Dixon. Right off the bat, make sure you are listening during the introduction. Many times in this situation we tend to be thinking of anything except the introduced person's name. "Is my hair neat?" "Do I have any tomato juice on my upper lip?" Put all that aside and repeat John's name to yourself three times.

Next comes observation. Is there anything unusual about John that might set him apart from any other three-piece suit? What about that tiny Masons pin on his left lapel? Here's your opportunity to make a connection between the pin and the name: Mason-Dixon. This observation and linkage phase can be accomplished within a brief span of time, but by the time you're through, your effort will have ensured John Dixon a lasting place in your memory.

Ultimately, you want observation to become a way of life. Here are a couple of easy ways to practice. In *Memory Fitness Over 40,* Dr. West suggests starting with a magazine photo of a person. Look at the photo and then close the magazine. List the features in the photo. What color were the eyes? What shape was the nose? What about hairstyle and clothing? Was there anything in the background? Having made a list, go back to the photo and study it, looking for two details you missed. Then start again. Do this until you've managed to list every aspect down to the most minute.

Another way to practice observation during the day is to think of a common item which you see regularly. It could be a fountain pen, a building you walk by, or a tile floor. Before you actually come across the item again, ask yourself some questions about it. What is it made of? What color is it? If you can't answer the questions immediately, take a moment next time you're confronted with the object and look for answers. A good example is the $20 bill. If you've got a curious bone in your body (and didn't know the answer), by now you've hauled out your wallet to see for yourself. Having raised a question and then made an observation to answer it, chances are you will not forget that particular information too easily.

With practice, observation becomes second nature. The way you look at things will change as you focus on details. And the attention you pay to detail will make each object rare enough that it will stand out in your mind and be easily encoded there.

TRICKS OF THE MEMORY TRADE

Memory and learning are not far apart, notes Dr. West in her book. When you learn something, you take random information and arrange it in a manner that has meaning to you. By concentrating in this way and noting specific details, you encode the learned material in your memory. But many things you might wish to remember, such as lists of items, phone numbers, dates, and random facts, are difficult to organize into a cohesive whole because they have no order or inherent meaning. Rather than remembering one thing which naturally flows into another, you must try to remember many different pieces of information that have no connection. A better way—and the secret of most memory techniques—involves organizing small pieces of material into larger groups, assigning the items a context you can understand, and making the information unique in your own mind.

ROTE MEMORY

While rote memorization is the most commonly practiced technique, it is the least useful for committing information to long-term memory. When you use the rote technique, you're simply repeating information over and over again. You do it when you look up a phone number in the Yellow Pages and then repeat it until you actually dial the number. "Rote repetition is effective for short-term tasks," says Dr. West, "but you'll find it very ineffective for long-term memory because it does not reorganize the information into a more convenient form. As soon as the repetition is interrupted, the information will be forgotten."

ASSIGNING MEANING

Rice farmers from the African country of Liberia were asked to memorize 20 words, divided into familiar categories. Not only did they remember a rather poor 9 to 11 words the first time through, they improved very little with successive tests. When the words were incorporated into folk stories, however, the farmers showed amazing improvement.

Two factors were responsible. First, since the Liberian farmers' culture has a tradition of oral storytelling, the folk story was a more familiar and meaningful form of receiving information to them than a random list of words could ever be. Familiarity and meaning increase memorability. Second, rather than memorizing 20 words, they had to remember only one story. By connecting the words to each other by way of a plot, the first word provided clues to the second word, and so forth. That gave the farmers an edge in remembering the next word without any hints.

The same technique can be applied to many everyday items you might want to remember, starting with new words for your vocabulary. "Many times, it's hard to draw a line of understanding between a word and its meaning," says Dr. West. "You might be hard put to remember that the medical prefix 'blepharo' refers to the eyelids, because it provides no clues. But you can take the sound of the word and incorporate it into this sentence: I'd blink if I saw a *pharaoh*.' The sentence reminds you of the word, and blink suggests eyelid."

To remember an address such as 1225 Turner Street, you might say to yourself, "I *turn*ed my life around on Christmas" (12/25). Can't seem to remember the name "Scheider"? Think of "shy deer."

While these may seem like make-work exercises that leave you with more to remember than before, they illustrate many of the necessary components of successful memorization. First, by thinking up a clever framework for the information, you are paying attention and concentrating. Second, you are making the information more familiar. One-two-two-five Turner Street means nothing, whereas "I turned my life around on Christmas" does.

MENTAL IMAGERY

Creating a picture in your mind of what needs to be memorized is one way to make the process fun.

This technique is especially useful for remembering names. "When I want people to remember my name," says Dr. Robin West, "I have them picture a robin flying west. To connect the name to my person, I ask them to include my most memorable feature, long hair, into the image. The end result is a mental image of a robin flying west with long hair streaming behind it in the wind. When they see my long hair, it triggers the image that contains my name."

If we go back for a moment to our old friend John Dixon, we can come up with a mental image that is even more unforgettable. We left off with the idea of the Mason-Dixon line. Going one step further, let's consider his first name, "John," in its capacity as a slang title for a bathroom. Now change that bathroom to one of those country outhouses with a little crescent moon on the door. Picture that outhouse perched majestically on the Mason-Dixon line, half in the South, half in the North. The next time you see the man with the Masons pin, it will trigger that image from which you can then derive his name. Just make sure you don't walk up to him and say, "Good morning, Mr. Outhouse."

ASSOCIATION

Basically, this is a retrieval trick for those moments when you can't quite put your finger on a name or piece of information even though you know it's in your head somewhere. The association technique takes advantage of the fact that often when we initially store information, it is linked with other factors prevailing at the same moment.

You and Jane spend an exhilarating day at the Museum of Office Supplies in New York City, for example, and later have dinner at the Purple Sloth Vegetarian Cafe. There, you engage in some light table conversation concerning quantum mechanics and eventually finish off your meal with a delicate mango mousse surprise. A year later you run into Jane at a sales convention and can't quite remember her name. Normally you would concentrate on the face and hope the name just pops out. But by using association, you can actively seek out her name under various memory files. Where did you go the last time you saw her? Perhaps her name is stored along with "Museum of Office Supplies." Or maybe it's part of the data filed under "Vegetarian Restaurants I'll Never Eat at Again." One way or another, the more you remember about the circumstances under which you learned a piece of information, the better your chances of retrieving that information by way of a side connection.

ORGANIZATION

Organization is more than just a trick; it's a priceless commodity when it comes to memory. Picture a fine meal including an appetizer, a large salad, and an entree of filet mignon. The filet is the main point of the meal, but if you fill up on the appetizer and salad, you'll have no room for it. When memorizing information, the same thing can happen. You can fill up on unimportant details and end up forgetting key points. That's why you need to organize. Ask yourself, What are the important points? Separate them from the fluff and apply your efforts to them.

Dr. West suggests organizing and memorizing written material through a method she calls PQRST. The letters stand for Preview, Question, Read, State, and Test. "First you should preview the material by reading briefly and identifying the main points," she says. "Then develop questions specifically targeted toward what you want to retain from the reading. Read the material carefully. State or repeat the central ideas and try to test yourself by answering your own questions. Follow all of these steps and you will remain focused on the information that is important for you to remember."

RETENTION

Okay. You've got a few techniques under your belt, but your status as a memory master is still one crucial step away. The tricks you've learned are a fine way to put information into a storable form. Now you need to make sure you are able to truly retain that information and find it again when you need it.

As unglamorous as it sounds, rehearsal is a mainstay of retention. "But do not confuse rehearsal with rote repetition," cautions Dr. West. "Instead of just reading the information or repeating a list over and over again, make sure you include these steps: Review the strategy you applied. Rehearse your mnemonic [memory device]. And rehearse your mnemonic with the information you learned."

How you schedule your rehearsal can be very important. Tests conducted by Harry P. Bahrick, Ph.D., of Ohio Wesleyan University suggest that information is retained longer and better if practice sessions are distributed over a period of time rather than having the practice jammed into one long session or several sessions with only short intervals in between.

"There could be many reasons why this occurs," says Dr. West. "First, when you distribute practice over several days, you consciously or unconsciously rehearse in between. Overlearning can also be a factor. Each time you approach a new study session, you have some material retained from the last session. In the second session you overlearn the material retained from the first session, and so on. This overlearning increases the likelihood that the information will be remembered."

RECALL

You've utilized good memory technique. You've rehearsed the material. Now that your mind has a viselike grip on the information, how do you get it back out?

"If you've formed good mnemonics, then using the cues you developed should access the information with no problem," says Dr. West. "But there is one additional little advantage-maker you can use to ensure good recall."

Pay attention to your mood and physical state. It is often easier to recall information when you are in the same condition as when you learned it. When you're sad, sad memories seem to come to the surface. Likewise, pain dredges up painful memories from the past. Obviously, it would be difficult to turn on and off your body and mind just to retrieve data you learned when you were in a particular state or mood. But there is a way around this. "Before sitting down to a learning task, try a few relaxation exercises," says Dr. West. "Later, before calling up the information for a test or speech, do those same exercises again so that your mental and physical state will be the same as when you learned it."

37

MEMOS

Question: How can you be in two places at once?

Answer: By sending a memo.

Question: How can you make a polished and precise presentation if you turn to jelly every time you need to present an idea?

Answer: By sending a memo.

Question: If a train traveling east at 85 mph leaves Denver at 3:00 P.M. and another traveling west at 60 mph leaves Philadelphia at 5:00 P.M., where will they meet?

Answer: Send a memo to one of your underlings requesting an answer.

They fall like snow from some celestial Xerox machine, covering the corporate landscape and forming little drifts on desktops and in mail slots. But memos, pain that they sometimes seem to be, are actually one of an executive's most effective tools.

For example, try to picture your company as a giant brain. You, as well as your co-workers, are neurons. The dendrites and tendrils along which messages travel can be thought of as your interoffice mail system. What then would be the electric impulses that are themselves the messages? Answer: memos. If your neurons were not able to send messages to each other, they would have to constantly be picking themselves up and meeting in tiny conference rooms somewhere in your brain to deliver the messages in person. With all those cells jogging around your head, you'd be lucky if you could figure out how to operate a light switch.

Likewise, if you and your co-workers spent all your time delivering messages in person, your corporation would have a hard time figuring out how to *produce* a light switch. Luckily, though, you can use memos. A memo allows you to remain in your office while writing it, thus letting you answer the phone, receive visitors, and generally remain "on-line" for various daily problems that have a habit of rearing their ugly heads. On the other hand, when you go off to meet with someone else, you are effectively "off-line," unreachable, removed from the flow of action. When you send a memo, you are actually in two places at once: You're sitting in your office, but your ideas may be in a completely different building, kicking their feet up on someone else's desk.

Your "memofied" ideas have a right to kick their feet up. Because you've taken time shaping them, they form a well-composed, orderly, and erudite body of information.

If you find that when it comes time to present an idea in the conference room you suddenly revert to one-syllable words and the occasional low, guttural animal noise, you may well want to consider the advantages a memo has to offer. You can write it in the peace and solitude of your own office. You can order and reorder your thoughts on paper until they are marching in better formation than a crack military parade squad. You can even use a thesaurus to throw in a couple of $5 vocabulary words. And the best part is that before sending it you can put the memo away for a day, come back to it, and see if you still think you're as clever as you thought you were yesterday. When all is done, you have a communiqué as precise as a heat-seeking missile. And this is only the beginning of the memo's usefulness.

5 USEFUL SUBSPECIES OF THE MEMO FAMILY

1. The taking-the-place-of-a-meeting memo. No question, it's generally far more efficient to send a sheet of paper than it is to organize and hold a meeting. "Even if you're just going down the hall to have a brief conference with somebody, you wind up doing a minuet; first you ask them how their weekend was, then you get off the topic at hand," says John Donnelly, cofounder and vice-president of Research America. "It's much easier to send a memo."

It's also simpler to dash off a note than it is to endure the logistical shenanigans required to gather a large group for even the briefest of meetings. So unless the meeting is one needed to brainstorm or one where the facts have already been digested and a consensus must be reached, consider a memo. If you are looking for feedback on a particular idea, ask recipients to jot down their ideas on the back of the memo and return it. If the opinions you are trying to solicit require very brief responses, make it easy by adding a list of options so people can check off their preferences.

You may also want to use this type of memo when you have a new idea to present but fear it will run into opposition. "When presenting an idea at a meeting, you're leaving yourself open to interruptions in the form of both questions and contention," notes Marie Timmins, founder and president of Corporate Word, a consulting firm which helps executives learn to communicate more effectively. "The problem with this is twofold. First, your presentation becomes stilted. Second, if the first few people who speak up are negative, it influences the dynamics of the group and could possibly lose you some allies who were on the fence during the presentation. Rather than risk this, a memo allows everyone to digest your idea in their own time and form an opinion unprejudiced by anyone else's."

2. The time-release memo. "I suggest this kind of memo when you know there is going to be opposition to your ideas," says Timmins. "What you do is study the list of people who are to receive the memo. From among those names, pick the person with the most prestige or power who you think is on your side. Then send the memo only to that person. Get his or her opinion and if it's a positive one, rework your memo to include that person's name and opinion before sending it out to the rest of the list. If your idea already has a semi-okay from the powers that be, everyone else will instantly view it in a more positive light."

3. The memo of praise. When an employee does something particularly outstanding, a memo of praise carries a lot more motivational weight than a simple pat on the back in the hallway. "It's rather like a scaled-down awards presentation," says Timmins. "First, it gives the employee something permanent to file away and perhaps pull out at review time. Second, if it is distributed to the entire department it boosts his or her prestige among co-workers. And third, a memo shows the employee that the boss was impressed enough to take a few minutes out of a busy schedule to draft and send the message."

Depending on just how outstanding the employee was, it is the manager's decision as to whether the memo goes strictly to that one person, to the whole department, or—as a token of truly excellent work—to a few upper-level executives. "Of course a memo such as this should always be followed up with an in-person pat on the back," says Timmins. "You don't want to have a piece of paper take the place of your presence."

4. The for-the-record memo. Sometimes you'll want to write a memo that officially establishes your point of view on a particular topic at a particular period of time. Such documents are often referred to as "for-the-record" memos, and they may be written solely to be filed away in your company's files. They may never even wind up in anyone's hands, but should trouble ensue, the memo can be retrieved and your blamelessness in the situation proven.

For example, say you've been approached by a colleague to do something you feel is not consistent with your company's policy. You tell the person you don't want to comply, but you also want it on the record that you resisted, along with your reasons for doing so. So you write a memo to your company's files explaining the situation. At the top of the memo, in capital letters, type the words, FOR THE RECORD. And be sure to date the memo. Then if your colleague makes trouble for you, you can pull out the memo and defend yourself.

"There are pros and cons to this type of memo," notes Timmins. "If you don't want to be a snitch yet do want to register disapproval, then popping a memo into the office files takes care of the situation and protects you should questions arise. On the other hand, there are certain situations which should be brought to the attention of your manager. A for-the-record memo is nice, but it doesn't rectify a full-blown problem that could have been avoided if you had only spoken up."

5. The insurance memo. The birth of a new project is always a delicate and somewhat confusing period. People make promises, take responsibility for certain phases, and generally offer all sorts of optimistic predictions which, while contributing greatly to the prevailing can-do spirit of the moment, are often forgotten (and even vehemently denied) when the project appears to be failing. If you are the point person in a new undertaking, it might be smart to take out a little "responsibility insurance," lest things fall apart and you are left holding the bag.

The way to proceed is simple. Take particularly detailed notes at the initial project meetings about who agreed to contribute what. Additionally, note who showed strong support and their reasons for doing so. For example, John Jones, the marketing analyst, liked the project because it would open up a new and highly lucrative market. The reason you want to record this sort of information is so that if the project fails and everyone bails out, you won't look like you dashed headlong into the undertaking without having gathered intelligent reasons for doing so.

Take the information and put it into a memo which begins "This is to summarize our meeting of March 3 . . . " In the memo mention people by name, their opinions, their suggestions, and the responsibilities they've agreed to undertake. Date it and circulate it to everyone having anything to do with the project as well as to your immediate superior. And don't forget to file one copy for later.

If the project fails and you are suddenly surrounded with people asking you how you could have been so stupid as to have thought it would work, pull out your insurance memo and suggest that they redirect that question toward themselves. Not only will the memo show everyone's full support, but should the project have failed due to someone's unfulfilled and conveniently forgotten commitment, the memories of the right people will be refreshed.

MEDITATIONS ON A MEMO: 8 RULES TO LIVE BY

1. Never mail an angry memo immediately after writing it; wait at least 24 hours.
2. Never write anything that you wouldn't want to reach eyes other than those for which it was intended. Who could forget that fateful memo in which "Today Show" host Bryant Gumbel made staffing suggestions to his boss, NBC executive producer Marty Ryan. He opened with the words, "I hope you understand that this note will be for your eyes ONLY. . ." (It was reprinted in at least one New York daily newspaper.) Gumbel soundly criticized several NBC employees, including the person to whom the memo was written. But Gumbel was lucky. He was able to issue an on-air apology. And because he is such a valuable commodity, he also was able to keep his job.
3. If your organization provides the capability of sending computer messages, assume that others have read confidential messages to you, regardless of the fact that a special computer password is needed to gain access.
4. Under most circumstances, you should get your boss's approval before sending a memo directly to someone over his head and to nobody else.
5. If you are concerned that your memo will get deep-sixed by the party to which it is intended, send it to several people, including those over her.
6. Don't use memos to belabor the obvious. And before you sit down to compose a memo, meditate on this phrase: Be concise.

7. Do send memos regarding a particular project to everybody involved. It's not appropriate to deny some people a copy of the memo
   (as a means of purposely offending them). "It's a breach of etiquette," says Donnelly. Also, by sending copies even to lower-level
   people, you may be inviting them to offer useful input.
8. Never send a memo when the matter is so sensitive that you don't
   want to commit it to the record. (Yes, even if your office does have
   a paper shredder.)

Bonus tip: If you want your memo to be read as soon as possible, make
sure there is a fair amount of white space and that your paragraphs are of
a neatly tailored size. Break the memo up with subheadings. Nothing is more
daunting than a page of solid print. If your memo looks long and boring, it
will be relegated to the bottom of other people's "to read" file. If it looks
light and inviting, chances are it will be read as soon as it's pulled out of its
interoffice mail envelope.

READING BETWEEN THE LINES

While a memo can certainly deliver the basic content of a message to
the reader, it can't impart the subtle nuances of body language, tone of voice,
and facial expression that are exchanged in person-to-person conversations.
Without those additional sources of information at your disposal, it's possible that you might miss the import of a message you are reading. The
problem is that all day long you receive memos calling your attention to this,
asking for that, and suggesting the other. So how can you tell which memos
to jump on and which ones you can get away with ignoring until your
current deadline rush is past?

For example: You are a newly made exec, and during your second week
on the job, you receive a memo from the VP of your division inviting you
to a brainstorming meeting with the purpose of discussing ways to increase
divisional productivity. Should you drop what you are currently doing and
start working on a list of 100 suggestions to present? "You can come up with
an answer by looking at who else the memo was sent to," suggests Marie
Timmins. "If you find that the memo was sent to everyone of your rank and
above in the division, then you don't need to drop what you are currently
doing. Sure, it would still be good to develop a few ideas to present, but even
if you don't, you'll be but one of a whole table of people discussing the issue.
It's not as if you personally are being singled out to save the company."

On the other hand, if you look at the list of recipients and find that it consists of you, the VP, and five other people whose rank is four levels above your own, it's time to start sweating. "While it isn't written out in plain English, the fact that no one else of your level has been invited basically means you are being summoned to a command performance," notes Timmins. "It could be that since you are new, they want to see what you are made of. In a case like this, it would be wise to drop what you are doing and give the memo a great deal of respect."

What about the "we've got a crisis situation" memo? "Anytime you get one of these, you want to be sure that you don't put it on the back burner too long," says Timmins. "But no matter how strongly it's worded, you should keep one thing in mind. If the house is on fire, you don't send a memo to the fire department. You call. And that's exactly what the memo sender would be doing if the Four Horsemen of the Apocalypse were truly riding the corporate halls."

Just the opposite is liable to be true, though, when it comes to reprimand memos. Whereas a crisis memo may be overstated, a reprimand memo is normally understated. "When you get one of these, you should get moving immediately," counsels Timmins. "If your performance is below par but not devastatingly so, a manager will probably invite you into his or her office and talk things over. A friendly word to the wise: If that same manager writes a memo to you, it means that friendship time is over. Your transgressions are being committed to paper and to the record. Be careful not to judge lightly a memo of this sort just because it is worded in the most civil of terms. People have a tendency to be more polite on paper than they would be in person. Even though the words aren't scowling, you can bet that somewhere, your manager is."

GETTING COPIED

"In general, a memo is an important symbol in an organization because your importance is judged by the fact that you are copied," says Terrence Deal, Ph.D., Vanderbilt University professor of education and human development, and coauthor of *Corporate Cultures: The Rites and Rituals of Corporate Life.* And when you think about it, it's true. When your name appears on a memo alongside a host of big guns, people who see it will assume that you are playing in the same league—even if in fact you are playing a minor role.

So when you find yourself left out, how can you ensure that you get into the "loop"? It may be a simple matter of asking the memo writer to be included in future memos. Explain that you may have some ideas to contribute and that you would like to be in the know. The subtle message you also want to get across is that you're willing to share any information that comes your way in exchange for inclusion on that person's memo circuit.

"I wouldn't be bashful about requesting a copy," says Donnelly, "particularly if it somehow affected me, my job, my performance, or my department." This is one area where the squeaky wheel may, in fact, get greased.

38

MENTORS AND MENTORSHIP

A mentor is a person who cares about you and goes out of his or her way to see that you get the best possible chance to fulfill your career potential.

Mentoring involves teaching, coaching, and, above all else, helping you build a high degree of confidence. But it is more than the sum total of these elements. Without some degree of affection, or warm friendship—comparable to what an older sibling might feel for a kid brother or sister—mentorship cannot work its full magic.

Perhaps because of this emotional component, there is little serious attention paid to mentorship in business courses, training sessions, or employee handbooks. You can't, after all, instruct one person to care about another. And it's somewhat awkward advising employees to walk around and find someone who'll take them under their wing, as if it were audition day at the orphanage.

Now it's quite possible to have a perfectly fine career without having a mentor, or being one. But participating in mentorship—at either end of the equation—can not only give you added momentum, but actually enrich the very quality of your working life.

THE 6 PRINCIPLES OF MENTORSHIP

One of the authors of this book (M.B.) gives the following account of his experience with mentorship.

When I first went to work as a reporter, I must have been the least prepared person in history to undertake such a job. For one thing, I knew absolutely nothing about journalism. Worse, I was shy, and the thought of interviewing politicians, police, and victims of various catastrophes terrified me. And to top it off, I couldn't type.

Why in the world was I even hired? That takes us to the first principle of mentorship.

A boss who is just a "boss" sees each employee as one more cog in his machine. A mentor-minded boss, however, is looking for signs of specialness that he or she can somehow work with and develop.

That may not be difficult when an employee comes with terrific credentials or a brilliant, even if short, track record. But the really top-notch mentor often sees great potential in raw, untested employees who may not even have faith in themselves.

In any event, six years later I became the city editor, running the whole news operation. Without my mentor, Fred, that would never have happened. Not in a million years.

Besides lots of coaching and practical tips, Fred began giving me special little areas of responsibility. As I mastered one, he'd give me another. And all the time, my confidence grew along with my technical skills.

A mentor has a vision of the employee that goes far beyond what she's going to do for him by Friday. He sees the future, and systematically grooms the employee to be ready for major responsibilities that may be four, five, even ten years down the road.

When I became the assistant city editor, Fred changed my desk. He put it right smack in front of his own executive-style desk in the newsroom. From that vantage point, I spent a good two or three years overhearing every conversation he had, every decision he made. From this massive exposure to management-in-action, I was able to develop "reflexes" that proved invaluable when I was promoted.

A mentor gives that special employee an inside view of what really goes on and how it gets done, of what really matters, and what can be safely ignored altogether. Most important, he manages to repeatedly "think out loud" in the employee's presence.

Most offices today have private cubicles, pretty much ruling out the "sit at my side and see what I do" approach. Special efforts may need to be made to compensate for the lack of this valuable apprenticeship technique. Regular, even if brief, private meetings. Sharing of important data and memos that few employees ever get to see (for no particular reason). Explaining the real reason why you or someone else made a certain decision. Doing that sort of thing not only educates the employee. Just as important, it tells him in the clearest possible way that he is important, responsible, and "on track" for a good future. That, in turn, creates loyalty to the mentor and the company. And makes him, perhaps, a bit more patient waiting for a promotion that sometimes can't come as quickly as he'd like.

One day, not long after I arrived at the *Philadelphia Tribune,* the publisher strode into the newsroom and asked me to write an editorial for him, based on his rough notes. I did, and the next day it ran as the lead editorial. Soon I was doing more and more editorials. Then my boss took me aside and said, "You're really doing a good job in the editorials. The old man is depending on you more and more. But I'll give you my honest advice: Don't get too good at writing editorials, if you know what I mean. Because you'll be spending half your time on them. And writing editorials is not how to get ahead in this business. People buy newspapers to read hard news. The big stories. See what I mean?"

I did. At least, I took his word for it. I managed to be "too busy" to write many more editorials. Instead, I put nearly all my energy into developing the kind of big, juicy, page-one stories that make people buy papers. Soon the publisher noticed that I had become a real asset—not just a convenience.

A mentor gives honest career advice when it's needed. Equally important, the employee must have enough faith in his or her mentor to take that advice. Otherwise, the mentorship relationship may well curl up and die.

Faith, which we are recommending, is one thing. Blind faith is something else. Perhaps blind-in-one-eye faith is what we need. If you're not sure the advice you've received is good but you aren't convinced it's wrong, either, the mentorship ethic says, Go with it. If you *are* convinced it's bad advice, then of course you must forget your mentor and strike out on your own.

Some people in my position would have thought, "Fred's just trying to keep me under his thumb. This is my big chance to work directly with the publisher—the owner! How can I refuse that opportunity?"

There are no real rules for making such a decision. Maybe I just liked my boss, and trusted him. And his advice seemed to make sense.

One of the classic roles of a mentor is to run interference for the employee: to not let him or her get ground up and spit out by corporate bureaucracy or office politics.

That kind of help can be invaluable. It's all too easy for a young person to find herself spending hours each day running errands, opening mail, or sitting on committees and task forces that will never accomplish anything. Worse, she could be the helpless victim of jealousy, or a petty power struggle.

A good mentor can fix all that—often with just a few words.

A mentor lets it generally be known that the special employee is a person with excellent potential—a person who is not to be trifled with.

One last job falls to the mentor. He or she ought to be your corporate publicity agent.

When the employee "lets his little star shine," the mentor puts it on top of a large tree. And he knows the credit will reflect back on him as much as it does on the employee.

The "negative mentor" has a habit of doing the opposite. Apparently fearing that his own contribution might be diminished, he tends to hide the individual contributions of his team members. But that hurts him at least as much as it does the employee. Most major executives realize that one of the most important contributions they can make to the company is to recruit, train, and promote talented individuals. Without a good supply of such people, a company is in deep trouble. So the manager who hides the great work of those who report to him is telling everyone that he is unable to produce a company's most valued asset—the leaders of tomorrow.

FINDING YOUR MENTOR

Your best potential mentor is your immediate supervisor. Failing that, the person just over her. Be sure to have that person "square" things with your supervisor, though, so no conflicts are created. Go any higher than that, and you may wind up getting your wings clipped when the big boss has no more time for you.

The potential mentor ought to be a person who is both respected in your organization and whose work is clearly of high effectiveness. He or she should also be engaged in work that is of central importance to the organization—or at least doing the kind of work you aspire to.

Someone reading over my shoulder just asked: What if your immediate supervisor is an idiot? And *his* boss nasty? Simple. Start working on a transfer—or a new résumé.

More often than not, though, you'll have a shot.

Now don't go into someone's office and ask, "Will you be my mentor?" That makes you sound like a six-year-old.

What you can do, though, is say, "Don, if you have some time available soon, could you explain to me why we only advertise in newspapers and on radio, and never in magazines or on TV?"

Or "Sharon, if you have some spare time soon, could you explain to me the actual skills I need to develop to become a senior analyst?"

Or "Hersh, I know you're real busy, but if you have 10 minutes, could you explain to me how you arrived at the fund-raising strategy for next year? I understand some of the little pieces, but I'd love to get some kind of overview—the big picture."

Most managers—especially those with the instinct to be a mentor—will respond very favorably to such requests.

And after a session or two, you can both decide whether it was time well spent. If so, you can ask another question.

Now some managers won't have the time or inclination to give you more than a 1-minute lecture. They may well, however, be quite impressed with your curiosity, even if they don't say so. And that can't hurt.

BEING A MENTOR

Whether you are near the top or not that far from the bottom of your organization, you probably have the opportunity to be *someone's* mentor.

There is much to be gained from it. Your department will grow stronger as people see a clear path upward. You will get a reputation for caring about people. You may get credit for producing the stars of tomorrow. And yes, you can (and *should*) get that credit even if the person you mentor leaves your department for another job in the company.

Best of all, helping others to bring out their best will enrich your own work experience.

You don't have to wait to be asked, either. Try taking the lead. If there's someone in your area who seems bright and energetic, ask him if he wants some special explanations, an inside view, a bit of tutoring. Ask him for a list of ideas. Ask if he's frustrated about anything.

Don't confuse mentoring, though, with repeated bouts of free-association blabbering or company gossip. Stick to the here and now, the practical, the achievable-in-real-life.

Don't give huge or complicated assignments to people who don't have the time or experience to handle them. A long series of small successes is far better than one killer assignment that takes months and months.

As time goes on, these small special assignments should have more and more direct relevance to the company's success. Projects that are "useful" but will never change the fundamental success of the company are not worth the time of anyone who has important potential.

Finally, be generous with praise, but make it very specific. "I like the fact that you had the perseverance to make 13 telephone calls until you found the right answer." Without such specifics, praise isn't all that helpful.

As for correction, be gentle. Don't point out *every* mistake made, or opportunity missed. Just one or two. And always use a tone of voice that conveys instruction, not disappointment or impatience.

The idea is to build confidence along with skills. One without the other doesn't work well. Together, they mold a better future.

39

MOTIVATION

Let's face facts. While the quest to improve employee motivation is certainly a noble one, it has of late become somewhat ridiculous. How many afternoons have been wasted watching overgrown cheerleaders (read "motivational consultants") rush up and down in front of the assembled troops yelling "DON'T POSTPONE ECSTASY!" What genius figured out the connection between increased productivity and letting employees beat managers over the head with foam-rubber bats? Add in those consultants who instruct their victims to scream in unison the company name at the top of their lungs for thirty minutes, and you've got another reason why the word "motivation" probably leaves a bad taste in your mouth.

Let's forget what kind of clown suit has been fitted onto the venerable science of motivational psychology for a moment and start anew. Here's the bottom line: The only kind of person who is not motivated is a dead one. Granted, the most you might be motivated to do today is heave your alarm clock through the window and go back to sleep. But you still felt a driving need to do it and to do it effectively. Why did you do it? Because sleeping late is rather pleasurable.

As behavioral psychologists never tire of saying, human beings operate on a pleasure/pain basis. In other words, we are motivated to seek pleasure and avoid pain.

There are many pleasures that people are actively motivated to seek: sex, food, and freedom, to name just a few of the big ones. But can you honestly say that any one of your employees has a job whose tasks provide anywhere near the level of pleasure as even one gourmet dinner? So why do they continue to perform their jobs? Because of lesser but still rewarding pleasures. They work to make money. They work for a feeling of accomplishment. They work to be successful and to know what it's like to be a winner.

But how much they will get of these things depends on their manager. To motivate your employees, you need to create a bonding of needs. You need them to perform their jobs, and they need you to give them a reason (i.e., pleasure) to perform their jobs well.

How to get 100 percent effort from your 50 percent employees

What does every sport or game known to man have in common? For starters, they all have some way of keeping score. Whether it's six points for a touchdown or a tiny slice of plastic pie for the right answers in Trivial Pursuit, all games have a built-in way for the players to know where they stand. All games have clear-cut rules: Hit the goalie in the mouth with your stick and you will be penalized. All games and sports also have an objective: Pin the sucker to the mat, accumulate more points than the other team, capture the flag.

The point? People enjoy games because of their clear-cut goals and scorekeeping characteristics (as well as for providing a lawsuit-free excuse to tackle people and make them eat dirt). Again, the point? There is a good chance that your employees are in the same position as a football player who doesn't know the score, has no idea how to win, and can't figure out the rules. If that player were you, would you be out on the field giving it your all, or would you be in a shower stall figuring out which knob turned on the hot water?

"As a manager, you want to create a motivational environment that parallels the one found in sports," says Joseph H. Boyett, vice-president of Atlanta-based management consulting firm Tarkenton Conn & Company, and coauthor of *Maximum Performance Management.* "As our president, Fran Tarkenton, says, the best thing about playing football is that when you leave the field, you know whether you've won or lost. Most workers go home at the end of the day never knowing."

To this end, the first thing you should do as a manager is define the mission or purpose of the group. This does not mean writing one line that says, "The purpose of this group is to make plastic fruit for the women of Borneo to wear on their heads." Focus not only on the product but upon the larger ramifications as well. Why does this group exist? What is it trying to accomplish within the higher mission of the organization as a whole? Who are the customers (internal or external) being served by the group? What does the group need to do to meet the customers' needs?

The next step is to communicate your vision to the employees so that there is no doubt in the group as to what they are all about and what kind of value they bring to the corporation. Make sure there is heavy emphasis on value. Perhaps the plastic fruit is not going to change the balance of world power, but maybe the cash derived from this profit center will allow the corporation's R & D department to create a new vaccine for its pharmaceutical division. People don't like to play a game if it seems meaningless. Let the group know that the stakes are higher than they thought.

"The manager should then create a good measurement and feedback system for his or her employees," says Boyett. "You know what the group is supposed to accomplish. Now you need to figure out the five to ten determinants that measure improvement, and then set a series of reachable goals in terms of those determinants." If possible your group, or representatives thereof, should participate in the choosing of the key indicators of success as well as the goal-setting process. Keep in mind that any competent employee is an expert in a small field, be it filekeeping or drill press operation. Solicit everyone's opinions and incorporate them when you can. You'll not only get some good ideas, but you'll get your employees to commit themselves to a plan which they helped create.

"Make large, colorful graphs that track the key indicators and pinpoint goal targets," says Boyett. "Post them in a public area where everyone can see them. Hold regular meetings to discuss the progress reflected by those indicators. Inherent in this is the idea that information should not be kept secret. All the behavior research on motivation shows that people want feedback, they want information on how they are doing. Making charts is an excellent way of providing it in an ongoing and constant manner."

The results of this fairly simple and basic technique can be astounding. "Research has shown that if you take people who haven't received feedback and you set up a scorekeeping method, you can expect an improvement in performance of anywhere from 20 to 50 percent," says Boyett. "Of course if all you do is keep score, this performance boost won't last over time. I call it the old consultant's trick. A consultant can go into an organization, determine performance indicators, set up graphs, focus people's attention, and get an instant leap in productivity. As long as she gets out of there in a month she's going to look great. But after she leaves, things will start to slide back to prefeedback levels."

Why? Because feedback is what is known as an antecedent. In the ABCs of motivation, an antecedent (A) is what gets behavior started. While B stands for the actual behavior, it is C that needs to be applied along with A to keep motivation high. C stands for consequences.

WHY POSITIVE REINFORCEMENT WORKS BEST

Consequences come in two flavors: positive and negative. The prevailing (albeit somewhat unconscious) practice among managers is to use negative reinforcement as a way to increase motivation. This is just the opposite of what will get people to work at their maximum potential level.

"For a negative reinforcement to work it has to be instantaneous, severe, and consistent," says Boyett. "A good example of this would be a hot stove. Touch it and you'll get a second-degree reinforcement about as instantaneously as possible. Not only that, but it will happen every time and it will happen impartially, burning you, your mother, or the President of the United States."

Think about the kind of punishment you can hand out at work. Obviously you can't torch your employees for low productivity. You also can't find out about poor work practices seconds after they occur. This rules out using punishment effectively as a motivator. "You can try chewing people out," says Boyett, "but they will stop listening after a while. You can threaten to fire people, but if you don't actually follow through in a consistent way and fire them, people will know it's an idle threat. And if you do fire them, all you'll end up with is a personnel problem."

Even if you do latch onto an effective negative reinforcement that doesn't break any federal felony laws, you have one other thing to contend with. "It's called the punishment effect," says Boyett. "When punishment is used to control behavior, people perform at a level just sufficient to avoid punishment."

Regardless of whether negative reinforcements are routinely applied, all of us still work in the shadow of an unspoken one that is taken for granted: Screw up and you will eventually lose your job. But unless we have some positive incentive that motivates us to work harder, most of us will only put out as much as it takes to continue eating in the company lunchroom.

Basically, positive reinforcement consists of praise and recognition. And before you groan, "I've heard this before," consider this. A survey conducted by Motivational Systems, a West Orange, New Jersey, management development firm, found that only 11 percent of managers recognized or praised employee work consistently. Of the more than 1,000 employees surveyed,

50 percent said they received due recognition "most of the time," 28 percent answered "rarely," and 10 percent said "not at all." Given the same benefits and salary, 27 percent of the employees questioned said they would move to another company that had a reputation for recognition and praise.

"We've found too many managers who either ignore or underestimate the power of praise," says Roger Flax, Ph.D., president of Motivational Systems. "It's not easy getting people to do their best when they would just as soon be working for some other company."

At its best, positive reinforcement merges the employees' personal quest for pleasure with your need for them to perform certain duties that may not in themselves be pleasurable. Naturally there are some guidelines. "First of all, you should be specific about the behavior you are reinforcing," suggests Boyett. "People engage in thousands of behaviors each day. If you aren't specific, then people get confused as to what they are doing right. They may think you are congratulating them on something totally different. So rather than saying 'Thanks for helping out yesterday,' say 'I appreciate the way you volunteered to help check inventory yesterday. It went much faster with two people working on it. Thanks for doing it without being asked.' "

Reinforce immediately after you observe the behavior. "If you forget to thank John for working late and only get around to it six weeks later, it's not going to have much impact," notes Boyett.

A great example of quick reinforcement is Xerox's "You Deserve an X Today" award, created by and for the corporate personnel department. The award, which can be given to anyone in the department by anyone else, is simply a slip of paper displaying an X and the reason for the reward. The recipient can redeem the slip for $25 from the company. While awards are subject to a management approval, this technique still remains fast and effective.

"Another important point is to make reinforcement contingent upon performance," says Boyett. "This means there should be a clear connection between people's actions and the recognition they get. Being generally nice and giving constant praise to people regardless of their behavior is not motivational reinforcement. That's why office birthday parties, while creating a friendly atmosphere, do not stimulate increased productivity. All you are doing is rewarding someone for living another year—not for performing an action that benefits the organization."

Reinforcement contingency can have a dramatic and precise effect on employee behavior, as was demonstrated in the case of Houston-based Oceaneering International, the largest underwater services contractor in the world. In mid-1987 the company's Western Hemisphere division was suffering an average of two to three serious accidents each month. In an attempt to curtail rising workers' compensation costs, vice-president Steve Helburn began offering a bonus to every technician, diver, and supervisor who partook in a safely conducted dive. In the first year that the program was initiated, work-related, lost-time accidents dropped from 31 to 18. For the $170,000 the company paid out in bonuses, it estimated it saved almost $500,000 in workers' compensation payments.

The Oceaneering International story illustrates yet another important point about reinforcement. Rewards should be proportional to what the employee did. Individual bonuses the first year averaged about $2,000. Not a fortune, but nothing to sneeze at. It's doubtful those divers would have modified their behavior for a thank you and a hearty handshake from the CEO.

Another reinforcement commandment is to make the reward fit the tastes of the employees. "I was working for one manufacturing client who had a lot of young women working in a plant environment," recalls Boyett. "As a way to motivate these employees, the highest performer each month, along with her spouse, got to go out to a nice restaurant with the executive vice-president and his wife. When this reward system didn't seem to be producing the desired results, we went and talked to the women. It turned out that most of them were less than favorably motivated by the prospect of dinner with the VP. As one woman put it, 'My God, I hope I never win! I don't have anything to wear and I have no idea what to talk about with the vice-president.' "

It could be that this reward was set up by executives who personally found the idea of dinner with a corporate officer an exciting prospect. But reinforcement is much like a Christmas present. The success of the gift is determined by how much the receiver likes it, not how much the giver does. The upshot of this is that you may have to spend a lunch hour or two with your employees. Listen to what they talk about. Do the boys on the drill press talk incessantly about baseball? A couple of tickets to the next game may be just the motivational ticket you're looking for. But don't expect to give tickets out from now until the final judgment. You'll need to vary the reward periodically to keep people's interest high.

Make sure you are consistent with your reinforcement policy. Your employees need to know that regardless of who they are or how many times they do well, there will still be a reward of some kind. Ask yourself this: If a light switch worked only half the time, how long would it be before you stopped reaching for it altogether?

Real responsibility, real rewards

"If you give your employees constant feedback and follow the rules of reinforcement, there's no reason why you shouldn't see your group operating at a motivational level in the eightieth to ninetieth percentile," says Boyett. But to push them over the top there are still two essential factors that must be considered: employee decision-making involvement and monetary incentive.

"We are telling managers now that their job is not to make decisions and solve problems. That's the old definition of management. Their job is to help people make their own decisions and solve their own problems. To coach and facilitate employee problem-solving. To let workers come to their own conclusions about what needs to be done. It's important that a manager do this because if the members of a group arrive at a decision themselves, they will be more likely to implement it. People don't resist their own ideas."

What this boils down to is giving people a sense of personal investment in their work. If they're merely following your idea, the bottom line is that they may carry it out, but they could really care less about the outcome. Whose baby would you give more care to—your own or someone else's? Boyett even goes so far as to say that if you have a particular plan of action and your employees come up with a slightly less brilliant one, you would still do better to see what can be done with the employees' idea. What is lost in brilliance may be more than adequately compensated for in elbow grease.

Of course this *is* the United States, birthplace of large amounts of money. No matter how much praise, feedback, and involvement you give your employees, there may still come a point when they ask, "Where's the green?" "Survey after survey has asked the American worker, 'Are you working as hard as you could?' and 70 to 80 percent said no," notes Boyett. "Why? Because the rewards of hard work go to the owners and management. But if we want high performance, we have to share those rewards as well. And we are seeing many companies doing just that. The wave of the future is pay for performance."

Feedback? More money? Decision-making powers? Who do these employees think they are—executives?

Well, why not? Is it so strange that the people working under you should want any less than you yourself do? Motivating employees ultimately comes down to a process by which you make each one a junior executive. After all, executives work hard because they have challenging jobs, good pay, and respect. Give these same simple pleasures to your employees, and they will work just as hard for you.

RECOGNIZE THE ROOTS
OF PROCRASTINATION

To paraphrase an old saying: Into every motivated life a little procrastination must fall. Everyone is guilty of procrastination at some point. Even Julius Caesar, renowned for saying "Veni, vidi, vici" (I came, I saw, I conquered), at some less historic moment probably said, "Veni, vidi, I'll get back to you tomorrow on this."

The problem with procrastination is that through a general misunderstanding of human nature the word has become a 15-letter synonym for laziness. But if you are automatically treating procrastination as a manifestation of laziness, you could be miles away from solving the problem.

"The bottom-line causes of procrastination are fear and low self-esteem," says Lenora M. Yuen, Ph.D., psychologist and coauthor of *Procrastination: Why You Do It, What to Do about It.* "When people have a low sense of self-esteem, they look to the work they produce as a constant measurement of their inherent worth. They don't fear failure on a project for normal reasons such as firing or missed promotion opportunities. Rather they fear failure because it would strike at the very core of their value as a person. This is where procrastination comes in."

If people like this were to give a project their best shot and not get rave reviews, they would have to say to themselves, "I tried my best and my best wasn't good enough. *I* am not good enough." So instead they procrastinate and then make a belated, all-out effort in the short period of time left to them. Then, at least, they can say to themselves, "This was not a true test of my abilities. With more time it could have been brilliant."

"Procrastination is a built-in safeguard that never allows the person's full potential to be put to any kind of critical test," says Dr. Yuen. "It allows a person to preserve an illusion of brilliance without ever having the illusion destroyed by reality."

Another possible explanation for procrastination is fear of success. "While most of us are hardly afraid of having a bigger salary and more prestige forced on us, there are those who only consider the additional responsibility that success may bring," says Dr. Yuen. "Part of that responsibility is that if you do well this time, you will have to top yourself next time. And where does it stop? Eventually you may run out of gas. So some people would rather never get started."

It's a rather perfectionist notion that you must constantly be better than you were before. And the need for perfection often is a reflection of a self-esteem problem.

Perfectionists will also spend inordinate amounts of time making sure that there is no room for criticism. "They patch up every little hole in a project, spending so much time on minor points that they end up far behind schedule," says Dr. Yuen.

The list goes on. Procrastination can be the result of undefined project parameters. "Many times a project is either poorly explained or never really fully conceived," says Dr. Yuen. "When this occurs, an employee, be it you or someone working for you, will rarely try to get more details for fear of looking stupid. So the project's very vagueness becomes cause for apprehension and an unwillingness to get started."

Procrastination can even be a form of rebellion. "I have a woman in my practice who works in a bank," says Dr. Yuen. "When her supervisor becomes dictatorial concerning her duties, she gets so resentful that she doesn't do anything for a while. On the other hand, she works very productively when her supervisor sits down with her, lists five things that need to be done by Friday, and then asks her how *she* would like to do them."

In other words, people who feel disempowered by a supervisor or organization will try to empower themselves by taking liberties with their own time management and production schedule. "Procrastination in these cases contains all the elements of a power struggle," notes Dr. Yuen. "The only problem is that it never comes to a head. You can't tell if they are doing it on purpose, because they can always say, 'I'm so sorry. I just forgot.' "

Fear. Perfectionism. Rebellion. With so many possible causes lurking behind procrastination, you still can't lose sight of the fact that, occasionally at least, the problem really is one of simple laziness. After all, your employee may just not give a damn. "The point, however, is that you cannot make any assumptions as to what is behind a person's procrastination," warns Dr. Yuen. "While it all looks the same on the surface, the underlying reasons can be numerous."

So how do you tell whether to give a deadline deadbeat the boot or a one-on-one attitude readjustment? "You can start by looking at the employee's whole work history," suggests Dr. Yuen. "If his procrastination is part of a prevailing pattern, then laziness or disinterest in the job is a definite possibility. But if you find yourself with a very industrious worker who's suddenly dragging his feet, then you've got to search elsewhere for a reason. You might start by asking yourself what changes the employee has recently gone through. A new position? New duties? What about the new supervisor? Any of these things, if they are upsetting the employee, could be at the root of the procrastination problem. The important thing is that you build a relationship with your employees which will allow them to feel comfortable expressing their fears or problems to you."

How to make any project
PROCRASTINATION-PROOF

While procrastination is a many-headed thing, it doesn't mean that you can't keep it out of any project right from the start. Once you understand some of the underlying reasons that it occurs, you can set up your marching orders so as to avoid procrastination in your employees as well as in yourself. Here's how.

Establish clear-cut goals and priorities immediately. "It's amazing what different people may consider to be clear-cut goals," says Dr. Yuen. "I spent an entire lecture explaining how to set specific goals, and at the end of it, all one man could say was, 'I want to change my life.' But you really need to be more specific. The first thing you might want to do is establish an ultimate deadline: 'I want this to be done by Friday, January 15th at 5:00 P.M.' Then you want to figure out priorities. Rather then ask yourself what are the most important factors in this project, you should ask yourself what is *the* most important factor. Don't give yourself three separate things to vacillate over. Focus!"

Once you've figured out the most important part of the project, ask yourself what the next most important part is, and so on. By doing this, you will end up with a linear progression of priorities that is easy to follow. Once you have this, you can set mini-deadlines for each and start working on them. Let's say the highest-priority component has a 2-week deadline. You might give the second-priority activity a 1½-week deadline, and a lesser component a one-day deadline. Work out the whole schedule in such a way that by meeting your various mini-deadlines you'll have enough time to give the most important factors the attention they need without missing your final deadline.

Come up with goals jointly. Whether it's between you and your employees or you and your boss, make sure a consensus is reached concerning the work schedule on the project. This will help avoid any feeling of being ruled over, which can lead to procrastination. Strive to let everyone involved have a say in the matter, and then reach a compromise which everyone can live with. Call it the "Deference to Autonomy" Rule.

Spell out clearly the consequences of not meeting the deadline. Let your employees know how important the work is and what kind of trouble they could put the division in if they don't finish the work on time. This makes the deadline all the more concrete to the kind of person who thinks there is always a little more time that can be squeezed out of any deadline. For personal motivation, you might imagine a worst-case scenario of what will happen if *you* don't finish your work on time.

Rely on feedback, feedback, feedback. Get it and give it. Check in with your employees when they meet one of their mini-deadlines. Do it consistently and let them know how they are doing. Encouragement always helps, but so does a little timely criticism if things are getting bogged down. "People tend to procrastinate alone and then try to hide it because they are ashamed," notes Dr. Yuen. "It can be a tremendous help to them if they have someone they can touch base with about their progress."

On a personal note, if you are the type who procrastinates, you may want to set up checkpoint meetings with your boss so that you don't find yourself working in a vacuum.

Remember that it doesn't have to be perfect. Only saints are perfect, and most of them have long since left their desk jobs for more spiritually lucrative careers. Let your employees know that you understand their abilities and limitations, and that you do not expect them to win the Nobel Prize. While some things do need to be perfect (accounting sheets and neurosurgery, for example), if most projects are 80 percent wonderful and 20 percent okay, you're ahead of the game. Remember that something is called average because that is about as well as the majority of people can do it.

To keep from intimidating *yourself* into procrastination because you aren't perfect, think about this. Studies have shown that most Olympic athletes are, on the whole, very accepting of themselves when they have a bad day. People perform better if they don't expect perfection. Granted, some athletes are perfectionists. But by the time the starting gun goes off, they've worked themselves into such a frenzy that there's a 50–50 chance they'll either break a record or break a leg. Instead, strive for relaxed confidence with room to forgive yourself the occasional error.

Finally, here is the "in case of procrastination, break glass and pull lever" tip. This is for when nothing else works. No feedback, reward, or punishment has succeeded in getting you started on this project. *Ask yourself what you can get done in the next 15 minutes and then do it.* "Anyone can stand to do just about anything for 15 minutes," says Dr. Yuen. "And for the surprisingly short amount of time it is, you *can* get something done. You don't have to have all the bases covered to take one step."

So get moving.

Motivation Is a Many-Splendored Thing

Do the same things that motivate American workers ring a Frenchman's bell equally well? Yes and no, according to psychologist Guvenc Alpender. After identifying a wide range of factors that influence motivation, Alpender asked first-line supervisors in five midsized manufacturing firms in France, the United States, and the Netherlands to rate the importance of 15 of them.

The results showed that while human relations factors—such as recognition, a sense of belonging, and fair treatment—ranked highest in importance, each country had a unique response when it came down to a choice among these three. In France, the most important motivating factor is a feeling of belongingness. In the United States, recognition was the number-one motivator, while in the Netherlands fairness topped the list.

One interesting conclusion that can be drawn is that while U.S. employees are primed by individual motivators such as personal recognition, their European counterparts are more easily moved by social motivators. Belonging to a group and being treated as well as others seems to be of more importance to them than the somewhat American desire to be a star.

40

NEGOTIATION

S*etting:* A hot and dusty marketplace somewhere in the Middle East

Time: 1500 B.C. (noonish)

Characters: Achmed—A man who owns a camel; Akkim—A man who is presently camel-less

AKKIM: [spoken in Arabic with subtitles] That's one fine looking camel you have there. If I had any interest in owning a camel, yours might be worth considering.

ACHMED: It is the best camel I have ever owned. And though I would never think of selling it, I could certainly ask for 100 gold shekels at auction.

AKKIM: 100 gold shekels! Surely your camel has stepped on your head once too often. Even if I could bring myself to consider buying your camel I would not offer more than 50.

ACHMED: This camel is like a brother to me. I could not part with him for 90 gold shekels, much less 50.

AKKIM: Perhaps he is worth 70, although his legs look a bit stringy.

ACHMED: At 80 shekels he is the best buy in town.

AKKIM: Done.

And so was born the fine art of negotiation. But a process that once had a traditional place in virtually every transaction has in recent years gathered around itself a high-priced cloak of exclusiveness. Today it seems that big-time corporate mergers, high-level international disputes, and blockbuster movie deals are the marketplaces where the complex techniques of negotiation are primarily practiced. If we look past those dramatic applications, however, we find that all of us use or need the tactics of negotiation every day. While we may not be cutting $500 million real estate deals, there are many situations where our negotiation skills can have a substantial effect on our careers and our lives in general.

Have you ever pulled off a successful negotiation? If the answer is no, think again. If you are currently involved in a romantic relationship, then you have done some fancy negotiating. Both your needs and a completely different set of needs—those of your significant other—have been met to a mutually agreeable degree (perhaps after some heated give-and-take discussions). If you don't think a simple relationship has need of some sublime negotiating principles, then you might want to perform this test. Take the basic text of your last lover's spat and substitute "building long-range, land-based ballistic missiles" where your partner accused you of spending too much time hanging out with your friends. It will amaze you how much the dynamics of your relationship problems resemble those of most international arms control negotiations.

And what goes for your personal affairs goes in spades at the office where relationships revolve around cash, power, and prestige. You negotiate with your boss for a raise or promotion. You negotiate with your co-workers to divide up duties, to line up backing on ideas, and for a host of other needs. Wherever there is a relationship between two people, there is negotiation. So you might as well learn how to do it well.

5 COMMON NEGOTIATION MISTAKES

You and your co-worker Mary both work in the same department. Your boss has asked for the creation and implementation of a new product line. Whoever comes up with the best idea and marketing strategy will probably be promoted to ruler of all that he or she surveys. You and Mary have each come up with a great idea and strategy. The boss likes both plans but only has the funds to develop one. It's time for you and Mary to do some serious negotiating. Here's what you *shouldn't* do.

1. Don't enter into a negotiation with artificially high demands hoping to spur a fast compromise born of haggling. To show trainees how problems can occur with that approach, negotiation expert Ted Higgens, director of sales productivity for the Forum Corporation, uses the story of the orange: "There are two men, each of whom has a son who is dying of a mysterious ailment. The only thing that can cure the two boys is an orange. Down the road from the two men's houses is a farmer, and all he has grown this year is one orange. The two men haggle over the orange, each wanting the whole thing. Finally they compromise and split the orange. Each of their sons only gets half better."

What neither man realized is that one son only needed the juice of the orange to get better, the other, only the skin. "By compromising on artificially high needs, the two men never took enough time to find a creative solution that would have helped them both equally," says Higgens. "There is room later for compromise, but first you need to find out what is really of value to you and what is of value to the other person."

If you take a little time with Mary, you may find out that she wants to go into creative development while you are interested in marketing. She could have her product implemented and you could do the marketing. There's no need to demand the whole world when you might only need to ask for the part that you want and that no one else needs.

2. Don't express disapproval or close the door on an unfavorable option too fast. "You rarely know all there is to know about a given situation," says Scott Brown, associate director of the Harvard Negotiation Project, coauthor of *Getting Together: Building a Relationship That Gets to Yes,* and consultant on U.S.–Soviet relationships. "By closing the door on an option too soon, you may never find out a piece of information which could suddenly make the situation worthwhile. Additionally, things change. What might not have worked last week may be subjected to a whole new set of variables which could make the situation profitable for you this week."

Besides cheating you out of a transaction that on closer inspection could be advantageous, quick disapproval can provoke an unwished-for reaction from the person on the other side of the table. "If you present a close-minded image to the other person, she is going to see little use in any further discussion or exploration," says Brown. "She will then revert back to what I call blind reacting, in which case actions will speak louder than words."

This put-up-or-shut-up attitude basically puts an end to creative problem-solving and leads to a war of attrition. Being firm is fine, but the line between firmness and narrow-mindedness is also fine. In your hypothetical dealings with Mary, initially keep a lid on the number of times you say no.

3. Don't try to handle the toughest issues first. "People tend to say, 'Here's the biggest problem, so let's nail this one and it will be easy from there on in,'" says Higgens. "But what usually happens is that you never get past that initial hurdle, and you create a lot of frustration. The best thing to do is start with minor issues which are more easily negotiable. Get the relationship going well and build some momentum before tackling the tougher problems."

4. Don't assume. "If you act as if an assumption is a fact, you're stuck with that premise and must proceed accordingly, ofttimes disastrously," warns Jacalyn Barnett, a partner heading up the matrimonial law department of Shea & Gould in New York City, in an interview with *Working Woman* magazine. In your current situation with Mary, don't assume you know what she really wants. Find out for sure. It may be she doesn't want to rule the department. It may be that she's getting ready to start her own business, but wants to make one more major splash in the corporate world to boost her credentials.

5. Don't get defensive and hoard information. "Rather than looking at the people on the other side of the table as an enemy army from which you have to hide your battle plans, think of them as part of a team solving a mutual problem," says Higgens. "The more information the team can combine, the faster you will reach your goal." Share what you know with Mary, and encourage her to do likewise. What if one of you has been told by a third party that the company will be ready to initiate another project in as little as eight months? Then there would be no reason to fight over this particular opportunity.

HOW TO PREPARE
FOR A SUCCESSFUL NEGOTIATION

Going to a negotiating session without preparing is like trying to find buried treasure with no clues and no map. You have no direction, no promising avenues to explore, and no clear idea what the treasure may actually be. You're bound to run into some unpleasant suprises. Higgens suggests mapping out a course of action by asking yourself these questions well ahead of time:

What are the areas of common ground that I share with the person across the table? Here, as with most of the other questions, research is the key. What is the other person's background? If you are both from marketing, then there is some validity in assuming that you will view problems from the same perspective. But if your backgrounds are totally different, take care. You need to reassess and be prepared to present your proposal from an engineering standpoint as well, if that happens to be his specialty.

What kinds of needs and wants does she have that I should think about? If the other person's company or division is cash-tight right now, for example, you'll want to focus on economy. But economy may be the last thing the other person cares about if his group is cash-rich. It may be he is interested in high market visibility at any cost. Make sure you know exactly what he wants and stress those points, or your proposal may have no appeal.

In what mode is this negotiation going to operate? Are you facing a ruthlessly competitive opponent who just wants to win at your expense? Or are you dealing with someone who wants to find an equitable solution? If you've had past experience with this person, those questions should be easy to figure out. If this is a first-time encounter, you may want to ask others what his negotiation style is like so that you will be prepared.

What is my opening package? What am I trying to get? At what point do I walk away? Without conscious awareness of your own needs and possible recourses, you won't be in any shape for dealing with those of the other person.

IN PURSUIT OF REASON: THINGS TO REMEMBER FOR A SMOOTH RIDE AT THE TABLE

You've now prepped yourself for just about anything short of having to perform an emergency appendectomy during the negotiation. But once you are face-to-face, there are a few additional things you'll want to keep in mind to facilitate clear thinking, and to help the proceedings move forward.

Monitor your emotions. Everyone you meet is going to have some emotional effect on you, be it major or minor. The person you enter negotiations with is no exception. "The problem is that most people normally do not take into consideration the effect their own emotions are going to have on their perceptions during the meeting," says Scott Brown. But trying to interpret what the other person is saying through your emotional haze is like trying to read a book underwater. Nothing is clear.

"The first thing you want to do is take a little premeeting time to anticipate your emotions," suggests Brown. "Take into consideration past meetings with this person. Does he frequently bring out anger in you? Do you find yourself slightly intimidated?" Realizing these things up front and keeping them in mind during the meeting will help you analyze the motivation behind your decisions. For example, if you don't like the other guy and understand this, you will realize that perhaps you've shot down a few of his marginal proposals that might have flown with a little encouragement. Or if the man intimidates you, it could be that you've given in on several details which might have gone your way if you stood up to him.

In his book, *Getting Together,* Brown makes the following suggestions for emotional first aid at the negotiating table. Become familiar with your body's emotional signs. Do you clench your jaw when annoyed? Does your stomach feel tight when you're nervous? Be aware of your body's condition during negotiations, and use that feedback as an early warning system for severe emotional stress.

When things start getting hot, take a break. By stepping outside for a glass of water, everyone gets a chance to cool down, reassess the situation, and focus on the rewards to be gained by making the relationship work.

When you are having a hard time distancing yourself emotionally from a negotiation, consult others before acting. Someone else's detached opinion can help balance your perspective on the situation.

When dealing with difficult people, use tactics that will keep them in line without offending. At some point in our career, we all have to deal with the man or woman whose genetic makeup is closer to that of a piranha than a human being. This person will try to eat you for dinner and will manage to jar every emotional nerve in your body, to boot. You'd love to return the favor in kind, but shooting the attacker would not only make a mess, it would probably end the relationship. What do you do?

"We counsel people in the use of certain tactics that let the other side know where the line has been drawn and when it has been stepped over," says Higgins. "The best part is that they are not anger-producing tactics, but they do get the relationship back on track when someone is being bull-headed."

The first tactic is asserting. It's useful when the other person repeatedly proposes something that is unfeasible, and you can't seem to get past the issue no matter how politely you phrase your refusal. "If you think that by giving in you'll alleviate the problem, you're wrong," says Higgens. "That's like trying to put out a fire with gasoline. The blaze only gets bigger. Instead, you can cut off further discussion on the subject with a short one-line assertion."

A few classic assertions are: "I'm sorry but that's out of the question, so let's look at the rest of the agenda." "We don't do business that way." "What you are suggesting is definitely not an option." Being definite and brisk without rancor will get the message across that it's time to move on to another subject.

The next tactic is silent listening. This can pay off when someone blows up at you, triggering that ancient fight-or-flee response. Since running out of a meeting screaming is generally frowned upon, you could immediately defend yourself or give in to the other person's loud demands. "But before doing anything, you should wait and listen closely for as long as possible," suggests Higgens. Silence has its advantages. "First, venting anger can be a very healthy and cathartic process for the other person. Second, and more important, while ranting the other person will probably divulge a piece of information that is very valuable for you to know."

Here's an example: You've been cutting a freelance deal to produce a product for a particular company. There are several points of contention involved, one of which is your fee. While the client had made mention of it, you did not think it was a very touchy subject, and you were not prepared to come down in price. Suddenly, the client has a fit during which you discover that his boss has been nailing him on budget all year. Having heard something of value, you can now talk to this guy about rearranging the package so that it will be more appealing to his boss and still bring you the money you need. Rather than caving in or killing an option, you've opened up a doorway for additional thinking.

The final tactic is disclosing. This is simply stating your feelings. While emotions are something to be controlled when you're trying to reach a clear decision, that doesn't mean they should always be kept hidden. Occasionally when things are getting difficult, it can't hurt to say, "I'm getting really frustrated here. I'm trying to understand your situation but you're not doing the same for me." If the other person says "too bad," *then* you can shoot him.

Be aware of partisan perceptions. Everyone sees the same thing differently. When two managers run onto the baseball diamond right after a tight home-plate steal, it's not because they want to know where the umpire got his neat face mask. They are more interested in how they can get their hands through the mask and discuss the call in a friendly manner. Just as a ballplayer can seem safe and out at the same time, there are always two ways to look at a problem. You may think you deserve a raise, and that your boss is being unfairly tight with the money. It seems simple enough, and yet each side has a different perception of the issue.

You think that you're not getting what is standard at other companies . . . that it's well within your boss's power to give you what you're asking for . . . that you've been working like a bunch of union beavers on time and a half. On the other side, your boss may be thinking that the salary you make is fair with respect to industry standards . . . that you're making more than he was when he had your job . . . that your productivity has been good but nothing deserving knighthood . . . that he's under pressure to keep his budget low. If each of you simply assumes your own perceptions are correct, neither of you will even bring them up. This means that from a list of eight topics to discuss with respect to your raise, you will only tackle one: Do I or don't I get one? Always try to see things from the other person's perspective, but don't stop there. Air your views, and then actively solicit the other person's.

Ask high-gain questions. "When you negotiate, you are in the information-gathering and idea-generating business," says Higgens. "High-gain questions ask the people on the other side of the table to evaluate, analyze, speculate, or generally express their feelings. You want them to divulge more information, so your discussions can get off a dead end and onto a more profitable line of thinking."

Rather than say to your boss, "So you're not giving me a raise?" you should ask, "If you can't give me a raise, is there some other option that might make my career with this company look more attractive?" Suddenly you've moved from a dead no to the possibility of additional suggestions. Perhaps you could take on new duties that might lead to a promotion in the near future.

In general, you want to stay away from closed-ended questions which demand yes or no answers, such as "Would you agree that X is the most important factor we are dealing with?" Instead, you should inquire as to what other factors are more important than X.

If things start to get bogged down and the other person feels that you're not giving enough, you might ask him this: "What would you do if you were in my situation?" An open-ended question may trigger some interesting suggestions and help the other person focus on the limitations you might be up against.

4 SIGNS OF A SUCCESSFUL NEGOTIATION

Scott Brown offers these four indicators as a scorecard on the success of your negotiation.

1. All your major interests have been met.
2. The critical interests of the other party have been met.
3. The relationship is good. This doesn't necessarily mean you'll be going golfing on weekends, but the next time you meet it should be at least as easy as this session was.
4. The outcome is better than any alternative you can think of.

By now you may have realized that this chapter has favored a rather low-impact approach to negotiation. There are no scams, coercive tricks, or samurai warrior techniques to be found here. Unless you are dealing with someone only once, such tricks will handicap you in the future. And unless you have a crystal ball, there's no way of knowing who you are going to run into again. But one thing is for sure: If you steamrolled them in the past, they'll be looking for restitution the next time around.

In the end, the most sensible way to look at negotiation is as a relationship working toward a win-win solution to a common problem. Keep an open mind, gather information, and remain calm. Then after you get your way, you can hire yourself out as a consultant on the Middle East problem.

Nothing New under the Sun

By now there isn't an arbitrator on Wall Street who hasn't heard about *The Art of War,* that 2,000-year-old book of venerable Japanese battle wisdom that seems to have a message for every modern-day paper-clip warrior. Virtually unknown, however, is India's book of perennial business wisdom called the *Arthasastra* ("The Textbook of Statecraft and Diplomacy"). Written around 330 B.C. by an early bureaucrat named Kautilya, this book was read and followed by the rulers of India centuries before Machiavelli was a gleam in his parents' eyes.

In the *Arthasastra,* Kautilya outlined four basic ways to approach someone who has something you want. The first is *Shaam.* This is the friendly and open approach. If Shaam alone doesn't work then you use *Daan,* which literally means "price." You offer a concession that doesn't hurt your position, warms the atmosphere, and perhaps makes the receiver feel obliged to offer a similar concession.

When Shaam and Daan do not work, your counterpart is probably trying to overpower you. This is when you apply *Dand,* which means "stick" in Sanskrit. Since you hold a few cards of your own in any negotiation, you should let the opposition know that you can hurt him and the proceedings if you must.

Finally, if the person across the table is too powerful to threaten, you must rely on *Bhed,* or cunning.

Of course the various applications and combinations of these four techniques approach the complexity of a chess game. But with the help of the *Arthasastra,* the kings and princes of India were able to play that game with a fair degree of success.

41

NUTRITION

Scientists have yet to determine whether the nutritional needs of the animal known as *Managerius executus* differ significantly from that of your run-of-the-mill *Homo sapiens.* But one thing is for sure: An executive does need quite a bit of mental and physical stamina to get through the average 60-hour, decision-making, nerve-trying work week. And a proper diet can contribute much of that stamina. The problem is time. Who has the time to read all the latest nutritional news, gather the necessary ingredients of a healthy eating regimen, and carefully ingest said ingredients at the right moment and in the correct amounts? When it comes to nutrition, what an executive needs to know are the fast facts: What do I need to eat so that I can function at maximum efficiency? How can I eat it in a way that will waste the least amount of time? And how do I use foods to minimize downtime due to illness?

STAMINA EATING

To the average executive, the concept of three square meals a day is little more than a fairy tale. Odd working hours, surprise business lunches, and deadlines which should have been met yesterday all conspire to keep you from maintaining anything close to the eating schedule your body and mind require to operate like a lean, mean, management machine. But even if you did manage to get in those three squares, you might still be falling short.

"One of the most important stamina rules is that your body needs its fuel in moderate doses throughout the day to keep energy nutrients optimally available at the cellular level," says Peter M. Miller, Ph.D., executive director of the Hilton Head Health Institute and author of *The Hilton Head Executive Stamina Program.* "To this end I actually counsel people to eat between four and five times a day."

At first you might think that following this advice would make you a fat executive rather than an energized one. But if we use an analogy which Dr. Miller is fond of, the logic becomes a bit more apparent. Think about your car. Do you fill it up only after it runs out of gas? Or do you quite sensibly top off the tank at regular intervals, making sure that you always have enough fuel to go the distance?

"Many executives will grab a cup of coffee and a danish at around 8:00 A.M. and then put off lunch until 2:00 in the afternoon. Meanwhile they run out of gas by midday and spend a couple of hours operating at well below their peak stamina level," notes Dr. Miller. "By eating four to five times a day, you avoid running low."

But this does not give you a license to stuff yourself regularly. After all, you don't try to cram ten gallons of gas into your car when you only need to put in five to top off the tank. "What I am suggesting is that you reduce the amount of food you eat at any one time so that you can spread the same amount of calories more evenly over the day," says Dr. Miller.

Eating less, but more frequently, makes good sense for another reason. "The larger the meal, the more time it takes to digest," notes Dr. Miller. "And the process of digestion requires increased blood and oxygen flow to the stomach and intestines. This represents energy which will not be available for the brain and muscles to use." In other words, the bigger the meal, the more time you'll spend operating in that groggy after-the-Thanksgiving-feast state of mind. It's not where you want to be when you have an after-lunch merger decision to make.

While your fueling schedule is an important component of your stamina level, the kind of fuel you use also makes a difference. A high-octane diet is one that is high in complex carbohydrates, like those found in whole grains and vegetables. "To ensure that you are receiving the large amounts of glucose that your body needs to maintain maximum energy, your basic fuel mix should be 60 percent carbohydrates, 15 percent protein, and no more than 25 percent fat daily," suggests Dr. Miller. "While many people subscribe to the old belief that protein is where you get your primary source of energy, this is not exactly true. Depend on foods such as vegetables, cereals, pasta, bread, potatoes, and fruit to give you the carbohydrates your body needs to manufacture a steady supply of glucose. Rather than having a steak and fries for lunch, for example, you would do much better ordering a fruit platter, salad, or perhaps pasta primavera. Less calories, more carbohydrates is the rule."

Late afternoon or midmorning (assuming you eat breakfast at 7:00 A.M. and lunch at 2:00 P.M.) is when you want to go for the additional mini-meal or snack. Dr. Miller suggests any of the following for a perfect pick-up when your glucose levels are sagging:

- 1 whole medium banana
- 1 whole medium orange
- ¼ cup of raisins
- 5 dates
- ¼ honeydew
- ½ medium cantaloupe

With a little preparation, you might also try these alternatives.

Executive Gorp

¼ cup raisins
¼ cup sunflower seeds
¼ cup dry-roasted peanuts, unsalted

Mix all ingredients together in a medium bowl.

Banana Boost

1 banana, sliced
½ cup sliced strawberries
1 tablespoon plain yogurt

Mix the banana and strawberries together in a medium bowl and top with yogurt.

Fruit Mix

3 medium apricots
½ medium apple, cored and sliced
¼ cantaloupe, cubed
2 figs

Mix all ingredients together in a medium bowl.

To counteract dehydration, make sure to drink fluids throughout the day. "One of the things we know about energy is that when your body loses fluid, you tend to get tired," says Dr. Miller. "Executives should take particular care since they frequently become dehydrated due to stuffy work environments as well as time spent in airplanes.

"But you want to be careful of too much coffee or other caffeinated beverages," cautions Dr. Miller. "Since caffeine is a diuretic, those drinks will only aggravate the problem. What I suggest is a 'stamina spritzer': 60 percent orange juice and 40 percent carbonated water, served very cold. I also find a 'stamina spritzer' to be the perfect way to get started in the morning."

In the quest for stamina, many an executive may well wonder if some additional vitamins are in order. "Basically, an executive has the same vitamin needs as anyone else," says Dr. Miller. "My feeling is that a well-rounded diet should provide all that's necessary. But if you feel that you're guilty of some rather patchy eating habits, you may want to take a multivitamin with a mineral supplement for nutritional insurance."

So in short, Dr. Miller's eating program for busy executives is this: small, nutrition-packed meals and snacks with a preponderance of complex carbohydrates; increased fluid intake; and a multivitamin/mineral supplement if necessary.

DINING OUT WITHOUT DAMAGE

It's a tough life: lunch with J.B. at the 21 Club; closing a deal over lobster thermidor at the Four Seasons. Business meals are a common part of every executive's day. But it is precisely during those meals that most people do the greatest damage to their bodies. No matter how good that hollandaise sauce looks on your plate, as far as your body is concerned it might just as well be edible glue.

This isn't to say that you've got to start taking your clients to restaurants with names like Guru Sam's All-Nite Soybeanery. You can still enjoy fine dining as long as you take a few precautions with your selections.

- Ask if fried entrées can be broiled instead. This works especially well with fish, shrimp, and chicken.
- Have your vegetables steamed or microwaved to keep in nutrients and keep out fat and sodium.
- Banish butter (at 100 calories per tablespoon) and ask your waiter for a small dish of cottage cheese or yogurt as a topping for your baked potato. These have less than one-eighth the calories of butter or margarine, plus additional calcium and protein to boot.

● Having salad dressings served on the side is a popular request, but why not do the same with sauces and gravies? Then you can add a small splash to suit your taste rather than rely on the chef to keep your best interests in mind.

● Choose these excellent appetizers when possible: sliced melon, a vegetable plate with low-fat dip, or fresh seafood items like baked oysters or shrimp cocktail with a lemon wedge. Avoid pâté, caviar, fried hors d'oeuvres, and high-fat dips.

● Gazpacho, minestrone, and other vegetable or bean soups get your dining off to a healthier start than do high-sodium broths and consommés or high-fat cream soups.

● Learn to recognize terms and phrases which serve as a sort of code for low-fat preparation. "Steamed," "in its own juice," "garden-fresh," "roasted," "poached," "in tomato juice," and "dry-boiled" (in lemon juice or wine) are all examples of the kinds of descriptive phrases you should be looking for on menus.

● On the other hand, you want to avoid foods that are described as "buttery," "buttered," "in butter sauce," "fried," "pan-fried," "crispy," "braised," "creamed," "in cream sauce," "in its own gravy," "with hollandaise sauce," "in cheese sauce," "scalloped," "marinated" (in oil), or "basted."

Combine these tips with choices from Dr. Miller's executive stamina food plan and there is no reason you have to give up your table at the 21 Club for a stand-up counter at Guru Sam's.

FITTING FIBER INTO YOUR SCHEDULE

By now you've heard about the benefits of fiber from the surgeon general, your mother, your spouse, and the person who bags your groceries at the check-out counter. You are tired of hearing vague eat-more-fiber advice from do-gooders and now would like answers to these basic questions: Where do you get it, what will it do for you, and how much do you need?

Technically, fiber is the term for the parts of plants that your body can't digest. You can think of fiber as falling into two categories, soluble and insoluble. Soluble fiber is the kind that dissolves in water. Insoluble fiber doesn't. The solubles are best for combining with cholesterol and escorting it out of the body. The insolubles stop constipation, and over the long term may help prevent colon cancer.

If you are interested in using soluble fiber to lower your cholesterol level, try including some of the following foods in your diet.

- Apricots
- Beans, kidney or pinto
- Beans, lima
- Beans, white
- Broccoli
- Cabbage
- Cauliflower
- Chick-peas
- Figs
- Kale
- Oat bran
- Oatmeal
- Onions
- Oranges
- Peas, black-eyed
- Peas, green
- Prunes
- Raisins
- Whole wheat bread

Insoluble fiber, the kind that does not dissolve in water, can easily be found in most whole grains as well as fruits, vegetables, and dried beans.

One possible advantage of high-fiber foods is that they may actually help you drop a few pounds while delivering the previously mentioned health benefits. Here's why.

- Most fiber foods are not calorically dense. This means that you can indulge in a feeding frenzy of fresh fruits and vegetables without getting many calories.
- Fiber foods take up a lot of room in your stomach. You'll feel full on fruits, vegetables, beans, and whole grains long before you've taken in a lot of calories.

Many experts recommend that we try to consume at least 30 grams of fiber a day. That's about twice as much as the typical American diet provides.

In general, the following are the easiest rules to remember when it comes to getting more fiber in your diet:

- Think brown when you think of bread. Whole wheat (or other whole grain) bread should be the rule.
- Eat potatoes and other vegetables with their skins.

- Eat vegetables that have edible stems or stalks, such as broccoli.
- Eat fruits that have edible seeds, such as raspberries, blackberries, and strawberries.
- Try brown rice, corn tortillas, bulgur wheat, or whole wheat pasta. Whole grain doesn't have to mean just cereal or bread.

FIGHTING FAT AT HOME

Home may be where the heart is, but it's also where many of us do serious damage to our heart every time we sit down at the dining room table—primarily by consuming foods that are too high in artery-clogging fat. Before we get into smart ways to get the fat out, let's pause a moment to understand exactly what we are fighting.

There are basically three kinds of fat, but only one that you need to worry about. The differences have to do with the varying numbers of hydrogen atoms that a fat molecule may contain. But since atom counting has yet to become a national pastime, all you need to remember is that saturated fats are your enemy. Chiefly of animal origin, saturated fats should be avoided because they are believed to contribute to elevated cholesterol levels and heart disease.

The other two fats, monounsaturated and polyunsaturated, are found primarily in vegetables. Not only don't these fats cause heart disease, they may in certain cases exert a protective effect.

If you have eating habits akin to the average American's, you are probably getting twice as much saturated fat from your diet as you should. The solution? Try adopting some of the following food preparation tips from the Rodale Food Center in Emmaus, Pennsylvania.

- Trim all visible fat from roasts, steaks, and chops and remove the skin and visible fat from chicken and other poultry before cooking. This can cut the fat content by up to one-half.
- Use nonstick pans or a nonstick vegetable spray for cooking eggs, pancakes, crepes, and similar foods.
- Sauté meat, poultry, and fish in a little seasoned stock or liquid instead of in oil or butter. Or saute chicken and fish in flavored vinegars.
- Cook roasts, chops, steaks, meatballs, hamburgers, and other meat patties on a raised broiler pan in the oven so the excess fat will drip away into the lower pan.

- To reduce the fat in salad dressings, replace at least two-thirds of the oil in a basic vinaigrette dressing recipe with plain, low-fat yogurt.
- Choose tuna (or other canned fish) packed in water rather than in oil.
- Buttermilk and plain, low-fat yogurt can be substituted for milk and light cream in sauces and soups, cold or hot. To avoid curdling when you heat them, first mix one teaspoon of cornstarch into one cup of the buttermilk or yogurt. You can also remove the pan from the heat and stir in the yogurt or buttermilk just before serving.
- Use stock, herbal tea, or juice instead of oil in marinades. If you're baking, cover the pan to keep the food moist. This is an ideal method for preparing fish, vegetable casseroles, and meat loaf.

Total fats should account for less than 30 percent of your caloric intake, according to the American Heart Association (AHA). What does that mean in everyday terms? The following is a fat breakdown of some everyday foods. Needless to say, if you want to stay within the AHA's target range you'll need to cut down on the foods with a fat content of 30 percent or higher.

Less than 10 percent fat: Puffed cereal, most fruits, potatoes, rice, most vegetables, beans, white meat turkey, tuna packed in water, bread, skim milk.

Between 10 percent and 30 percent fat: Bluefish, saltines, low-fat cottage cheese, collard greens, lobster, oysters, oatmeal, chicken breast, pea soup, plain popcorn, onion soup, plain bran cereals, beef liver, mussels, buttermilk, low-fat milk, low-fat yogurt, scallops, king crab, pancakes.

Between 30 percent and 40 percent fat: Canned pink salmon, loin lamb chops, sirloin steak, cheese pizza, chicken wings, french fries, flank steak, waffles, beef gravy, cheese crackers, rump roast, tuna packed in oil.

Between 40 percent and 50 percent fat: Ice cream, whole milk, lean ground beef, part-skim ricotta cheese, sardines, ham, porterhouse steak.

50 percent or more fat: Hot dogs, mayonnaise, oil-based dressings, bacon, Brie cheese, eggs, potato chips, blue cheese dressing, chocolate, most hard cheeses, heavy cream, sausage, peanut butter, cream cheese, sour cream, nuts, spareribs, butter, margarine, avocados.

42

OFFICES

Did you ever stop to consider the fact that you spend almost as many waking hours in your office as you do in your home? Yet how much time do you spend sprucing up your office as compared to your home? At home most of us are constantly rearranging furniture, painting the walls, and acquiring the odd curiosity that will set off the coffee table in the living room. At the office? If we're lucky we clean our desks once a month and pick up the crumpled paper balls that never completed their two-point trip to the wastebasket.

Granted, most of us have homes that provide considerably more decorating options than do our offices. Granted, homes are to enjoy and offices are to endure. And granted, we seldom move into homes that have already been predesigned and decorated by someone who has an industrial-green filing cabinet for a soul. But that doesn't mean you can't take matters into your own hands and make a few changes for the better in your personal work environment.

Why should you? Consider this. When you ask someone what time it is and he yanks back his sleeve to gaze at his Rolex, sparkling expensively in the sun, what are you prone to think? The fact is that we do notice people's personal accessories and draw conclusions from them. The same phenomenon occurs with offices. Whether they are neat or unruly, sport a shrunken head or a Harvard diploma on the wall, offices send messages to fellow workers about who the occupant is. And that can be used to your advantage.

A second reason to consider an office makeover is you—your personal comfort. If you can't stand working in the presence of that Holiday Inn-style winter wonderland oil painting that someone hung in your office, you should take it down. Put something up that stimulates you. You're the one who has to look at it all day. Once you start taking steps to personalize your office, you'll not only like working there better, you'll work better in general.

Of course an office makeover goes far beyond the banishment of one tacky oil painting. Factors such as color, the placement of your desk, and the objects on your desk all send subtle messages to the people you invite into your space. Those same factors will also influence your own state of mind and effectiveness.

COLOR YOUR WORLD FOR MAXIMUM EFFECT

Most of us divide colors into three groups: those we like, those we don't like, and those that don't seem to strike us one way or the other. But at the Wagner Institute of Color Research in Santa Monica, California, the study of color isn't based on personal preferences. It focuses instead on how people respond psychologically to various hues.

"You may like a color very much, but it doesn't necessarily mean that if you painted your office that color it would improve your productivity," says Carlton Wagner, head of the institute and color adviser to firms such as General Motors, DuPont, and Ford Motor Company. "As a matter of fact, my experience has shown that just the opposite normally occurs. Anxious, flighty people—the kind who often fly off the handle—tend to gravitate toward the color yellow, for example. But the color yellow actually *causes* people to become anxious and lose their temper. Generally speaking, when people select their own office colors, I find that it further emphasizes the negative aspects of their personalities. The reason for this is that subliminally, people gravitate toward a color which reinforces a direction in which they are already moving."

While one might think that this is taking the subconscious color connection just a shade too far, Wagner is willing to make an even stronger statement. "Sixty percent of an environment's appeal is predicated on color," he says. "And what's even more interesting, I've found that a one to two percent change in color is enough to cause a difference in reaction."

In other words, if you took 100 tinting steps in changing the color white to black, there would be a measurable effect on the psyche after the very first step, the most minute change from white to grayish white. "We've actually shown this to be true by doing two employee break rooms in two slightly different shades of beige. During the first few days of use, employees favored both rooms equally. But then they started to use one room a little less and one a bit more. By the end of a month, one of the break rooms was consistently empty—shunned because of a color difference which most of us would hardly notice. That's how important color can be."

Now that you are sitting there suddenly aware of the many colors around you playing Ping-Pong with your emotional well-being, you're probably wondering how you can tame this natural force for the good of career and personal productivity. "Well, the first question I ask my clients is how the space will be used," says Wagner. "Will your office be a place in which you do your own work, or will it be used to interact with people coming to see you? Many times I have to color a space so that the effect is less for the particular manager and more for the people who interact with her—so that they are aware of the position she holds in the company."

If you are primarily interested in your office's effect on others, then the next thing Wagner would want to know is exactly who those others are. "While the general population does react en masse to certain symbols of respect, there is definitely a difference between the color reactions of people from different socio-economic backgrounds. Fortunately, the people who work for you will all probably fall within a certain pay range."

If you were managing a department of 15 men and women making between $18,000 and $25,000, you would probably want to do your office in an air force blue (a dusty, midrange blue) to command their respect. "You do need to be careful in your color consideration," notes Wagner. "For example, I could give you so much prestige that your employees would actually feel uncomfortable interacting with you."

Potential despots interested in colors that would make an employee genuflect before approaching their desk should try maroon or forest green. "There is a historical consciousness that surrounds these as well as any other dark or rich colors," says Wagner. "Back in the Middle Ages, because color production was expensive, when any new or totally saturated color was introduced, it went to the aristocracy, the clergy, and the richest merchants. The scarlet of the cardinal's robe and the royal purple of the king's cloak are good examples. So when you saw someone wearing rich colors, undiluted by any tint of white, you knew that person had money and power."

Forest green seems to hold the highest degree of respect because it used to be especially hard to produce. During the period when the Adams brothers were decorating the manors of England's landed gentry, they often painted entire rooms in forest green to denote the wealth of the family. This historical class consciousness can still be seen today in the range of automobile colorings. Just compare the kinds of colors a Mercedes comes in with those of a Hyundai.

"I would use a forest green to decorate the office of a Trump or Iacocca because the people whom they deal with are of a sufficient socio-economic background that they would not find the color daunting," says Wagner. But if you are thinking of using a rich color in a bid to impress your superiors, forget it. "It would seem incongruent with your position, and upper-level executives would be put off by it. Where color can work the most powerfully *against* you is in situations where it doesn't mesh with your persona or position."

While an air force blue may be a safe bet for most managers, it isn't necessarily the color you would want if your office is strictly a place to get some work done. "In a case like this, where personal comfort and productivity are the important factors, the first thing I would want to know is whether a computer terminal is in heavy use," says Wagner. "If a person does a lot of work on a monochrome screen, then I would color the wall behind the computer to compensate so that he or she can avoid eye fatigue and work for the longest amount of time in relative comfort."

The best way to accomplish this is to use the screen color's direct opposite. "In the case of amber, the truest opposite would be a somewhat off-putting purple-lavender," says Wagner. "But what I would do instead is use a subtle lavender gray. If the screen happens to be green, I would opt for a dusty peach on the wall directly behind it."

For overall effect, Wagner might choose a dusty mauve for a relaxing work environment. "But it would have to be for either a woman, or a man of sufficiently high socio-economic level that he would feel comfortable with the color."

In general, if you aren't sure what to do with your office, Navajo white is not a bad choice. "It's easily the safest color to use, and in fact about 85

The Sweet Smell of Success

Certain scents boost productivity by advantageously affecting employee behavior, say Japanese researchers. A study of computer operations found that when liquid perfumes were compressed into a fine mist and pumped through office air-conditioning systems, lemon-scented air decreased errors by 54 percent, jasmine by 33 percent, and lavender by 20 percent. The underlying theory is that pleasant smells help relieve mistake-causing stress.

Ever practical, the Japanese have already packaged this discovery for home use in the form of an alarm clock which, ten minutes before sounding, sprays a scented mist to make mind and body more alert. (Unfortunately, the product is not available in the United States.)

percent of all offices are done in Navaho white," notes Wagner. "Basically it's a soft, brown-beige white that wouldn't even read as a tan." The advantage to this color over basic plain white is that it cuts down on glare and won't lead to a type of "indoor snow blindness" that so many high-gloss pure whites can induce. "If you can't get professional guidance," says Wagner, "at least you won't go wrong with this color as the primary influence with perhaps one wall done in lavender-gray or dusty peach to offset your computer terminal."

OBJECTIFY YOUR PRESTIGE WITH THE RIGHT OBJECTS

If you had walked into the office of the late Armand Hammer, the first thing your eyes might have rested upon would have been the 50-million-year-old hunk of fossil shale lying on his desk. That is, of course, if you could have drawn your attention away from the $1,000,000,000 check encased in Lucite, an impressive reminder of a past debt repayment. If you hadn't already known exactly how important the man sitting behind the desk was, the objects *on* his desk would probably have given you a strong clue.

While most of us have yet to carve our name upon the world à la Hammer, we can still use a few well-chosen objects to let the world know that it's dealing with a person of no small importance. And importance is not the only thing you can convey with a well-planned desktop. All those activities, hobbies, and talents you pursue outside of the office can easily be transferred to your desk via a few mementos and photographs. One small photo of you standing in a Jeep on safari in Kenya, for example, might build your office reputation as a world traveler. When other people are trying to get a bearing on who you are, small clues loom large in their minds.

The first thing you want to do before embarking on Project Prestige is take a look at the desks of the high and mighty in your company. In a *New York Times* interview, University of Michigan psychology professor David Winter, Ph.D., notes that the things that exude the appropriate aura of prestige do change depending on the corporate circumstances. "If having a fancy computer is part of the cachet of the office culture, then those high in the need for power will be sure to get one. But in other office cultures, not having a computer on your desk might be more prestigious, because it means that someone else does the work for you."

Beyond the realm of office equipment, the same considerations apply. "Is it appropriate to put up your college diploma?" asks Jason Michaels, an office design consultant in New York City. "It depends on what others in your company do. If most people don't, then it may look a little pompous on your part to have the sheepskin displayed prominently. On the other hand, if you happen to know that the CEO is a Yale man and so are you, you just might want to take a chance and hang your diploma on the wall. Alma maters build bonds."

Accessorizing is another way to lend a little prestige to your office. A Montblanc pen, a solid-gold paper clip holder, a fine leather appointment book—these are the things which executives are made of. "You want to be careful, though, not to overdo it," cautions San Francisco psychologist Jana Meyers. "If you have more finery on your desk than the executive VP, it's going to look a little out of place and people will notice. Rather than thinking of you as elegant, people will leave with the impression that you're either a showoff or overly concerned with your image. And the last thing you want to do is appear to be consciously creating an image."

The same goes for personal mementos. "Take a moment to decide what is the most interesting aspect of your life outside the office, and then choose one or two objects that best depict that aspect," suggests Washington, D.C., image consultant Debbie Ross. "If it happens to be golf, then perhaps that trophy you won at the last country club tourney would do well on your desk. If you collect stamps, a particularly interesting set, well mounted and framed, would look great on the wall. In general you want to choose an object which will attract attention and stimulate a little conversation. But keep in mind that you are dealing with an office and not your den. One or two objects are fine; a trophy case would be just a little boorish."

If the memento of your choice happens to be in the form of a photograph, you want to be careful that you don't create a shrine for yourself. Eleven inches by 14 inches is the absolute limit on outside dimensions of any photograph, according to organizational psychologist Marilyn Machlowitz, Ph.D. Anything larger is going to look a tad precious. Additionally, scenes of swimsuit-clad spouses are a no-no, and so are wedding pictures. Finally, if you are going to use photographs, be sure that they don't look terribly outdated.

With all the image making which you're engaged in, remember that not everything in your office needs to look like it came from Versailles. "Comfort items such as the pen holder your son made in his middle school shop class also have a place in your office," says Mark Snyder, a psychologist at the University of Minnesota. "Not only do items such as this make you feel more at home in your office, but they provide a nice balance when juxtaposed with trendier accoutrements. While such an object may look somewhat out of place, people visiting your office will recognize it for what it is, a thing of sentimental value."

USE THESE SECRETS OF LIGHT AND SPACE

The Steelcase Furniture Company surveyed thousands of office workers nationwide to determine what the most important aspect of a good office was considered to be. While you might think that a big desk, a lot of space, and close proximity to the candy machine would all be candidates for the number one slot, this wasn't the case. In fact, 88 percent said good lighting was the most important factor.

Admittedly, light is one of those things we take for granted. You flip a switch on in the morning, do your work, and turn that same switch off when it's time to leave. But in actuality, there is far more to light than meets the eye.

Consider, for example, those fluorescent tubes that hang over your head all day at work. While they may seem to be providing you with a constant stream of light, they are in fact flickering on and off approximately 60 times per second. And although you can't actually see it happening, some experts believe this constant on-off action can cause headaches, eyestrain, loss of visual acuity, and fatigue.

Another example: Have you ever been stuck in a windowless office? Do you remember that vague feeling of discomfort you got, as if you were continually missing something? According to Gary Gordon, a New York City–based lighting consultant, what you were missing was variation. Natural light subtly yet constantly changes position and intensity throughout the day, and those changes stimulate us. But electric light never changes. So on a subconscious level, we perceive the windowless environment as sterile and somewhat unnatural. Time passes in strange ways when we don't receive cues from the sun.

For both problems the solution is the same: Provide some additional light sources. But what kind? Lighting designers use three terms to denote different kinds of light usage. Ambient light, the kind which is produced by ceiling lights, is for general illumination. Task lighting, such as you would get from a desk lamp, is purpose-specific. Reading, writing, or other tasks are performed in close proximity to this type of light source. Finally, focal lighting highlights a specific item or space for show.

There is a place for all three types of lighting in your office. Besides the ambient light, which most offices already have, you should get a desk lamp with an incandescent bulb. By blending the two kinds of light, you can dilute the effects of flickering fluorescent bulbs. Add a small clip-on light for a painting or poster, and you have three light sources with which to change the mood of your office throughout the day. Now even if you don't have a window, you can still create enough variations in lighting to preserve your sanity.

Combining light sources has yet another purpose in the workplace: It can actually make the office seem bigger. James A. Wise, a professor at Grand Valley State College in Michigan who has been helping NASA design space stations that seem larger than they really are, has found that when you mix fluorescent and incandescent lighting, subtle differences in color rendering break the space apart and make it seem larger. If the illusion of spaciousness is what you are seeking, another Wise suggestion is to light from the periphery of the office rather than from overhead. Make sure the light washes over the wall rather than directing it toward the center of the room. However, if you must stick to overheads, ask a lighting store salesperson for something to help diffuse the light so that it spreads horizontally.

In general, more office space equals more prestige. After all, it's hard to look important if you've got an office the size of a small rabbit hutch. But since you were probably assigned your present office, there is no way—short of knocking out a couple walls—to actually increase your physical space. Fortunately, there are some additional tricks that can work wonders with our perceptions.

The first is for those of you who have a small rectangular office. Wise has found that if you angle your desk, rather than placing it flush with the wall, it will actually make the room seem larger. And while we are on the topic of desks, here's a fast tip: Avoid clutter. If your primary concern is to increase the illusion of space in your office, the best way is to keep your desk clean, according to Jan Yager, Ph.D., author of *Making Your Office Work For You.* And that also goes for the rest of your work area. Hang your coat in the hall closet rather than over the back of your chair. If you have boxes of files lying around, see if you can't tuck them into a cabinet. The less stuff you have lying around, the more surface and floor space will be exposed, increasing the illusion of space.

Granted, no one will ever mistake your office for the Taj Mahal. But a little rearranging, a smidgen of accessorizing, some paint, and 20 minutes of housecleaning can work wonders on your workspace. And once your office looks like a place where important work is being done by an important person, you may be surprised at the additional respect and regard you get from fellow workers.

43

ORGANIZATION

Consider this. An alien scout lands on Earth to determine the behavioral patterns of the ruling life form on the planet. The scout randomly picks a human being and watches his every movement for several days. The man he picks gets up every morning, walks the dog, fills its food and water dish, goes to work, comes home, and walks the dog again. The alien returns to his planet and makes this report: The dominant life forms on this planet lead a life of relative ease completely supported by a slave class of bipeds who provide them with food and shelter. Whenever a ruling class member chooses to stroll about the community, a slave is required to follow three steps behind and has the insulting job of cleaning up the mess anytime his master wishes to relieve himself.

The alien scout thought that dogs ruled the world.

Believe it or not, an analogy to your office situation can be drawn here. If that same alien were to land at your place of business, blend in (quite easy to do, since these aliens bear a striking resemblance to office supplies), and observe your daily routine, he would be very likely to think that your primary duty was to clean your in-box and arrange the constant tidal flow of papers across your desk into ever-changing piles and patterns.

If you are not well organized, the alien would have assumed correctly. While your duties as a manager may include planning for the future, developing new marketing concepts, implementing new production procedures, and generally riding motivational herd over 30 or 40 employees, the fact is that if you aren't organized, then you probably are a slave to paperwork.

You're spending too much time reading data for which you have no use and too much time finding the information you actually need.

On the other hand, good organizational skills are not a panacea for all your woes. A person can have the most orderly files in the world and still be a bad manager. Simply put, good organization is an elementary tool which accomplishes its purpose when it frees you up to take care of important matters. Looking at it in this light, what you want is not to have the most orderly office in the universe, but an office which lets you get your work done. This can be accomplished more easily than you think.

DEALING WITH PAPER FLOW AT THE SOURCE

"A lot of people never get organized because they think there are complex rules, etched in stone, which must be followed," notes Barbara Hemphill, an organizational consultant and the president of Hemphill Associates in Washington, D.C. "For example, people think that being organized means being neat, or that being organized means handling a piece of paper only once. I find that for 90 percent of the people I work with, rules such as these do not work. If you have to deal with every piece of paper you pick up on an immediate basis, you may find that while you get a lot done, none of it is prioritized. You worked all day but the task that most needed doing was not even touched. But more importantly, following organizational rules in a blind manner doesn't work for a very simple reason: Everyone has his or her own needs and everyone must tailor his or her setup to answer those needs."

So the first organizational question to ask yourself is what kind of information is important to the successful fulfillment of your particular duties. The first area to which this question should be applied is your incoming interoffice mail. This is the point at which a great deal of your paperwork enters your office. "You can think of your incoming mail as a river that runs across your desk," says New York City organizational consultant Josh Thompson. "If the flow is too high, there are two ways you can handle the ensuing flood. First, you can bail frantically. This is what most people who have an organizational problem are currently doing. They read everything that comes through as quickly as possible, wasting time on the large percentage of incoming communiqués which have virtually nothing to do with their specific duties. The second way to control the flow is to build a dam at the source."

A dam can turn a torrential flood of paper into an easily managed trickle, but it needs to be done in a manner which does not prevent you from seeing the information which you *do* need. "An important point to remember is that in management, one distinguishes between information and data," notes Linda G. Sprague, Ph.D., professor of operations management at the University of New Hampshire's Whittemore School of Business and Economics. "They are not the same thing at all. You get an awful lot of data but not very much information. The difference between the two is that information is a subset of data which is relevant, accurate, timely, and concise."

Here's an example. At Massachusetts General Hospital, every pharmaceutical transaction has to be recorded due to governmental requirements. At the end of each month what the pharmacy manager might typically receive is a neat printout stacked about 3 feet high that includes every transaction from three aspirins dispensed on the 3rd of the month to a shot of morphine given on the 23rd. "That's raw data, and the manager of the pharmacy doesn't need to look at it," notes Dr. Sprague. "But he will get all 3 feet of data unless he sits down with the pharmacist and the data processing people and tells them, 'I need narcotics summaries, nonnarcotics summaries, and floor stock summaries by units.' One of the first steps of good organization—or good management, for that matter—is making sure that you are not getting inappropriate amounts of data and that you are getting appropriate amounts of information."

So the first step in your quest for order is to make sure the people you work with are sending you only what you need. Naturally this requires you to *know* what you need, but it also demands that you give your people some hard guidelines. The best way to put it to them is exactly how Dr. Sprague defines information.

It needs to be relevant. Let the people you work with know that out of all the data they send, you are concerned only with the information which normally ends up in paragraphs 8 through 18, for example. The rest can be jettisoned.

It needs to be accurate. Now that your people know what you want, they can dump the extraneous data and use the extra space and time to make the information they send as precise and detailed as you request.

It needs to be timely. If the info is from three weeks ago, you don't want it unless you are making future predictions based upon previous patterns and have specifically requested the material. "You need to be careful with this one," cautions Thompson. "Many managers get so caught up in facts and figures that they will look at useless, dated data, thinking that they should stay on top of any and all data."

It needs to be concise. 'Nuff said here.

Another place where you can curtail incoming data is in those situations where memos, as a matter of course, are sent to everyone. "This is the type of memo you receive concerning the customer service department's latest doings, even though *your* duties deal specifically with personnel," notes Thompson. "In a case such as this, it isn't out of line to request that your name be taken off the list. Many managers make the mistake of thinking that just because someone took the trouble of sending them data, they should read it. Well just remember, it's more trouble for you to read it than it is for them to send it."

Having paper-trained your co-workers, it's time to do the same with yourself. "Part of any manager's incoming mail consists of a number of industry periodicals and reports to which the company maintains a subscription," notes Thompson. "I'd estimate that most people do not read 60 to 70 percent of the material. Instead, they leave it lying around the office or constantly relegate the material to different slush piles, promising themselves that at some point they will get to it. Quite frankly, they will never get to it. The material will simply take up space and add to the general confusion."

In this case it is best to ask yourself a few honest questions. First, when was the last time you actually read a particular periodical? If the answer is more than a year ago . . . get rid of it. You aren't missing anything you weren't already missing, and it obviously isn't affecting your work. Second, when was the last time you found a piece of truly useful information in the periodicals you *do* read? Again, if the answer is an extended period of time, dump them. "It's good to remember the 80–20 rule in a case such as this," says Thompson. "Eighty percent of the useful information you find will come from about 20 percent of the material. Find that 20 percent and get rid of the rest."

SETTING UP YOUR OFFICE
FOR MAXIMUM ORDER AND EFFICIENCY

Consider the humble automobile. In many ways it is a masterpiece of ergonomics. Everything you need is within reach of the driver's seat, be it headlights to see by or tunes to cruise by. Information? By shifting your field of vision a matter of inches, you can determine your speed, the engine temperature, and who's behind you. In other words, your car is perfectly set up to provide you easy access to everything you need for the business of driving.

Now consider your humble office. Can the same thing be said? According to engineer Vladimir Stibic, author of *Tools of the Mind: Techniques and*

Methods of Intellectual Work, many offices contain amazing infringements on ergonomic rules. What does this have to do with organization? Everything.

Let's go back to the car for a moment. What if the speedometer were in the back seat? How often would you check it? While this may seem like an absurd image, there's a good chance that your office has its own back-seat speedometer in a different form. How many times, for example, do you get phone calls and need to write down a piece of vital information only to find yourself scrambling for a scrap of paper to scribble on? To answer that question, simply look at all the ragged scraps which dot your desk like an outbreak of dandruff.

If you were to be ergonomic about things, you would have your office set up so that there was always a notebook resting just beside the phone, with a pen ready to go and a place to file the notes when you were done. Simple as it may seem, if what you need is there when you need it, organization is not a problem. If those things aren't there, you'll just "make do." But confusion will prevail just as surely as you would get a speeding ticket if your speedometer were in the back seat.

So again you need to ask yourself the same question you asked in the last section: What do you need in order to get the job done? But while the last section addressed information, this time you are focusing on the actual physical needs of the job. You want to start by figuring out what activities you engage in most often.

"If you do in fact spend a great deal of time on the telephone, then you should make sure you have a clear working space around the phone and the tools you need within easy reach," says Thompson. "But if you spend most of the day writing and are rarely on the phone, move it to a less prominent place. And taking this even further, if you do most of your writing by hand, there's really no need for that word processor and printer to be taking up half your desk. They can be moved to a stand on wheels and rolled into position when occasionally needed. It's amazing how many people I've seen working in a cluttered little corner of their desk simply because the rest of the desk is taken up with objects seldom used. Part of the reason people have such a hard time organizing is because they never have the proper amount of space to do things in. The space becomes cluttered and things are pushed aside haphazardly to make room which would already be there if they'd taken the time to relegate less important objects to a place out of the way."

All you really need to do is take a look at your office and you'll probably be able to pinpoint where some rearranging needs to be done. If you have books piled everywhere, then you probably do a lot of reading and should have bookcases put in. If it's the pile in your in-box which has crept across your desk like ivy, it could be you need a larger in-box on a separate table.

It can't be stressed enough that having the right tools in the right place is half of the fight for organization. "I've worked in companies where they wouldn't think of manufacturing a product without the right mold, and yet they try to run an office without a stapler," notes organizational consultant Hemphill. "The problem is that we haven't been taught to notice or assign importance to minor details such as these, but they do make a difference. If you don't have that stapler, papers will remain loose for an unbelievably long time. They get lost, they get mixed up. It's little occurrences such as this that add up to a large mess eventually."

And speaking ergonomically, those tools shouldn't just be stashed somewhere in your office. They should be within easy reach. "If you have to open a drawer, reach into the back, and grope around in a little box every time you need a paper clip, chances are you won't bother most of the time," says Thompson. "A major rule of organization is that if you use it often it should be where you can get at it with the absolute least amount of effort."

"Making things easy for yourself is mandatory in organization," adds Hemphill. "If it isn't easy, you won't do it. For example, if you read a great deal of information, there should always be a highlighter handy to mark the most important parts. That way you won't need to reread everything later. But if that highlighter isn't handy, you'll find yourself rereading the same useless material over and over again."

The 80–20 rule can be put to good use in setting up your office for organizational efficiency. "Sit where you normally would when doing your work and extend your arm," suggests Thompson. "Swing your chair around 360 degrees and note the radius of your reach. Within that reach you should arrange the few (20 percent) tools which you find yourself using a majority (80 percent) of the time. Conversely, if you find objects within that circle which you seldom use, banish them out of reach."

If you frequently stash a great deal of information in your personal files, for example, and your filing cabinet is somewhere you have to get up and walk to, move it within the circle. Odds are you'll instantly eliminate those intermediate piles of paper that used to collect on your desk in between treks to the filing cabinet.

On the other hand, be realistic about your need concerning objects which already lie within the circle. Some people will keep a ten-volume set of product information on their desk even though it's already collected an inch and a half of dust. It's always been there, and at one point two years ago it was very useful. Now? Get rid of it. "In setting up your office for the smooth control of work, you do need to realize that your arrangement isn't permanent," notes Hemphill. "Duties and needs change. As they change, your office setup will need to change. A big problem some people have with organization is that they stick to an old system even after their needs have radically changed."

RIDING HERD ON PAPERWORK . . .
PAINLESSLY

If you've considered and implemented some of the guidelines previously discussed, you're already well on your way to being organized. You've brought the level of incoming data down to a manageable level, and you've turned your office into an environment which is truly designed to deal with the work which passes through it. Now it's time to focus on the actual paperwork itself.

Part of the reason people have a difficult time getting organized is because they act upon any given piece of paper in an all-or-nothing sort of way. When they pick it up, they either decide to take care of it right away or they decide not to do a thing about it and put it back in the pile. Obviously, the problem with this is that there is only so much you can do right away and even more that you can't. The end result is an ever-growing pile of papers which have no semblance of order.

If this behavior seems familiar to you (not that any fingers are being pointed), consider how you are actually robbing yourself of precious time. If you do nothing with a piece of paper except read it and put it back in the pile you are actually wasting the time you took to consider it in the first place. Having made no initial decision as to the fate of that paper, when you come back to it later you're only going to have to read it all over again. It seems a lot like that infamous army exercise where a raw recruit is ordered to dig a hole in the morning and ordered to fill that same hole in the afternoon.

To a certain extent, a good organizational system can help alleviate this problem by allowing you to make bite-sized decisions each time you handle a piece of paper. If you can make some sort of decision and then move the piece of paper to a pile or file which reflects that decision, then the next time you look at it you are already a little ahead of the game.

In *The Organized Executive*, author Stephanie Winston writes that there are only four things you can do with a piece of paper: Throw it away, refer it to someone else, act on it, or file it. These are the starting criteria through which every piece of paper that comes to your office should pass. If you pick up a piece of paper and decide you should throw it away, do so immediately. If you put it down and come back to it later, you may need a second reading to redetermine its content. Referrals follow the same rule. If you think it should be referred, you probably already know to whom it should be referred. Do it. (*Hint:* If you find yourself referring things frequently, be sure you maintain a supply of interoffice mailers. Otherwise you know these items will lie around on your desk forever.)

This leaves us with the act-on-it and file-it categories. "You should be wary of acting on anything until you've processed enough of your mail to have a fair idea of what your priorities for the day will be," Thompson cautions. "You may pick up a piece of paper, devote an hour to it, and then afterwards find that the very next thing in your in-box is of even greater significance and should have been done first."

So here is where we create our next organizational category—as a subsection of "act on it." In this subsection will go all those papers that you've chosen to work on, but they will now be further divided into time-frame categories. One pile/file might be labeled "do it today." Another could be "do it by the end of this week." Everything in a third pile might have a two-week limit in which it must be attended to.

Naturally you will need to develop your own categories which parallel the typical deadline situations under which you work. But once you've done so, try to make a time-frame judgment on every "act on it" paper you pick up, and then relegate it to the appropriate file. "And in keeping with the ergonomic setup of your office, try to have a special place within easy reach that will always be where you will put your now-segregated piles of 'to act on' papers," reminds Thompson.

One hint: As you handle papers and relegate them to different categories, you'll want to keep alert for those papers that are just getting eternally shuffled. Whereas the "you should only handle a piece of paper once" rule is one of the biggest myths in organizing, you don't want to handle it a hundred times, either. "I tell clients to put a red dot in the upper right hand corner each time they handle a piece of paper," says Barbara Hemphill. "Handling something two or three times is not a problem; but if the sheet starts to look like it has an outbreak of the measles, then it's time to take some decisive action. The best thing to do is re-ask yourself the initial toss-it, file-it, act-on-it, or refer-it question, and then do something immediately. Odds are if it has been shuffled around *that* long, you can probably get rid of it or file it for later use."

Finally we have that information designated as "to file." This is information that you know you are going to need at some point, maybe today, maybe next year, but it doesn't require specific action. Well . . . file it! That is, of course, if you've got a filing system. If this isn't the case, not to worry. It's easier than you think. Hemphill suggests that rather than trying to file everything in your office at one time, you start by working on today's inflow. "Make sure that everything you receive today has a place. Your backlog isn't going to get any worse for the wait, and then when you have the time to deal with it, you'll have already started your system. But if you try organizing everything at once you'll be overwhelmed and, quite frankly, discouraged."

The best way to come up with headings for your new system is to look at a piece of information and ask yourself, If I needed to find this piece of paper again, what would I look under? "As you come up with file headings, be sure to keep an alphabetized list handy so that you know what titles are currently being used," advises Hemphill. "This is so you don't end up forgetting you have a file named 'car' and start a new one entitled 'auto.' Before making a new file, check your list to make sure there isn't something that's already appropriate."

When starting your new system you want to try to avoid obsessive behavior as much as is humanly possible. "Most filing systems are far too complicated because people have a tendency to over-specify," says Hemphill. "A basic principle to follow is to put things into their largest category first."

So if you traveled infrequently, you might have a folder named "travel." As your traveling stints multiply, you might move on to subsections of travel with the titles such as "Northwest" or "East Coast." Or it might be by branch office. Finally, you could have 50 state-by-state subdivisions within the travel folder. "But most people err by breaking files down too much initially," Hemphill points out. "In actuality, it takes less time to go through one file with 20 pieces of paper in it than it does to go through ten files with 2 pieces each."

What we've just discussed is what Hemphill calls file management: the nuts and bolts of paper organizing, so to speak. The second component is file mechanics, which addresses questions such as whether to color code, are you or is your secretary going to do the filing honors, and what kind of folders should you use. These are all dilemmas which you must solve yourself since you are the one that needs to feel comfortable with your system. But keep in mind these two tips: (1) Always keep extra folders and labeling tabs stashed somewhere in the filing cabinet. If you have to go hunting for these items, you're probably going to be more likely to see humans land on Mars before you see those new headings you need incorporated into your system. (2) If you're going to color code, pastels are definitely out this year (good organization is nothing if not fashion-conscious).

The third component of your system is file maintenance. "The tips here are real simple," says Hemphill. "When you've got a file in your hand, if you see even one piece of paper in it that's out-of-date or has lost its usefulness, throw it out. I've seen people who know that something should be thrown out actually put it back in the file to be thrown out during their annual spring cleaning. This is ridiculous. If you throw it out when you notice it, by the time you get around to spring cleaning, most of the work will already have been done in an almost effortless manner." And when it does come time to purge and you find yourself wavering over some attractive piece of paper to which you've become attached, ask yourself, What is the worst thing that will happen if I throw this out? Answer this and you'll know what to do.

Now having set up your system, what happens if things go wrong? Is it a bad system? "Not necessarily," says Hemphill. "It could be the system was good but that your needs have changed. Part of organization is recognizing that it's never finished. It's an ongoing process. To know whether your system is good, just ask yourself two simple questions: Does it work, and Do I like it?"

If you can answer yes to both, it's unlikely that any intergalactic scout will ever mistake *you* for a paper slave.

44

POLITICS

T he great, rarely discussed half-truth about life is that it *matters* who you go to lunch with.

First of all, when you work in an organization, whether it's IBM or Planned Parenthood, you ultimately are trying to achieve certain goals both for the organization and for yourself. It's true that an organization can be successful while you fail, or you can succeed while your company falls apart. But—even without profit-sharing—if you take a personal interest in your company's success, you will at the very least work harder and be more productive.

What all of this has to do with your lunching ritual is simple. If you accept the fact that dedication to your organization's goals and hard work will eventually help both of you get ahead, you're only half right. The reality is that you also have to engage in what many define as politics: keeping yourself in the information flow, making sure people know who you are, understanding how power is wielded, aligning yourself (or at least appearing to align yourself) in power plays, and, yes, going to lunch with the right people.

Office Politics Tragedy #1. Stuart Schmidt, Ph.D., professor of human resources administration at Temple University's School of Business Administration, recalls the case of an MBA candidate who had returned to school after five years of working as an engineer. On the one hand, the engineer had earned merit recognitions and numerous awards for his prolific work. But he was the only member of his work team who received no promotion during those five years. And he was bitter.

As Dr. Schmidt tells it, the engineer complained that he got to work early and stayed at his bench long after office hours were officially over (while his colleagues and boss went out for an after-work beer). He generally worked through lunch (while the same crowd was out schmoozing over burgers). He even came in on Saturday mornings (while—you guessed it— the others played golf). Can you spot the flaw in his approach?

"Nobody got a chance to know who he was," explains Dr. Schmidt. "And they just assumed he couldn't work with others, which is an important skill for anyone who wants to advance in administration, which he wanted to do. In an office environment, you have to engage in social relationships— some would call it politics—or you might as well be an attachment to a word processor." A *Newsweek* article on the subject put it this way: "It may be the only game in which the person who doesn't play is guaranteed to lose."

Office Politics Tragedy #2. A banking MBA who prefers to remain anonymous was fired from her first job and told that she "didn't fit in." As she lamented in the pages of the *National Business Employment Weekly:* "All through school, if I did a good job, I got an A. Then in my first job, I was doing the work well, but I didn't realize that how I played politics would count as much as it did. In the end, it was the reason I was let go; I didn't know that it mattered whom I ate lunch with, but it did."

DON'T COUNT YOURSELF OUT

No, you don't have to become a conniver, back-stabber, or any other sort of politician who would make Machiavelli proud. But you can't afford to avoid politics totally, either. If you find the whole matter of office politics distasteful and unnatural and possibly counterproductive, what you *can* do is work to at least minimize your involvement. Kathleen Shea, Ph.D., a Libertyville, Illinois–based organizational psychologist, routinely offers her clients a strategy for getting ahead despite the politics.

Wake up to reality. "I encourage people to recognize their own naïveté about the business world and competition," she says. "For people who don't even know they have to be political, the first thing to do is to accept the situation and play [at least] some of the games themselves. Playing a political game is not so bad as long as you recognize it as a game." (Dr. Shea, by the way, won recognition for her research on high-achieving executives. Much of her work involved drawing parallels between the behavior of kids on playgrounds and the behavior of executives. Her bottom-line finding: "There's no difference between the games played as kids and what goes on in executive suites.")

Stop sabotaging yourself. If you're already heavily involved in office politics, Dr. Shea suggests you reexamine your assumptions and motives. Are you merely using politics to get around your own (often self-imposed) shortcomings? All of the gossiping and plotting is likely to get you nowhere if you operate under such loose-logic assumptions as: "Before I can be successful, I've got to [pick one] get my MBA, lose 20 pounds, . . ." Another self-defeating message: "If I bring the doughnuts in every Tuesday morning, everybody will be nice to me." Don't pin your hopes on it. Says Dr. Shea, "Stop sabotaging yourself, and the rest will follow."

Discover the impact of your personality. "If you're aware of your personality and how it affects yourself and others, you can control the negative aspects and concentrate on the positive," Dr. Shea says. Then you won't have to worry so much about other people. Once you understand, for example, that your narcissistic ("look at me! look at me!") personality and inability to share the spotlight with other team players cause colleagues to exclude you, you can take corrective action. To improve yourself, start telling people things like "This really was a team effort." Give others some of the credit. Eventually, predicts Dr. Shea, "you won't have to be so political. People will want you to be successful because you're such a beautiful person."

Work smart. Sure, if you start to emphasize the positive aspects of your personality, people may think you're great. But that still won't get you very far unless you can *work*, too. So focus on your performance. Substance counts.

SUBTLE (EVEN SUBCONSCIOUS) WAYS PEOPLE PLAY POLITICS

Most people frown upon such activities as apple-polishing and lying, notes Philadelphia-based management consultant John P. Fernandez, Ph.D., in his book *Survival in the Corporate Fishbowl*. They deny any involvement in such activities, yet they do them anyway. "In fact, I would caution you to be very wary of those who protest that they do not engage in politics, that they are always honest, straightforward, fair, and on the up and up. If they are truly all of that, they will not need tell you so, certainly not too much."

Do the planet a favor and don't bore anybody with the details of your political abstinence. And don't believe anyone who says he is above it all. Machiavelli contended that politics begins whenever two people begin to act.

Organizational gamesmen and gameswomen often politic in a number of ways without knowing they're doing it.

Hiding the information. They hold back information that could help others (so they themselves will look good by comparison).

Becoming Mr. Helpful. They do solicitous things at dinners and cocktail parties. When a higher-level person finishes her drink, for example, a politicker may say, "Oh, I see you need a refill; I'm going up to the bar, anyway. May I get you one?" The same person is likely to volunteer to get a drink for a lower-level sort only if he wants to extract himself from a conversation.

Emulating the boss. It's amazing how many people don't even know that they're trying to align themselves with a boss or other organizational power force through emulation. Suddenly they find themselves wearing polka-dot ties (just like the boss). Suddenly they love squash on Saturday mornings (and we don't mean the vegetable). Suddenly they develop a fondness for post-impressionist paintings or rare coins or Wagner's *Ring* cycle . . . just like you-know-who.

Pleasing Daddy. They do things which they know will please the boss, like bringing in only oat-bran doughnuts (which the boss, of course, prefers) instead of an assortment.

Coordinating restroom excursions. Men are notorious for this. They see the boss leave his office and head in the direction of the men's room. Suddenly, they have an urge to go . . . and then, while washing up, they may say, "Hey, I *love* that suit." Or, if that's inappropriate, they may say, "I just read your memo. You made some really good points."

HOW TO RECOGNIZE AND ALLY YOURSELF WITH POWER

The act of hitching yourself to a star may seem like the disingenuous sort of behavior you decry in others. And you may think it amounts to nothing more than using people. Think again. You're simply *helping* someone who is powerful (or is in the process of attaining power). In exchange, that person is helping you. Not such a big deal, huh?

"These kinds of alliances are often a two-way thing. People who are good at moving up often are also good at developing a team which moves up with them. All those involved gain loyalty and support because they help each other. It's the most straightforward way that politics works, and I don't think there's anything wrong with that," says Michael Maccoby, a Washington, D.C.–based management consultant and author of the books *The Gamesman*, *The Leader,* and *Why Work?*

So alliances are a reality of organizational life. And if you suspect other people will condemn you for aligning yourself with the powerful or the powerful-to-be, keep in mind that there are ways to do it and ways not to do it. Some of the best advice on the subject comes from Maccoby, who suggests that if you're friendly with *everybody,* you won't be resented if you happen to be a little friendlier with the important people. "The ones who just suck up to powerful people and are nasty to others, I think, are less likely to get to the top," he says.

Should you always be the first to volunteer when power types are seeking help? Not necessarily. You first should stop to consider how much you legitimately support what they're doing—and whether their goals and your goals are compatible, says Robert A. Lefton, Ph.D., an industrial psychologist and president of Psychological Associates, a St. Louis–based consulting firm. Don't blindly assume that they are. "Be a good observer. Listen to dialogue," he cautions. "Look and listen and piece it together."

Then there's the art of recognizing power. In smaller organizations, there's no question who has the power: He or she probably sits a few feet away from you. The larger the organization, though, the farther you're likely to be from the real influence. Which means you'll have to become acquainted either with those who serve the powerful (power service-class) or with those destined for power in the future. An example of a power service-class type to be aware of (and dare we use the word utilize?) is the consultant. Often he is a power behind the throne. If the chief executive relies heavily upon a particular consultant, it may be worth your while to get to know that person. If possible, find a way of engaging his services yourself.

Then there are the people who are likely to experience a meteoric rise through your organization. Maccoby says it's better (not to mention easier) to ally yourself with such a person as she's moving up, rather than when she's already there. The trouble is, that requires you to figure out who is on the power track (so you can then figure out ways to help her succeed). "You can tell fairly quickly that some people are in contention by taking a look at their performance and their style. They act like leaders. People start deferring to them, asking them their views," explains Maccoby.

"If you want to ally yourself with somebody like that, it becomes a question of what you have to offer. People often approach each other tentatively. If you feel it's a good deal, that the person is going someplace, then you have the opportunity to respond."

If the person never does approach you, remember that there are many small opportunities for you to establish contact and a relationship. "You might start talking to him about what he's doing and say that it interests you," says Maccoby. But it can't be too forced. Subtlety is indicated. Also, there's usually some mutual chemistry involved in personal alliances.

Maccoby adds another note of caution: "Some people do these things in a way that adds value and is legitimate, helping the companies and themselves. But some people do it in a purely political way, just trying to be in the right place with the right people. We all know the difference," he says. The question is, does the boss? "He may, or he may not. We're all subject to a certain amount of flattery," Maccoby concedes.

No matter how you decide to proceed in the murky world of office politics, don't overdo it. Don't spend the bulk of your waking hours agonizing over who's in and who's out. Don't treat every shred of grapevine news as an occasion to abandon your work at hand for a full afternoon of office gossiping. (You *must* pick up the phone to check out what you've heard with a few sources, though; it can be destructive to stay out of the information flow.) Just remember that while you're keeping alert to the goings-on around you, it also helps if you're competent and nice and useful to people (and we're not talking about just bringing in the doughnuts).

WHAT TO DO IF YOU'RE CAUGHT BETWEEN CLASHING TITANS

Remember when Apple Computer was virtually split up between co-founder Steven Jobs and chairman John Scully, the professional manager Jobs had brought in to run the company when it got too big for him? Eventually, the struggle for control was won by Scully. But Dr. Lefton knows of managers who, although they had aligned themselves with the defeated Jobs, were still retained by the victor Scully. How did they do it?

"They were people who conducted themselves in an open, honest way, and Scully realized they had a right to disagree," he says. "Scully was someone who built dissent into the system." The problem is, not all bosses allow for dissension. So before deciding which power function to align yourself with, stop for a moment and assess what kind of people you're dealing with. Are they the professional types who understand and encourage disagreement? Or are they the type to hold a grudge? You may be able to avoid a great deal of anxiety, not to mention cross fire, if you make a careful assessment of the situation before choosing sides. In the end, you may even opt for neutrality.

Find out as much as you can about the two disputants—particularly their histories, their displeasures, and what drives them. Then understand the source of the conflict. If one titan is motivated by ethics that you find questionable, for instance, how comfortable will you be with yourself if you support him? Or what if the issue that divides the two competitors is, to your mind, a trivial one? How do you choose an alliance based on something so insignificant? Says Dr. Lefton, "Most people who survive such situations are those who have been honest with themselves, with their boss, and even with the people they're competing with."

Dr. Fernandez suggests that if you're a subordinate to competing titans, you should consider who will be *your* best ally. "Help the one who's helping you the most, the one who you predict will support your goals and aspirations," he says.

Neutrality poses its own tricky problems. If the rivals are peers of yours, for instance, it may be easier to elect not to take sides. But if you do, you may find yourself unable to recruit any allies later when you yourself are in a battle.

One option is to build your own independent base of power so that the rivals (whether they're bosses or peers) are both dependent on *you*. "Do you have a critical skill or specific knowledge that they'll both need from you?" asks Dr. Schmidt. "Maybe you're the only one in the office who really knows his way around junk bonds." Try to create a situation in which both parties need you.

Politics by the numbers

Organizational psychologists say you can predict with reasonable accuracy the kind of office politics to expect in a new job by looking at the number of people you will be working with. Here, with the help of *National Business Employment Weekly,* are some examples.

The two-person office. If you're the number-two person in a satellite operation of the home office, you're in the trickiest political situation. With only one other party, the relationship takes on many of the pressures of a marriage: the necessity of getting along, the lack of other people to whom you can appeal for help or with whom you can ally, the suppression of disagreements. And remember, if you're the newcomer, it's probably someone else's rules by which you are going to play.

On the plus side: You have the undivided attention of your boss. If he likes you, he probably will become your mentor—and keep the home office abreast of your fine qualities.

On the minus side: He's all you've got. If he's out of favor with the home office, you're likely to go nowhere. If you try to circumvent him and appeal to home-office types, you'll possibly find yourself in a sticky, acrimonious divorce.

The Political Power of Newcomers

Joining a new organization? Surprisingly, you may be in one of the strongest political positions. Most workplaces afford new arrivals a honeymoon period in which to prove themselves (or prove what dolts they are). The length of time permitted varies greatly, often depending on what sort of timetables the operation works under. If the company is involved in selling big-ticket items or services, for example, and it takes weeks or months to close a single deal, the honeymoon may last for months. If it's a television newsroom in which frantic daily dead-lines are the norm, the window of opportunity may be a mere week.

By their nature, organizational honeymoons afford you the chance to assess which of competing factions would serve your political needs the best. So don't jump in and join a clique on your first day at a new job; in haste, you'll possibly select the wrong one. But neither should you take too long to make your decision. A sure sign that time is running out: Colleagues start getting impatient with you to reveal your leanings.

The three- to five-person office. If you're good at blending into groups, this may be the easiest arrangement politically, because the numbers are so small. If you're not a team-player type, though, it may be the hardest. The reason? Deviant behavior is more noticeable in a group of three to five people than it is in a larger group, according to Dr. Shea.

On the plus side: The team's rules will be clearly spelled out. If there are split factions (a sure sign: when folks split off into distinct groups for lunch), you'll probably be recruited by both. The factions are likely to afford you some time to decide which you want to join.

On the minus side: A failure to join in with the group or one of its factions will label you an untrustworthy loner. Any deviant behavior will be quickly noticed. Surprisingly, the flow of crucial information is slower in offices of three to five than it is in larger office groups.

The 30-person team. As a rule, the larger the group, the more competi-tion you'll find for everything from resources (the biggest offices) to rewards (the biggest salaries). There's competition, too, for the boss's time and good will. And he probably doesn't have enough of either to go around. Teams of this size are typical in corporate training programs.

On the plus side: You'll have a variety of cliques from which to choose. Decide on the one you feel wields the most influence and with whom you feel comfortable; then make sure you have something important to offer (a terrific pitching arm may be all you need). In large groups the grapevine is a marvelous and active source of crucial—but sometimes inaccurate—information. Again, try to confirm anything you hear with several independent sources.

On the minus side: Today's "in" clique may be out of status tomorrow. You've got to carefully juggle the need to stand out (in the boss's eyes) with the need to fit in. Star performers are often sabotaged by others unless they develop a wide base of support (i.e., friends). And you've got to ask yourself if you're really up for all the competition.

45

PROMOTIONS

To be honest, the whole matter of promotions can be boiled down into one simple question: *How do you get one?* Actually, there are two ways. The first involves a little-known discipline of the occult called execucraft. As prescribed by the ancient bylaws, the promotion-seeking initiate must wait for the first full moon that falls after the beginning of the corporation's second fiscal quarter. Standing within a circle of flaming memos, the initiate then reads the company rules and regulations backwards while simultaneously genuflecting in the direction of corporate headquarters. Finally, the boss's desk must be carried to an open field and, by the light of the full moon, buried at a depth of approximately five feet. (*Note:* Rutherford's *The Occult Office* suggests that you bury the desk an extra foot for each additional $1,000 of raise you wish to accompany your promotion.)

Does it work? Actually it works about as well as what most people who want a promotion do, which is simply *wish* for one. Now you might argue that people don't just sit around idly wishing for a promotion. After all, you are out there striving, toiling, and achieving, confident that your efforts will not go unrewarded. But working is different from working specifically toward a promotion—the latter requires a game plan of sorts.

Suppose that in the last year you were responsible for a total of six different projects. On three of them you rolled your sleeves high and, in all modesty, outdid yourself. On the other three you did what was required but nothing more. Come review time, it turns out that the three projects you aced weren't quite as important in your boss's eyes as the other three on which you merely did enough to get by. Overall you may have done a great deal of work, but because you didn't know where to direct your energies you failed to make a promotion-winning impression on your boss. It's rather like being a football player standing on the 50-yard line and not knowing which end zone is your opponent's. It's a 50-yard run in either direction. But obviously if you run the wrong way, your manager, teammates, and fans are not going to be impressed with your legwork.

Knowing which way to run with the ball is just one component of our second, and less mystic, way to get a promotion. Not only do you need to determine what is promotable behavior in your boss's eyes and adjust your allocation of effort accordingly, you also have to make sure your boss notices your effort.

8 WAYS TO MAKE YOURSELF PROMOTABLE

Promotions are a delicate subject. It doesn't take a mind reader to know that just about everyone in your office wants one. On the other hand, hardly anyone wants to appear so brazen as to actually ask for one.

Fortunately, there are more subtle ways to get your message across.

1. Figure out what your employer wants without actually asking him. After you've seen two or three people advance at your company, sit down and write a list of the factors that seem to go into promotions where you work, suggests Karolus Smejda, a Chicago-based human resources management consultant. Does the boss base promotions solely on performance? Is he looking for creativity over detail-orientation? Does he select people with whom he feels particularly comfortable—the ones who hang out with him? Answer these questions, then work on developing the appropriate skills or behaviors.

2. Let your boss know you've got more to offer. A golden opportunity to do this is during your performance review, although there's no reason to delay your conversation for such a formal occasion. Simply ask what you can do to make yourself more valuable to the company, according to Robert O. Snelling, Sr., chairman of Snelling & Snelling, the world's largest employment service. He suggests a conversation along these lines: When talking with your boss, say, "I love my job, I love what I'm doing, I think this company is going places, I want to go with it. What can I do to make myself more valuable to the company?"

Another bit of advice: Never say "I want a promotion." Instead, ask how you could "make a larger contribution" to your organization, recommends Marilyn Moats Kennedy, managing partner of the Wilmette, Illinois, management consulting firm Career Strategies.

What all of this does is give your boss the impression that you are operating from a basis of personal interest in your work and in the company: a very promotable characteristic. At the same time, the unspoken thought that will be planted in your boss's mind is that you can hardly fulfill your desire to do more for the company unless you are elevated to a position from which more can be accomplished.

3. Keep precise records of your accomplishments. A catalog of accomplishments speaks more eloquently in your own behalf than you ever could. If you can quantify your stellar performance—particularly how it impacts on the bottom line—little more needs to be said. It's hard for a boss to dispute your worth when you can show hard data indicating, for example, that you've saved the company $200,000 over the last year through a project you proposed. The odds are that your boss is too busy to keep careful track of such things himself, says Snelling, who adds that most supervisors remember the bad performances, not the good ones. "When you supervise people, you tend to look for mistakes, because you don't want them repeated." An appropriate time to give your boss your list of accomplishments is a few days before your next performance review.

4. Show some initiative by making constructive suggestions or developing new ideas. "There is always the danger that if you simply concentrate on doing your specified duties well, management will never see any reason to take you away from a position for which you have an obvious aptitude," warns New York City–based management consultant Josh Bellamy. "What you want to do is show your boss that while you can easily handle your current duties, they obviously don't even begin to plumb the depths of your potential. And the way to do this is by making suggestions and developing new project ideas."

Once again, this kind of action sends a subliminal message to your boss that you not only want a promotion, but that you obviously deserve one (depending on the merit of your ideas, of course).

5. Volunteer. This is another way of showing initiative. But you've got to look for the opportunities. Say it's 6:30 P.M., you're still at the office, and your boss is still there, too. You pop your head in his office and say, "I see you're working late. Is there anything I can help you with?" Snelling explains that even if your boss doesn't feel you're qualified to handle whatever he's working on, he may give you a shot, just to see what you can do. Also, explains Snelling, "the boss sees the volunteer in a different light. He appreciates the fact that you're concerned about him and not yourself." By fostering good chemistry with your boss, you boost your chances of being promoted. "You cannot get a promotion without having a relationship with the person who's giving it," says New York City–based career consultant Adele Scheele, Ph.D.

6. Ask to further your training. Tell your boss you'd like to take a computer course at a local college, for example, and explain how it will help you help the company. Sign up for any in-house seminars your company offers that might be appropriate to your career goals. Once again, you are sending an unspoken message to your boss that you are motivated to move up the corporate ladder.

7. Gain more visibility. Compete for professional awards sponsored by your industry or trade group, says Dr. Scheele. She also advises you to do as she does: Get published or be interviewed by the press. "If you have strong skills and opinions about what you do, write articles for trade or popular magazines. Or make yourself available as a resource in your area of expertise to the press, radio, and television in your town." Snelling, whose name also frequently appears in the press, concurs: "If you don't toot your own horn, you're in trouble." Dr. Scheele also recommends getting involved in the civic and philanthropic activities that are supported by those at the top of your organization. She points out that in addition to the generous devotion of time, "it's a way of forging relationships."

8. Be well positioned for promotions. Take careful note of the career paths of others. In heavy industries, for instance, advancement generally is greatest for those with experience in plant management. In consumer goods companies, it's marketing, advertising, and sales people who are most likely to reach the higher rungs. Sure, it can happen that a company will occasionally promote from a different department, but it's not likely. To get advice on how to best position yourself, Dr. Scheele recommends you find yourself a mentor who is, if possible, a couple of levels above you—and who looks well positioned himself. (See "Mentors and Mentorship" on page 307.)

How to find out
why you weren't promoted

Let's suppose that you've volunteered to do just about everything except chew your boss's food for her. You've proposed enough projects to keep a country the size of Canada busy for the next 20 years. Your list of accomplishments is longer than a roll of toilet paper, and you've earned a doctorate in advanced nuclear physics in your spare time. But you didn't get the promotion. Now what?

After you've done the mature thing and drop-kicked your computer terminal across the room, it's time to find out what happened. The way to start is by approaching your boss and asking her what the factors were that took you out of the running. Keep in mind, however, that you should be open to hearing some negative news. "Often you won't want to hear what you're being told," says consultant Smejda. "But remember not to be defensive. If you become defensive, you shut down the information flow."

Ask what goals you need to achieve. Your boss may tell you, for example, that she was looking for a candidate who had more experience than you did. Even if you think it's a bogus reason, ask what you can do to broaden your experience. This tactic also nails down your boss to some very specific requirements. Fulfill those requirements and she will be hard put to use the same excuse next time.

If the person who *was* promoted is the type whose interpersonal exchanges are flawless, ask your boss if "people skills" or "management abilities" were an issue. If your boss conveys that they were, ask if the organization will enroll you in a training workshop so you can improve. (Hint: If your company expresses no interest in providing for your training, it's a pretty sure sign it doesn't see you as going very far.)

Sometimes there may be unspoken factors lurking just beneath the surface of your discussion. For instance, don't expect your boss to tell you that you weren't promoted because you weren't educated at an Ivy League institution. Those sorts of biases, if they exist, can best be gleaned by studying the biographies of those who *do* get promoted in your company. Here's an example of an unspoken factor that may not be so obvious: You don't inspire trust (because nobody can predict how you'll behave in any given situation). If you suspect that's your problem, ask others for their views on the matter. "The grapevine will tell you if you didn't get promoted because you're unpredictable," says consultant Kennedy. She suggests you change your behavior so that you *are* more predictable. Trouble is, changing other people's perceptions may be more difficult.

In any case, by learning what it takes to get ahead, you'll also have the chance to evaluate whether your organization is right for you. In fact, if you ask Kennedy how to find out why you weren't promoted, she'll tell you that if you have to ask, you haven't done your homework. "Promotions are utterly, utterly predictable," she says, adding that many people don't want to accept the fact, for example, that they need two years of sales experience before they can get promoted. "They probably already know what kinds of experience they need, but they're hoping they can beat the system," she says.

Here's another promotion problem that should be fairly obvious: when your boss is blocking your promotion because he or she doesn't like you. One of the best methods for making yourself promotable is to have a good rapport with your superior. On the other hand, a conflict of opinion or personality between the two of you is likely to prevent your advancement. If you feel your career is being dead-ended because of the bad chemistry, Kennedy suggests you approach your boss about it (and remember not to lapse into defensiveness). If your sincere efforts are rebuffed, "decide how long that person's likely to be in place or likely to block you," she says. If it's too long for your timetable, start looking elsewhere. "Above all, don't sit there and do nothing. It's absolutely the worst strategy."

CREATING A POSITION
FOR YOU TO MOVE UP TO

You started with your company just out of college and for the first three years you were charging up the corporate ladder faster than a fireman saving people from a burning apartment building. Your bosses couldn't do enough for such a bright and motivated person. Then it all came to a halt. Your current title? You've had it so long it's collecting dust. Given the fact that in your last three reviews you scored the highest rating possible, you can't figure out why you've been booted off the fast track.

"This is a fairly common occurrence," says Los Angeles career consultant Rory Galleger. "And it has nothing to do with the employee. The problem lies in the fact that a corporate hierarchy is shaped like a pyramid. Each higher level has less room in it. While there might be 25 assistant managers on one level, there are only 10 managers on the next, and then 5 supervisors, 2 vice-presidents, and 1 CEO. The higher you go, the more you have to contend with the possibility that there are no empty slots to fill."

The problem is compounded by the fact that as you move up in the hierarchy, the people holding positions above yours tend to be settled in for the long run. In other words, assistant managers may come and go, but vice-presidents are forever (or at least three to four years).

So what do you do if there's no room at the executive inn? You could wait it out. Or you could leave. Jumping ship is a definite possibility. But rather than doing either, why not consider a third option? Just as a family will often build an addition to their house when they need more room to grow, you can add a new and previously unimagined position to the corporate hierarchy when it's time for your career to grow.

"Maybe you've pinpointed a definite company need that no one has been assigned to fulfill," says Galleger. "Perhaps you've created a new product that is just begging for a new product manager. Whatever it is, you need to keep in mind that just because the corporate structure currently appears as it does doesn't mean that new positions can't be created. And when there is no room to move up otherwise, creating a new position to which you can be promoted may be the only feasible way to escape a deadly career plateau."

Whether the new position grows out of a proposed new product or service or whether it comes from defining a hitherto undetected need, there are some basic steps to take, according to Natasha Josefowitz, Ph.D., a San Diego–based management consultant and the author of *You're the Boss* and other books.

- After you've decided on a new product or pinpointed needs that are going unfilled, determine the resources that would be required.

- Then decide to whom you would report.
- Then determine the staff that would be required.
- Then construct a budget.
- Then put your new position within the organizational chart.

The time has never been better to make such proposals. "Organizations today are much more flexible than they've ever been," says Snelling. "Instead of trying to make a silk purse out of a sow's ear—that is, first designing a job and trying to mold a person to fit it—they're packaging jobs for individuals. They'll take people and work on their strengths. They'll pick up a piece of work from here, a little job from over there. They'll put all the things an individual is good at doing together in one package."

To succeed at creating a new job, Snelling says you should be acutely aware of what's going on in the company. "Point out to your boss that there's a particular work area that isn't getting much attention, and that you're the perfect person to handle it. Companies are showing a willingness to do this."

There are two possible mistakes, though, worth warning you about in advance. Mistake Number One: coming up with a scheme that is so half-baked that it tarnishes your reputation. Mistake Number Two: coming up with a great idea but failing to adequately convince your superiors that it's you who deserves the new position. "The interesting thing about these two mistakes is that they are actually interconnected," notes Galleger. "You may come up with a half-baked idea which does have a kernel of value hidden within. What will then happen is that the company may indeed create a new position but opt not to put you in it because you don't seem to have a comprehensive grasp of the situation. So you want to be sure to think the matter completely through and tailor the job description so that you are the only person who can possibly fulfill the requirements."

Another option, and one that many times seems more feasible, is to create a new position by building on your current job. If you can make a good dollars-and-cents case for expanding some of your responsibilities into a new full-time job that would be considered a promotion, you may be able to tailor your own advancement.

"The way to travel this path is by initially volunteering for additional duties which no one else seems to have time to undertake," Galleger suggests. "What you are doing in effect is giving your boss a free trial run of your abilities. If it doesn't work out, then he or she hasn't lost anything. But if you handle the additional duties well and can make them a regular part of your work schedule, you'll make yourself indispensable enough that a formal expansion of your job title will seem quite feasible."

46

PUBLIC SPEAKING

Q*uestion:* What could possibly be worse than death?

Answer: Believe it or not, 85 percent of people surveyed said that public speaking was more to be feared than the prospect of a date with the grim reaper. How much worse is revealed in a recent edition of the *Book of Lists:* Fear of public speaking ranked first. Death? A pale sixth.

Why all the panic concerning something that is less painful than a root canal, is shorter in duration than open heart surgery, and typically ends with applause?

Granted, if there were a choice between facing 102 staring eyes and watching an afternoon of "Brady Bunch" reruns, no one would fault you for putting on a Florence Henderson Fan Club pin and hitting the couch. There *are* things more pleasant than getting up in front of a crowd. But when you start hearing stories such as the one media adviser Roger Ailes tells about a decorated Marine Corps general being reduced to petrified wood at the prospect of a television interview, you have to wonder why there's such terror about talking. After all, the man used to have large guns fired in his direction.

One source of stage fright is a simple misconception most people have about what makes a successful speech. Think back to the last time you had to give a talk. What was the last thing you thought before stepping up to the podium? Was it (A) "I hope they like me," or (B) "I hope they understand what I'm saying and find it useful"? In terms of potential for generating stage fright, the difference between A and B is immense.

Speaking to an audience with thought A in mind puts you in the same realm as any entertainer. This is fine if you spent your childhood taking public speaking lessons and have made a career of podium pounding. But if you're the typical up-and-coming executive who gives perhaps three or four important talks a year, you are not a well-practiced, professional speaker. By basing the success of your speech on whether or not your personality and verbal fireworks wow the audience, you are putting the same amount of pressure on yourself as if you suddenly had to stand up and sing in front of a capacity crowd at the Metropolitan Opera (and the only place you've sung before had a shower curtain for an audience).

But while you might be an amateur speaker, chances are that you are a pro when it comes to the subject you are speaking about. Thought B helps you capitalize on this idea. You are an expert on direct-mail marketing. The audience wants to know more about it. You are going to explain it to them. Suddenly the center of your concern is not you, it's the information. When you come right down to it, you explain this information every day to the people who work for you. It's no different explaining it to an audience. So let's forget about personal charm for the moment and focus on ways to make your speech as useful as possible to your audience.

SPEECH PREPARATION 101: ASKING YOURSELF THE RIGHT QUESTIONS

"I always spend the first 30 percent of my speech-planning time considering exactly who I'm going to be talking to," says Margaret Bedrosian, a Rockville, Maryland, public speaking consultant and author of *Speak Like a Pro.* "What is my audience's area of expertise? How do they feel right now about the economy and their industry? What are their specific interests concerning my topic? You want to ask yourself as many questions as possible about who the audience is and what they care about right now."

Other things to consider are the location and the reason that your audience is there. Is it a business meeting, a convention, or a vacation write-off? Try to gauge the mood of the event, or else you may find yourself giving a highly technical speech to a group of people who are more interested in the hotel's hot-tub facilities.

"After I know who I'm speaking to, I spend another 30 percent of my planning time figuring out what it is I can do for these people in one speech," says Bedrosian. "What is it that I want them to get out of my speech, and how can I do it in such a way that I don't give them too much?"

According to Bedrosian, one of the cardinal (and most commonly committed) sins of public speaking is giving the audience more information than they can use. "This is particularly important to remember when you are giving presentations in a business-meeting environment," she says. "As a rule, upper-level executives want you to present them with information that has already been streamlined and digested. They don't mind a certain degree of narrative, but if you can wrap it all up into a bumper sticker kind of idea, they appreciate it."

If you've been asked to study a particular topic and then make a presentation, you've already taken the time to analyze your subject. Your superiors want to hear your report so that they don't have to go through the same time-consuming fact-finding work you just completed. But if you make them listen to every detail rather than focus on your conclusions, then you've managed to waste their time anyway.

"For speeches in general and meetings in particular, you can take a cue from television news shows," says Bedrosian. "They present information that people want, weeding out the irrelevant material and packaging the rest in bite-sized nuggets that don't outlast the viewer's attention span."

SPEECH PREPARATION 201: PUTTING YOUR THOUGHTS IN ORDER

As you may have noticed, 60 percent of your preparation time has already been spent before you even begin to think of an outline. This is as it should be. Unless you know your audience and understand what you can give to them, your speech will lack usefulness. And if it lacks usefulness, you'd better hope you've got a sparkling personality and winning smile.

"When it comes time for me to start the actual outlining and ordering of my presentation, I like to use a technique called mind-mapping," says professional speaker and career development consultant Adele Greenfield, president of Greenfield Resources in Charlotte, North Carolina. "You begin by drawing a circle in the middle of a sheet of paper and writing your central idea in that circle. For example, you might write 'new flooring product' in there. Then you draw a line toward the upper right-hand corner of the page and draw another circle in which you might write 'research & development.' From that circle you might have three more lines branching off to three more circles, all having to do with R&D.

"Once you've gone that far along the R&D branch, you may want to start a totally new branch toward the lower left-hand corner of the page with a circle labeled 'marketing.' Off that circle would be a line to another labeled 'packaging.' By the time you are done, there may be 20 to 30 circles on the page with lines not only connecting them in a linear progression but also cross-connecting. For example, off the R&D circle you may have a circle marked 'tested durability of new flooring product.' This might be used as a sell line in an advertisement for the product. Therefore a line might cross from this circle to one way over in the marketing area labeled 'advertising.'

"The advantage to using this method is that it allows you to bring out all your ideas in a semiordered fashion without being too linear," says Greenfield. "The brain does not necessarily think in terms of well-ordered lists. It cross-references and leaps back and forth between subjects. Brain-mapping allows your mind the freedom to do this, whereas simple outline preparation forces you to think in a rigid order from start to finish."

Once you've finished this mapping process, take a look at what you've got and make some assessments. Which topics and ideas flow into one another with cross-connecting lines? What is the relative importance of each circle to your audience? Maybe some can be weeded out. Which ideas overlap? Once you've answered these questions, your outline and the ordering of your speech will practically fall into place.

One additional thing you'll want to take into account is that people have an attention span ranging anywhere from 3 to 7 minutes. Arrange your speech so that there are natural peaks that coincide with people's interest levels. Think of it not as one big speech but as several mini-speeches that intertwine.

Now that you've got the order, you'll want to decide which parts of your presentation could benefit from some additional emphasis by way of handouts and overhead transparencies. "The audience generally likes to have some handout material to write additional notes on and also to take home with them," says Greenfield. "If they see it as well as hear it, the information can be doubly effective."

SPEECH PREPARATION 301: REHEARSING

The remaining 10 percent of your planning time should be spent on rehearsal. At this point you may be wondering what happened to the section entitled "How to Actually *Write* a Speech That Will Make Me Look Brilliant." Actually, you are never going to write a speech word for word. You want to talk to the audience, not recite to them.

"When you speak in normal conversation, there is more information being conveyed than simply the words out of your mouth," explains Michael T. Motley, Ph.D., communication consultant and chair of the Department of Rhetoric and Communication at the University of California,

Davis. "The pauses, the inflections, and the facial expressions we use all add a wealth of additional information and meaning to what we are saying. What the person who memorizes does is throw that natural system out of kilter."

When rehearsing, don't imagine yourself addressing the multitudes. Pretend you are talking to a friend. As a matter of fact, get hold of a friend and try out the speech on him or her. "But don't sit the person down, say 'I'd like you to hear my speech,' and then plow right through it," says Dr. Motley. "Instead, say, 'Let me tell you what I'm going to talk about in this speech. I'm going to start off by saying this, and then I want to make this point about . . . ' Talk to your friend about the content rather than actually giving the speech. In other words, make a conversation out of it."

You may also want to forget that old advice about practicing in front of a mirror. "The problem with this is that by both delivering your speech and assessing it, you'll be doing two things at once—and neither of them well," notes Bedrosian. "What I normally rely on is a tape recorder. After two or three run-throughs, I usually have a speech I like. Then I listen to it about ten times in the car or on the plane. This is wonderful practice, because when I get up to give the speech, it never seems like I'm giving it for the first time."

During the rehearsal stage you'll also want to make sure your notes are functional. The key thing to keep in mind is that when you actually do use the notes, you'll probably be experiencing a mild panic. So make your notes as easy to read as possible. This means writing them in a dark, highly legible ink, and spacing the lines generously if you've got a lot of notes. That way you'll avoid the telephone book effect where you dial three numbers, look at the page again for the rest, and are unable find the line you were looking at. Another widely used option is index cards. Turn them over as you deliver the information and you'll never get lost.

In summary, the thought of getting up to speak without a word-for-word prepared speech may be slightly frightening. Keep one thing in mind, however: If you didn't know more about the subject than your audience, you wouldn't be the one doing the speaking.

Stage fright: "speak? i can't even breathe!"

First the bad news. Most speakers (even seasoned ones) will experience two stages of mental and physical arousal each time they give a presentation. The first begins a few minutes before the speech starts. From a normal resting heart rate in the 70-beats-per-minute range, you will experience a rapid acceleration that can boost your heart rate as high as 140. Then as you begin the speech, you will be gripped by what Dr. Motley calls the "confrontation" surge. This is a tremendously stressful period in which heart rates can soar to as high as 190 beats per minute.

Scared? Now for the good news. This "confrontation" surge normally only lasts about 30 seconds. "Even in the most nervous of speakers, you can practically guarantee that the initial stage fright as well as the physiological signs of it will begin to subside," says Dr. Motley. "That doesn't mean it will go completely away, but with each additional minute it will become less and less."

Since you know the first 30 seconds are going to be especially rough, it wouldn't hurt during rehearsal to work until you have an especially sure-footed introduction. "Plan what you are going to say in the first 30 to 60 seconds," says Roger Ailes, who wrote *You Are the Message* and directed President Bush's media campaign. "If you have to write it down word for word, do it." But generally the best medicine for a case of "confrontation" surge is reminding yourself that it will soon be over. Just tell yourself, This is not representative of how I will feel for the rest of my speech.

And now for some more good news. Studies have shown that uninitiated audiences (audiences not versed in the signs of stage fright) are surprisingly bad judges of a speaker's nervousness. What's more, audiences that were not only trained to detect stage fright but were actively on the alert for it did only slightly better. Both groups consistently rated the speaker as being calmer than he really was.

"My experience as a consultant has put me in touch with many executives who didn't worry about speaking until recently," says Dr. Motley. "What happened is that now they are speaking to more high-powered people, and they are afraid their stage fright will show through and blow their image of being confident, decisive executives." But knowing that virtually no one can tell how nervous you are means that your reputation as the Rambo of the boardroom is well protected.

"To reassure yourself, find a buddy after the meeting and get an opinion about your speech," suggests Dr. Motley. "The turning point in my getting over stage fright came when people constantly commented on how calm I seemed on stage. Finally it got through to me that I didn't have to worry. Even though I was nervous, they couldn't tell!"

WHAT TO DO 10 MINUTES
BEFORE GOING ON

Your mouth is as dry as the Sahara and you've got butterflies on pogo sticks in your stomach. Here are a few ways to turn yourself into a lean, mean (and calmer), speaking machine.

1. Mingle a bit with the audience and make friends. "First of all, it takes your mind off your nervousness," says consultant Greenfield. "But additionally, when you get up to speak, the audience will no longer be a roomful of strangers. There will be what psychologist Leo Buscaglia calls friendly eyes to whom you can speak while you get your stage balance."

2. Breathe. Hopefully you are doing this anyway, but pay some attention to it. "Breathe from the diaphragm rather than from high up in the chest," suggests Greenfield. "As you breathe in, the lower part of your ribcage and abdominal area should expand." Recite "Re- " while you inhale and "-lax" as you exhale. Your breathing will naturally begin to slow down.

3. Tense and release the muscles around your chest and shoulders. "Do it a couple of times and you'll start to get a feeling of physical looseness," says Greenfield. "Tense the muscles. Hold it . . . aaaaaaaaand let go. I don't suggest this exercise if you suffer from high blood pressure or heart problems, though."

A FEW ODDS AND ENDS TO REMEMBER WHILE SPEAKING

About your judgment: "I was giving a speech to an audience some time ago," remembers Greenfield, "and no matter what humorous things I said, I was getting nowhere with them. They never cracked a smile. At best, they were simply polite. Although they listened attentively, they did it like good little students rather than a truly interested audience. I exhausted myself trying to get a reaction. But afterward, the comments they put on the evaluation cards I passed out were some of the most glowing I've ever received. They fairly raved about how I had changed their lives."

The moral of this story is that you are not a mind reader. Don't try to judge the success of your talk by audience reaction, because in your mistaken conclusion you may be doing yourself a disservice. Unless the members of the audience are beginning to heft overripe food products in their hands, you've got no worries.

About your gestures: Another thing *not* to worry about is your gesturing. "We use our hands naturally, and if you deliver your talk in a conversational mode, you will use them just as naturally at the podium," says Dr. Motley. "A problem typically arises when people get up to speak and make a concerted effort to be physically animated. It breeds self-consciousness and throws off their natural rhythm."

Getting On Speaking Terms with a Microphone

You've got a speech that would put Winston Churchill, Marc Antony, and Abraham Lincoln to shame. You are calm, confident, and dressed to kill. But there is still one thing that can sink your presentation faster than a torpedo can scuttle a ship. And that thing is staring you right in the face: the microphone.

It's not your fault. Most people don't spend their life talking to their family and friends through a mike, so it's not as if you should be used to this device. But according to Tom McManus, author of *The Friendly Microphone,* remembering the following tips will keep you from committing any public address system faux pas.

- To test the microphone, tap on it gently with your finger. Don't blow into it.
- Speak directly into the microphone from a distance of 4 to 6 inches. Most mikes will have trouble picking up your voice if you speak under, over, or on either side of them.
- Don't handle the mike unless you are sure it's designed to be hand-held.
- Adjust lavaliere and lapel mikes so they are a few inches below your chin.
- Don't get too close to the microphone, because you'll probably produce a popping sound when you use the letter *p* and a hissing sound when you use the letter *s*. If you find that you overemphasize these letters in normal speech, fit a light foam cover over the mike before using it.

While you shouldn't worry about using your hands to express yourself, you should at least make sure they are free to do their thing. That means releasing your grip on the podium and not mauling your notes.

About your voice: "In general, men tend to suffer from what is known as 'lazy lips,' while women often pitch their voice a little too high," notes Margaret Bedrosian. "Anyone has the ability to bring his or her voice down a note, but the problem is making sure it doesn't creep back up. When I began training myself to speak lower, I used to put little blank Post-it Notes all over the auditorium at eye level. As my eyes wandered around the room, every time I saw one of those little squares I was reminded to bring my voice back down again. After continuous reminders and training, I began to naturally maintain the tone I wanted."

"Lazy lips" can be a little bit more of a problem. Typically, men do not take advantage of the mobility of their lips or the full articulation capabilities of their entire mouth. "The best way to rectify the problem is to practice in the mirror," suggests Bedrosian. "Enunciate clearly and exaggerate your mouth movements. Then bring it back closer to normal with only slightly higher mouth movement. The upshot is that if you do nothing more than open your mouth a little more while talking, that in itself will go a long way toward improving the situation."

IN CONCLUSION

Even with all of these tips in mind, you may still feel nervous and make some mistakes. But that's not the point. The point is to be natural and informative. Make it your mission to make your audience, be it 6 or 60 people, understand and remember the information you are providing.

Be interested in the information yourself, and you can't miss. As some wise person once said: A good speech is one in which the speaker has a message. A great speech is the one where a message has a speaker.

47

RÉSUMÉS

Ask people what they do for a living and you'll probably get a one- or two-line answer. Ask them how they got into the business and maybe you'll get an additional 1-minute synopsis. But take those same people and ask them to write a résumé, and suddenly all that brevity beats a fast exit as their work history magically takes on the proportions of a saga next to which *War and Peace* looks like a short story.

And modesty? That left through the same door as brevity. In the blink of an eye, mere mortals transform themselves into titans with "highly effective communications skills, vast creative resources, and strong problem-solving skills." The Mormon Tabernacle Choir couldn't sing praises any louder than most folks do on their résumé.

On the other hand, you may well ask whether there's anything wrong with a fully packed résumé that makes you look like the avatar of management. The answer is no. There's nothing wrong with it as long as you do it the right way. And the right way is to keep in mind the person who has to read your résumé as well as hundreds of others. What does that person want to see? And what will turn that person off faster than salt on a slug's back?

Basically, all you want your résumé to do is get you in the door for an interview. Once in, then you start working on getting the job. So you can think of your résumé as a direct-mail marketing piece. Keep the "buyer" in mind and strategically dispense well-chosen, but brief, information so that the reader's interest is piqued quickly and then sustained long enough to reach for the phone and give you a call.

OPENERS: SURVIVING THE FIRST CUT

"Realistically speaking, your résumé will receive about 10 seconds' worth of a personnel department's attention initially," says Bill Keough, author of *The Successful Résumé Writing Guide*. "So right from the top of your first page you want to provide the kind of information they will be looking for. In the upper left-hand corner, put your name, address, and phone number. In the upper right-hand corner, put your salary and geographical requirements."

To this day, the debate rages as to whether or not you should mention salary. After all, if you go too high or too low, you may be taking yourself out of the running. "You should keep in mind, however, that salary levels do say something about your experience and current career level," notes Keough. "If your asking price is too low, there's a good chance that you may not have the experience necessary for the position. And if you're asking too much, it could be that you are overqualified. Doing an interview in either of these cases would just end up being a waste of your time. But if your salary requirement jibes with that offered by the position, then a potential employer will receive the message that you are indeed already playing in the right ballpark and probably have experience commensurate with what the job requires."

When it comes to geographical requirements, the same logic holds. Employers like to know if you are willing to move. Right under salary requirements put down the following: "Geographical Requirements: Willing to relocate in the U.S." Of course, that applies only if you are indeed willing to move. If you aren't, make that clear: "Geographical Requirements: Philadelphia metro area (or whatever)." Again, you may cut yourself out of a potential interview. But if you aren't willing to move, why interview for a job that requires you to start shopping for a home in Nome, Alaska?

With the corner information out of the way, the first thing that should pop up center stage on page one is your job objective. In this case there are two schools of thought. Keough opts for brevity. "Simply put down the job you are applying for and leave it at that. If it's production manager in a publisher's art department, then write 'Job Objective: Production manager, art department.' What you don't want is 'I am looking for a position with a publishing firm where my design experience can be put to best use.' This doesn't tell the reviewer what job you want. And it certainly isn't his job to decide what would be best for you. Vagueness wastes those initial 10 seconds of consideration your résumé will receive."

On the other hand, you can expand on your job objective to good advantage. "Take this opportunity to quickly highlight some special advantages that you offer a prospective employer," says Richard Payne, vice-president of Fox-Morris Associates and author of *How to Get a Better Job Quicker.* "For example, if you were applying to a company that frequently does business with Japan, and you happen to speak Japanese, rather than writing 'Job Objective: vice-president of marketing,' you could write 'Job Objective: vice-president of marketing for an international firm where a command of the Japanese language would be valuable.' "

One additional heading you may want to include in the introductory portion of your résumé is a general summary. "This should be no more than a paragraph in which you briefly mention work experience that directly pertains to the job you are applying for," says Keough. "If you are applying for a job as controller of a major corporation, for example, under General Summary you could write: 'BA degree, MBA accounting, 10 years' experience with emphasis on financial management and administration, budgeting, general accounting, cash management, auditing, profit planning, credit analysis, data processing systems, personnel supervision, foreign exchange, and trend analysis.' With no more than a brief scan, a potential employer will be able to tell that you've certainly got some extensive experience in the areas that count. This is the point at which he or she will make the decision to allocate extra time to read the rest of your résumé."

WORK HISTORY: FOCUSING
ON YOUR ACCOMPLISHMENTS

If you've been succinct, and if your salary, objective, and summary match the position's requirements, then you've bought yourself another 5 minutes of the reviewer's attention. He or she knows you've got some experience in the appropriate areas. Now it's time to detail the quality of your experience.

"This is the section where many people tend to blow it," says Payne. "They forget to ask themselves what the reader will be interested in and instead mar the information with vague descriptions, irrelevant facts, and an unfocused presentation. When writing this section, you must keep in mind the two prime considerations of the reader: Does this applicant deserve to play in my ballpark? Is he a heavy hitter?"

In extensive tests conducted by Payne and his company to find what sort of résumé spurs a potential employer to call the applicant, one thing became crystal clear: Short wins out over long. "To this end, you want to sum up key points concerning your employment as quickly as possible but still give the reader the information needed to make a decision," says Payne. "The first rule is no matter how important a position you hold, you should be able to describe it in three or four sentences."

Within those three to four sentences you want to cover the following ground.

Whom do you report to directly? Whom do you report to indirectly? If you report directly to the CEO, it certainly says something concerning your importance in the company. On the other hand, if you report to an assistant manager but work with a VP on special projects, this could mean you are being groomed for serious promotion.

Who reports to you? Your importance is also gauged by the importance of the people who report to you. Mention titles if possible. If the inventory control manager reports to you, say so. Besides showing that you have department managers under your supervision, you are also indirectly saying that you have a working knowledge of inventory control.

How many people report to you? "A staff of 10 people says one thing about the scope of your responsibility; a staff of 500 says another," notes Payne. "State specific numbers. One advantage is that if you've had several jobs with successively more people working for you, it will quickly highlight your professional growth."

How big is the operational budget you control? Again, use figures. If you control a $5 million ad budget, that's a much different story than if you have ten grand and a unicycle at your command.

What do you do for the organization? "If you can hone this answer down to a 1-sentence, broad-brush description of your role, you'll probably hit closer to the mark than if you used 20 sentences," says Payne.

So what does all this add up to in print? Here's a typical Payne-penned example.

United Plastics Corporation, Wilmington, Delaware.
Chief Engineer:
Report to vice-president of manufacturing, and during his lengthy overseas business trips, directly to president. Direct engineering staff of 50 professionals plus 30 clericals. Responsible for department operational budget of $2,000,000 plus payroll of approximately $1,500,000. Responsible for all engineering functions for this plastics manufacturing company with annual sales in excess of $100,000,000.

At this point you may be saying, "Sure, I'd throw around figures too if I had a $2 million budget. But I don't have any budget. I am what you'd call budgetless. Now what?" "Simply describe what you do and who you report to," says Payne. "It's better to keep it brief rather than fill up the page with unnecessary details."

In addition to the short-and-simple rule, there are a few other important guidelines to keep in mind. "Use abbreviated but dynamic sentences when writing your résumé," suggests Payne. "You can leave off the 'I did this' and 'I did that.' The 'I' is understood. You are writing an outline, not prose."

Another rule, which you may already have noticed, is that you don't need to provide a detailed list of your daily duties. If you are a copy editor and you are applying to a newspaper, they already know what a copy editor does. Describing the position in minute detail will only waste the reader's valuable time. All he or she wants to know is how important a copy editor you are—magnitude.

"Speaking of magnitude, always use facts, figures, and accomplishments whenever possible," says Payne. "One of the biggest mistakes résumé writers make is that they are constantly foisting self-assessments upon the reader. 'I am an excellent writer.' 'I am a highly motivated manager who gets things done.' These are the writer's own opinions and are completely worthless to the person reading the résumé. On the other hand, if you write 'The last two projects I managed contributed $500,000 to company profits last year,' or 'Currently responsible for a staff of 100,' then the résumé reader will assume the best. Approach résumé writing in this manner and you'll give the impression of quiet competence rather than come across as a hornblower."

Once you've sketched out a general job description, it's time to get down to brass tacks: all the veritably superhuman things you accomplished while working for a particular company. "Your job description answers a résumé reviewer's first question: 'Does this person have the experience to play in my ballpark?'" notes Payne. "Your accomplishments, or worth

Restricted References

Don't list references on your résumé. If called too often, they're likely to become indifferent to endorsing you, suggests Robert Half International, a San Francisco–based recruiting firm. Instead, give prospective employers a list of references *only* when they request it. And to keep their enthusiasm high, notify your references *each time* they might be contacted. Never list references without first getting their permission.

points as I call them, answer the second question: 'Is this person a heavy hitter?' "

In an attempt to highlight their accomplishments (or worth points), many people will list them under a heading separate from work experience. "The problem with this is that it requires a reviewer to spend time matching up accomplishments with the job where they were achieved," notes Payne. "Instead, list your worth points directly under each job experience heading."

Here's an example of how it would look:

Product Manager 1984–1986
   Responsible for Weekender Paints, a $6 million brand.

- Conceived and implemented the repositioning of brand (including new copy and package graphics) to counter a 10-year sales downtrend averaging 10 percent a year. Repositioning increased test-market volume 16 percent and national volume 8 percent the following year.
- Initiated development of new and more competitive copy than advertising used during repositioning. Test-area sales increased 35 percent.
- Developed plastic packaging which increased test-market volume 10 percent.

"Again, state your worth points in a matter-of-fact way. You won't need to do any bragging," counsels Payne. "But make sure you can give the reader specific results."

What sort of achievements deserve to be headlined as worth points? According to Payne, the best ones are those in which you increased profits, saved money, or solved overlooked problems. If you were instrumental in the training and development of new talent or if you established new products and programs, put that down also. "Keep an eye out for the worth points which graphically prove that you have what the reviewer is looking for," says Payne. "But once you have that aspect covered, don't continually repeat yourself. Put down other worth points which hint at a broad range of experiences and skills. For example, a controller might be tempted to put down six worth points which all seem to demonstrate how well he can balance a budget. But that's not the best approach. He should also highlight the fact that he introduced new computer technology into accounting, and that he helped people in that department adjust to new procedures. Instead of putting down all six budget-balancing examples, the controller should use the most impressive one and save space for worth points in other areas."

Once you've assembled your entire work history, replete with as many worth points as you can muster, it's time to stand back and assess the information with a critical eye. One thing you want to look for is whether your collected experience seems to move toward an ever-increasing specialization in the area of most interest to your potential employer.

Another thing to be careful of is that you don't look like the high school football hero whose glory days are over. "If your most recent job seems less spectacular than a job you held four years ago, the reviewer may think you've peaked and he's catching you on the down side," says Payne. "To avoid this, you can cut back on the worth points of a former job so that your current one looks better in comparison. That way it will seem as though you are still in an advancement phase of your career. The main thing to keep in mind is that your most recent job is the most important one. The past should never outshine the present."

Once you have mastered the strategic subtleties of this section, there is one very important factor concerning your work history that cannot be overlooked: chronology. "Use a reverse chronology," suggests Keough. "There's no reason why a reviewer should have to wade through a page and a half of information just to find out what you do currently. Besides, you don't want the first thing he sees to be '*Chicken Delight*: delivery boy,' when you are now vice-president of marketing."

Besides proper order, you also want to make sure there are no gaps in your work history. "While you can't cover up a two-year layoff, you can gloss over six months by simply listing years instead of precise dates," says Keough. "If you list being at one job from 1987 to 1988 and your next one from 1989 to 1990, you could very easily hide a period of unemployment that ran from February 1, 1988, to March 2, 1989."

PERSONAL INFORMATION: ICING THE CAKE

You've given the nitty-gritty. The reviewer knows that you make money faster than the mint and possess leadership qualities that make Alexander the Great look like a second-rate tour guide. What else could you possibly need?

"Even if you graduated from college 25 years ago, an education section should be included in your résumé," says Payne. "But don't make the mistake of putting it before your employment history unless you don't have much of a history with which to impress the reader. Remember, people want to know what you've done lately, not what you did 10 years ago in college. That's secondary information."

On the other hand, your educational history does allow you a chance to outshine the competition. "College is the only time when you and your peers were all judged and graded on the same scale," notes Payne. "If your grade point average was 3.9 or 4.0, then that really says something about your abilities in comparison with everyone else. If you ranked number 2 out of a class of 450, that says the same thing. So when you put down your education, make sure it includes the name of the college, your major, the type of degree and especially your grade average or class rank."

"If you graduated from college less than five years ago, you should also include extracurricular activities," adds Keough. "Class president, school newspaper editor, track—any of these will help you look like a more accomplished and well-rounded person even though your employment history is still on the light side. But after five or six years, you don't want these things cluttering up your résumé, drawing attention away from more important, work-related factors."

Continuing education should also be included on your résumé under a heading of its own. "Highlight courses you've taken that will advance you in your chosen field," suggests Payne. "Management seminars, night school, and company-sponsored training sessions are all excellent ways to show that you are a motivated person who never tires of gaining additional expertise. On the other hand, you may want to avoid mentioning certain kinds of education that may actually hurt your employment chances. For example, if you are applying for an engineering position and happen to mention that you've been taking a real-estate course, your potential employer may wonder whether you might suddenly leave one day to pursue that alternate career path."

When it comes to purely personal data, you may want to take a little extra time to consider what you write. "While personal data is not necessary, it can put a little character into a faceless résumé," says Keough. "At the same time, it can also put you in an unattractive light to a potential employer."

Payne remembers one résumé that struck him as somewhat unusual in the personal data department. "The man had a wonderful résumé up until the personal section, where he listed his interests as bird-watching and playing the cello. Now in themselves, these are wonderful pastimes. And yet a potential employer may read this and say to himself, 'This isn't someone I'm going to have a few friendly beers with after work.' You have to remember that most people are more likely to hire someone who reminds them of themselves. So you want to be careful not to go too far out on a limb with personal data."

Dot Your *i*'s and Cross Your *t*'s

When surveyed by Olsten Services, a Westbury, New York, temporary employment agency, one of every three employers considered a typographical error on a résumé to be grounds for rejection.

If you are applying to a stodgy law firm, for example, you probably shouldn't mention that in your spare time you like to skydive. On the other hand, there would be nothing wrong with mentioning that you enjoy golf and sailing and you are a member of the Lions Club. Good, solid, stable.

Likewise, there is no need for anyone to know that you are divorced, belong to an aura-balancing therapy group, or enjoy taxidermy. Get the picture? A good way to gauge the personal section is to pretend it's someone else's and then try to imagine the kind of person who would typically list the things you just did.

When all is said and done, there are still two more things you should keep in mind when it comes to résumés. The first is a trick well known to book and magazine designers: Maintain a fair amount of white space on your pages. People are more likely to read a body of printed matter if it doesn't look too imposing. So to make your résumé more easily digestible, put a line of space between separate bodies of information and leave a wide margin on the right side of the page.

The second thing to remember is that a résumé isn't necessarily something to think about preparing only when you are looking for a job. "To prepare a résumé properly, you should know the effects your work has had on the companies that employed you," says Payne. This means that whenever you solve a problem, save some money, or introduce a new product line, you should research and note the outcome so that someday you can put the hard facts into your résumé. Once a year, regardless of your current situation, take the time to make a summary of what you've done. Then when the time comes to look for a job, you'll be well prepared to deliver the kind of information any employer would be happy to see.

48

REVIEWS

It's review time once again, and you find yourself sitting in one of two chairs. If you occupy the chair behind the desk, then your assigned role is that of judge, jury, and monarch. You decide how an employee has performed over the last year and you decree what rewards or disciplines are to be dispensed. Like a king or queen, you may advance one of your minions to high and exalted office, or banish the poor serf to the dungeons of cubicle obscurity.

On the other hand, if you are sitting in seat No. 2, then you are the supplicant seeking blessings from your master and answers from your oracle. You are quite aware that the person in front of you can make your life either a paradise of easily-afforded European vacations and split-level, suburban comfort, or a living hell played out against the tacky interior of a four-year-old Yugo.

Perhaps this is a somewhat exaggerated description of the true feelings people have during a performance appraisal—but it isn't exaggerated by much. There's a reason why managers and employees alike seem to dread review time.

Managers are keenly aware that how they mark those ten little boxes on the appraisal form is going to affect the employee's disposable income, social status, and self-esteem. Correcting someone's inefficient work habits is one thing; exerting a major influence on someone's life is another. Many managers therefore tend to favor one of two courses of action. The first is the "good guy" approach: Everyone gets a raise and everyone is doing just fine. This type of philosophy manifests itself in companies where 75 percent of the employees are receiving either an "exceptional" or an "exceeds requirements" rating on their review. While this is wonderful, it's hardly realistic. If the majority of people were exceptional, then exceptional would be average. By treading so lightly, these easily satisfied managers not only waste company money, they also lower performance appraisal standards. This in turn makes it harder to get better performance from their employees. How do you tell an "exceptional" employee that he needs to improve?

The other course is what could be called the "facts of life" path. These managers know that some people do better than others and that you've got to reward based on performance, not good intentions or a great personality. So they grit their teeth, make an assessment, and try to have the disgruntled employee out of the office in 10 minutes or less.

From the employees' viewpoint, the review is dreaded because no one likes to lose control over his own destiny. Employees resent the fact that what the person with the pencil marks down could make the difference between a new house for the family or another year in the same apartment. While employees understand that those pencil marks are directly tied to performance (over which they do have control), the problem is that they often don't feel that the manager's assessment is well informed or fair. Employees also tend to react in one of two ways: pure resentment or total despair.

To rectify this cycle of avoidance, resentment, and misunderstanding, two things need to be done. First, both manager and employee must move away from a framework of "How much of a raise am I going to get?" and "How much of a raise should I give this person?" Reviews should be a time to plan for better performance. Once there is improvement, the employee will receive his just reward and the manager will have no problem recommending that reward.

The second thing to keep in mind is that while reviews have never typically been a joint effort by manager and employee, there's no reason why they can't be. By extending the power of participation to the employee, a manager can avoid the monarch-supplicant relationship which causes so much resentment. Additionally, no one knows an employee's work better than the person doing it. By getting that person to open up, a manager just might receive some insightful information which could help boost performance in the future.

WHY TWO REVIEWS ARE BETTER THAN ONE

"The first thing I counsel managers to do is separate pay and promotion decisions from the discussion of an employee's performance," says William Weitzel, Ph.D., professor of business administration at the University of Oklahoma and former vice-president, administration, for Target stores. "The reason for this is that the first topic conflicts enormously with the second."

From a manager's viewpoint, the most important thing that gets done at a review is that decisions and plans are made to improve employee performance. That means a little constructive criticism is going to have to take place. On the other hand, the employee knows that what is said during this meeting will have a direct effect on personal income. So he will do just about anything to influence a favorable outcome. Past mistakes will be glossed over with excuses. Weaknesses brought up by the manager will be met with denial on the part of the employee.

"To circumvent this kind of conflict, managers may want to consider a semiannual review schedule," says Dr. Weitzel. "In other words, rather than have the typical year-end meeting where performance and pay are discussed at the same time, conduct a performance appraisal at six months and a pay review at the end of the year. At the first meeting, problems and solutions can be approached openly without the employee fearing monetary repercussions. And the manager can then act as a coach without having to change coats and become a judge by the end of the meeting."

In effect, Dr. Weitzel is suggesting a kind of institutional mentorism. A mentor takes someone under his wing and gives advice about what's being done wrong, what's being done right, and what direction needs to be taken for success. Beneficiaries of the mentor's advice take the information in a nondefensive way because they know that the suggestions are coming from someone who wants them to succeed.

Likewise, the manager who implements the semiannual review is in a more comfortable position. Salary and promotion decisions are still six months away. Now is the time to discuss problems with the employee, find solutions, and give encouragement. If employees can be convinced that final judgments are not being formed at this time, then they have a great deal of incentive to absorb and implement your suggestions. They realize that it is within their power to take your advice, solve their problems, and subsequently receive the year-end appraisal they want by giving you the kind of performance you asked for.

HOW TO GET EMPLOYEES INVOLVED IN A QUEST FOR EXCELLENCE

Having transformed yourself from an enemy into an ally, it's time to revamp your review-time manner to get even better results from your employees. You may first want to know what the employees feel is most often wrong with the way you and your managerial compatriots currently handle reviews. A survey of almost 200 companies by ODT Associates, an Amherst, Massachusetts, consulting firm, came up with these four most frequent gripes.

1. Managers hold no real discussion with employees and give them little opportunity to participate, said 71 percent of people interviewed.
2. Managers avoid being specific, said 68 percent.
3. Ratings sometimes are inconsistent with actual performance, said 55 percent.
4. Employees aren't given information on how to improve, said 56 percent.

Basically, all of these problems can be summed up in one phrase: lack of communication. You make your assessments, the employees nurse their resentments, but a barrier of silence prevents any real discussion of discrepancies between those views. To breach that barrier, you need to extend an invitation to your employees. "Before your meeting, ask employees to prepare their own self-evaluation," suggests Dr. Weitzel. "You can even go so far as to let them fill out a formal review sheet. Although common logic might dictate that people would take advantage of the situation by giving themselves unduly high marks, in reality this is not the case. Study after study shows that while employees often feel that they are being assessed unfairly, when given the chance to make their own judgment they are harder on themselves than their managers would have been."

When asking employees to make a self-appraisal, encourage them not only to document triumphs, but to mention problems as well. Remember, now that you are using a semiannual review system, it is to the employees' benefit to get trouble out into the open so that it can be rectified before the pay review rolls around six months later. Ask employees to also include plans for the future—their suggested ways to improve performance and take on additional responsibilities. "This accomplishes two things," notes Dr. Weitzel. "First, your employees will feel that they are being heard and that their opinion is not only trusted, but will be used in some way during the appraisal process. Second, ideas for improvement are more readily followed when they are self-suggested."

Having already sought the employee's opinion ahead of time, you have now set the stage for a truly interactive performance appraisal. "To make sure it's a successful one as well, there are several things you want to accomplish," says Dr. Weitzel. "You want to be sure that the employee knows where he stands with respect to you. That person should also understand how he is being evaluated, what his strengths and problem areas are, and how he needs to change his behavior to get even better appraisal marks next time. The employee should also come away feeling as if he now has a plan of action to get from where he is to where he wants to be in the company."

Of course this doesn't mean you have to accomplish everything in the first 5 minutes of the review. Instead, ease into the meeting, making sure that the employee feels comfortable from the start. "You may want to begin by sitting down together at a table or even arranging a side-by-side chat, rather than opting for the typical across-the-desk face-off," says Bob Mezoff, president of ODT Associates. "Sitting behind a desk tends to cast you in a position of rigid authority, which will then make it harder to encourage employee participation."

"The best way to get the ball rolling is to ask the employee to tell you about performance positives," says Dr. Weitzel. "It starts the meeting on an up note and may alleviate some of the employee's natural defensiveness in this situation. As you listen, vocalize your agreement with the employee's assessment, but go on to ask how each particular area can be improved upon even more. Show the employee that it would be to his best advantage to capitalize on his obvious strong points."

But when you don't agree with what the employee says, stress that while you can understand how he made that judgment, you see things from a different perspective—and then explain why. Disagreement frequently occurs when the employee values certain accomplishments which are relatively unimportant to the manager. In this case you need to consider the possibility that you never made your priorities crystal clear. If this is the case, take a moment to give the employee an overview of the department: Show where his work fits into the plan and which of his responsibilities are the most important. Then say that while you are pleased with the excellent work the employee is currently doing, you'd like to see him concentrate that same talent in areas which are more important to the department.

"The other obvious time you and your employee won't see eye-to-eye is when he thinks he did a bang-up job and you don't," notes Dr. Weitzel. "In a case like this, you want to be sure that you don't attack the employee's

When It's Your Turn

Unless you are the chairman of the board, you, too, will have your moment of judgment. While it may seem that the only personal power you have over the situation is to refrain from perspiring overly much, this is not the case at all.

"Employees constantly grumble about the unfairness of the review process, but rarely seem to understand that there is a great deal they can do for themselves," says Dianne LaMountain, ODT associate and coauthor of *How to Receive a Performance Appraisal*. "The first step needs to be taken long before review time rolls around. At the beginning of the appraisal period, meet with your boss and set up some performance guidelines so that there is no mistaking what you need to accomplish. This will help you to avoid unpleasant surprises come review time."

Since you probably already have a good idea of what the job entails, write your own version of the guidelines beforehand and ask your boss to correct the parts that are off target. "It's easier and faster to be an editor rather than a creator," notes LaMountain. "Your boss will appreciate the time saved." Be sure that your description covers your responsibilities, goals, priorities, and the criteria you think your boss will use to make quality determinations.

"The second thing to do is not wait until the end of the year to find out where you stand," says LaMountain. "Periodically, go to your boss and ask, 'If the performance appraisal were done today, how would I do?' Again, employees can take on a lot of the responsibility for this by doing their own appraisal and asking if they are on target."

During the actual review, there are two additional things to keep in mind. First, no matter how glowing your ratings are, be sure to ask for some advice concerning areas of improvement. "You may have a boss who as a matter of course gives everyone a wonderful review," cautions LaMountain. "If this is the case, it could be that there are some problems which are being ignored. If those problems are not taken care of, you may someday find yourself in the ludicrous position of actually being fired after receiving a string of 'outstanding' ratings."

The second thing to remember is not to sweat the small stuff. This means that there are bound to be several points of contention between you and your manager regarding performance that you should handle intelligently. In other words, let your boss have her say and then at the end of the meeting pick the two or three most important points you want to discuss. This is a much better way of handling the situation than leaping to your own defense every time your manager gets critical. You could wind up wasting time on unimportant matters.

viewpoint or intentions. The fact that he honestly feels the way he does could mean that he doesn't know your criteria for excellent performance. Let him know what you are looking for and then ask for suggestions as to how he can meet your expectations."

Emphasizing a joint plan of action can also be helpful when you ask the employee to tell you about performance difficulties. (Be sure to refer to them as difficulties, not weaknesses.) Make it clear that if you and the employee can get problems out into the open, then joint solutions can be found and the situation can be rectified in time for the pay review. When the employee then brings up a problem, ask him what he thinks can be done to clear up the situation.

"A very important rule to remember is never to be patronizing in a performance-appraisal meeting," says Dr. Weitzel. "It's so easy to do that. The employee has a problem, and since you already know the solution you haul off and let fly with a half-hour lecture detailing what to do. Meanwhile the employee is sitting there saying to himself, 'This person must really think I'm an idiot.' The odds are that the employee already knows 70 percent of what you are about to say. But instead of picking up the 30 percent that's new, he'll be sitting there fussing and fuming, and the information will fall on deaf ears."

Instead, you should always first ask the employee how he would solve the problem. Listen, agree, and then say, "Those are all great suggestions, but here are a couple others you may want to consider." Then you simply mention only your top ideas, the 30 percent that the employee didn't consider. This way you avoid patronizing, you cut down on speeches, and the employee leaves your office remembering the three great things you said rather than the seven spoon-fed ideas which anyone could have figured out.

Naturally there will be problems that employees will not bring up because of oversight or fear. Again, use tact. Rather than saying, "I noticed you didn't bring up this problem," try asking if he or she is having any problems in a specific area. Employees will understand that you *have* noticed problems, but will appreciate the chance to answer for themselves. Again, ask for suggestions as to how the situation can be rectified.

"An important thing to remember is that any suggestions for future improvement should be molded into concise, easily understood, short-term plans of action," says Dr. Weitzel. "Agree on what specifically needs to be done, write it down, and set a time period for implementation. Try to stay away from hazy directives such as 'Show more initiative' or 'Get more done in less time.' When you've agreed and put it in writing, have the employee sign it."

While the emphasis is on short-term improvement, however, long-range prospects shouldn't be overlooked. Let the employee know that the discussed improvements will strengthen skills needed for successful movement up the corporate ladder. Give him the feeling that your discussion is not simply a basis for performance improvement, it's a training ground for his future career. In other words, give him a reason to excel.

A GOOD GRADE AND HOW TO GET IT

At this point you've discussed the employee's highs and lows for the last six months and you've also signed off on a definite course of action for the next six. Now it's time to check boxes. If you had the employee fill out an appraisal sheet on his own, start making comparisons. If the employee is true to form, then he probably underrated himself, in which case you come off as the good guy. On the other hand, if the employee's assessment is overrated, then you'll need to talk.

"One thing to keep in mind is that everyone is interested in grades," says Dr. Weitzel. "So at some point you can expect an employee to ask, 'What do I have to do around here to get an outstanding rating?' You should already know exactly what constitutes an excellent rating, but keep it to yourself for the moment. Instead ask the employee what he thinks would earn him an 'outstanding.' Agree with his on-target suggestions but at the same time be sure to explain why you don't agree when he is off base. Make additional suggestions when you think the employee has missed something."

Building upon the employee's initial suggestions, create a comprehensive picture of "outstanding" performance. When both you and your employee have reached an agreement on the definition, write it down and sign it. "What you are doing is creating a contract for excellence," says Dr. Weitzel. "Should the employee meet these requirements, then he will receive the desired rating."

"One thing to keep in mind, however, is that you don't want to be discussing the criteria for a top rating with an employee who is currently doing only marginal work," says Dianne LaMountain, an ODT associate and coauthor of *How to Receive a Performance Appraisal.* "Instead, focus on the rating level that is one rung above the employee's current status. So if the person is operating at a marginal level, make the contract for 'good' or 'meets requirements.' Keep the goals short-term and within the employee's grasp."

Creating a contract really comes in handy when a manager is faced with that most uncomfortable of situations: dealing with an employee whose work consistently falls short. The reason managers typically have a problem giving out a "not acceptable" or "below requirements" rating is that deep down inside they are afraid their judgment may be too arbitrary. Self-doubt as to whether the guidelines and goals were made crystal clear also plays a role. On the employee's part, a bad rating is always viewed as arbitrary. But if you and your employee cut a definitive contract, then the final outcome no longer becomes a matter of judgment. Instead it is simply a question of whether the agreed-upon obligations have been fulfilled.

"When the pay review rolls around, ask the employee to be prepared to discuss how well he met the letter of the contract," says Dr. Weitzel. "When it becomes obvious that he didn't fulfill his end of the bargain then you have to say, 'We both recognize that you didn't do what you said you were going to do. I'm disappointed, as I know you are. I think you recognize that I have to mark the form to show that you did not perform at the level that both you and I wanted you to. Now let's plan to make sure it doesn't happen again.' "

The more specific the contract, the less room you leave the employee to argue, should this scenario occur. But the main thing to keep in mind is that you don't want to be harsh, patronizing, or autocratic. Focus on ways that you and your employee can become team members working on the problem together.

The last thing to remember is that hope is the greatest motivator of all. Maybe this time around the employee didn't do so well, but the words "Let's plan to make sure this doesn't happen again" imply that the employee does have a brighter future to work toward. He knows that you are not disgusted with him and have no intention of throwing him to the dogs. He can leave your office with his sights set high for the next review.

49

ROMANCE

Cupid is more likely to strike at the office than anywhere else. And strange as it sounds, you would be wise to have a strategy in place for that magical moment when his arrow connects with its unsuspecting target.

At its best, office romance is something that makes two people delirious about coming to work each morning and leads to a solid, lasting relationship: a healthy marriage, a good working alliance . . . the whole trip. Nobody gets hurt, colleagues are unaffected, and the lovers themselves create a workplace synergy that results in high-energy output and creative new ideas.

At its worst, office romance becomes a divisive mess. Consider the boss/subordinate liaison in which the subordinate gets favored treatment and greater access to resources—alienating, demoralizing, and stalling the career of everyone else. (In some cases, it's against the law, as you'll soon read.) Or consider the boss-subordinate partners who hide their relationship, but the subordinate goes around surreptitiously polling co-workers on their honest feelings about the boss—which she dutifully reports back to him. (Yes, office romances have been used as fronts for such spy operations.) Or take the case of two office peers who fall in love, marry, and then a year or two later wind up in divorce court. They get to play out their bitterness for eight hours every day in an office that becomes a nasty battleground. Co-workers take sides. Bad vibes permeate the air. Cooperation simply grinds to a halt.

Despite such possible complications, the average workplace is virtually flooded with surging hormones. When Lisa Mainiero, Ph.D., author of *Office Romance: Love, Power & Sex in the Workplace,* randomly polled 200 employees, she found that 76 percent of them either were currently involved in an office romance or knew of a couple at their office that was. "It's a real soap opera out there," says Dr. Mainiero, who is a professor of management at Fairfield University in Connecticut.

In the olden days, before women started to gain their rightful place in corporate hierarchies, there was basically one variation of the office romance theme. Woman takes job as secretary. Woman is assigned to attractive boss (single or otherwise). Woman and boss get romantically involved. If woman and boss marry, she quits her job.

As women began advancing beyond the secretarial pool, the opportunities for office entanglements began to get far more complex. Here's an example of a scenario for the 1990s: Male subordinate hooks up with female boss. When relationship cools, male subordinate sues corporation for sexual harassment because female boss has sent the word up that he is not to be promoted.

While such cases sound extreme, they are becoming more and more common. So to succeed in today's working environment, you have to be aware of the downside risk of getting involved. (Yes, there are office romance success stories, and we'll get to them in a moment.) The word from the experts is that it's not always necessary—let alone natural—to "just say no" when the possibility of romantic involvement presents itself. But you *must* remember this: The rules are different for office romances than for any other kind, and you can suffer a lot more potential damage than a mere broken heart.

WHY PEOPLE FIND LOVE AT THE OFFICE

It's no wonder so many are doing it. For one thing, there's the proximity of it all. There may be half a dozen potential lovers sitting within 30 feet of your desk. Right now. For another, time is on the side of office lovers. The average person spends more waking hours with co-workers than with family or friends. Here are a few other contributing factors you should know about.

Common interests. If you're single, it's possible that you'll have more in common with a co-worker than with anyone you're likely to meet at Club Med. If you're married and are heavily involved in your career, you may find you share more interests with your office mate than with your house mate.

Power is sexy. "People tend to be attracted to bosses, peers, anyone with positional power," says Marcy Crary, Ph.D., an organizational psychologist and professor at Bentley College in Boston. "And it can even be the power to help and support, the power that comes from mentors."

People are looking their best. Because they're dressing to impress—not to sit in front of the tube—folks at work tend to look a lot better than the typical at-home lover or spouse.

Creative energy. The excitement of getting the merger off the ground or bringing a new product to market generates an atmosphere that lends itself to romance.

Emotional support. A co-worker may offer emotional backing to help you through an office rivalry dilemma or an impending project you're laboring to complete, and it's easy to "sexualize" (translation: put in a sexual context) that emotional support, says Dr. Crary.

So when you fall in love with the person over the desk and are convinced that he or she is the perfect someone that you've spent years looking for, here's a question to ask yourself: Would I still like this person if he or she weren't head of my department, but were someone operating the elevator?

HOW AN ALLIANCE CAN GO WRONG

When do office romances succeed and when do they fail? Dr. Mainiero says the chances for a successful office alliance are best when it's between two peers from different departments. "It can be ideal when they work in different areas and when their career paths are distinct—for example, if one's a marketing person and the other's an engineer." On the other hand, she warns, "There's no question that relationships between bosses and subordinates are a bad idea." For the record, here's what can go wrong when you mix business with pleasure.

Professional jealousy may develop. While relationships between peers in the same department frequently do work out, Dr. Mainiero reports that peer competition can loosen the tightest of romantic bonds. "I've seen cases where marriages were in jeopardy because one partner was promoted before the other," she says. Adds Stewart D. Friedman, Ph.D., an organizational psychologist and professor of management at the University of Pennsylvania's Wharton School: "The organization expects you to compete, which ruins expectations you have for each other to be cooperative."

Higher-ups will question your judgment. Whether you're a boss or a subordinate, you put yourself in a compromising position. Even if you bend over backward to keep your personal life separate from your work life, there will be the suspicion that the boss is making things easy for the subordinate/lover or that the subordinate is trading sex for office favors.

Co-workers may get demoralized. This can happen when they see favoritism, real or imagined, or when a broken-up couple polarizes the office.

There may be a conflict of interest. An example is a bank auditor who is dating a bank branch manager. Foolish people who get involved in such blatant conflict-of-interest situations without volunteering for transfers deserve to get axed.

The subordinate may be trapped. If the relationship cools and the subordinate wants out, he or she may feel the not-so-subtle threat of a career that gets dead-ended by the potentially bitter boss.

Work performance may suffer—and not because of preoccupation. "People might sacrifice themselves so that their partners look good," says Dr. Friedman.

Lovers will feel the subtle impact of their different work levels. Explains Dr. Friedman, "In any love relationship where there's unequal social status, there's the basis for inequality."

For the clandestine couple, making the liaison public can destroy the magic. Ever notice how excited a couple gets talking about how they maneuver to keep their relationship a secret? It may, in fact, be the romance's main attraction. "The idea of sharing a secret is something that creates a bond between people. It reinforces a relationship," says Dr. Crary. Once the excitement of subterfuge is eliminated, there may be nothing left.

CAN YOU MAKE AN OFFICE ROMANCE WORK?

Talk about advance planning! Dr. Mainiero once met a couple who actually spent part of the first date devising a contingency plan for that day when their relationship would turn sour—this is before they even *had* a relationship. They agreed that if one person couldn't handle the breakup, the other would transfer to another department. And the last time anyone checked, the lovers were still happily aligned, which comes as no surprise to Dr. Mainiero. "It ended up being a positive sign when they could communicate honestly from the word go. They were on solid footing." She suggests that anyone who takes his career seriously would be wise to plan for the end right from the start.

It may be a waste of energy to hide your office romance. "Most couples try to keep it a secret, but that rarely works," says Dr. Mainiero. "Co-workers pick up on the signals—the subtle glances, the touching of an arm." While she says it is generally futile to hide your love from co-workers, it is sometimes a good idea to keep a budding romance a secret from the boss. It simply depends on your company's norms. Take your cue from observing how other office couples were treated. And be aware that even if you do hide it, you may eventually be found out.

WHEN SOMEONE ELSE'S AFFAIR BECOMES YOUR BUSINESS

When Chicago attorney Paul Cherner spoke at a personnel administrators' conference about legal issues that the courts are considering, the audi-

For Bosses: How to Discourage Office Romances

You can't.

Policies that ban intraoffice dating don't work, proclaims Robert L. Mathis, D.B.A., professor of management at the University of Nebraska at Omaha. "You simply cannot prohibit people from being attracted to each other," he says. Employees will conduct their affairs in secret, and you'll become the object of widespread resentment.

What you can do is make it clear that any office dating that results in diminished productivity, demoralized employees, or the appearance of sexual harassment will not be tolerated.

"Romance should not be the issue, but rather work performance," explains Dr. Lisa Mainiero. "So there need to be policies concerning such performance, designed to curb any negative impact of the romance on the workplace, and not the romance itself." It's really no different than the way people with alcohol or drug problems are to be treated: Only step in when the workplace feels the negative effects.

If a couple's work performance falls by the wayside, or if the romance is impacting on the performance of others, a manager's first step is to have an informal chat with the couple or just one of the partners. "In most cases it does the trick," says Dr. Mainiero. Dr. Mathis even offers a little script:

"You know, John, your personal life is your personal life. But around here we like to keep things separate. We can't dictate what you do, but you could be affecting both your career and Sally's. People are talking, and it's creating some awkward situations . . ."

If the complaints about the couple continue, a formal, written warning should be issued. If that fails to accomplish anything, the partners might be transferred or terminated.

So you think this is probably a bit extreme? Here's an example of what can be at stake. Dr. Mathis points to cases in which a subordinate partner in an office romance attempts to end the relationship, but is threatened that he will have his career stalled. Regardless, the relationship ends. Months or years later, the subordinate fails to get a hoped-for promotion. He may claim sexual harassment—that the former lover blocked the promotion. "The company can end up being liable for a discrimination charge unless it proves it took steps to deal with the problem—such as disciplining the offending manager," Dr. Mathis says.

ence paid particularly close attention to his comments on something called paramour sexual harassment.

Generally speaking, you're a victim of paramour sexual harassment if you are discriminated against in your career advancement by a superior who is romantically involved with one of your co-workers. Fortunately, you may have the law on your side. According to Cherner, there are at least two cases in which paramour sexual harassment has been held to violate federal and state laws that cover sexual discrimination.

In a typical case of sexual harassment, a person is treated unfairly in the workplace for failing to accept a boss's advances. But in this reverse form, a worker is treated unfairly because the boss is showing favoritism to someone else who *is* accepting those advances.

Should you call your lawyer? "If it becomes an intolerable situation, you can file a claim. But that might end up making it impractical for you to work in the organization," says Cherner. "On the other hand, sometimes higher-ups at the company simply don't know that either the affair or the discrimination is going on, and they wouldn't tolerate it if they did know."

A good alternative first move would be to take advantage of your company's anonymous grievance procedure—assuming there is one. If there isn't, you may have nothing to lose by writing a strictly anonymous and untraceable letter to your company's president. Explain that so-and-so and such-and-such are romantically involved and that it is impacting on the workplace and other employees. "It's important to address not only the moral issue, but the fact that the affair is clouding business decisions," explains Cherner.

And if you are aware of any other conflict-of-interest situation that results from an office romance, you've got a right to anonymously blow the whistle.

50

SELF-ESTEEM

San Jose Assemblyman John Vasconcellos took a lot of heat a few years back when he created a California State Legislature task force to (get this) promote self-esteem. Everyone from editorial writers to comedians found the notion irresistibly funny: a governmental body actually trying to cure social ills by making people think more highly of themselves.

But the connection is so obvious that only a fool would downplay the importance of feeling good about oneself. When you like yourself, you also feel confident enough to take the kind of chances that will enable you to succeed in your job, explains Arthur Huntley, M.D., professor of psychiatry at the Medical College of Pennsylvania, in Philadelphia. Or, in the words of Assemblyman Vasconcellos himself: "If you own, appreciate, accept, and are comfortable with yourself, the more self-esteeming you'll become, and the less and less situations will seem to be fraught with peril."

Also, once you've sold yourself on yourself, you'll discover that others will buy, too. "Other people respond to you based on the verbal and nonverbal messages you send out about yourself," says Dr. Huntley. A simple example: If you've got high self-esteem, you'll be able to comfortably look people in the eye. Sensing that you are a confident person, people will be more likely to respond in a positive way.

WHERE'S THE LOW SELF-ESTEEM COMING FROM?

So you're well educated, experienced, and talented. Low self-esteem *still* may thwart your best-laid career plans, says Philadelphia psychologist

Suzan Greenberg, Psy.D. Many of her clients have their careers hampered in this way, when low self-esteem inhibits their ability to be effective on the job. Often the low self-esteem stems from feelings of guilt. Some feel guilty because of their aggressive impulses. Others may experience guilt because of their desire to succeed—if success represents something unacceptable such as doing better than their parents.

The roadblock could also be the result of feelings triggered by reminders of past problems. A typical example: A person takes a job where the smart, powerful female boss makes her feel just as inferior as she felt in the shadow of her smart, powerful older sister. Suddenly, what happened throughout childhood is happening at IBM: She finds herself unable to be innovative, or even productive.

"Examine what circumstances are bringing out these feelings of low self-esteem, and try to understand what other forces may be at work," says Dr. Greenberg. You may find, for instance, that you're working for a boss who simply never showers approval on you or anyone else—regardless of the job performed. His behavior triggers the same feelings of inadequacy you experienced when your father never gave *his* approval. If you had a stronger self-concept to start with, you probably wouldn't mind. But the negative feelings drawn up from the past zap your energy and enthusiasm for work. Short-term solution: Solicit feedback from others as a means of gauging your performance, or establish your own system of ranking how well or how poorly you do. Long-term solution: Find a counselor to help you tackle the self-esteem issue.

Remember that low self-esteem is often a symptom of depression. (Other symptoms include fatigue, hopelessness, sleep disturbances, and loss of pleasure.) In any event, talking over feelings of low self-esteem with a psychologist or career counselor can get you to the first step of mastery: understanding the dynamics of your underlying problem.

How risk taking improves self-esteem

For ten years Layne Longfellow, Ph.D., of the Institute for Human Skills in Arizona, took executives and other thrill-seekers on "personal explora-tion" wilderness seminars in the Canadian Rockies. One of the major pur-poses of the seminars was to demonstrate that if you take a risk in one area of your life and succeed, the impact will be felt in other areas. Under Dr. Longfellow's guidance, many people found they were capable of performing physical feats in the outdoors that they never dreamed they were capable of—climbing to near-stratospheric heights or enduring weather so frigid it would give polar bears goosebumps. How *couldn't* one's self-respect increase under such circumstances? "So when participants went back to work, their improved self-confidence enabled them to be more assertive with their bosses. They were able to show more initiative in getting new projects off the ground," explains Dr. Longfellow.

Swell, but what about those people whose lack of strength or endurance may have prevented them from reaching the top of the mountain? "Actually, some of the most beneficial lessons were learned by those who failed," says Dr. Longfellow. "In many cases, they came to understand that failing is just failing. It's not a tragedy. It's not a condemnation. They simply didn't get something done. But life goes on." Such a realization is all part of the maturation process: You find the limits that define your identity.

So there you have it: Risk taking can be a win-win situation.

SOME POINTERS ON TAKING RISKS

Taking risks at work can produce wide-ranging effects. When you discover that you can be constructively assertive, for instance, you'll start to see results. And then those results will inspire you on to a new level of risk taking. But here are some things to keep in mind.

Start out small. You're almost guaranteed to fail if you begin by taking big risks, warns Dr. Huntley. So don't overextend yourself. Take a small risk. And if you succeed, take a larger one. Perhaps you want to become more sociable with your colleagues. Don't begin by inviting the entire department over to your home for a party. Start out by asking one of them out to lunch.

Seek out people who will support you. Dr. Huntley explains that folks with high self-esteem are likely to be those who grew up with supportive families, friends, and teachers. With the support of others, you'll feel more secure in taking risks. So surround yourself with nurturing people, and be open to their feedback.

Beware of your negative filter. The low self-expectations that result from low self-esteem are hard to shake. So as you begin to take risks, be aware that you may instinctively be minimizing or not even acknowledging any positive results you may be gaining. If you habitually *expect* people to respond negatively to your ideas, for example, you may now have to convince yourself that they really do like what you suggest—that they're not just pretending. Trade in the negative filter for a positive one.

10 THINGS TO DO EACH DAY TO FEEL GOOD ABOUT YOURSELF

1. Be a kid again. Set aside 15 minutes for play. Pay a visit to a toy store and buy something that looks like fun. Blow bubbles, chase your cat around the house, or squish your toes in the sandbox, advises Perry W. Buffington, Ph.D., an Atlanta psychologist and author of *Your Behavior is Showing.*

2. Expand your horizons. Read the classics for 15 minutes a day. A daily peek at the troubles in Dickens's novels will make your own difficulties seem insignificant by comparison.

3. List five of your strengths. Change the list daily. And don't be afraid to include "Always bowls above 180."

4. Help someone without telling him. Pay the toll for the guy in the car behind you.

5. Change something about yourself. Buy new eyeglass frames. Polish your shoes—for once. Try a different belt buckle or other accessory.

6. Accomplish something small that you've been avoiding. Clean up your desk. Rehang those curtains. Arrange to have your car lubricated.

7. Talk with a good friend. Meet a buddy for breakfast. Phone a pal long-distance. Pay attention to what they say.

8. Get some regular exercise. A half-hour jog. A quick session with the stationary bike. Some stretches. A mile-long walk. "Exercise is a mastery experience," explains Dr. Greenberg. "There are the relaxation benefits. The sense of being in control. And you get to see the physical results."

9. Get in touch with your spiritual side. Meditation, prayer, or simply a quiet moment spent communing with nature can help you feel more balanced, and confident about life.

10. Relax. Try progressive relaxation, self-hypnosis, or any other stress-busting technique that will take you on a revitalizing "mini-vacation." Wash away all the negative energy that's accumulated.

POSITIVE THOUGHTS, POSITIVE FEELINGS

"Most of what we think the world is doing to us, we are doing to ourselves." Things haven't really changed much since Shakespeare penned those lines for *Othello.* Too frequently, our own negative thinking and negative self-talk are the culprits that dead-end a career.

Learn to identify the self-put-downs that may be sabotaging your success. Some examples:

Do you think only in terms of black and white? This response pattern is as common as non-winning lottery tickets. Too many folks routinely think that if they don't do something perfectly, then they must be doing it miserably, and that as a result they're total failures. Solution: Maintain a balanced perspective, suggests Dr. Greenberg. Instead of thinking "I'm a lousy negotiator," for example, try out "Sometimes I don't negotiate as well as I'd like to. Perhaps I can learn some negotiating tactics from someone who's good at it."

Do you magnify your flaws? Okay, okay. So your business memos aren't as crisp and focused as you'd like. Yes, you should learn how to do better. But no, this isn't the sort of personal shortcoming that will banish you to the streets to collect returnable cans for a living.

POSITIVE SELF-TALK IN 5 STEPS

Jay Knippen, Ph.D., a management professor at the University of South Florida, provides this example of how to raise your self-worth with self-talk. The situation: You want to propose a particular project to your boss. The problem: He rejected the last one you proposed.

Step 1: *Objectively* state what it is that's causing you doubt. "I'm going to propose a project, and he rejected the last one."

Step 2: Objectively interpret what the incident *does not* mean. "That doesn't mean he'll reject this proposal."

Step 3: Objectively indicate the cause of the incident. "He rejected the last proposal because it was too expensive, not detailed enough, and didn't cover contingencies."

Step 4: Identify positive ways to prevent the incident from recurring. "This new proposal is cheaper, more detailed, and covers contingencies."

Step 5: Use positive imaging. Says Dr. Knippen, "See yourself not only getting the project accepted but enjoying the eventual outcome down the road. Getting promoted. Driving your brand new Porsche."

51

STRESS

If stress had a sound, it would be that of a buzz saw ripping into sheet metal. If stress were an object, it would be a shattered mirror. But the question is, if stress had a face . . . would it be yours?

The business community loses $100 billion annually because of stress, estimates Donald T. DeCarlo, senior vice-president of Commercial Insurance Resources. "That figure may sound large, but if you take into account decreased worker efficiency, sick days, and workers' compensation paid out because of stress, there are some experts who think the estimate may be on the low side."

You personally may have been good for a few thousand of that $100 billion lost last year, and if your misunderstanding of stress is that of the average person's, you should be good for even a little more this year. We all are victimized by stress at some point in our career. And quite frankly, as the information age intensifies, we can expect to be dealing with even more stimuli at an accelerated rate in the future. This means more stress.

Luckily, information can be positive, too—it can go a long way toward lowering not only your own stress levels, but those of your employees as well. If you *understand* what causes stress, you may be able to nip it in the bud. And if you know how to relieve stress, your down-time can be minimized.

ARE YOU A VICTIM OF STRESS?

Stress can be hard to detect. It builds up gradually and its physical and mental manifestations take many forms. To confuse the issue even more, there is *good* stress and *bad* stress.

"Good stress is the exhilaration you feel when you've won the lottery or you've rallied mentally to successfully meet a challenge," says Hal Meyers, Ph.D., of Thought Technology. "You need this type of stress to operate at peak levels. Once the thrill is over, however, your body returns to normal operative levels. But bad stress takes your body and mind to a fever pitch of tension and then does not let go."

The reason bad stress often goes undetected is that the cause goes undetected. Even if you do notice what's bothering you, you probably don't realize that the tension from stress hangs around long after the cause is gone. To use an analogy, consider a violin string. Tightening the string could be considered the initial stress. But once the string is tight enough to hit a high E, what you've got is sustained tension. Likewise you may initially get overwound by a problem. But once the problem *seems* to be rectified you may still be stuck at high E; your body and mind never got the chance to loosen their strings.

The best way to tell whether stress is getting to you is by monitoring your behavior and listening to what your body has to say. In his book, *Kicking Your Stress Habits,* Minnesota psychologist Donald A. Tubesing, Ph.D., pinpoints some of the most common stress signals.

- Headaches
- Tightness in the neck
- Loss of appetite
- Excessive eating
- Indigestion
- Pounding heartbeat
- Forgetfulness
- Depression
- Loss of interest in sex
- Loss of self-confidence
- Trouble sleeping
- Feeling keyed up
- Feeling preoccupied
- Anger
- Hostility
- Quarreling

"While these are the most common signs of stress, we as individuals each receive unique signals from our bodies," says Dr. Tubesing. To begin developing your personal stress mug shot, start by thinking back to the last time you *knew* without a doubt that you were stressed. Maybe it was the day your boss harangued you in front of the whole department. Did you have a headache the rest of the day? Maybe you went home and screamed at the kids. Write down anything you can remember. Add to the list as new sources of recognizable stress arise and soon you will discover some physical and mental signals which pop up with amazing regularity.

Once you know how you react to stress, you can turn the equation around. If you suddenly start getting stress signals without any apparent cause, you'll know something is bugging you. Then you can begin examining your environment for possible culprits.

THE 4 BIGGEST EXECUTIVE STRESSES

Back in prehistoric times when customer service was largely a matter of dragging animal carcasses home to the tribe and morning commutes to the forest were backup-free, the stress response had a very definite and useful place in the scheme of things. When the vice-president of meat acquisition happened to run into a long-toothed and furry product sample, he had only one executive decision to make: Should he fight or should he flee? Either choice made great energy demands on the body, and the stress response helped the body meet those demands.

That same prehistoric response operates within us today. The only problem is that the challenges we need to meet have changed. There are very few situations in the modern workplace which can be solved by either running out of a room screaming or chucking a spear through someone.

In a study of 300 managers from 12 major companies, John H. Howard, Ph.D., professor and management psychologist at the University of Western Ontario, pinpointed four factors in executive jobs that seem to produce the most stress.

1. A feeling of helplessness. You've probably run into a situation where you knew what was wrong with a project and also knew how to fix it. The only problem was you couldn't apply what you knew because of organizational constraints. Whether for lack of sufficient power on your part or ignorance on the part of upper management, you had to let the problem continue to grow.

2. Urgency. It's funny how many people consider the life of an executive to be a cushy montage of short hours, long lunches, and days at the golf course. In fact, 50- to 60-hour work weeks are not uncommon for most people in management. And during those hours it has been estimated that an executive ends up performing a different task every seven minutes. The worst part is that there isn't one of those tasks that is not marked urgent.

Race horses get rest periods after a strenuous performance, but executives don't.

3. Uncertainty. When a drill-press operator gets his instructions, there is usually very little that is left to the imagination with respect to his duties. On the other hand, an executive's responsibilities often demand that decisions be made based upon inconclusive or insufficient information. Adding to the feeling of uncertainty is the additional burden of nebulous goals and unspecified quality criteria from upper management.

4. Overwork. This one goes hand-in-hand with urgency. Since executives don't punch time clocks and are expected to achieve, the line between busy and overworked is almost nonexistent.

While these four factors get down to the daily stress nitty-gritty, there are also what could be called umbrella stressors which build up tension peripherally. Donald DeCarlo points his finger at two in particular: merger mania and techno-stress. "It used to be if you had a position with a company, you had it for life," he says. "But with the current popularity of the merger as well as the merciless downsizing many companies are now going through, a person has to wonder if he or she will have a job tomorrow. And if a merger doesn't get you, it could be that your position will be easily filled by a computer at some time in the future."

How to beat the 4 biggest
EXECUTIVE STRESSES

As we said before, you can't run from these problems, and yet they're too pervasive to actually fight. They also tend to pop up in a variety of changing forms. Uncertainty rears its head every time you get passed over for promotion. (What the heck do they want from you anyway?) Urgency is the constant byproduct of upper-level mismanagement. So what do you do to stressproof yourself while under this constant siege?

"First of all, you need to realize that while there is some stress that is unavoidable, there is also stress that you create," says Steven Sideroff, Ph.D., head of Stress Strategies, a stress management center which has helped executives from companies such as Lockheed and IBM. "People are constantly creating stress for themselves via their unbalanced perceptions of a situation and their style of time management."

For example, the last time you made a mistake and were read the riot act for it, were you devastated? Was it really that horrible? Was it the End of the World? If you think about it, these descriptions are better suited to a weekend stay with the Spanish Inquisition rather than a minor altercation with your boss. The point is that if you label something as horrible, it will be horrible. And horrible things tend to be stressful. Instead, try perceiving events in a slightly softer light. That same situation that was devastating could instead be thought of as merely uncomfortable. The End of the World could be downgraded to a temporary pain in your butt. Perceiving situations in softer terms programs your mind and body not to hype themselves up for World War III when in fact you're dealing with a pillow fight.

During his six-week course in stress management, Dr. Sideroff teaches a variety of techniques to bring more objectivity and less hysteria to his students' situational perceptions. "One thing I tell people to do is think of someone they know who handles challenging situations in a positive way. Then imagine this person handling the problem that is currently bothering you. What would this other person think about the situation? How would she interpret it? What would she do?"

Cultivating hardiness

During the 1983 Bell System breakup, stress was a palpable entity stalking the hallways in search of fresh executives to devour. But when researchers Suzanne C. Oullette Kobasa, Ph.D., and Salvatore Maddi, Ph.D., professors of psychology at City University of New York and University of California, Irvine, respectively, took a firsthand look at the situation, they found one group of execs that seemed immune to the mental and physical tolls of tension.

The factor which set these people apart from the twitching masses was something the two researchers labeled as "personality hardiness." In this case, being hardy does not mean you can fell a redwood tree with your teeth—but it's the ability to feel you could if you wanted to. The executives who displayed personality hardiness had a set of attitudes and beliefs which allowed them to look at an unmanageable situation and find something in it that they could control. They could look at a problem and see the importance and fascination of it rather than its menacing aspects. To them, every threat became a challenge. Attitudes like these actually allowed some Bell execs to enjoy the turmoil of the breakup while others were huddling under their desks.

To develop a little personality muscle of your own, Dr. Maddi and Dr. Kobasa recommend the following techniques.

Situational reconstruction. After a stress-producing event, try to imagine specific ways that the event could have been better or worse. Then visualize what you could have done to make the better outcome a reality. At the same time, you can also congratulate yourself on the things you did do to avoid the worst possible scenario. What you'll begin to realize by practicing situational reconstruction is that you aren't helpless. No matter how uncontrollable most problems may seem, you do have some options available that can change the circumstances.

Compensatory self-improvement. This is what you resort to when situational reconstruction doesn't work. You've tried and there just doesn't seem to be anything that can be changed. "At this point, the first thing you should do is realize the stress situation is a given and is best accepted as such," say Dr. Maddi and Dr. Kobasa.

But the second thing to do is realize that the situation does not constitute the whole of your life. Turn your attention to something you *do* have control over. If you're hitting a brick wall at work, brush up on your piano playing at home. Or become the master rose-grower you always wanted to be. This compensating technique will leave you with a sense of power and accomplishment that you might miss if you tend to focus on a single unsolvable problem.

RELAXATION TECHNIQUES THAT FIT INTO YOUR SCHEDULE

"Ninety percent of the executives I run across could use some type of stress-management technique," estimates Dr. Sideroff. "The bottom line is that just about everyone needs some way of training themselves to relax."

You may have read up to this point with mild interest tempered by the mental reservation that you are not truly stressed. But unless you think you're the one in ten that just seems to ease on down life's highway, there's a good chance that stress *is* affecting your performance and health. The following techniques are meant to be used regularly as a means of easing tensions you recognize as well as those that are subconscious. Think of these as quick tune-ups that will keep you running at maximum efficiency with minimum wear and tear.

Walking. Nothing could be simpler and better for fast tension relief than a 20-minute stroll. But to get the full benefit, try following these suggestions from David and Deena Balboa of the Walking Center in New York City.

- Walk somewhere that allows you to maintain a sustained rhythm without interruptions. You'll want to head for a park with winding paths rather than cruising down Main Street with all its traffic lights.

- Consciously relax your shoulders. Keep your head erect to avoid contracting the windpipe and thereby shortening your breath.
- Lower your eyelids a bit to decrease the amount of visual stimuli.
- Allow your arms their full range of motion.
- Take a few really deep breaths and let them out with a gentle but audible sigh.
- Rather than dwell on your problems, focus on your breathing. Don't try to control it. Simply pay attention as you inhale and exhale. If you find your mind wandering, don't worry. Just coax it back to your breathing.
- Every once in a while, recheck to make sure your shoulders are dropped and relaxed.

Li Shou. Even simpler than a walk, this thousand-year-old Chinese technique can be done right in your office. "In Chinese, *Li Shou* means 'hand swinging,'" says Edward C. Chang, Ph.D., of Albany State College in Georgia, who is translating into English an ancient text describing the use of exercise as a therapeutic technique. "If done correctly, you can use Li Shou to acquire a meditative state and experience the same stimulation and euphoria usually associated with vigorous forms of exercise."

Here's how to get into the "swing" of stress relief.

- Rub the palms of your hands against each other for a few seconds until you've created a pleasant warmth. Then, using both palms, massage your face from forehead to chin as if you were washing your face. Repeat this several times, making sure to always massage in the same direction.
- Consciously relax your entire body and smile.
- Stand with your feet at shoulders' width apart and your toes pointing straight ahead.
- Without slouching, let your arms and elbows sink naturally downward. Spread your fingers slightly.
- Close your eyes partially, with your lids not quite meeting, and without bending your head, mentally focus downward to your toes.
- Raise both hands, extending them frontward only to navel level, and swing them to the back no higher than your buttocks with sufficient force that your arms bounce back and forth rhythmically like a pendulum. Do this 100 times, counting on each backswing.
- As you do this, focus your attention on your toes while maintaining a constant awareness of what your arms are doing.

Should your mind wander, gently bring it back to your arms and toes. Feel the tension in your hands and arms on the backswing. Appreciate the sense of release on each frontswing.
• Eventually work your way up to 1000 swings.

Biofeedback. It used to be that to do biofeedback, you'd need to high-tail it to some laboratory where they would hook you up to a big machine that looked like a prop from *Forbidden Planet.* We've come a long way since then. A company called Thought Technology offers the perfect executive biofeedback device in their GSR2 unit. Since it easily fits into your briefcase or pocket, the GSR2 leaves you with no excuse to be without a means of relaxation at the office.

The principle of biofeedback using GSR2 is wonderfully uncom-plicated. When you experience stress, your skin pores change size. The GSR2 measures this change and translates the information into a sound. As the sound rises in pitch, it indicates that you are getting more tense. When the sound starts to travel down the scale, you begin taking the road to relaxation. All you have to do is listen and try to "influence" the tone.

"I teach biofeedback techniques in my six-week course because people tend to experience a great deal of success with it," notes Dr. Sideroff. "It's not necessarily because biofeedback is better than any other methods, but it is more uniquely suited to our society."

What he means by this is that we Westerners find it hard to sit still and simply relax. "Downtime! Unproductive interval!" our minds scream. But with biofeedback, you are *doing* something to relax. You are controlling tone levels. Besides the active aspect of biofeedback, there is also something else we Westerners like: positive reinforcement. The biofeedback unit tells you instantly when you are doing something wrong or right. It takes the guess-work out of stress reduction. To find out more about the GSR2, contact Thought Technology, Ltd., 2180 Belgrave Avenue, Suite 693, Montreal, P.Q., Canada H4A 2L8; phone 800–361–3651 (for U.S. only).

ARE YOU YOUR EMPLOYEES' BIGGEST SOURCE OF STRESS?

Everyone knows one of those bosses who doesn't think honest work is being done unless his employees are a veritable chorus line of nervous tics. He measures efficiency with a stopwatch and has occasionally toyed with the idea of starting off the day by firing a starter's gun. It's this type of manager who is the most common source of employee stress, right? Maybe not. You can be as mellow as elevator music and still cause a mountain of stress for the people that work for you. Rather than actively harassing employees, you may simply be overlooking some basic needs which most human beings require to function at an optimal, stress-free level.

When Mark J. Tager, M.D., coauthor of *Working Well: Managing for Health and High Performance,* interviewed employees all over the country to determine how managers put undue stress on their workers, he uncovered these three common complaints.

Behaving unpredictably. Jekyll-Hyde mood swings in a manager, although the most colorful manifestation of unpredictability, are not necessarily the *most* frequent reason that employees often feel lost at sea without a compass. You may think you are operating in a logical fashion, but if your employees do not know your agenda or the criteria by which you judge their work, your decisions may seem arbitrary in their eyes.

The answer is communication. When your employees do good work, praise them consistently. When bad work appears, let them know in detail what's wrong and how it can be improved. When you promote, make sure your employees understand your decisions. And as much as possible, let them know your short-term and long-term departmental goals. A little extra information goes a long way toward providing a secure work environment.

Whittling away at self-esteem. We won't even begin to insult you with the suggestion that you may be recklessly doling out unwarranted criticism. But maybe you've been a tad too hard on someone who's made a mistake lately. Before speaking with the employee, remember the last mistake *you* made and how you felt. After the recrimination job you did on yourself, did you really need to be laid any lower by your boss? With that in mind, try to deal with the employee's mistake quickly and effectively. Rather than crying over spilled milk, focus on how to clean it up and keep it from spilling again in the future. Also, keep your criticism private. No one likes to be poked at in front of co-workers.

Providing too much or too little stimulation. There are some bosses who take a certain pride in the fact that they are not overly demanding. They allow their employees a leisurely pace and wouldn't dream of creating a stressful blizzard of activity in the office. Curiously enough, this kind of management style may cause more stress than it avoids. Animals, when deprived of stimulation, commonly display signs of stress ranging from depression to outright aggressiveness. Humans are even more demanding in their need for stimulation. Most people would rather be working briskly than sitting at a clean desk watching the clock tick.

Don't expect everyone to do the same amount of work, though. For some the load will not be enough, for others it may be an exhausting burden. Keep an eye out and adjust assignments accordingly. If you do things right, everyone will remain busy and no one will be complaining of overwork or unfair division of labor.

How Head Honchos Beat Stress

While the rest of the world tends to focus on the jet-setting, deal-making, limo-riding facets of being a CEO, there is a less glamorous side: the 60-hour-plus workweek that the average top dog maintains. Living with 20 fewer leisure hours than the rest of us mere mortals, how do CEOs stave off stress? Exercise is the top choice.

Among 3,000 executives surveyed by the University of Massachusetts Medical School, two of three say they exercise regularly—and nearly half say they do so in order to relieve stress. Other studies have found that as many as 80 percent of CEOs are regular exercisers—nearly twice the rate of the general population.

According to cardiologist James Rippe, M.D., who headed the Massachusetts study, calisthenics are the most popular fitness routine among corporate executives, done at least three times a week by 94 percent of those surveyed. By comparison, 72 percent say they run regularly, 66 percent participate in fitness walking, 64 percent use a stationary bicycle, and 57 percent lift weights. Less common forms of exercise include racquetball, reported by 26 percent, and golf, reported by a surprisingly low 2 percent.

But exercise isn't the only escape from the stress of corporate responsibility. The vast majority of responding CEOs say they frequently read for pleasure and relaxation. As a matter of fact, the typical CEO reads about six times as much as the general population.

Music also helps to soothe more than half of the surveyed CEOs, with classical and easy-listening being the top choices. Not far behind was country and western, as well as opera.

52

TEAMWORK

J ames E. Bernstein, M.D., is an entrepreneur's entrepreneur. He founded General Health, Inc., a health-risk management firm, and Age Wave, Inc., an information company that studies the marketing implications of the aging of the United States population. He is also the president of Brooklawn Associates, a small business development firm based in Washington, D.C.

Like most successful people, Dr. Bernstein has a proven strategy for getting individuals to work together as a team. His method does not rely on manipulating others, nor is it based on any other form of trickery. He doesn't spend a fortune on team-building seminars in the wilderness or similar programs. Instead he simply sets aside a special time so that he and other members of his team can meet to get to know one another better, to enable members of the team to discover what makes each other tick—and what ticks each person off.

In Dr. Bernstein's team-building sessions, a member may disclose such personal matters as how she falls apart at the seams—and become hopelessly demoralized, as well—when someone excludes her from social functions. Or someone may mention how one simple statement of praise can literally motivate him to work around the clock. Through such insights, others in the team learn what they can do to bolster the group's motivation level; they also learn how to minimize behavior that will send team members into the doldrums.

Dr. Bernstein suggests that no more than ten people should be included in such sessions. He adds that the process will run most smoothly if it's held in a setting that enables people to relax. Participants shouldn't be required to perform any work other than the task at hand: to discuss what motivates them and to share details of their biggest turn-offs. And by all means, refreshments should be served.

The leader should start out with a brief speech such as: "My goal is to get a team working for the company. To the extent that you feel comfortable talking about these things, I think it would be very helpful. And I want to reassure all of you that I'm trying to create an environment where there can be a safe exchange." Of course, it will sound a bit too staged if you use that exact script. But whatever you say to get the ball rolling, Dr. Bernstein warns that people have to trust you "or they won't own up."

Such discussions evolve naturally after a leader sets the tone by sticking his own neck out. "A leader does it by example, and he has to be sufficiently candid that he's credible," Dr. Bernstein explains.

Not speaking for himself, Dr. Bernstein says a leader might kick off a session by confessing how he totally freaks out when people don't come through on time—even in little things like promising to phone at 3:00 P.M., and them calling at 3:15 P.M. He relates a possible monologue: " . . . In fact, I have to tell you that I'm irrational about it. I don't know whether it comes from my father or my mother, but when I was a kid growing up, I sort of got it in my bones that if you're late, you don't love me, you don't care. You're disrespectful. Whatever it is, it's a real hot button for me, and it's good for you to know it. I may be very immature, but I can't get it out of my system."

By honestly divulging our own quirks and explaining where they come from, you get people to loosen up. And you send the message to them that you're not afraid of being honest, that it's okay to be honest with members of the team.

Even if you're not the official leader of a team, you can informally use this method to create a cohesive clan out of a collection of disinterested folks, particularly if you're all together on a special project. It can be as simple as organizing an after-work gab session with the others. You can start by sharing the details of what inspires you and what turns you off. You'll be surprised how infectious your honesty will be.

CREATING ESPRIT DE CORPS

Okay, you're the coach. You're the person who knows more about the game than any of the players. And you're the one who knows everybody's strengths and weaknesses. But now, to get the most out of your players, you really have to step out of the arena and let the others show their stuff. By doing this, by authorizing a team to work together unencumbered by any ongoing interference on your part, you send a strong message that will help build esprit de corps: Teams work best when members surrender their individuality for the benefit of the group itself.

Also, teams work most productively if there's a guiding vision that pulls (not pushes) each team member in one direction, explains Wolf J. Rinke, a Rockville, Maryland, management consultant. If an organization doesn't operate under a strong philosophy, it's up to the team leader to provide one—and to clarify that philosophy and the team's mission. Here's how:

Speak in terms of the team's successes, not your own. If you're more concerned about the successes of others than with your own moments in the limelight, you will set a tone of cooperation that will generate good group energy.

Get people to compliment other members of the team, instead of themselves. Robert Lynch, vice-president of The Miller Consulting Group in Atlanta, suggests you begin meetings by saying something like: "Anybody have something good to say about another member this week? Who helped you out this week? Who saved you?" It gets people to publicly acknowledge the contributions of others.

Treat each person as if he or she is the most important member of the team. This is especially true of those on the lowest rung, those who Rinke believes *are* the most important members of the team. He cites the example of the high-class restaurant manager who dismisses the lowly dishwasher as insignificant. "But when first-class, gourmet food gets served up on dirty dishes, it isn't first-class, gourmet food, is it?"

Inspire folks to share the credit. "When you give people credit for something, they have more of a stake in the outcome," says George Prince, founder of Synectics, Inc., a management consulting firm in Cambridge, Massachusetts. Sharing credit can change an employee's stance from adversarial to supportive. Prince suggests you set the tone by saying things like: "You really have to credit Sally; she gave me the idea." Trouble is, such statements fly in the face of the competitive education that most of us underwent, an education which taught that you simply don't admit anyone else has helped you.

Take an interest in your team members as people. "High performance groups are managed by supervisors who spend a lot of time with employees talking about personal issues, as opposed to talking about getting work done," says Rinke. Dr. Bernstein concurs: "I spend a lot of time trying to figure out what makes a person tick, what people like to do, what they think is fun. I like to keep track of what's going on in their personal lives, to take an interest in them as people.

"If someone comes to me and says 'It takes me four hours to get to work and back because of traffic, and I can't stand the roommate I'm living with,' I'll ask what I can do to help. If he says he doesn't have five minutes to find another apartment, I might tell him to take Friday off and let me know his new address on Monday."

Recognize and reward good teamwork. "We tell people to go out and be a team, but performance evaluations and rewards are usually based on individual merit," says management consultant Lynch. The solution: Peg at least part of any performance-based reward on the accomplishments of the team.

The benefits to be gained from all this esprit de corps are obvious, but we'll point one out anyway. With such team spirit, predicts Lynch, "You may get 10 people going home each night worrying about the problems and looking for solutions, instead of just you."

HOW TO BLEND THE RIGHT PEOPLE
FOR A PERFECT TEAM

Sure, your instinct is to accumulate a bunch of clones—people who think a lot like you (maybe even look like you). But the best teams are an aggregation of contrasting styles and values. "The trick," explains Lynch, "is to not have any one mold." So when staffing up, look for diversity. "Conflicts are a part of a good team," he says, "and disagreement is good."

Here are some of the personality types he suggests you ideally should have.

The action-oriented type. These are folks who tend to plow ahead (sometimes thoughtlessly) on any given task. They want results *now*—which may be too soon.

The analytical type. Such people put the stern eye of reality on everything they see. These are the ones who don't want to act until they've carefully studied (again, possibly over-studied) the situation, until they've understood every possible ramification. You can identify them easily because they tend to begin sentences with the words "What if . . . "

The administrative type. You know the sort. They're the ones who are forever saying, "Let's keep track of this."

The synergistically oriented type. These folks have the ability to pull things out of people. They're magicians at drawing strengths out of others (that may be their *only* strength, but it's a talent any team could use).

The visionary type. In another context (say, the third grade) these people were known as "dreamers." Regardless, their ability to overlook the minor details of this morning's problems and focus clearly on the future is invaluable in any team. And remember, you'll be cheating the team by coaxing them back to reality.

So, how many of the above are represented on your team? As a leader, it's your responsibility to recruit and balance the above assemblage into a finely working troupe. Like many worthwhile endeavors, it's not likely to be easy. If you're an action-oriented type, for example, you've got to recognize that you *need* a slowpoke analytical type to keep you in check—even if she drives you crazy, which is probably what will happen.

4 UNEXPECTED ROLES OF A TEAM LEADER

As leader of a team, you're supposed to inspire, motivate, develop, challenge, and reward. That's old news. But here are some additional roles you probably never considered.

1. Equalizer. When consultant Prince teaches team building to client companies, he names as team captain someone who is relatively low in company status. As members watch senior people serving on the low-ranking captain's team, they come to understand that rank-consciousness must be minimized if a team is to be effective. To set a tone of equality, it's up to the leader to move as if he's on equal footing with others—no better, no worse. The message: Resist the urge to pull rank. "In high-performing teams that we see, leaders don't say, 'That's the way it is because I say it is.' If leaders want coffee, they get up and get it themselves. They don't ask others to do it," says Prince.

So how do you surrender status? How do you avoid using the power you're so happy you have? For starters, Prince suggests you call a halt to one particularly destructive habit: putting people on the spot. Join them instead.

Bad: "This is your baby. If you blow it, you blow it."

Good: "This is our baby. Any help you need, let me know."

Bad: "This is your risk."

Good: "This is our risk. How can we be prudent about it?"

2. Anxiety-defuser. One of the big, undiscussed tasks of a team leader is to avoid putting people on the defensive. It's not easy, given our competitive instincts, which tend to bring out the defensiveness within us. According to Prince, most folks screen everything that passes their ears for the subtle put-down. Since people are so fine-tuned to pick up on criticism—and so turned off when it occurs—you should avoid language that contains what Prince calls "hidden discounts."

Don't say: "What Mary meant to say is . . . " "That won't work . . . " "To be practical . . . " "To be serious . . . "

Also avoid such anxiety-producing behavior as:

- Preaching or moralizing
- Being critical, unless you initially cite positive aspects of whatever behavior or idea you're criticizing
- Emphasizing how much you misunderstand something; it sends the message that a person isn't good enough to explain things clearly
- Quickly disagreeing; it sets up a win-lose relationship
- Being cynical
- Interrupting
- Cross-examining
- Not listening

It's not enough to try to stop *yourself* from behaving in subtly adversarial ways. You also have to point out such behavior in others (and, as tough as it may sound, do it without putting *them* on the defensive). Begin by first looking for—and complimenting—the value in what you hear others say and do.

3. Supporter of confusion. Your impulse may be to attack anything you don't immediately understand, but productive teamwork requires a bit of uncertainty. There's nothing wrong with supporting something even though you're not certain how it will turn out. "A great many enterprises have an uncertain outcome. If you insist on knowing the outcome in advance, you won't get any innovation," says Prince. Even if your trust in others turns out for the worse, remember: A good team leader learns how to tolerate unexpected outcomes (also known as "mistakes").

4. Visionary. Team leaders are at their best when they provide vision. So think ahead, and share your free-wheeling dreams of group accomplishments. If you're good at it, you'll provide an excitement that will give folks a joyous sense of direction and purpose—and it will encourage them to be visionaries, too. "The really great leader is the one who helps others develop a vision, but doesn't develop it for them," explains Prince. "He's stimulating and he's a catalyst."

When a person does great work but alienates others

It's bound to happen sooner or later: the emergence of the player who makes all the scores, but who sends the rest of the team thrashing around the locker room in disgust. (You know the type. You may even be one yourself.) When that happens, there are basically two paths to take: You can deal with the individual, or (if the person is that crucial to the team's performance) you will have to deal with the rest of the team.

First off, you can give the offender the benefit of the doubt, and assume that he's not aware of his effect on other team members. He probably is, but assume otherwise when you sit down to explain the situation to him. "When having your discussion with the person, put it in the context of how his behavior is a problem for both him and the team. Avoid generalities, and try not to make him defensive," says consultant Lynch. He offers this example:

Bad: "We're having trouble with you. You're a bad team player."

Good: "Joe, when somebody brings up an idea and you fire back immediate harsh criticism, it turns him off and he stops offering ideas. It cuts off a source of good ideas."

If such people won't change, you may eventually be forced to expel them from your team. "Their good work won't make up for all the bad stuff they cause," says consultant Prince. "You work with them as best you can, but if you then realize they can't make it, get rid of them. They're a poison."

For his part, Dr. Bernstein occasionally finds it necessary to go directly to the others, the alienated team members. "Sometimes you have to say to the other people, 'I know you recognize Susan is abrasive and I know Susan turns you off, but she does really great work. So when you see her coming, dive for cover, smile, and just recognize that we're all putting up with her.'

How to turn loners into team players

Highlight positive interdependence. Explain that they can't succeed unless everybody succeeds. Make it clear to loners that they need you for what you can contribute, and that you need them for what they can contribute. "The greater the sense of positive interdependence, the less anyone will want to be alone," says David W. Johnson, Ph.D., professor of social psychology at the University of Minnesota.

Point out the benefits of teamwork. Perhaps they've never experienced the rewards of team membership. "I would find out what special skills such people have and think of a way to apply them in a group context," explains Patricia M. Carrigan, Ph.D., former manager of General Motors' Bay City, Michigan, plant, now president of Pat Carrigan Associates, a management consulting firm. Give them an opportunity to reap the rewards of a group accomplishment.

Help them develop interpersonal skills they may be lacking. When people gravitate toward careers that enable them to operate independently, it may be because they never developed the skills required of those who work well in groups. If your loners have poor interpersonal communication ability, for example, help may be as close as a training session. They could learn how to improve such skills as persuasiveness, listening effectively, and reading verbal and physical cues from other team members, suggests Bernard Rosenbaum, president of MOHR Development, a Stamford, Connecticut, business training firm.

Maybe they shouldn't be on the team after all. "People who have high needs for autonomy make poor team players," explains Robert Bramson, Ph.D., an Oakland, California–based organizational psychologist and management consultant with Bramson, Gill Associates, and author of *Coping with Difficult People.* "They tend to become demoralized if you make them part of an integrated team, one in which everyone's work depends on others." He suggests you begin by including loners in the group, but let them retain some independent functions. This way, you can point out (and they can see) the benefits of teamwork. "If they gain confidence in the abilities of other people and in their own ability to operate within a group, it may work well," explains Dr. Bramson. "But if it doesn't work, it doesn't work." In that case, you could try accepting the employee as he or she is.

53

TELEPHONE SKILLS

Good Morning! Telephone Doctor's office! This is Becky!"

"Um, this is David Diamond. Is the Telephone Doctor in?"

"I'm sorry! She's traveling to New Orleans this week and will be back in the office on Thursday! How may *I* help you?"

"Uh . . . I'm working on a book about. . . . "

"The Telephone Doctor's assistant Cathy is in, and she works closely with her! Would you like to speak with *her*?"

"Er, sure."

"Are you able to hold?"

Just when you thought you heard of everything, here comes the Telephone Doctor. Seven years ago St. Louis–based Nancy Friedman, a former receptionist and secretary, set herself up in the business of teaching and preaching telephone etiquette to the ill-telephone-mannered masses. There apparently are enough communicators out there suffering from telephone manners anxiety that her business has not only survived but thrived. She employs a staff of 17 people to arrange her speaking engagements (with corporations like IBM, AT&T, and Union Carbide) and to produce her audio- and videotapes on the topic of telephone usage. If her receptionist's telephone-answering technique is any indication, the Telephone Doctor must be doing something right on the telephone front: Check out how helpful, direct, and thorough the receptionist was in the above conversation.

No, you probably don't need to rush to St. Louis for a personal consultation. If you're like most folks, you've developed enough of a telephone style to at least get by. But still, there are some useful and effective telephone skills that most people tend to overlook. "Hundreds of thousands of dollars are leaking through phone wires each year because of the way people use the phone," asserts Friedman (who, in case you're wondering, is not a real doctor). She tells her audiences and customers that it's not unusual for companies to change suppliers or vendors merely because they were treated rudely over the phone. In fact she preaches that as a culture, our biggest telephone offense is that we're simply not friendly enough over the wires. "A caller should be treated as a welcomed guest," she says, "not as an annoyance."

One of the points Friedman always makes is that you should *expect* that your party won't be in when you try to get in touch by phone. Her surveys reveal that only 30 percent of all business calls are completed on the first try. She suggests that since 7 out of 10 people will not be there when you try to reach them, you should have a complete message prepared and ready to give to a secretary. The point: If that secretary knows exactly what you want, he or she may be in a position to find someone else to help you.

7 WAYS TO AVOID PHONE FOUL-UPS

1. Beware of background noise. You may well be the type who can't operate at maximum capacity unless you have Keith Richards blaring from your office radio. But consider, for a moment, how your favorite background music sounds to the ears of the operaphile on the other end of the line. What's more, he probably can't hear what you're saying.

2. Silence those swallows. Maybe you can drink coffee and talk on the phone at the same time. But if you want to keep your listener from feeling like he's second fiddle to a mug of caffeine, you'd better raise the receiver so your gulps aren't amplified and transmitted. An even smarter approach would be to resist the urge to gulp while you're doing the talking.

3. Have notes at hand. If you've got an agenda to cover, have ready a list of the topics you want to discuss. Then cross off each one after you tackle it. After all, how many times have you hung up and later realized that you forgot to raise an important issue?

4. Be careful with your language. Since you're not speaking face-to-face, the listener can't rely on your facial expressions and gestures to help interpret what you're trying to communicate. So without the nonverbal accompaniment, such phrases as "As I said . . ." may be interpreted as "You clod, you were too stupid to understand me the first time around . . ." Try instead, "Let me just review again some of the major things that are impor-tant . . . " This advice comes from Anthony Alessandra, a La Jolla, California–based professional speaker on sales and communications matters, who offers another example:

Bad: "I'd like to ask you a question." (This can come out sounding like an interrogation.)

Good: "Do you mind if I ask you a question?" (This conveys positive vibes, whether or not you bother to wait for an answer.)

5. Don't be afraid of pauses. When there's a pause after the other person finishes speaking, don't jump right in and say something. Give her some time, so you can make sure she's finished. Also, if you allow for a brief pause, it shows the other party that you're more concerned with what she's saying than you are with what you have to say. Alessandra suggests that your pauses be no longer than 2 seconds. Any longer than that and people start to get nervous.

6. Don't have your secretary juggle calls. Talk about obnoxious habits. You know what it's like to receive a call from a secretary who explains that her boss is calling and asks if you'd mind staying on hold until he's available to speak with you. So why do it to anyone else? Only the President of the United States and a few deserving others should have the right to such a degrading time-saving technique. Thankfully, this little custom is out of vogue for the moment.

7. Be well equipped. If you want to save telephone time, get yourself a telephone equipped with an automatic redial feature, speed dialing, and speaker phone attachment. But for heaven's sake, only use the speaker phone until you get the party on the line (it will give you maybe 20 free seconds to use your hands for other chores). When your party answers, switch off the speaker phone—that is, unless you actually *want* the other person to think you're a pompous creep.

If you spend the better part of your day on the telephone, do your back, neck, and shoulders a favor: Buy a telephone headset. It also frees your hands for other uses (hopefully something other than pouring yourself coffee).

A DIFFERENT KIND OF NAME-DROPPING

You're speaking on the phone with someone you don't know very well, and the guy isn't some bigwig type. Do you call him "Mr." or do you go by the first name?

Alessandra suggests you try to get a sense of how likely the person is to *want* to be called by his first name. If in your conversation he comes off as being aloof and impersonal, you probably should call him "Mr." Listen carefully to his responses. If he tends to reply to your questions in one-word answers, there's a good chance he doesn't want you to call him by his first name. If you feel it's appropriate, you may ask, "How do you prefer to be called?"

Whether it's Mr./Ms. Smith or Joe/Joan, it's still true that the most beautiful sounds to a person's ears are the utterance of his or her name. So instead of punctuating your conversation with "uh," "you know," and the like, remember to mention your listener's name when you can. In a subtle way, it makes the conversation seem a bit more personalized, almost as if you're communicating face-to-face. Or as Alessandra puts it, "When you call someone by his first name, it's one more strand in the cable of trust you're building."

Also, in cases where you're apt to forget the other person's name, repeating it a few times during the conversation will help you remember. But don't go overboard. Few things are more annoying than to hear someone mindlessly beginning every sentence with your name.

A final word about secretaries: Allesandra points out that secretaries are more likely to put your call through to their boss (or be forthright about the best time to reach him) if you develop a rapport with them. Call the secretary by whatever he or she initially uses to identify himself or herself, whether it's Mr./Ms. or a first name.

54

TIME MANAGEMENT

Manic Time-Management Mania. It's a disease that primarily strikes down frantic, harried people with poor time-management habits who, ironically, possess a powerful, completely unrealized desire to someday become the most efficient force in the known universe.

The means of transmission? All it takes is a single time-management book in the wrong hands, and whammo! A zealot is born. Yesterday he left his wristwatch in the bathroom soap dish. Today he's at work with a stop-watch dangling from his neck, reflecting an occasional ray of the sun like some armored breastplate of the righteous. He's Mister Time Management, who in the course of 24 hours and one slim how-to book, has rearranged his entire existence into two-hour sessions, one-hour meetings, half-hour slots, 15-minute briefs, 7.5-minute assessment periods, and 3.75-minute bath-room breaks.

He's got personal time-management spreadsheets neatly done in five different colors (they only take four hours each week to make) and enough priority lists, files, folders, and charts to time-manage every inhabitant of the Northern Hemisphere. He's divided his paperwork into 22 different piles, each denoting a priority and time slot (e.g., the third pile is "as important as the fifth pile if the second and fourteenth piles have no more than four items in each and it's Thursday"). The problem is this: He has become the ultimate truant officer of his moments, but making sure those unruly min-utes and hooky-playing hours are where they belong has become a full-time job. That makes two full-time jobs he now has.

This type of malady is not uncommon. Converts, be they religious or managerial, have a tendency to overdo. But when it comes to time management, putting into practice every new tip and technique that comes along will surely bury you under a mountain of routine. The most futile part of the story is that if your routine is too complex and the techniques are too hard to get used to, after about three weeks you'll find yourself slipping back into old habits.

When it comes to developing positive time-management habits, the phrase "easy does it" comes to mind. Most of us don't need a box of tips, a bag of techniques, and ten laws etched in stone. We can begin using our time to greater advantage by implementing a mere handful of commonsense practices. The simpler the tips, the easier it will be to continue practicing them over an extended period of time.

KEEPING SIGHT OF THE BIG PICTURE

Ever wonder why it seems as if your life is slipping by while you are standing still? One reason may be that you spend your time each day accomplishing only those things by which your performance will be judged over the short term—things that will be noticed and generate complaints if they don't get completed.

So you dash off that memo to Sam in sales. You report to your boss the findings of your committee. You meet with the person who will write up that press release. Your to-do list is always full of such chores, and sometimes you even end a day having successfully completed all of them.

But your to-do list probably fails to include such items as "Develop relationship with someone who may be helpful in the long run," "Explore what other parts of the organization are doing," or "Do some self-exploration." "People rarely carve out time from the present in order to invest in the long run," explains Ross A. Webber, Ph.D., a management professor at the University of Pennsylvania's Wharton School and author of *Time Is Money: The Key to Managerial Success*. "Programmed and immediate tasks tend to be handled before more ambiguous and longer-run matters." In other words, we rarely bother to stop and think about what it is we want to achieve with our lives, or even where we'd like to be five years from now. This is not just a matter of losing sight of the big picture; we never bothered to develop one in the first place. It has always been so much easier to study for tests, apply for jobs, accomplish the clearly structured day-to-day objectives. As a result, says Dr. Webber, "the present tends to tyrannize the future."

To avoid being overwhelmed by short-term demands, Dr. Webber suggests you reformat your to-do list along the following lines. Two-thirds of the items should be chores that must be accomplished today or tomorrow. One-third of the items should be tasks that are linked to the long run. Include objectives you would like to meet one month in advance ("Become acquainted with a member of the chairman's support staff"), a year from now ("Become a member of that staff"), and five years from now ("Learn enough about this business that I can consider starting my own firm").

Here are some additional tips for getting a grip on your long-term objectives.

Know what you want. You can't even hope to manage your time wisely unless you have a strong sense of your own objectives. That means you should know what you want out of life and what you want to achieve from all your hard work. "Once you understand what you want to accomplish, you'll be in a position to evaluate activities that either help you or hinder you," says Larry Baker, president of Time Management Center, a St. Louis–area consulting firm. You'll also feel more comfortable with the decisions you make regarding how you spend your time. Here's an example: You've determined that your key objective in life is to develop solid relationships with your children. Saturday morning approaches and you have the option of attending your daughter's swim meet or going 18 holes with a foursome that includes a fellow who is rumored to be in line to head your division. By keeping sight of the big picture, and deciding accordingly, you'll feel less pressured by conflicting demands on your time.

Be flexible. You change; your objectives change; your priorities change. So make sure you have a flexible system of prioritizing each demand, problem, opportunity, objective, and activity, says Dru Scott, Ph.D., consultant and author of *How to Put More Time in Your Life.* By keeping your objectives open for fine-tuning, she says, you'll be less likely to abandon them at a crisis point.

Visualize your objectives. Sit down and envision yourself attaining your goals, advises Dr. Scott. The visualization communicates to your subconscious mind more powerfully than words do, so it gets your subconscious working on the mission.

Maximize your time investment. Dr. Scott defines *essentials* as "what you must do in the course of the day to stay alive, healthy, and able to pay the rent." She defines *central concerns* as your major priorities, "what you most want and value in life." Since you must devote a lot of time attending to essentials, Dr. Scott suggests that you increase the value of those time investments by making them coincide with your central concerns. A simple

A Word of Caution about To-Do Lists

We cheat ourselves when we conscientiously tackle our to-do list items one by one. The world doesn't operate in perfect, sequential order. "Effective managers are simultaneous people who can easily make transitions between topics," explains Dr. Ross A. Webber of the University of Pennsylvania's Wharton School. So be prepared to accomplish more than one thing at a time. A simple example: At 10:00 A.M. a manager phones you to get a handle on some scheduling assignment you're completing. Near the bottom of your to-do list is the item "Ask someone in the company for advice on expanded disability insurance coverage." So use this as an occasion to ask the manager for that advice. Even farther down on your to-do list is the item "Solicit ideas for trade group speech." While you have her on the phone, why not pick the manager's brain for ideas?

example: You are called upon to deliver a speech before an industry group. The subject of the speech is of little concern to you, but among your central concerns is the development of an effective communication style and the generating of contacts outside of your company. So concentrate on those aspects of the task. "When you feel you have to do something, ask yourself how you can turn it into an opportunity to accomplish something you want to accomplish," she says.

Know how you spend your days. If you want to keep track of what's wasting your time, you have to know how you're spending it. To that end, keep a daily log of everything you do, advises time expert Baker. When you see black-and-white proof that you spend far too much time performing tasks that could be delegated or haggling over lunch arrangements, you're likely to start taking corrective action.

Rethinking interruptions

There's a wonderful sign that's sometimes spotted behind retail counters: "The customer is not an interruption of your work. The customer *is* your work." Although the message is meant to encourage employees to treat customers politely, it also hints at the complex nature of interruptions. Many of us are in the *business* of getting interrupted. When Henry Kissinger was Secretary of State, for example, he talked about arriving at work at 7:00

A.M. armed with a list of daily objectives. Fifteen minutes later, however, he might get word of a revolution in some remote locale, and his day would be blown to bits.

Few of us get interrupted on an almost daily basis to respond to global crises. But many of our interruptions loom as catastrophic in our own little corner of the universe. If we hope to be serious about managing our time, we have to understand that many of those interruptions (let's call them positive interruptions) are a predictable and necessary part of our work, and should be dealt with as such.

Anticipate interruptions. A lot of management advice involves setting aside specific blocks of time to perform specific tasks. That approach is still the best method for staying on top of things. But our schedule should never be so tight that we don't have time for the incidental, the unexpected, the interruption with a silver lining—for example, the 2-minute water-cooler conversation with an associate that leads to a brilliant idea.

Beware the deadly self-interruption. If truth be told, most of us haven't become much more self-disciplined than we were at age six. We tend to put off things we dislike, things that are difficult, and things that won't produce immediate results, says Baker. So we go around looking for interruptions. Maybe we're in the middle of writing up a report and we're having trouble thinking up a perfect phrase. Suddenly, we'll remember we have to schedule a haircut appointment for next Saturday. Instead of simply jotting a quick note to ourselves to make the phone call later in the day, we'll pick up the phone and do it now. After we hang up, we'll suddenly notice some mail on our desk and feel the urge to investigate the finer points of a frequent flier club solicitation. Then we start fantasizing about our next vacation, or we suddenly notice some new entries that have been dumped into our in-basket. Solution: To isolate goofing-off time and keep it limited, *schedule* brief breaks as part of your regular work routine.

Understand the difference between positive interruptions and negative interruptions. Positive interruptions are work-related. Negative interruptions are not. If your boss interrupts your flow of concentration with a new, fast-breaking, high-priority assignment for you to complete, obviously you're going to have to respond. But if she constantly wanders over to annoyingly check on the status of your performance, you should be assertive in letting her know that the interruptions are time-wasters. How? Say, "Whenever I have to stop and explain what I'm doing, I lose my concentration and have to start from square one. Can we schedule regular times at which we can go over the progress I'm making?"

How Would You Handle These Interruptions?

Interruption No. 1: You're in your office, happily on schedule as you plan a test-marketing strategy for an upcoming potential product. In walks a subordinate with a question concerning a discrepancy in the budget figures for the test marketing campaign.

Interruption No. 2: Your buddy in accounting phones to share with you the details of last night's date. You need a friend in the accounting department.

In the first case, if you're the only person who can help the subordinate understand the budgetary discrepancy, you sit down with him and double-check the figures until you see the source of the problem— so you can have the subordinate solve it. If someone else can help the subordinate, you say something on the order of "Helen or Jim can go over that with you." In either event, don't fall into the trap of using the visit as a time to socialize, warns time-management consultant Larry Baker. Once you've helped or directed the subordinate, be firm in terminating the conversation. "Don't let the other individual control your time. Be assertive in telling him that the conversation is over," he suggests. Stand up, walk to the door, and say, "I'm glad I could help you with that problem," or "Thanks for bringing that to my attention." It's your turf. Protect it.

The second case is a negative interruption. Even though you need a friend in the accounting department for political reasons, put off the conversation until a time when you can socialize without jeopardizing your schedule. (It's unlikely that the office politics could be more important than whatever work you were accomplishing before the interruption.) Be friendly and suggest you meet for lunch to discuss the romantic endeavor, because you want to hear the entire story.

Note: Dr. Dru Scott, who wrote *Time Management and the Telephone,* has a strategy for answering the phone when she is busy. First, she says her name. Next, after the caller identifies himself, she warmly adds, "It's good to hear your voice," or "Thanks for calling back." Then she asks: "How can I assist you?" It lets the person know you're available but that you don't need the small talk. "If you have a warm spirit," she explains, "the caller will not be offended."

When someone phones and asks if you have time to chat, you can say, "Sure, but just a little time."

9 EFFECTIVE TIME-SAVING TIPS

1. Schedule a call-back period. Don't interrupt the flow of your work by returning calls throughout the day. Instead, set aside one or two periods to make your calls. Trial and error will help you determine what time of the day your parties are most likely to be in their offices to receive your calls. Some folks find that the period immediately following lunch is best for concentrating on call-backs. It's a relatively undemanding "productive ritual" designed to get you back into the work mode.

2. Schedule regular reading periods. Each morning Dr. Webber scans the *Wall Street Journal* and draws red circles around articles that look promising. Those articles are clipped by his secretary, who puts them into his to-read file, which he attacks at night while watching television with his family. That's one strategy for dealing with the information explosion. Another is to set aside a half-hour each day to read mail, memos, and anything else that crosses your desk. Or make a habit of keeping your mail and other contents of your in-basket in a file folder that can be slipped into your briefcase and read during waiting periods.

3. Schedule paperwork time. Why waste precious office time handling routine paperwork? Instead, slot it for a slack-time period (perhaps Tuesday mornings at 8:30 A.M., before anyone else arrives in the office, or Wednesday evening while your spouse is out at a class).

4. Try to shrink your deadlines. Challenge the well-accepted theory that work expands to fill the time allotted. Shave a day or two off of your deadlines to see if it makes you more efficient.

5. Arrive early or leave late once or twice a week. It's amazing how much you can get done when nobody is around to distract you.

6. Block out larger chunks of time to work on projects that need serious concentration. Set aside private time for assignments that can't be handled in fits and starts. Close your office door and have your calls intercepted, or work from home.

7. Break large tasks into small ones. Sometimes a time-consuming project can be done more efficiently on a piecemeal basis. That may be the best way of fitting it into your hectic schedule (and it might make it more bearable, too).

8. Learn how to say no. If you truly don't have the time to coach the office softball league or train the new intern or speak before a professional organization that lacks influence, say, "I'm sorry, I just don't have the time."

9. Use a day-planning calendar. Join the ranks of executives who credit their success to those small day-planning calendars that enable them to continually see where the time goes, half-hour by half-hour. A number of varieties and formats exist on the market, so find one that fits your needs.

How to Add an Extra Month to Each Year

Think you could benefit from a 13th month each year? Here's how to get one. Simply wake up 1 hour earlier each day during the work week. That will give you 5 hours per week, or 250 hours per year. Divide those 250 hours by 8 (assuming you have 8-hour days) and you get 31 days—a free month. (What you accomplish in that extra month is your responsibility.)

Why not go to bed an hour later instead of waking up early? Time-management expert Dr. Dru Scott explains that for most people, the early hours are far more productive than are later hours. "Most people find it much easier to be in a 'proactive' mode in the morning," she says. (By contrast, you're likely to be in a "reactive" mode at night, when you're exhausted from the day's activities.)

If the thought of dragging yourself out of bed an hour early seems a bit too much to take, Dr. Scott suggests you start with a half-hour.

55

TRIPS

Your boss's boss ushers you into his office and tells you he has a perfect advancement opportunity for you. Then the first question out of his mouth is, "Are you free to travel?"

At many organizations, it would be like slitting your professional throat if you turned down a job on the grounds that you'd rather spend the best years of your life watching your children's school galas than watching DC-10s line up on taxiways. Since the best business is conducted on a face-to-face basis, travel is the time-tested way of getting things done—and there's no sign of it letting up. The U.S. Travel Data Center estimates that the number of business trips of over 200 miles increased by about 34 percent in the last decade. That boom happened despite a wave of corporate cost-cutting, the proliferation of transcontinental teleconferences, and changes in tax laws that discourage business travel.

The boom in business trips is little consolation, however, for those in corporate America who just can't hack the jet lag, the missed Little League games, the lost luggage, and those look-alike Holiday Inn rooms bearing endless in-room advertisements for prime-rib specials. If they're lucky, they work for one of those few employers who are particularly supportive of nontravelers. At those places, an employee need only be honest and tell the boss's boss how much she loves the organization, but that she isn't particularly suited for travel. And, by the way, what future homebound opportunities are available?

More likely than not, though, travel is viewed as a necessity for fast-track advancement at the place where you work. And Richard F. Bloom,

Ph.D., a New York psychologist with TriSource Group, says that if you turn down an opportunity at your company because you simply don't want to travel, "there may be some risk." He adds, "There are companies where travel is the rule, rather than the exception. And if you aren't interested in traveling, it isn't the company to be in."

In a moment we'll discuss the toll that travel takes for some, but first let's give some attention to the folks who actually live to travel. Experts know that taking trips can be stimulating—and even help you do your job better. The same adrenaline that pumps while you're running to catch a plane can also help heighten your awareness and make you think clearer when you eventually meet that client in Denver. In fact, just getting out of the office and into new surroundings can offer a boost. There's also the independence—being able to avoid the hassles of demanding bosses and ringing telephones. Some people can get more work accomplished during a three-hour layover in Kansas City than in an entire day back in the office.

Sounds like something to which you could become addicted, huh? You're not alone. The term "travelholic" is commonly used among employee assistance types. It applies to those who simply can't function well without constantly being on the go. Often, these travelholics like to travel for all the wrong reasons.

A subgroup of travelholics, for example, includes those with a propensity for alcoholism. Life on the road affords ample opportunities to imbibe (on the plane, at the hotel bar, at corporate hospitality suites), often away from the critical eyes of bosses and spouses. It's well known that some alcoholics, when given the opportunity, tend to gravitate toward jobs that mask their drinking. Another group travels as a way of dodging problems on the home front. And there are those who keep on the move to avoid the sort of intimacy one gets by staying at home with the spouse and kids. (We're not even going to mention the legendary types who have lovers waiting for them in every airline hub city.)

For those of us who travel without any of these sorry motivations, life on the road can be a real bummer. Away from friends and family, one learns the meaning of the terms "loneliness" and "alienation." No wonder frequent traveling can result in a wide array of stress-related illnesses, encompassing everything from psychological problems to digestive disorders. And then there's the toll on the family left behind. Kids may develop an I-don't-give-a-darn attitude when Dad or Mom isn't around to participate in everyday family matters. Since the families of a traveling parent typically are run by the spouse at home, there's a cycle of readjustment each time the traveling parent returns home. He or she may find it a tough task to regain equal status at the head of the household.

With that in mind, let's see how the experts—those who spend much of their time on the road—make the best of the situation. The following tips were contributed by business travelers Leonard Zweig, publisher of *Family Business* magazine and vice-president of its parent company, MLR Publishing; Henry Cohen, a senior manager of a multi-billion-dollar, multinational corporation; Julia Lawlor, a writer for *USA Weekend* and *USA Today;* Gary Garb, a senior engineer at a major computer corporation; and Dr. Bloom.

45 TIPS FOR SUCCESSFUL BUSINESS TRIPS

1. Find a good travel agent. If you deal with the same person all the time, your profile of travel needs and preferences will be kept in a computer file. Your ally at the travel agency will always know where you prefer to sit when you fly. He or she will know all your frequent flier numbers, your credit card number (so booking can be done quickly), and your dietary preference. "They know I'm a vegetarian, so they immediately put in the request for a vegetarian meal," explains engineer Garb.

2. Leave messages for the loved ones back home. Dr. Bloom has clients who, whenever they take extended business trips, leave numbered letters (or even audio tapes) at home to be opened on a one-a-day basis. This can work both ways. Have your family write you letters (or compile tapes) to last the duration of your trip.

3. Keep a separate toiletry kit packed for travel. With doubles of everything, you'll always know you have enough contact lens solution, dental floss, and vitamin supplements ready to go.

4. If you travel often, have doubles of everything in your wardrobe. Or at least have two of every color. That way, one outfit can be at home being dry cleaned while the other is on the road.

5. Always keep enough clothes, toiletries, and work material to get by for one day in a carry-on bag. If your checked luggage goes astray, this could be a lifesaver.

6. Join an airline club. For a moderate initiation fee plus annual dues, you get a comfortable place to wait between flights and possibly an office space in which to work. The club can also be a great place to meet clients.

7. When possible, avoid being routed onto connecting flights for domestic trips. Not only do they add time, but they multiply the chances of missed flights and lost luggage. Especially try to avoid connections at Chicago, Atlanta, and New York's JFK. (*Note:* Writer Lawlor discovered she *preferred* taking connecting flights when she traveled during a pregnancy. She discovered that she felt better taking two 3-hour flights and walking around a connecting airport than she did sitting still for a 6-hour direct flight.)

8. To revive yourself and help reduce travel fatigue, break up long overseas flights. On a six-nation business trip to Asia, Henry Cohen broke up the long haul across the Pacific by making brief stopovers in Hawaii. Returning from New Zealand to Philadelphia, for instance, he landed in Hawaii at 6:00 A.M. (after 15 hours in the air), showered in his hotel, took a five-hour nap, ate a meal, and was back on a plane by 6:00 P.M.—greatly refreshed. "It accomplished two things," he reported. "The nap supplemented the not-very-sound sleep I had on the plane. And the stopover cut my adjustment to the time change in half."

9. For more legroom in economy class, request the bulkhead seat. But beware that airlines frequently assign the bulkhead to kids who travel alone. (On the other hand, it could be fun to sit next to a youngster.)

10. Check out a flight's on-time record. The U.S. Department of Transportation keeps record of on-time performance of regular air carriers. Ask your travel agent for the record of a specific flight. Wouldn't it help to know in advance that the flight arrives on time only 14 percent of the time?

11. For safety, pick an aisle seat near an exit.

12. If you'll be visiting several destinations, rotate your luggage. Cohen keeps everything he needs for the first stop in a carry-on suit holder. Everything else is in a suitcase which he checks. When he's preparing to leave the first destination, he rotates clothes for the second stop into the suit holder and moves the clothing from the first stop into the suitcase. That way, he always has the clothes he needs with him—right on the flight. And during his various stops, he never has to open his suitcase until he's ready to leave.

13. On international trips, make sure to meet any visa requirements.

14. Use a heavy-duty luggage carrier. "The last thing you feel like doing after getting off a lengthy flight late at night is carrying your luggage a long distance," says Garb.

15. Eat lightly before getting on a plane. When he's traveling to Europe or the Orient, publisher Zweig eats lightly beforehand and refuses airline meals or drinks. He skips the in-flight movie. Instead, he covers his eyes with a sleeping mask and tries to doze.

16. Before lengthy flights, avoid caffeine. Among other devious things, it will keep you from sleeping.

17. If you take motion-sickness medicine, do so on the ground. That way, it has a chance to work its stuff by the time you're in the air.

18. Don't race for the airport. Lawlor makes a habit of arriving 45 minutes before a flight.

19. Plan to arrive at your business destination early. If possible, arrive the night before doing business on domestic trips and a full day before on foreign trips. If you're traveling to Europe for Monday morning business, take a Saturday night flight, suggests Garb. You'll arrive on Sunday morning. Stay up all day; sleep all night. You'll wake up in great shape. If you must arrive Monday morning for a Monday meeting in Europe, don't try to catch a little sleep before heading to the office, warns Cohen. It will throw you off balance and make you more tired.

20. If possible, wear loose-fitting, casual clothes while traveling.

21. When they begin seating for your flight, don't rush to the gate. Traveling is inherently stressful, but you don't have to make things worse by waiting in line when you can be comfortably seated and reading a book.

22. Hate airline breakfasts? Have the flight attendant save dinner for you. On overseas flights, Zweig refuses the dinner (there's usually a beef selection) but asks the flight attendant to save it for him for breakfast, when he needs more protein than is generally offered by airline breakfasts, with their soggy croissants.

23. Order a special in-flight meal. If you request a special hypoglycemia (low blood-sugar) meal, for example, you might get the seafood salad offered to first class—even if you fly coach. When shuttling between interviews, reporter Lawlor requests vegetarian meals, which are lighter than meat dishes and thus help prevent jet lag.

24. Bring your own fresh fruit and cheese. Julia Child does.

25. Walk around inside the plane. (See "Beware of Deep Vein Thrombosis" on the opposite page.)

26. Do some isometrics or other exercises on the plane. Alternately relax and then tense your shoulder muscles, thighs, and buttocks in sequence. While waiting to use the lavatory, do a few deep knee bends.

27. Don't leap out of your seat the moment the plane reaches the gate. Instead of standing crouched, waiting to exit (like everybody else), take a few minutes to de-stress yourself.

28. Roam around the hotel before checking in. Determine where the most desirable rooms are located and request one at the desk.

29. Get a money belt and keep some cash or traveler's checks in it. These are not only a hedge against pickpockets, muggers, or a misplaced wallet. Engineer Garb has been hungry, tired, and newly arrived in the wee hours at places where credit cards were not accepted.

Beware of Deep Vein Thrombosis

Midway through a 16-hour flight between London and Singapore, businessman Henry Cohen woke up from his snooze and felt a cramp in his calf. Several days and two doctors later, he learned that he had deep vein thrombosis (DVT)—a serious blood-clotting condition that's brought on by dehydration and sitting or lying in one position too long. Treatment with intravenous blood thinners was begun promptly, but it took three months for the blood clot to fully dissolve.

Caucasians with high cholesterol levels are prime candidates for a blood clot in the leg, which if left untreated could travel to the lungs. There are two steps to avoiding this potentially dangerous ailment. First: Keep yourself from getting dehydrated. If that sounds simple, it's not. Fact is, there's virtually no moisture inside a pressurized jetliner's cabin, so dehydration can come rather quickly. This is especially true if all you drink is coffee, tea, or alcohol—beverages with a diuretic effect that can dry you out even faster. Instead, drink plenty of water or juice. Second: Get up and walk around the cabin every now and then. The exercise will help keep blood from pooling in your legs.

---

30. Bring a favorite photo of your family. Put it on the bureau or desk in your hotel room.

31. Bring your favorite pillow. Dr. Joyce Brothers does.

32. Bring your favorite alarm clock.

33. Take down those tacky in-room advertisements and shove them in a drawer. They should string up whoever it was that first suggested covering hotel-room bureaus with advertisements for the hotel's restaurant and such.

34. Take advantage of room service. As a woman traveling alone, Lawlor finds it awkward to eat dinner at the finer restaurants in each city she visits. Instead, she lunches at those restaurants and enjoys a room-service dinner—while wearing casual clothes.

35. Whenever possible, take a suit-carrier instead of luggage you have to check. Almost every plane has a space for hanging garment bags. With a suit-carrier and a small carry-on case, there's no need to check (and possibly lose) your luggage.

36. Have a racquetball partner in every city you regularly visit. Or a squash partner. (Racquet clubs can help you arrange it.) Or select hotels with swimming pools, or ones located near jogging paths. In short, don't use travel as an excuse to abandon your exercise routine.

37. Reserve an economy rental car. Frequently, rental companies will not have one available when you arrive but will offer you an intermediate-sized car at the same rate. If there actually is an economy car available but you prefer intermediate, you can always request and pay for an upgrade.

38. Join a rental car "express" club. It will speed your trip.

39. Count your luggage. Traveling with five pieces? Keep the number five in your head. Going and coming, count out each piece.

40. Arrange connections according to the weather. Why book a connecting flight in Chicago, Minneapolis, or Milwaukee during the winter when Dallas is also available?

41. On your return trip, drop off any baggage you want to check at the departure curb before returning the rental car. That way you don't have to carry your luggage from the car to the rental return office to the courtesy bus to the check-in line.

42. Complete your expense reports while flying home. Otherwise, says Cohen, you could wind up forgetting half of the expenses.

43. Select hotels with superior business amenities. The New York Hilton and Towers, for example, offers a late-night dictation service and next-day delivery of documents.

44. Discuss the impact of your traveling with your family. Dr. Bloom suggests that before you take a job that will require a great deal of travel, "talk it over in detail with family members to see what their concerns are, and what the impact will be."

45. Think before removing your shoes on an airplane. It's true that removing your shoes can help keep your blood flowing smoothly. But because your feet tend to swell on long flights, you may have trouble getting your shoes back on. Another option is to loosen your laces for the flight. Or you can remove your shoes, and upon landing, slip your feet back into them without tying the laces. Once you've walked halfway down the concourse, your feet will be back to normal size—so you can tie your shoes again.

56

WRITING SKILLS

There are all sorts of organizational horror stories about rising managers with great potential whose careers were dead-ended by their inability to write (or to be more accurate, by their disregard for learning how). That's not surprising, because for years, writing skills have been viewed as a method of pinpointing promotable executives. And it makes sense: Writing is thinking. Writing is persuasion. Writing is observation. Writing is deciding how to communicate to others without needlessly talking down to them. In short, writing is a powerful and necessary tool of communication, and any successful manager must know how to wield it effectively.

So face it: You're going to have to learn how to write effectively, the sooner the better. It can be a 20-page report, a minor memo, or even a thank-you note, but each time you put pen to paper, you share a piece of yourself—and you create a semipermanent archive that reflects your strengths or shortcomings. Don't just take our word for it. For example, Benjamin Franklin attributed much of his success to his ability to write well. It was a skill Ben had worked hard to develop, principally by rewriting popular essays and by building his vocabulary through extensive reading.

GETTING A GRIP ON THE BASICS

What are the two most important things to consider before you write anything? Your purpose and your audience, says Judith Yellin, whose New York City–based Successful Writing Group works with managers to develop their writing skills. Here's how to improve yours.

Know why you're writing. Writing comes a lot easier if you spend a few moments beforehand gaining a clear understanding of what you are trying to communicate—and why. To achieve this, simply complete the following sentence: "The point of this (report/memo/proposal/letter) is to . . ." Throughout the writing and rewriting process, never take your eye off this mission. And remember that you must also let the reader(s) know why they're reading it.

Know your audience and anticipate their reaction. Think about the questions you know they will want to have answered, suggests Yellin. And imagine readers' responses to your writing—it will help you tailor a product that is suited for them.

Understand the tone you need. In conversation, that's simple enough to do. You wouldn't greet an old friend that same way you chastise your daughter for some major infraction of household rules. In conversation, you have the benefit of the listener's immediate reaction to help you adjust to the proper tone, but writing is more difficult. Depending on the occasion, you may need to be abrupt, polite, personal, or something else. Yet most people fall into the trap of always writing in the same tone, regardless of the situation. That's like driving only in second gear.

LEARNING THE WRITING PROCESS

"Most of the people that we train have not been educated for writing in the real world," says Yellin. "They have no idea of audience awareness or of the purpose and the power that the written word can have." As a reflection of previous struggles in high school or college writing classes, most of her students have negative feelings and attitudes to overcome toward the writing task.

Most nonprofessional writers take an unnatural approach to writing. They try to do everything at once: generate material, edit it, organize it. So Yellin, who believes writing is a biological act akin to listening or speaking, teaches managers the "natural process" that most pros eventually stumble upon. Here's the short course.

Prewriting. This is the stage in which you think about what you're trying to accomplish. You write notes to yourself.

Writing the rough draft. Here you generate the raw material, based largely on your notes. You get started by taking a free-form approach. Don't stop to find the perfect word for the perfect sentence—not at this stage. And don't worry: Nobody will see this except you and the person who empties the office wastebasket.

Organization. This is what Yellin calls the "discovery" process. You take a careful look at what you've written and suddenly you may discover, for example, that it's two memos—not one—that you really need to write. You break the material in two, and begin rearranging paragraphs.

Revision. Here you become your own critic—replacing words, editing out the duplications, and expunging the damaging or the unnecessary.

All of this doesn't necessarily come easily. "If the author does not labor with the written word, if the discourse seems to flow effortlessly, the writer probably is not communicating as well as he or she could or should," writes Robert W. Goddard, director of publications for Liberty Mutual Insurance Group. "You can always make it better than the first time around. You always see places where you can add, subtract, massage." Remember the words of the late sportswriter Red Smith: "Writing is easy. I just open a vein and bleed."

KEEPING IT SIMPLE

Writing communicates best when it's clear and brief. That means you use uncomplicated words. It means writing in short, simple sentences. It means keeping your paragraphs small, and not including too many ideas in any one paragraph.

"The idea is more important than the words," explains Hank Wallace, a writing consultant in Washington, D.C., who teaches business managers and government officials to write in the short, to-the-point style of broad-cast journalism. "You get a short-term gain by using big words. The reader knows you know a big word and have more than a first-grade education. But in the long run (after a few paragraphs, that is) the reader will be more impressed by your intelligence or lack of it—which is ultimately what makes you win or lose," he says. Clear, simple writing can convey that intelligence.

Wallace believes a newswriting style is best for communicating within organizations, particularly because in newswriting, the main point of the story—the main message—always comes first. "Most people, except news-people, put their main point last," he explains. A notable exception: State Department types, who are used to briefing busy ambassadors. The biggest offenders: lawyers, who are used to building a logical case before reaching a conclusion.

Publications director Goddard echoes this sentiment: "Most people who write a five-page memo will outline their analysis of the problem for three or four pages and reach the conclusion only on page five. By that point the reader has to reread the memo all over again to see if he agrees with what the writer said. But if you put the conclusion up front, the reader will have it in his mind while he's reading the rest of the memo."

Then there's the issue of unnecessary wordiness. Why write "management personnel" when "managers" would suffice? Why say "it has been my observation that . . . " when you could write "I feel . . . " Here are a few other common culprits.

- Instead of "At the present time," write "Now"
- Instead of "Without further delay," write "Immediately"
- Instead of "It has been my observation that," write "I know"

Make yourself familiar with spelling, syntax, and the rules of grammar. (At the very least, it will impress your seventh-grade daughter.) *The Elements of Style,* by William Strunk, Jr., and E. B. White, is a useful book to keep in your office. And a good dictionary should be a required item of office furnishing.

WHEN YOU *SHOULDN'T* PUT IT IN WRITING

Your comments in a meeting may linger in the minds of the attendees for roughly three days. By the time they get reported to every new set of ears, they are likely to be distorted beyond recognition. Your written words, on the other hand, can last much longer and become solid testimony to your poor judgment (not to mention your erroneous grammar). You should always assume that your writing will eventually fall before unintended eyes. Here are some things that are better left unwritten.

- Maligning comments about others
- Salary details of any sort
- Any type of office gossip
- Personnel plans
- Confidential information about employees or corporate strategy that may be read by someone who does not have the proper right to know

Yellin suggests that if you do happen to commit your negative feelings to paper, wait 24 hours before sending them. You may feel differently by then.

HOW TO AVOID WRITER'S BLOCK

With so much at stake, it's no wonder that even the best of writers sometimes get blocked. If you can't get yourself started, try these tricks.

1. Turn to the person closest to you (real or imagined) and say what it is you can't write. Example: "Our department is going through some rough changes and everybody must take on extra work."
2. Pretend you're writing to a friend or someone else who is sympathetic—someone who will like you regardless of what you write.
3. Work on your outline. Take each point and write a few sentences to elaborate. You may soon find yourself writing more than you expected. In most cases, small steps will help motivate you to take bigger steps. And you'll be getting organized at the same time.
4. Work on the part you like best. It may help get you geared up for the other parts.
5. Put it away for a few days, "When you're in it too deep, try putting it away for a few days." suggests Goddard. "Then go back to it with a fresh view."

A Case for Unclear Writing

There's a time and a place for memos that are not easily understood, according to John Fielden, Ph.D., professor of management communications at the University of Alabama and writing consultant to major corporations. Dr. Fielden believes that one's style of writing should be altered to reflect the message being conveyed and the effect that you want. Unclear writing, he says, can be a tool that's somewhat akin to polite and diplomatic speech.

Here's the case. Your boss comes floating in one Monday morning with copies of a proposal he spent the weekend crafting. He thinks it's terrific, and he wants you to give him your opinion of it in writing by tomorrow morning. You think the proposal stinks, but you don't have the kind of relationship with your boss in which you can simply wander into his office and say, "Hey, Joe, this is a terrible idea."

According to Dr. Fielden, "It would be poison" to write a very brief, clear response telling the boss—in simple, direct sentences—that his proposal is a bad idea and why. "You run the risk of being viewed as too abrasive." On the other hand, if you beat around the bush in offering your criticism, introducing your remarks with something on the order of "While it's clear that you devoted a great deal of your time to this project . . . ", you run the risk of sounding too manipulative. So you're really caught between a rock and a hard place.

(continued)

A Case for Unclear Writing—*Continued*

When you're conveying negative information to a superior, Dr. Fielden says, it's best to avoid the rules on clarity and adopt what's considered a passive style of writing. For instance, if you have problems with your boss's proposal, you could avoid taking responsibility for your objections by attributing them to a vague third party. Here's an example (as included in a controversial article Dr. Fielden wrote for *Harvard Business Review*). Don't write: "I have several objections to your plans." Instead write: "It is more than possible that several objections to your proposed plans might be raised by some observers." Or "Several objections might be raised by those hostile to your plans."

He also suggests you use long sentences and heavy paragraphs to slow down the reader's comprehension of sensitive or negative information. "We don't teach managers to write dishonestly, we teach them to be realistic," explains Dr. Fielden. "You don't have to learn to tell the truth in ways that will get you slapped in the face."Another advantage of unclear writing: It will reduce the incidence of nosy third-party readers picking up the negative memo and saying, "Boy, did she tell Joe off . . . "

Another note on communicating bad news. Rely heavily on the word "although," suggests writing consultant Hank Wallace. For example: "Although we value your great intelligence, we've chosen a more qualified candidate for the job." This approach softens the blow by linking negative news with something positive.

INDEX